THE HUSSITE KING

OTAKAR ODLOŽILÍK

THE
HUSSITE KING
Bohemia in European Affairs
1440-1471

RUTGERS UNIVERSITY PRESS
New Brunswick   *New Jersey*

To the memory of my parents

PREFACE

George of Poděbrady, called by some authors the Hussite king, holds a prominent place among the national heroes of the Czech people. His reign (1458–1471) followed upon a period of concentrated efforts to consolidate the kingdom of Bohemia, in which he played a significant role. Born in 1420, George was soon drawn into the whirlpool of public life and came to the fore as the head of a powerful aristocratic faction at the age of twenty-four. No other member of the Czech nobility, Catholic or Hussite, was strong and astute enough to challenge George's bid for the highest position in the kingdom. The Poděbrady era has been recognized by the Czech people as a glorious age, comparable to the fourteenth-century reign of Charles IV, "the Father of the Nation."

George was a distinguished figure, no less successful on the battlefields than in conducting negotiations or presiding over representative assemblies. He impressed both Emperor Frederick III and Pope Pius II by his personality and statesmanship. He was immensely popular among the Hussite Czechs and slandered viciously by his fanatical Silesian opponents. He was married twice and had several sons and daughters. Some of them were married to members of illustrious families, the Hohenzollerns, the Hunyadis, and the Wettins. The basic biographical data can in part be found in contemporary sources, and in part established by combination of indirect evidence; but there is not enough material for a story dealing exclusively with his private affairs.

The chances of success get better when one passes from George's family life to the study of his position in his native Bohemia. His apprenticeship in public affairs was relatively short and he did not spend those years in a remote place or in subordination. The geographical position of the family residence, the castle of Poděbrady, in the fertile lowlands of Central Bohemia, as well as the ramified connections established by his father and other relatives, gave George a promising start. He joined the vanguard of the Hussite party and advanced rapidly. His personal story soon merged with the course of public life in Bohemia and became one of its essential components.

As a leader of the Hussite party, and since 1458 as the king, George was confronted with vast problems, domestic and international. He endeavored to regulate the relations of Bohemia, the kernel of the kingdom, with the incorporated provinces, deeply estranged during the Hussite wars. Realistic and tolerant, he attempted to mitigate the deep-seated antagonism between the "two peoples" inhabiting the kingdom, the Czechs and the Germans, the Hussites and the Catholics. He hoped to obtain from the papacy a solemn sanction of the agreement concluded in 1436 between the Council of Basel and the Hussites, known as the Compacts. He sought friendly contacts with Bohemia's neighbors and had a genuine ambition to contribute to the regeneration of the Holy Roman Empire. In promoting reform schemes, he wished to enhance the security of his own country and make more effective the defense of the Christian inheritance against the enemies of the Cross.

To do George justice, his biographer cannot limit himself to the study of the sources relating primarily to Bohemia. It is necessary to weave into the description of his activities the frequent contacts with Emperor Frederick III and a fairly large number of German princes—the Hohenzollerns, the Wettins, and the Wittelsbachs. Hungary and Poland often call for attention as well. At certain junctures the framework must be widened to include the distant courts of France, Burgundy, Venice, and Milan. The Turkish expansion is a theme which none can pass over in silence if he wishes to grasp the meaning of some bilateral treaties, and even more, of such a bold scheme as the League of Christian Princes. Above all George's concerns and occupations towered the task of reconciliation of the Hussite Czechs with Rome. On its success or failure depended not only the pacification of the kingdom but also a smooth course of international relations, as the tragic events of 1467–71 were to show.

While a simple biography would hardly be feasible for lack of family chronicles and personal records, a comprehensive study of George's ambitions and endeavors can be undertaken with a good chance of success. Czech, German, and French scholars had prepared the ground for it by general surveys and by critical studies of specific problems, as well as by publications of sources of Bohemian, imperial, and ecclesiastical history in George's lifetime. Collections of official documents, private letters, and narrative sources are accessible almost without exception in earlier or modern editions.

American libraries have expanded their sections devoted to Central Europe so that no worth-while publication has remained out of my reach. Widener, Columbia University, and New York Public Libraries, and the Library of Congress undoubtedly lead in that field. Gaps in their holdings could be filled by search in European institutions, in the Nationalbiblio-thek in Vienna, in the British Museum, and in the Vatican library and archives. Hours spent in the main library of the University of Pennsyl-vania (known today as the Charles Patterson van Pelt Library) and espe-cially in its section, the Henry C. Lea Library of Mediaeval History, gave me more pleasure and satisfaction than plain words could express.

Twenty and some years ago, while associated with Yale University as an honorary research fellow, I wrote two sketches of the Poděbrady era. One of them entitled "George of Poděbrady and Bohemia to the Pacifi-cation of Silesia—1459" was accepted by my friend, Professor S. Harrison Thomson for the *University of Colorado Studies* (vol. I, no. 3, pp. 265–288). The second one, "Problems of the Reign of George of Poděbrady," was published by the late Professor Samuel H. Cross in the *Slavonic and East European Review* (vol. XX, 1941, pp. 206–222). The subject, once treated, did not lose its appeal to my mind and heart even when other tasks claimed my time and energy. My interest in it was not ephemeral and it could be traced to my first reading of Palacký's *History of the Czech People* at the age of ten. The five-hundredth anniversary of George's election and coronation, observed in 1958, gave a new impetus to my research from which came this book. In planning it I have decided not for a heavily documented description of the Poděbrady era but for an interpretative study of its problems.

I recall gratefully the leave of absence which the University of Penn-sylvania granted me for the spring of 1961. The time and facilities for research and compilation of the story would not have been properly used if I had not been supported, especially in moments of uncertainty, by my old friend Professor Matthew Spinka who helped me invaluably by patient reading and careful revision of my manuscript. To him I shall be always thankful.

I am also indebted to Professor Peter Charanis of the Department of History at Rutgers University, who recommended my manuscript for publication. The assistance of Mr. Liam Dunne, who designed the maps, is also appreciated. Unusual competence and experience on the part of both publisher and printer was needed to produce this book.

Otakar Odložilík

Philadelphia
April, 1965

CONTENTS

THE HUSSITE KING

FROM REVOLUTION TO RESTORATION

The Hussite revolution, in many respects, transformed the traditional pattern of life in medieval Bohemia and exerted its potent influence for many decades afterwards. Both the advocates of Church reform and their opponents were aware of the significance of the profound changes which had taken place in the stormy years after the martyr death of John Hus in 1415. A wide gap separated conservative segments of the population of Bohemia, faithful to the Roman Church, from the Hussite party, since their aims were diametrically opposed. Whereas the Hussites endeavored to unite the Czech people under their banners, their adversaries aimed at a suppression of the new concepts and at the restoration of the old order both in religion and in politics. Situated in Central Europe, the kingdom of Bohemia could not be isolated from the other parts of the Christian orbit and allowed to exist as a haven for heretics and rebels. Attempts to defeat the Hussites alternated with peaceful offensives, but neither proved successful.

Threatened after the death of King Wenceslas IV (August, 1419) by their enemies, the Hussites resorted to arms and organized their military forces under the supreme leadership of John Žižka of Trocnov, a faithful follower of Hus and a strategist of genius. Under his command the Hussite forces resisted all foreign invaders for five years and in the intervals between defensive campaigns they dealt heavy blows to their foes among the nobility and patriciate of Bohemia. Žižka's lieutenants, with Prokop the Bald in the forefront, carried on the struggle for seven more years and finally convinced the initiators of the anti-Hussite crusades of their futility. An expedition against Bohemia was organized in the summer of 1431 on a larger scale than ever before, but it ended in confusion and a hasty retreat from the border town of Domažlice before it had actually started. Its dismal failure impressed even the most fanatical opponents of the Czechs and strengthened the moderate elements advocating peace, provided it could be obtained by compromise.

The Hussite movement originated in opposition to the decisions of the Council of Constance, and since 1417 to Pope Martin V. After the death of the legitimate ruler of Bohemia, King Wenceslas IV, the Hussites turned against his younger brother, Sigismund, King of the Romans and of Hungary, refusing to recognize his claims to the crown of Bohemia. As Sigismund's successive expeditions against the rebels were organized as crusades with the Pope's blessing, peace could not be concluded on one front only. Religious and political issues were intertwined from the very beginning of the Hussite struggles, and to settle them it was necessary to proceed along two lines: first, to bring the Czechs back into the fold of the Church; and second, to facilitate Sigismund's accession to the throne.

The long and laborious negotiations looking toward these goals opened soon after the panicky flight from Domažlice in 1431. Prominent church dignitaries, assembled at Basel to prepare the General Council, requested the Czechs to send their spokesmen to that city for preliminary discussions of controversial matters. Despite technical difficulties, contacts between the respective parties were soon established and in May, 1432, a meeting was held at Cheb (Eger) between the envoys from Basel and the Czech delegates. In the latter delegation there were represented three Hussite factions: that of Prague, commonly known as the Utraquists; of the Orphans, observing Žižka's tradition; and of the Taborites, the left wing of Hussitism.

A general agreement was soon reached and the Czechs were assured that the doctrinal differences would be dealt with "by the law of God and the practices of Christ, the apostles, and of the early Church, along with the teachings of the Councils and of the doctors conforming truly thereto." This article, known as the "Judge of Cheb," was often invoked in the course of negotiations, and represented the most significant concession the Church ever made to the Hussite point of view.[1] As it was granted by spokesmen of the General Church assembly, it was highly valued by the Hussites, who were distrustful of the Pope and remained deaf to his appeals that they return to his obedience.

Negotiations with the Council opened early in 1433. The parties accepted as the basis for oral and written exchanges the Four Articles of Prague, formulated in 1420, and acknowledged by all Hussite factions.[2] In an abridged form the articles read as follows:

    1. That the Word of God shall be freely and without hindrance proclaimed and preached by Christian priests in the kingdom of Bohemia.

    2. That the Holy Sacrament of the body and blood of Christ under

the two kinds of bread and wine shall be freely administered to all true Christians who are not excluded from communion by mortal sin.

3. That since many priests and monks hold many earthly possessions against Christ's command and to the disadvantage of their spiritual office and also of the temporal lords, such priests shall be deprived of this illegal power and shall live exemplary lives according to the Holy Scripture, in following the way of Christ and the apostles.

4. That all mortal sins, and especially those that are public, as also other disorders contrary to the divine law, shall be prohibited and punished by those whose office it is so that the evil and false repute of this country may be removed and the well-being of the kingdom and of the Bohemian nation may be promoted.

Four Hussite leaders, John of Rokycany (Rokycana), Ulric of Znojmo, Nicholas of Pelhřimov, and Peter Payne, an Englishman living in Bohemia since his escape from Oxford in 1413, defended in Basel the cardinal tenets of their faith as expresesd in the Four Articles. The Council designated four theologians, John Stojković, Aegidius Carlier, Henry Kalteisen, and John Palomar, to reply to the Hussite speeches and to present the official doctrine. It soon became clear to the assembled prelates that no accord could be reached by means of disputes and polemics or by the application of the "Judge of Cheb." The Council decided to assert its authority over the Hussites by a recourse to the traditional methods.

The Council never was prepared to accept the Four Articles unreservedly, and the Hussites requested that the arbitration be conducted in accordance with the terms of the "Judge of Cheb." When contacts were established, it was the fixing of the line at which they would be willing to meet that proved to be the main task. By steady pressure and diplomatic maneuvering, the Hussites were split; and while the leaders of the military brotherhoods insisted on the original terms of the "Judge of Cheb," the war-weary Prague party leaned to a compromise both with the spiritual and the secular authorities. The envoys from Basel during their first visit to Bohemia in the spring and summer of 1433 had correctly diagnosed the situation and reported it faithfully to the directors of the Council. It was not the chief delegate Bishop Philibert, but John Palomar, the Archdeacon of Barcelona, who recommended partial concessions to the Hussites to make them more tractable. A keen observer, he compared the Czechs to wild and unharnessed horses or mules and recommended that a halter be put on their heads so that they could be captured, tamed, and fastened to the manger.[3] Successes scored by the Council at various meetings with the Czechs were largely due to Palomar's tactics. Reference was often made by both sides to "Palomar's halter."

The first draft of an agreement later known as the Compacts (Compactata) was finished on November 30, 1433.[4] It indicated the limits which the Basel delegates had set up for tactical purposes. None of the Four Articles was flatly rejected, but elaborate interpretations and subtle clauses were attached to each of them, toning down their revolutionary spirit.

Passing in silence over the doctrinal differences concerning the presence of Christ in the Eucharist, the contracting parties approved communion in both kinds (*sub utraque*) as demanded by one of the Four Articles and as practiced by all Hussites irrespective of their political or theological orientation. Administration of the sacrament in both kinds to laymen was not permitted universally, but granted only to those who had practiced it before the drafting of the Compacts. Priests officiating at the service were requested to teach the faithful that under either one of the species Christ is just as fully present as under both kinds. The concession accorded to the Hussites fell short of their hope that the Chalice, if not restored generally in the western Church, would at least be sanctioned all over the kingdom of Bohemia to prevent divisions and conflicts.

An agreement in principle was reached on the demand for energetic steps against public sins. The Hussites accepted a restrictive formula by which the right of punishing the guilty was not granted to individuals, but to the legitimate authorities, and even then only under the observance of valid laws. The article stressing the need of unfettered preaching was also modified and the concept of freedom was obscured by a stipulation that the authority of the Church should not be impaired. Finally, the vexing question of temporal possessions by the clerics was answered to mutual satisfaction by a retreat of the Hussites from insistence on evangelical poverty to tolerance of church endowments. Those who were entrusted with their administration were to be left in their offices, and no goods rightly belonging to the Church were to be held by secular owners. None of the parties requested clarification of the most difficult problem, the restitution of church properties that had changed hands during the revolutionary period, as not only the Utraquist but even the Catholic lords, including Sigismund, were involved.

The first draft, compiled after the sharp exchanges of arguments by a small body of negotiators, aroused indignation among the resolute Hussites, including some sections of the Prague party. The envoys of the Council remained in Bohemia for some time afterwards but made no attempt to calm the spirits by a conciliatory gesture. The Council, after having heard their report, assumed the same attitude, indicating that the Hussites must either accept the November agreement or risk a rupture of negotiations.

In the early stage of negotiations, matters of faith commanded attention of both the Hussites and of the Council. When some progress was made in discussions of doctrinal points, both parties became aware of weakness of the political interim which had set in after the rift with King Sigismund. The Hussite leaders, though elated by successful campaigns, realized that their resources were not limitless and that without substantial help from abroad they would not be able finally to crush the claimant to the throne. They hoped that negotiating from a position of strength would enable them to hammer out the terms of an honorable agreement. In 1431 they felt strong enough to face not only the Council but also the pretender to the throne.

After his return from Cheb in May, 1432, Prokop the Bald turned to Sigismund, requesting him to attend the Council and to take direct part in the negotiations.[5] Drawing a lesson from their earlier experiences, the Hussite leaders were anxious to have their accord with the spiritual authority supplemented by a settlement of their differences with their chief enemy, and to ward off danger of political conflicts. Although seriously interested in the recognition of his claims by the Hussites, Sigismund dallied in Italy for more than a year and only in the early fall of 1433 betook himself to Basel.

The leading members of the Council were favorably impressed by Sigismund's conduct and cultivated his good will. They knew that he lived on friendly terms with Pope Eugene IV, by whom he had been crowned Emperor on Whitsunday, 1433. It was no secret that Sigismund was eager to hasten the dealings with the Czechs to gain their recognition. Mutual understanding between him and the Council was quickly achieved and the two main issues—religious conciliation and political restoration—were merged. Enjoying the Council's favor, Sigismund soon played a far more active part in Church affairs than had usually been accorded to the emperors, and he used this opportunity for the promotion of his own interests.

Acceptance of Sigismund's claims required a good deal of time and of diplomatic dexterity on both sides. The Catholic inhabitants of the kingdom of Bohemia regarded his coronation in July, 1420, as legitimate. On the other hand, the Hussites rejected it as irregular, as it had been performed hastily and did not agree with the *Ordo coronationis* (order of Coronation), once compiled by Sigismund's father, Charles IV, and with the unwritten traditions.[6] No less serious an obstacle was the Hussite aversion to Sigismund, roused by his indifference to the fate of John Hus and Jerome of Prague while these two reformers were under trial at Constance. Memories of Sigismund's active part in organizing the crusades against Bohemia lingered among both the moderate and the resolute Hussites. Not entirely forgotten were the invectives against

Sigismund by the radical preachers, one of whom, John of Želiv, branded the King as the great red dragon, a transparent allusion to the beast from the Book of Revelation and to Sigismund's red beard.[7]

Loathing the idea of dealing with the Hussite war leaders directly and on equal terms, Sigismund established contacts from Basel with powerful magnates who either remained faithful to the Church or adhered to the Hussite right wing.[8] The mightiest of the Catholic lords, Oldřich of Rožmberk, journeyed to Basel to pay homage to Sigismund as his sovereign. Well known as the inveterate foe of the Taborites, Oldřich could not be used as a mediator. Instead, his neighbor, Menhart of Jindřichův Hradec, owner of vast domains in southeastern Bohemia, was chosen for that role. Menhart communicated in both kinds and had many friends among the moderate Hussites. Only a handful of people knew that he observed the Hussite rites merely for tactical purposes. A realist with unconcealed leanings toward cynicism, Sigismund needed no lesson from the shrewd Archdeacon of Barcelona in how to select men who could fasten a "halter" on the Czech head.

Reports coming to Sigismund through various channels agreed on the whole with the accounts presented by the delegates of the Council to their superiors. The theologians of the radical factions, the Orphans and the Taborites, were supported in their opposition by the military brotherhoods which operated in various parts of Bohemia and were determined, if conciliation could not be effected by a rigid application of the "Judge of Cheb," to pursue the struggle.

The foremost task confronting Sigismund's partisans in Bohemia was the organization of a bloc strong enough to crush the military brotherhoods. Shielded by the authority of the recently elected governor of Bohemia, Aleš Vřešťovský of Rýzmburk, Menhart forged the links between the lords of the Catholic and the Hussite orientations. They were joined, in the spring of 1434, by the nobility from Moravia and by the conservative elements in the Old Town of Prague as well as by some other royal boroughs. Soon after its creation, the League of the Lords appealed to the military brotherhoods to stop their operations against Plzeň and other Catholic centers. The war leaders paid no heed to the appeal and allied themselves with a fairly large number of royal boroughs governed by the Orphans or the Taborites. An armed conflict became inevitable. In a fierce battle at Lipany in central Bohemia (May 30, 1434), the Prague troops and the contingents mustered by the conservative nobility defeated their opponents.

Summing up his description of the bloody encounter, František Palacký wrote: "In that battle vanished the force of the Taborites and Orphans forever. Their chief leaders, the two Prokops (Prokop the Bald and his aide, said Prokop the Lesser), lost their life, and in addition to them fell other captains and many priests, and as many as thirteen thousand of the warriors who for several years had been feared as the scourge of Europe; for although many of them were prepared to surrender, their foes did not spare them but slaughtered them persistently so that only about seven hundred fighting men were taken into captivity." [9]

Both the Council and Sigismund entertained a hope that after the catastrophe of the military brotherhoods negotiations with the Czechs would proceed rapidly and smoothly. Their optimism soon proved to be a miscalculation. Since the victory at Lipany had to be shared with other partners, Menhart's reactionary faction could not play the decisive role in dealings with the pretender to the throne. Similarly, in the negotiations with the Council, priest John of Rokycany, representing the Hussite center, played the leading role, whereas the conservative theologians were almost entirely eliminated from active partnership.

When early in the summer of 1434 contacts were resumed among the negotiators, Sigismund acted more resolutely than the representatives of the Council. On more than one occasion he overstepped his limits and was discreetly warned by the prelates not to encroach on their rights. Conditions in Bohemia seemed fully to justify Sigismund's conduct. Ecclesiastical organization, which had been laboriously built by the first archbishop of Prague, was completely disrupted during the revolutionary era. On the other hand, Aleš Vřešťovský, more conciliatory and more popular than Menhart, acted with authority as the head of the provincial administration.

The Czech nobles did not resent Sigismund's meddling with the religious affairs. During the interregnum they themselves had usurped rights and powers that in normal times had been out of their reach, and they wanted to involve Sigismund in their effort to reach a compromise with the Council. Although Sigismund had no genuine interest in theological subtleties and made no secret of his aversion to Hussite rigorism, the representatives of the Czech factions included problems of church organization in their demands, and often received from the claimant of the throne assurances which the Council was reluctant to grant.

The most significant concession made by Sigismund to the Hussites pertained to church organization. The Archbishop of Prague, Conrad of Vechta, who in his advanced age had collaborated with the conservative Hussites, had died in 1431. The See of Litomyšl was vacant, so that no bishop existed in Bohemia to ordain the candidates to priesthood and to perform other rites reserved to bishops. Approached at Brno by the Hussites in July, 1435, Sigismund promised, among other things, to assist them in their efforts to fill the vacancies with competent candidates. A charter was drafted incorporating, along with other provisions, Sigismund's consent to an election of an archbishop and two suffragans by the provincial Diet of Bohemia.[10] In order to placate suspicious negotiators, Sigismund promised to intercede with the Church authorities for the confirmation and consecration of the elected clerics. In private he spoke slightingly of the qualifications required for high spiritual offices. He shocked one of the representatives of the Council by a cynical remark that he cared little whom the Hussites nominated, "even if they elected an ass." [11]

Encouraged by Sigismund's pledge, the Hussite laymen and clerics assembled in Prague in October, 1435, and appointed a committee of sixteen, who in turn in a secret session elected John Rokycana as archbishop, and two other clerics, Martin Lupáč and Václav of Mýto, as his suffragans.[12] Held without the authorization by the Council, the election aroused indignation in ecclesiastical circles. The Basel delegates bestirred themselves to avert Sigismund's prompt endorsement of the act and obtained from him an oral pledge that he would abstain from interference in religious affairs.[13] Allaying suspicions of the Hussite leaders by vague assurances, Sigismund delayed his confirmation of the elected dignitaries and refrained from making binding statements without a previous consultation with the spokesmen of the Council.

The desire of the Czechs to end the interim was so strong that they promised to come to a provincial Diet and meet there with Sigismund and the delegates from Basel. In normal times the Diet was held in Prague; but this time it was called to convene in the mining town of Jihlava on the border of Bohemia and Moravia. It was well attended by the lords, the lesser nobility, and representatives of the royal boroughs. The Council sent as its representatives Bishop Philibert of Coutances, John Palomar, Martin Bernerii and Thomas Haselbach. Sigismund and his consort Barbara arrived in the company of their son-in-law, Albrecht, the Duke of Austria.

A snarl interrupted negotiations between the Hussites and the Council's delegates. The Hussite spokesmen insisted that the delegates confirm Rokycana and his suffragans along with the signing of an agreement on the articles of faith. Once again Sigismund appeared on the stage as a mediator and assured the Hussites, both in his own and Albrecht's name, that they would intercede with the Pope and the Council for confirmation of the elected dignitaries.[14] The Hussites accepted Sigismund's pledge so that the Diet could proceed to its main task, the reading and approval of a rather ponderous document, the Compacts (*Compactata*).

In the lengthy charter prepared by members of the royal chancellery were included three agreements of earlier dates: a condensed text of the Four Articles of Prague, with explanatory notes and reservations formulated in Prague on November 30, 1433, by the delegates from Basel and the Hussite leaders; an additional accord approved at Brno in July, 1435, by the Basel envoys and the Czechs; and finally, a resolution adopted in Prague on September 21, 1435, by the assembly of the Estates of Bohemia, approving the earlier agreement with the Council. Connected by conventional phrases and supplemented by corroborative formulas, these agreements represented the maximum concessions which the Council was willing to grant to the Hussites.[15]

The Latin version of the Compacts was read publicly in the spacious square of Jihlava on July 5, 1436. Translations into Czech, German, and Magyar were prepared simultaneously to give the Compacts wide publicity in Bohemia and the neighboring countries. The Hussites insisted that they should be protected by representatives of the Council against defamatory campaigns. By a solemn proclamation, the stigma of heresy was lifted from the Czechs and they were recognized as good Christians and true sons of the Holy Church.[16]

The course of negotiations between the Council and the Czechs was determined by the decision, respected on the whole by both parties, to regard the Four Articles of Prague as the summary of the Hussite views and to reach an agreement on their meaning. A good many questions on which the Hussites were at odds among themselves were left untouched, as even a passing reference to them would have complicated the task of the peacemakers. They related to minor doctrinal points or to ceremonies, and it was tacitly assumed by the contracting parties that they would be settled amicably, once an accord had been reached on the essential points. Elimination of spokesmen of the radical wing after the Lipany battle made the concentration on basic points easier as the moderate party, headed by John of Rokycany, earnestly desired to re-establish unity with the Church and therefore dropped the excessive demands formerly raised by either the Orphans or the Taborites.

Sigismund's charter, drafted at Brno in July, 1435, was not added to the three documents making up the Compacts. Some of its stipulations were resented by the Council as excessive. The Czech negotiators continued to press for the confirmation of the Hussite bishops. Anxious to avoid rupture at the rather advanced stage of the negotiations, Sigismund endorsed, on July 13, 1436, the election of Rokycana and his two suffragans and promised intervention in their behalf with the Pope.[17] Thus the matter was exempted from the accord concluded with the Council and proved to be one of the most onerous obligations accepted by the pretender to the throne.

Sigismund's connivance in the election of bishops cleared the path for the final settlement of the outstanding problems. Presented with a long list of demands, he adopted a conciliatory attitude to shorten the period of discussion. His charter, issued at Jihlava on July 20, 1436, contained twenty-five points and was regarded by the Czechs as the secular complement to the Compacts.[18] It was not carefully drafted and the articles upon which an agreement had been reached in the preliminary conferences were not grouped organically. Two of them expressed Sigismund's willingness to respect the privileges and freedoms granted to the Estates of Bohemia by his predecessors. Other articles pertained to concrete problems created by the rift in 1419 and the ensuing wars.

Six articles expressed the king's obligations arising from his approval of the Compacts. In addition to the general endorsement of the accord with the Council, Sigismund offered protection to the communicants in both kinds. Utraquist clerics were assured of a free access to the royal court. Nobody was to be forced to repair damaged castles, forts, monasteries, or churches. Provisions were made for the recall of monks and nuns to their former residences. The problems arising from at least the partial revival of monasticism in Bohemia were to be settled amicably by the archbishop and the local authorities. Sigismund also promised to consult with the archbishop and the general assembly of the clergy on appropriate measures by which the University of Prague could be reorganized.

Preliminary exchanges of views showed Sigismund that even the conservative lords made his admission to the ancestral throne dependent upon substantial concessions. In the third article, he expressed his willingness to rule with a Council of the realm, elected by the Estates, and to fill the vacancies in high administrative offices only after a consultation with them. He also pledged to bring back the crown and the other royal insignia, charters, privileges, and records both of the aulic and the provincial tribunals, which he had taken with him after the hasty coronation in July, 1420. The fear of foreign meddling was dispelled by Sigismund's agreement not to appoint aliens to offices in Bohemia and to observe in the incorporated provinces the rules and practices sanctioned by Charles IV and other kings. During the king's absence from Bohemia, no alien should administer the country. Charters issued by Sigismund during the war period were to be submitted to the Council of the realm for examination and confirmation. The royal boroughs were not to be pressed for payments due to the monarch but not delivered during the wars. To stabilize the currency, Sigismund promised to coin again the *grossi,* which had been introduced in 1300 by one of his predecessors, Wenceslas II, but had suffered from gradual depreciation. By the twentieth article, Sigismund granted a general pardon to his former opponents and thus closed the long drawn-out feud.

Although the charter was comprehensive and well-defined as to concrete problems, it covered the field only partially, leaving gaps and loopholes of which the contracting parties were undoubtedly well aware.

Such a complex problem as the restitution of ecclesiastical domains in which both the Church and secular lords, including the King himself, were vitally interested, was not included in the charter of July 20, 1436. Attempts to arrive at a compromise gave rise to bickerings and mutual accusations and were soon abandoned. As the Basel delegates had done, Sigismund likewise committed himself to a peaceful settlement of the conflict, and judged therefore that a tacit elimination of knotty items from the written documents was preferable to protracted conferences. Obstructions had to be removed from the road connecting Jihlava with Prague at almost any cost, as nothing would have been more painful than an admission on his part of another setback and a hurried retreat to Hungary from such an advanced position.

On August 23, 1436, Sigismund and his wife Barbara, with their retinue, entered Prague. They took up their residence in the royal court in the City, as the castle at Hradčany was severely damaged and uninhabitable. The Council delegates, headed by Bishop Philibert, had arrived two days earlier to supervise the practical application of the Compacts. To all appearances the rift had been healed and Bohemia had been brought back into the comity of nations. Nevertheless, no thorough scrutiny of the principal documents, the Compacts and the charter of July 20, 1436, was needed to reveal how frail were the ties between the Hussites and the supreme authorities—the Church and the king.

Nevertheless, a hope of reconciliation was entertained by the majority of the Hussite party. The radical factions, weakened as they were by the defeat at Lipany, were unable to challenge the terms approved at Jihlava. If Sigismund and the Council delegates had been guided by practical considerations, they would soon have realized that co-operation with the moderate center offered them the best chance of success. Rokycana, the Archbishop-elect, had a large number of followers both among the clerics and the nobles, and the designated suffragans also enjoyed popularity in their own circles. They were all prepared to join in any constructive effort to stabilize both the political and the ecclesiastical conditions.

Bishop Philibert was reluctant to make a step that could be interpreted as at least a tacit recognition of the three Hussite leaders in the dignities to which they had been elected. More familiar with the Czechs than Philibert, King Sigismund pursued a friendlier policy so as not to drive Rokycana into bitter opposition. Sigismund feared that the Archbishop-elect, if deprived of any hope, might ally himself with the remnants of the radical factions, the Orphans and the Taborites, and stir up new difficulties. He was even more cautious in dealings with the Hussite laymen. He granted the office of the supreme burgrave of Prague to Menhart of Hradec as a reward for his unswerving loyalty, but did not exclude from the provincial government men known for their sincere attachment to the Hussite cause. Municipal administration in Prague was entrusted to conservative aldermen and some popular figures from the revolutionary era were pacified by grants of sinecures. Sheer opportunism led Sigismund to conclude a pact with the city of Tábor, which since its foundation in 1420 stood in the forefront of his foes and symbolized by its very name the most radical tendencies.[19] Opposition in other parts of Bohemia was allayed by his dexterous moves or minor concessions.

One problem required careful handling and was solved to Sigismund's satisfaction only after protracted discussions. The bone of contention was the distribution of seats in the provincial court, and Sigismund acted as a mediator between the lords and the lesser nobility. On his recommendation, twelve seats were assigned permanently to the lords and eight to the knights. Using his right to appoint the judges, Sigismund filled the bench partly with Catholics, partly with conservative Hussites.[20]

Sigismund succeeded in winning over, or at least in pacifying, the various factions or individuals. One of the radical leaders, John Roháč, defied the King from his castle, called symbolically the Zion. Although abandoned by his former allies, Roháč resisted the besieging forces for four months, but ran out of resources and was captured by the royalists. In September, 1437, he and his cohorts, a group of over fifty men, were executed to intimidate the latent opposition. The hard sentence was hailed by Sigismund's staunch supporters, but caused consternation among the Hussites, especially in eastern Bohemia. Sigismund was sensible enough to realize that instead of buttressing he had weakened his position in Bohemia; but he made no attempt to pour oil on the troubled waters. In the agitated atmosphere, the hope that genuine collaboration could be established between the Catholic ruler and the mass of the Hussites vanished completely.

Practical application of the Compacts was hindered by even more serious difficulties than those encountered by Sigismund in political matters. Bishop Philibert acted as the chief representative of the Fathers of Basel, but wielded only limited powers. The Council claimed the right of confirming the Compacts in a plenary session, and of defining more precisely what should be believed about such tenets as the communion in both kinds.

Philibert's position was rather precarious. Rokycana's election, combined with other impediments, precluded Philibert's elevation to the See of Prague, an act which alone would have given him prestige and jurisdiction over the clergy, both Catholic and Utraquist. The Bishop took his task seriously, but his endeavors were marred by disturbing influences which originated partly in Basel and partly in Bohemia. The bulls

of January 15, 1437, by which the Council sanctioned the Jihlava negotiations, were received by the Utraquists with mixed feelings, as the passages pertaining to the Chalice were not precise and gave rise to doubts
whether the Council authorized or merely tolerated the communion in
both kinds.[21] The assembly of the Utraquist clergy elected two delegates,
who soon left for Basel to clear up the matter. They were John of Příbram and Prokop of Plzeň; both held moderate views on the points to
be discussed with the Council.

During the several months that the envoys spent in vain attempts to
dispose the Council favorably toward their position, the prospects of ecclesiastical reunion in Bohemia decreased markedly. Bishop Philibert realized that the Hussite majority linked the Compacts closely with Rokycana's cause. Since he could neither recognize Rokycana's claims, nor
challenge him openly, he cast his lot with the conservative Utraquist
clerics, among whom the Archbishop-elect had implacable enemies. In
this alliance Bishop Philibert gained some ground; more, however, among
the propertied classes than among common people, who were still imbued
with the spirit of defiance.

Sigismund was in no hurry to intervene in behalf of Rokycana, as he
was bound by his previous assurances. His dilatory policy pleased Philibert, as it prolonged the interim and afforded him opportunity for intricate maneuvering. By chicanery and under the guise of legality, Rokycana was deprived of the benefice at the leading church of Prague, the
Holy Virgin of Týn, which was promptly awarded to an archconserva-
tive cleric. Other hostile acts, involving either Rokycana or his ardent
supporters, followed in quick succession. Sensing the danger of persecution, Rokycana left the city and put himself under the protection of
mighty lords of his own religious orientation in eastern Bohemia.

Rokycana's escape facilitated the reorganization of the Utraquists. On
Sigismund's suggestion, an elderly cleric, Christian of Prachatice, was
elected administrator of the Utraquist party. He was of unimpeachable
character, and as he once had supported Hus as his good friend, he was
respected at least by the older generation. Bishop Philibert did not favor
this step, as it helped to keep the Hussites together as a distinct unit;
but he soon waived his objection, as Christian made no claim to the
episcopate and respected the Council. Christian selected as his assistants
some clerics, thus organizing the highest organ of the Hussite party,
known as the "Lower Consistory," with the church of the Holy Virgin
of Týn as its headquarters.

Philibert's relationship with Czech Catholics was not as smooth as he
had originally expected. The population of Bohemia was not won entirely for the Chalice, although Žižka and other leaders had worked assiduously toward that objective. Even when the tide of Hussitism rose

to its highest crest, some areas were not reached and remained faithful
to the Pope. The Cathedral of Saint Vitus never passed into Hussite
hands and after 1436 it served as the rallying point for Catholic clerics.
Members of the metropolitan chapter who survived the years of adversity returned to their prebends. They constituted themselves as an administrative body, known from its situation on the Hradčany hill the
"Upper Consistory." Along with them many secular as well as regular
clerics and nuns returned to Prague and other centers, not waiting for
a formal approval, as had been stipulated in Sigismund's charter of July
20, 1436.

Their claims and activities gave rise to suspicions and fears among the
Hussites of Rokycana's party, to say nothing of the more resolute adherents of the Chalice. Along with Sigismund's attempts to restore the
monarchy to its former strength, the growth of the Catholic party revealed the limited value of the Jihlava agreements for the Hussites. Rokycana's hard luck seemed to symbolize the danger confronting Hussitism,
irrespective of local differences or shades of opinion.

Philibert's endeavor to gain universal recognition for the Compacts fell
short of results worthy of his zeal and expectation. From the Catholic
clergy he did not get much support for his scheme. The "Upper Consistory" did not feel bound by the Compacts, as they had been negotiated without their participation. Such actions as the election of Rokycana and of his suffragans, which Philibert could not openly repudiate,
had no validity in their eyes. Only incorrigible optimists could hope that
the metropolitan chapter would ever consider Rokycana or any other
Hussite theologian as a worthy candidate for the archbishopric. As the
scheme of pacification was based on the idea of equality of the Catholics with the Utraquists adhering loyally to the Compacts, the canons of
Saint Vitus could not be expected to further it.

The Catholic clergy of Bohemia were encouraged by reports that a
new conflict between the Council and the papacy was in the offing. They
sympathized with Pope Eugene IV and moved closer to him when the
tension became acute. In consequence, they showed even less interest in
Philibert's endeavors than before, and their aloofness made his position
in Bohemia rather precarious.

The Utraquists continued to deal with the Council and expected op-
timistically that the negotiations conducted in Basel by John of Příbram
and Prokop of Plzeň would lead to an amicable settlement. Nevertheless, they were not indifferent to the Pope's statement of September 18,
1437, by which the Compacts were neither expressly confirmed nor
bluntly rejected. Although Eugene IV resolved to call a general Council to Ferrara, he postponed for thirty days the dissolution of the Basel

assembly, so that the final decision concerning the Chalice could be made by the same body which had approved the Compacts.[22]

As the leading members of the Council were anxious to bring the dealings with the Czechs to an end, the demands presented by John of Příbram and Prokop of Plzeň were put on the agenda late in the fall of 1437. After several weeks of deliberation, the Council issued, on December 23, 1437, a decree relating to the Eucharist.[23] According to it, communion in both kinds was not made obligatory by the Lord's commands, for laymen or nonofficiating clerics, so that the Church had the authority to determine what rite should prevail. The decree expressed the belief that both practices, in one or in both kinds, bring equal blessings to the communicant. Nobody should be misled into believing that in the bread alone is the body of Christ and in the wine alone his blood, for Christ is present fully and integrally in either or both. To dispel any doubt about the matter, the Council declared that the communion of laymen in one kind should be regarded as lawful. The decree buried the hope that the Chalice would be introduced generally, at least in Bohemia and Moravia. The differences between the Catholics and the Utraquists were to continue, although the Compacts envisaged a uniform organization under one archbishop.

The arrival and publication at Prague of the December decree caused disillusionment among the Utraquists. They resented the Council's retreat from the line marked by the Compacts and lost interest in any further negotiations by which the remaining problems might be solved. Philibert's position was seriously shattered, as few people, indeed, were interested in such a settlement as he had in mind. At that critical time he was almost completely isolated. Sigismund, who otherwise had shielded him by the royal authority, departed from Prague on November 11, 1437, having Hungary as his destination. His health was so impaired that he could not ride and was to be carried in a chair on men's shoulders. A strong unit or horsemen escorted the sickly king. At a respectful distance followed a band of jesters and prostitutes, the latter under their own banner. The procession moved from one stage to another and reached, after ten days, the royal borough of Znojmo in southern Moravia. There Sigismund succumbed to his illness and died, sitting on the throne, on November 9, 1437. His body was not carried back to Prague but was taken by Queen-Empress Barbara to Hungary for burial.

Bishop Philibert was not discouraged by the increasing difficulties and dwindling following from further attempts to heal the rift between the Hussites and the Roman Church. During his long absence, first at Basel and since 1436 in Bohemia, he apparently lost contact with his own diocese and had no desire to return to Coutances in faraway Normandy. He died in Prague in June, 1439. Although he had not been appointed to the See of Prague, he was buried in the Cathedral of Saint Vitus, where bodies of many Czech prelates had been interred. His chief collaborator among the Utraquists, Christian or Prachatice, died early in September, 1439. With him the Hussite clergy lost one of its distinguished members who was generally respected, as even the radical elements retained memories of his friendly relations with John Hus during the latter's life.

Thus in the course of several months the effort at conciliation on the basis of the Compacts lost its two principal champions. No Catholic prelate came to Bohemia to occupy the position held formerly by Bishop Philibert, and Christian's successor, John Příbram, was not destined for a role of mediator. After three and a half years of concerted efforts to restore Bohemia to its traditional rank among the countries of the Roman obedience, the country seemed to be pushed back to the position from which the negotiators started at Cheb in 1432.

IN SEARCH OF POLITICAL STABILITY

Bohemia rose to prominence under the kings of the House of Luxemburg. Their era began in 1310, when Prince John, the only son of the Emperor Henry VII, was offered the hand of the Czech Princess Elizabeth, who ascended the throne along with her husband. Elizabeth, the second sister of the last male member of the native dynasty of Bohemia, was regarded as the lawful heiress to the throne; but according to the prevalent ideas, she could not rule alone. Her marriage was approved by the leading lords, who preferred the Emperor's son to any other candidate.

Three members of the Luxemburg family ruled Bohemia before the outbreak of the Hussite revolution: John (1310–1346), Charles IV (1346–1378), and Wenceslas IV (1378–1419), the eldest of Charles's sons. The Luxemburgs retained their family possessions in western Germany, but resided permanently in Bohemia, the solid basis of their power. While John spent most of his life out of the country, participating in knightly activities and warlike adventures, Charles came to be attached to the land of his birth and was proud of his origin, on his mother's side, from the Přemysl House, whose members had ruled Bohemia for several centuries up to 1306.

The territory which John took over after his coronation was much larger than the Luxemburg patrimony, and was for the most part rich by nature. It was divided into two provinces, Bohemia and Moravia, which the descendants of the mythical Přemysl had regarded as their family domain and had saved from fragmentation by internal conflicts. The international position of Bohemia had been weakened by obligations imposed on its rulers by the Holy Roman Emperors in the earlier Middle Ages, long before the extinction of the native dynasty. John contributed very little to the internal stability of his kingdom, but added to the original boundary new territories to the north and northeast. Charles IV followed in his father's footsteps. He not only made new acquisitions, but also regulated by several charters the relations between Bohemia, the nucleus of the kingdom, and the incorporated provinces.[24]

Although the Luxemburgs promoted the welfare and expansion of the country and were, on the whole, popular, Charles did not assign to the dynasty the highest position in the political organization of his domains. Knowing the constitutional problems by which his father's reign had been aggravated, he espoused the idea that the dynasty and the people, represented by the upper social classes, should recognize the Crown as the supreme factor in the nation and as the symbol of unity. Such a concept of government was gaining ground at that time, not only in Bohemia but also in other countries, especially those which had lost their native dynasties and had called in rulers of foreign origin.

The language of pertinent charters was not always clear and simple, but Charles and his contemporaries made a distinction between the jewelled diadem and the Crown as a symbol of sovereignty, independence, and unity of the realm. To support this concept, Charles procured for himself and his successors a new magnificent crown of gold and precious stones and issued a statute requiring that after each coronation ceremony it should repose on the skull of the patron saint of the country, Prince Wenceslas. By linking the constitutional issues with the ancient religious traditions, Charles added to the prestige of the Crown and made the concept both popular and inviolable. When he confirmed his father's acquisitions and defined the ties between the various parts of the kingdom, he subordinated them not to the dynasty but to the Crown.[25]

At the end of Charles's life, five provinces were united under the Crown of Saint Wenceslas: Bohemia, Moravia, Silesia, and Upper and Lower Lusatias. Although under the same rule, they were only loosely connected with each other and preserved their distinct traditions and local constitutions. Their populations were of different origins, and several languages were used in their official and private intercourse. Bohemia and Moravia were preponderantly Czech in blood and speech. In Silesia the upper classes were mostly German, while the rest of the population were Slavs, either Czechs or Poles. In both Lusatias the nobility and the townspeople were also almost entirely German; the peasants, known as the Lusatian Serbs, spoke their own tongue, which belonged to the group of West Slavonic languages and was closely related to the Czech. It was not always easy to secure harmonious collaboration between the two racial elements. Both the Slavs and the Germans were interested in the preservation of their rights and domains, and were unwilling to yield to pressures from a neighbor of the other race.

Of the five parts of the kingdom over which Charles and his successors ruled, Bohemia was the largest and strongest in every respect. Its provincial capital, Prague, held a unique position, as it was the permanent residence of the kings. It was also recognized, though not without opposition, as the administrative center of the entire kingdom. Supreme officers of Bohemia served as the governing body for that province, and endeavored also to extend their authority over the other provinces. As such matters were seldom regulated by written documents, usurpations occurred frequently and provincial administrations raised objections against repeated attempts to institute the provincial board of Bohemia as the supreme administrative body of the kingdom. The practice of entrusting the key positions to the natives of Bohemia was one of the sources of resentment. It has to be admitted, however, that the combination of provincial and national offices helped to keep the five provinces together. Other links were established by appointments of Bohemian nobles as royal captains in Silesia and in the Lusatias. Some aristocratic houses of Bohemia purchased estates in the incorporated provinces or intermarried with the landowning nobility there.

The charters on which the political organization of the kingdom was based dated mostly from 1348. During the period of stability under Charles IV and Wenceslas IV, they were either supplemented by other documents or practical measures, so that no separatist tendencies hindered the peaceful coalescence of the diverse territories which the Luxemburgs held under their scepter. Charles liked to emphasize his ancestral links with the House of Přemysl, and that endeared him to the Czechs in Bohemia and Moravia. Under Wenceslas IV the Czech language gained the dominant position at the royal court and the dynasty came to be assimilated to the pattern of national life. In the circle of Wenceslas' friends and favorites, persons born in Bohemia were in the majority, but some court offices were assigned either to Moravians or Silesians, as the personal qualities more often than the family background determined the selection.

The Hussite movement threw the system, which Charles had laboriously constructed, into disorder, and put the loyalty of the incorporated provinces to a severe test. Although the spiritual and military leaders of the Hussites tried hard to win the Czech people for the communion in both kinds, they never met with full success. The percentage of those who remained faithful to the Pope was higher in Moravia than in Bohemia, in which the movement had originated. The German-speaking inhabitants of the kingdom held on to the official church doctrine, so that the linguistic boundary marked also the differences in religion.

The division of the population of the kingdom in matters of faith was a serious problem which neither the secular nor the spiritual authorities could dismiss from their thoughts. It gained immensely in importance after the death of Wenceslas IV. Knowing of the Hussite opposition, Sigismund made common cause with the German-speaking subjects and accentuated by his decision the feud between the Czechs and the Teutons. In the spring of 1420 he made the capital of Silesia, the populous and prosperous city of Breslau, his headquarters, and from there he marched with large armies against Bohemia. Sigismund's coronation in July, 1420, was recognized as lawful by the Catholic sections of the population, irrespective of language, whereas the Hussites contested its validity.

The rift caused by religious dissensions threatened to destroy the network of statutes and legal provisions by which the five provinces were kept together. The Hussites of Bohemia opposed Sigismund resolutely for about fifteen years. Of the two groups of inhabitants upon whose support Sigismund could count, one, the German-speaking townsfolk, was decimated, while the other, the Catholic lords, were kept in check by the Hussite captains.

In the struggle for Moravia, which the Hussites wanted to attach to their domain, no decisive victory was won. The province was not a compact unit. The larger part of its territory as the royal domain was under the direct control of the ruler. The bishop of Olomouc owned properties which for their size and organization could, indeed, be regarded as a state within the state. The Duchy of Opava was loosely connected with Moravia, forming a transition territory from Moravia to Silesia. The royal domain in Moravia changed hands several times, and in October, 1423, Sigismund gave it into the temporary possessions to his son-in-law, Albrecht of Austria.[26] By this transfer the position of the anti-Hussite elements in Moravia was considerably strengthened. Royal boroughs there did not pass under Czech control, as it happened in Bohemia, but continued to exist as German-speaking enclaves in the compact Czech area. It was of great significance that the See of Olomouc never was vacant, so that the Catholic party in Moravia always had its visible head.

The provinces of Silesia and the Lusatias, though in many respects similar, presented problems which could not be solved by recourse to arms. Silesia, originally a portion of Poland, had disintegrated before its attachment to the kingdom of Bohemia, and as a consequence several princely houses ruled over the Silesian lands. A fairly large portion of the Silesian territory came, after the extinction of the local families, under royal control. The administrative system of the royal domain resembled that of Bohemia, with the higher and lesser nobility in leading positions. The royal city of Breslau, the seat of the assembly of the Silesian princes and nobles as well as the bishop's residence, was in the hands of the German patriciate and stood invariably in the forefront of opposition to Hussite designs.

The internal structure of the two Lusatias was looser and had its peculiarities. In Upper Lusatia, six royal boroughs were traditionally a league; in Lower Lusatia, the big estate was the characteristic feature. Lusatian resistance presented less danger to the Hussite cause than the determined opposition of the Silesian upper classes, supported by the national wealth of the province.

In the protracted struggle for the throne, Silesia and the Lusatias served Sigismund for several years as a base from which he could launch expeditions against Bohemia. As long as the Hussites adhered to Žižka's idea that the enemy should be allowed to cross the mountain ridges and then be attacked on Bohemian soil, the incorporated provinces were spared the horrors of war. With the change of the Hussite strategy, for which Prokop the Bald was responsible, hard times set in for the less protected areas that could be reached without too much risk from the strongholds of the Hussite brotherhoods. Their methods of warfare, especially the use of armed wagons, facilitated swift raids by smaller units and their return with booty and prisoners. Some expeditions were carefully organized and developed into major operations against the castles of Sigismund's partisans and the walled cities allied with the landowning nobility. During the most daring invasion in the spring of 1428, the Hussite units entered the suburbs of Breslau, but their artillery was not strong enough to break the system of fortifications around the inner city.

The forces commanded by Hussite captains were not large enough to make possible the permanent occupation of any of the incorporated provinces. The military brotherhoods pursued more modest aims and were satisfied when they prevented there the concentration of troops for another invasion of Bohemia. Recognizing the military superiority of the Hussites, the leagues of nobles and cities were willing to enter into agreements with them. Conversions to the Hussite faith were rare, but some nobles like Bolek, the prince of Opole, joined the Hussite brotherhoods in military operations.

When contacts between Sigismund and the Hussites were established, his admission to Bohemia was the chief problem awaiting settlement. Second in importance was the release of Moravia from Albrecht's control and its reunion with Bohemia. This objective arose not only from traditional sentiments, but also from the desire to extend the benefit of the Compacts and other agreements of 1436 to the Hussites in Moravia. Sigismund tenaciously resisted the pressure, as he had no money with which to compensate his son-in-law for the services rendered during the Hussite wars. No legal problems stood in the way of a reunion of Silesia and of the two Lusatias with Bohemia; but Sigismund's reign, after his entry into Prague, was too short to make possible more than a formal resumption of peaceful contacts.

A serious crisis beset the kingdom of Bohemia after Sigismund's death in December 1437. The Estates contested the principle of hereditary monarchy and claimed the right to elect a new king. A strong faction, in which Oldřich of Rožmberk and Menhart of Hradec held the commanding position, favored Albrecht of Austria, the husband of Sigismund's only daughter, Elizabeth. Another and more numerous party, headed by Hynek Ptáček of Pirkštejn, opposed Albrecht's bid for the crown of Saint Wenceslas, fearing that once established, he would show less interest in upholding the Compacts than his father-in-law had done.

As the resources from which Ptáček's partisans could support their campaign against Albrecht were rather limited, it was necessary to agree on a candidate to the crown who could send forces to Bohemia and help to win a victory. The decision was neither quick nor easy, and in the end proved to be ill-starred. After protracted discussions, the majority of Ptáček's party chose Prince Casimir, the younger brother of King Władysław. In selecting a Polish prince who at that time was only thirteen years old, Albrecht's opponents were guided not only by the sense of close kinship between the Czechs and the Poles but also by the memories of the former attempts of the Hussite statesmen to secure help against Sigismund from Poland and Lithuania.

In these schemes Silesia played an important role on account of its geographical position. Anti-Albrecht sentiment was particularly strong in northeastern Bohemia, and the roads thence to Poland led through Silesia. If the Poles had decided to ally themselves with Ptáček's partisans effectively, their armies could reach Prague only through Silesia, as Moravia was under Albrecht's control.

The conflict did not develop into a war on a large scale. Polish troops, which in the early summer of 1438 penetrated into northeastern Bohemia, were not strong enough to defeat Albrecht's party. Reinforcements were rushed to Silesia, but they did not adequately coordinate their operations with Albrecht's opponents. This failure caused disillusionment among the Czech sponsors of Casimir's candidature, and strengthened conservative elements in Poland. Grouped around the Bishop of Cracow, Zbigniew Oleśnicki, the Polish foes of Hussitism turned the scales in favor of negotiations with Albrecht to settle the conflict.

Albrecht's position, originally rather weak and precarious, had improved considerably before the Polish offer reached him. He had been crowned in Prague and had reached the capital of Silesia, Breslau, without encountering any strong opposition. He knew well that Hungary, which he also claimed after Sigismund's death, was seriously threatened by the Turks; therefore, he favored a speedy understanding with the Poles. To conclude an armistice more easily, he did not insist on severe terms for his opponents in Bohemia, but authorized his plenipotentiaries to treat with them and induce them to lay down their arms. Peace in Bohemia was not fully restored, but local clashes between aristocratic coteries were not so serious as to require the King's personal intervention. Albrecht was fully occupied in Hungary and entrusted the administration of Bohemia to two governors, Oldřich of Rožmberk and Menhart of Hradec.[27]

The expedition against the Turks progressed slowly, as Albrecht's forces were too small and too badly organized to make possible a vigorous offensive. Late in August the Sultan's troops took an important fortress on the Danube, Smederevo, and started preparing for an invasion of Hungary. Albrecht's army suffered from a lack of supplies, diseases, and disorder. Only the advent of rainy season saved the decimated forces from a complete disaster. The King also fell ill, and was anxious to leave the Hungarian marshlands as quickly as possible, hoping that a mere sight of his beloved Vienna would restore him to health. On his sad retreat he reached only central Hungary and died not far from Esztergom on October 27, 1439.

On February 22, 1440, less than four months after Albrecht's death, his widow Elizabeth gave birth to a boy who received at baptism the name of Ladislaus (László), popular in Hungary and current among the Czechs in the form of Ladislav. The laws valid in Bohemia contained no unequivocal clause which could be invoked to dispel doubts concerning Ladislav's right to the throne. Closely linked with the question of succession were other problems brought into the open by the Hussite revolution, which Ladislav's father and grandfather had failed to solve.

Those who favored Ladislav's recognition as a candidate for the crown of Bohemia could point to a charter, issued by Charles IV on April 7, 1348, which granted hereditary rights to both male and female members of the Luxemburg family and stipulated that only after its extinction the prelates, the nobles, and the community of citizens of the kingdom could proceed to an election.[28] Some other less solemn charters made even clearer Charles's intention to extend the right to the throne to both his lineal and collateral descendants.[29] Sigismund's only daughter, Elizabeth, had been married to Albrecht long before her father's death, so that it was not her succession but the recognition of her husband's claims that split the ranks of the nobility of Bohemia. Ladislav was a legitimate child, and the great-grandson on the maternal side of Charles IV; but so many stormy events had taken place since that wise ruler's death that serious disputes and disharmony in interpretation of his charters were to be expected. Some members of the pro-Habsburg party also invoked the treaties of mutual succession, concluded in 1364 and 1366 between Charles IV and Rudolf IV of Austria; [30] but that seemed to be the second line of defense, rather weak and unpopular in wider circles.

The infant prince lived first at the court of his mother in Hungary, and after her death in December, 1442, was moved to Austria. Apart from him, the main line of the Habsburgs (Albertine) had no male members. The family was represented by the senior member of the younger (Leopoldine) line, Frederick. A feud between Frederick and his younger brother Albrecht VI hindered the efforts of Ladislav's partisans for a speedy recognition of his hereditary rights. Frederick had a stronger position than Albrecht and his chances of victory were considerably enhanced when the Electors of the Empire decided, early in 1440, to offer him the imperial dignity, vacated by the death of Albrecht V. He accepted after several weeks of deliberations and came to be known as Frederick III. In August, 1440, he was recognized as Ladislav's guardian and accepted that function, pledging to support the boy's claims to the thrones of Bohemia and Hungary.[31]

Although no serious difficulties were to be expected in the incorporated provinces, the Estates of Bohemia held different opinions on the constitutional issues arising from Albrecht's premature death. In the winter of 1439–40, attempts were made to build up a solid front of the lords and knights and, indeed, various factions of the nobility showed willingness to stop bickering and unite on some co-ordinated action. On January 29, 1440, they reached an agreement on a "letter of peace," pledging solidarity and mutual support in the defense of their liberties.[32] It was of great importance that the Catholic lords accepted the Compacts as one of the basic laws of Bohemia, thus nipping in the bud the danger of a revival of the wars of religion. No governor was elected by the assembly to administer the country during the interregnum. Instead, in the counties into which Bohemia was traditionally divided, leagues were organized to secure co-operation of the local lords, lesser nobility, and royal boroughs, irrespective of their religious affiliation. In the documents relating to them, the term "landfrid," borrowed from the German, came to be used more frequently than before, indicating that the preservation of peace in the country was the chief purpose of regional agreements. The "landfrids," indeed, reduced the danger of local feuds, but gave the population of Bohemia less protection than could have come from a king, or at least from a duly appointed and generally respected provincial governor.

Making full use of the vacancy of the throne, the lords of Bohemia were averse to a public scrutiny of the documents regulating the succession and maintained that Ladislav's tender age was the main obstacle to any consideration of his claims. The situation presented a much better opportunity for asserting the elective principle than had been the case either after the death of Wenceslas IV in 1419 or of Sigismund in 1437; and the lords were determined to promote energetically their own aims. They were also on the whole agreed that the right to elect a new king belonged exclusively to them, and that the nobility in the incorporated provinces should play a passive role. Little attention was given to the text of Charles's charter, which was by no means explicit in granting the monopoly to the Estates of Bohemia.[33] Serious difficulties arose when the lesser nobility and royal boroughs challenged the lords, claiming the right of active participation in the election. When confronted with tough opposition from so many sides, the lords gave up their attempts to establish an oligarchy and consented to the formation of a body of electors in which the lords had eighteen, the knights fourteen, and the royal boroughs also fourteen members.[34] Several candidates were considered, and finally the majority of the voters decided for Albrecht, Duke of Bavaria. As in his childhood he had resided at Wenceslas' court, he knew Czech and thus seemed to be better qualified for the office than the other candidate, Frederick of Hohenzollern, Markgrave of Brandenburg.

Albrecht's rejection of the proffered throne caused consternation among the Estates and shattered their ranks. No solid majority could be found to support Frederick of Brandenburg. At this juncture the radical Hussite wing revived the idea of a dynastic union with Poland. The most articulate among the radicals were the former members of Tábor, who survived the catastrophe at Lipany and paid only lip service to the Compacts. Their candidate was no longer Prince Casimir but the King Władysław III himself. The Hussite champions of the Polish candidature were encouraged by the news from Hungary, where a large portion of the nobility, out of opposition to the infant prince Ladislav, espoused Władysław's cause. They hoped that by co-ordinated efforts the Habsburgs could be driven out both from Hungary and their own country. The scheme of an anti-Habsburg campaign was quickly concocted, but was not promoted effectively enough to give the Pole a fair chance of success. In Bohemia the calls for the election of a ruler of the "Slavic tongue" evoked but a faint echo, as the former allies were split on that issue and nobody came to Bohemia from Poland to re-establish their unity.

The most influential among the Hussite nobles, Hynek Ptáček of Pirkštejn, who once had favored the Polish candidature, kept aloof when the plan was revived. His coolness was of paramount importance, as he headed the strongest of the competing groups, indeed the majority of the Hussites. As captain of the Kouřim county in central Bohemia, he exercised strong influence in the political and religious developments and attached to his domain four other counties, those of Čáslav, Chrudim, Hradec Králové, and Mladá Boleslav, all administered by his partisans. Supported by this solid bloc, Ptáček was able to hold the ground against the conservative forces whose power had increased under Sigismund and Albrecht.

It was to Ptáček's great advantage that the conservative elements among the Czech nobility were split on several issues and could not be welded into a single party. One of the causes of disharmony were the Compacts. On some rare occasions, as that of the signing of the "letter of peace," the Catholic lords acquiesced in general references to the Compacts, since a negative attitude would have precluded their agreement with the Hussite nobility. Personally, they did not regard the Compacts as binding, since they were not sanctioned by the Pope. The church organization on Catholic domains was seldom adjusted to the Compacts, but remained under the full jurisdiction of the "Upper Consistory," whose members recognized only the Pope as the supreme authority in matters of faith.

The foremost representative of this orientation was Oldřich of Rožmberk, whose property formed the largest economic and administrative unit in Bohemia. There was no parish in that part of the country in which the Lord's Supper was administered in both kinds. The center of the Rožmberk domains, the castle and the borough of Krumlov, situated at the bend of the river Vltava, was one of the Catholic strongholds in Bohemia. During Oldřich's life Krumlov flourished and was visited by many envoys or travelers from other Catholic areas. It was of great importance for Oldřich's political designs that his property reached the Austrian and Bavarian borders at various points. He could travel into those two countries or send his emissaries there without any difficulty, and there was really little danger that his correspondence with his allies abroad would be intercepted by his Czech foes. Oldřich's implacable enemy was the party of Tábor, not only the city of that name, but also the other boroughs in southern Bohemia which had been allied to Tábor prior to the Lipany battle. The resentment against him was shared by many landowners in that area whose estates were too small to compete successfully with the Rožmberk property. The Taborites often talked of Oldřich as the "lame devil," referring to the physical handicap with which he had apparently been born.

Ambitious and unbalanced, Oldřich was not a safe ally. As he had developed the art of dissimulation almost to perfection, not even his friends were able to unravel, in critical situations, his thoughts and designs. Some Catholic lords in southwestern Bohemia usually sided with the Rožmberk, whereas others, guided more by political aspirations than religious allegiance, maintained friendly contacts with the Hussites, especially with their right wing. Personal animosities often hindered formation of solid blocs.

There was only a slight difference in matters of faith between Oldřich and Menhart of Hradec. The latter communicated in both kinds and paid lip service to the Compacts, but otherwise conformed entirely to the doctrine and rites of the Roman Church. Menhart had a fairly strong following among conservative laymen and clerics, but he did not control a compact area in any part of Bohemia. The alliance between Oldřich and Menhart did not develop into an honest and lasting attachment. Selfish motives on both sides were stronger than the concern for political stability and peace in Bohemia. Menhart derived considerable benefits from friendly contacts with his powerful neighbor. On the other hand, Oldřich and his partisans could not ignore Menhart's ability to rally around himself the conservative Hussites who would not have submitted to Oldřich's leadership. As the Supreme Burgrave of Prague, Menhart enjoyed not only social prestige but wielded much power when the throne was vacant. The royal castles at Hradčany and Karlštejn were under Menhart's control, and thus he had in custody both the coronation jewels and the archives of the realm.

As the staunchest supporter of both Sigismund and Albrecht, Oldřich seemed to be destined to play the leading role in the Habsburg party. Both the Queen-dowager Elizabeth and Frederick III were anxious to preserve his good will. They realized, however, that their family interests would be jeopardized if too closely linked with the Catholic cause in Bohemia. Therefore, Menhart's sympathies were no less valued by the Habsburgs than Oldřich's support of their cause.

After the failure of the negotiations with the Bavarian prince, both the Catholics and the moderate Hussites re-established contacts with the Queen-dowager and the Habsburg princes. Nobody reproached them for their temporary desertion of Ladislav's cause, as they were too powerful to be estranged. With no suitable candidate in sight, nothing would have been simpler than to endorse unreservedly Ladislav's rights and to agree to a governorship during his minority. There was, however, among the aristocratic coteries no desire to proceed along that straight line, as most of them wanted to exploit the situation by either stressing the elective principle or by securing promotions for themselves through bargaining with the custodians of the prospective candidate to the throne. Ladislav's infancy often served as a mere excuse for delays in taking the decisive step.

While both Oldřich of Rožmberk and Menhart of Hradec hindered the formation of a solid bloc of the Estates by dallying, Ptáček moved ahead to break the deadlock. Several weeks after the death of the Queen-dowager, he journeyed to Vienna to negotiate with Frederick III. It took him but little time to find out that the King had no intention of getting directly involved in the political and religious problems of Bohemia. Ptáček did not press the matter, but withdrew discreetly the offer of the crown of Bohemia to Frederick, which he had made in the early stage of his negotiations. Thereupon, he declared himself for Ladislav, though not without reservation. He urged Frederick to move from Vienna to Prague and to administer the kingdom in Ladislav's name. Nothing but evasive answers came from Frederick, and Ptáček realized that his mission had ended in failure.

Ptáček's dealings with Frederick III could not escape the notice of the conservative lords, always jealous and distrustful of their more energetic rival. They knew from their sources of information that contacts between Ptáček and Frederick were to be resumed in September, 1443, and exercised influence on the composition of the delegation to Vienna, ostensibly to make it truly representative. When the time arrived, both Oldřich and Menhart rode to Vienna, whereas Ptáček's party was represented by one of its less distinguished members. Ptáček's decision not to attend the conference strengthened automatically Oldřich's position, as no other member of the delegation could compare with him in wealth and social contacts. About a month was spent in efforts to make Frederick III more tractable, but the results were far from satisfactory. The King declared his intention to act as Ladislav's guardian, and pledged to observe the confirmation of ancient privileges by Albrecht II.[35] He was not satisfied with informal assurances of loyalty but requested categorically that the Prince's rights be confirmed by the provincial Diet. Pending that, he was not ready to move from Vienna to Prague.

Frederick's answer to questions presented to him by the Czech envoys was hotly debated at the provincial assembly in January, 1444. Spokesmen for Ptáček's party expressed their dissatisfaction with the King's policy. They recommended that more energetic steps be taken to get Frederick's support for their scheme of political and administrative consolidation. The Diet failed to restore unanimity among the Czech factions and nothing was adopted but a general declaration in Ladislav's favor.[36] The vote was not followed by any concrete steps toward regency, but it helped the Habsburgs indirectly, as it precluded in the years to come any serious consideration of another candidate than Ladislav. As Frederick III refused to participate actively in the pacification of Bohemia on Ladislav's behalf, the country was destined to exist for almost a decade without stable government.

Since the resumption of political activities in the fall of 1443, Oldřich's prospects had been improving. The acquiescence of the January Diet in half measures prolonged the interregnum and created almost unlimited possibilities for maneuvering. Another improvement of Oldřich's chances came in August, 1444, when his rival, Hynek Ptáček of Pirkštejn, was stricken by a contagious disease and died at a not very advanced age. Although much nearer to his goal than ever before, Oldřich was not ready for an all-out offensive against his opponents. He was wealthy enough to finance any ambitious scheme, but more was needed than money to bring all the conservative groups under his banner. Oldřich's personality was not attractive enough to qualify him for leadership of a bloc to be formed of Catholics and conservative Hussites. Even Menhart of Hradec was not prepared to go beyond mere temporary alignments with him.

The league of the Hussite nobility controlling east-central and eastern Bohemia was not thrown into confusion by Ptáček's death. At a well-attended assembly at Kutná Hora in September, 1444, one of Ptáček's lieutenants, George of Poděbrady, was recognized as the leader, and his position was not seriously challenged by any of the wealthy lords who had stood by Ptáček during his lifetime. The party ranks were so firmly closed that no defection occurred to play into the hands of either Menhart or of Oldřich.

Neither George himself nor his close relatives recorded the date of his birth, but it has been believed that he was born in April, 1420, at the castle of Poděbrady. George's father, Victorin, was a member of the Bohemian branch of an old noble family of Kunštát, and apart from Poděbrady, situated east of Prague on the river Labe, he owned land in other parts of the country. A fairly large portion of that property came into his possession when he married Anne of Vartemberk, from a family no less distinguished than that of the lords of Kunštát. Through the Vartemberk relatives, the lords of Kunštát and Poděbrady established relationship with the Rožmberks and the lords of Hradec. It is assumed that George was a nephew of Oldřich of Rožmberk.

Religious differences weakened the family ties. Victorin espoused the Hussite cause and had his share in its defense against Sigismund. A close friendship between him and Žižka gave rise to a story that the latter visited Poděbrady and acted as George's godfather. Born at the very beginning of the war period, George was not brought up in a comfortable and cheerful atmosphere. His father died in 1427, and it seems likely that his mother either preceded her husband in death or passed away soon afterwards. Thereafter George lived with his relatives in Moravia, but returned to Bohemia after some years. As a lad of fourteen, he participated in the battle at Lipany and witnessed the disaster of the Orphan and Tábor brotherhoods.

The castle of Poděbrady was not a sumptuous edifice and it was not Victorin's ambition to attract to it poets, artists, or theologians of the Hussite orientation. A simple way of life prevailed there in keeping with Hussite rigorism. George received the rudiments of education from the priests who lived either in the castle or in the adjacent town, but his training was not rounded off and was apparently no higher than the average. George never learned Latin and had hardly more than an elementary knowledge of German, so that even at his advanced age he was able to converse with envoys and visitors from abroad only through interpreters. It was rightly said of him that in the school of experience he matured into a wise man "whose sense had been sharpened by nature, not by training in letters." [37]

George's appearance at Lipany on the side of his uncle could not have been more than an episode, but not much time was to elapse between that date and George's first appointment to a public office. When Sigismund settled the dispute concerning the distribution of the seats in the provincial tribunal, George, then seventeen, became one of the judges.[38] At that time he was probably released from guardianship and took over from his uncle the family domains in Bohemia. His attachment to Hynek Ptáček also dated from that time, so that the year 1437 may be accepted as the starting point of George's amazing career. As one of the captains of the Mladá Boleslav county, George rendered Ptáček valuable services and in loyal co-operation with him he moved to the front.

By marriage in 1440, or thereabout, to Kunhuta of Šternberk, George enlarged the network of family contacts and increased his following. It was important to his future career that by these new links he came into relationship with families formerly attached to the Orphans or the Taborites. While these families were reserved in their attitude toward Ptáček, they allied themselves with George and, after the change of leadership in 1444 gave a wider basis to the League of Poděbrady, as the party was often called.

George's chief concern was a speedy suppression of the rivalries which were sapping the strength of the country. He soon realized that no energetic intervention could be expected from the lackadaisical guardian of the infant prince Ladislav, and that all constructive forces in Bohemia would have to be mobilized to induce the recalcitrants to loyal co-operation. Frederick III once more refused to be involved in the affairs of Bohemia and declined an invitation to a meeting with the Czech envoys in a place not far from the Austrian border. For several years no step was taken by him to establish regency, the best safeguard of Ladislav's interests. Bohemia was saved from ruin partly by George's efforts, partly by the favorable constellation of forces in its vicinity. No German prince was strong enough to attack it, while the eastern neighbors, Poland and Hungary, were experiencing serious troubles after the catastrophe at Varna in November, 1444.

It is not a purely academic question to ask which of George's opponents was more dangerous, Oldřich or Menhart. The Rožmberk domains could be converted without too much expenditure into a base from which the Catholic party could advance into other parts of the country or in which it would be invulnerable if attacked. Oldřich's widely ramified connections with the Bavarian and Austrian nobility were also to be taken seriously into consideration. Oldřich also was in a better position than any Utraquist leader for closer contacts with Frederick's court or the Holy See. It was rather risky to leave such a formidable foe, unreconciled or unbroken, on one's flank. Oldřich, true to his traditional tactics, evolved complicated maneuvers to avoid an open clash. Even when induced to participate in general congresses of the nobility, he eschewed formal obligations, and if forced to attach his signature and seal to any resolution not according to his inmost thought, he had no scruples in openly sabotaging it or in working clandestinely against its realization.

For about two years following Ptáček's death Oldřich evaded his political opponents and pursued his selfish designs. His contacts with the Austrian and other aristocrats connected with the Habsburg court gave him a good deal of personal satisfaction, but he sensed a danger of isolation from the aristocratic factions in Bohemia. When approached directly by George,[39] he promised to participate in a congress of representatives of the nobility and of the royal boroughs. It was held in June, 1446, at Pelhřimov in southeastern Bohemia and initiated proposals which had to be presented to the provincial Diet, scheduled for November.[40]

It was of great importance that the Diet was attended not only by the members from Bohemia but also by delegates from the incorporated provinces. Oldřich was present only to convince himself that George's authority had considerably risen during the two years of intensive activity in the areas which once had obeyed Ptáček. No opportunity presented itself to Oldřich to challenge George directly, but he carefully watched dissensions among the lords and the lower Estates, the gentry and the royal boroughs. Curiously enough, the spokesmen of the third Estate played, unwittingly, into Oldřich's hands, as they were, for their own reasons, opposed to the appointment of a governor with far-reaching powers.

One resolution adopted at the Diet was addressed to Frederick III and was to be delivered to him by special delegates.[41] The Estates urged him to send Ladislav to Prague so that the boy could be trained for kingship and crowned at an opportune time. The delegates were instructed to point out that Ladislav's presence would weaken the centrifugal tendencies in the incorporated provinces which were reluctant to obey the Czech leaders. In one point the instruction hinted at the Estates' determination to open negotiations with foreign princes, if Frederick III persisted in his dilatory policy and neither authorized a strong regency nor sent the boy prince to Bohemia.

Oldřich gave his consent to the instruction for the delegates to Vienna but soon after his return from the Diet to Krumlov he resumed contacts with Frederick III and gave him a biased report of the Prague deliberations.[42] Encouraged by Oldřich's account, Frederick III felt no urge to heed the requests for Ladislav's extradition, and invited the Estates to appoint a more representative delegation with which he was prepared to discuss the relevant questions.[48] He suggested late September, 1447, as the date of the conference, so as to gain more time for himself and such key figures in Ladislav's patrimony as the double-faced Rožmberk.

Looking at matters from a different angle than that of the Czechs, Frederick believed he had good reasons for procrastination. Ladislav had claims not only to Bohemia but also to Hungary, and his transfer from neutral Vienna to Prague would have imperiled his chances in the other kingdom. After the Varna battle the consolidation of Hungary was even more urgent than the establishment of a regency in Bohemia. To avoid litigation with the Hungarian nobles, Frederick was determined not to release Ladislav from his custody, and he proceeded to deal with the Czechs accordingly. He made no arrangement for a meeting in September, 1447, so that even the optimists among George's partisans lost hope of a speedy settlement of the long-pending questions. In order to prevent an outburst of indignation, Frederick approached both Oldřich and Menhart through intermediaries, to assure that at least their party would not change its orientation.

There was really not much danger that the conservative leaders would break off the ties with Vienna and seek close contacts with the Poděbrady party. Personal and ideological differences were so profound that nothing more could be accomplished than a temporary alignment if both parties saw good reasons for it. At this juncture George and his lieutenants resolved to act independently of the conservative party to reach the immediate objective—the appointment of a governor for Bohemia. Apart from the troubles arising from the competition of leagues and factions, centrifugal tendencies in the incorporated provinces made the appointment of a competent administrator a matter of utmost urgency. The Dukes of Saxony, Frederick and William, watched the developments in Bohemia more closely than any other German princes and made no secret of their desire to extend their control over some portions of the kingdom bordering on their own domains, especially Lower Lusatia. Bohemia, which in normal times was able to paralyze separatist movements and frustrate aggressive designs of her neighbors, lost much of her influence in the remote, predominantly German and Catholic areas. The policy of Frederick of Saxony encountered for some time only one barrier—the alertness of the Markgrave of Brandenburg who hoped that the disputed areas would one day drop into his lap. The rivalry of the two princes reduced for the time being the danger of alienation of Lower Lusatia, but could not be relied on permanently.

When George took all these matters into consideration, he concluded reasonably that Menhart's strength was to be regarded as a greater obstacle in the way toward political consolidation of Bohemia than Oldřich's wealth and cunning. No governor could effectively administer Bohemia, an ideal geographical unit, from any other residence than Prague. As Supreme Burgrave, Menhart controlled that city from the Hradčany heights, and as he showed no inclination to consent to a compromise, he had to be removed from the position which King Sigismund had granted him as a compensation for his unwavering loyalty.

The winter of 1447–48 was spent in manifold preparations for a vigorous offensive, diplomatic against Ladislav's guardian and armed against the Supreme Burgrave. As had been hinted in the instruction for the envoys from the Prague Diet to Frederick III,[44] the Czechs decided to approach some foreign courts to elicit from them sympathetic reaction to the plans hatched out in George's inner circle. Letters to Henry VI of England and several other rulers were prepared for expedition, but it is not quite certain whether they ever reached the addressees or were intercepted by Oldřich of Rožmberk.[45] In them the Czechs complained of Frederick's indifference to their requests for Ladislav's transfer to Prague. The possibility that the Estates would be forced by Frederick's inertia to cut the ties with the Habsburgs and proceed to a free election was vaguely mentioned in the correspondence with the foreign courts. At one time rumors circulated in Bohemia and elsewhere that William of Saxony, the husband of Ladislav's older sister Anne, was considered as a candidate for the crown of Bohemia; but they soon proved to be false. According to all indications, George's partisans did not intend to break away from Ladislav but maneuvered diplomatically to arouse Frederick's fears and thus to incline him to a more energetic support of their endeavors to set up a provisional government for Bohemia.

While these activities were in progress, the Poděbrady party prepared for a less hazardous step—an attack on Menhart's stronghold. Its ranks were consolidated at a congress in June, 1448, at Kutná Hora.[46] Those present reaffirmed their adherence both to the Compacts and of the "letter of peace" of January, 1440. They pledged to help against anyone "detracting from the glory of God or disturbing the commonwealth." Bonds binding the eastern counties and the domains of George's sympathizers scattered all over the country were tightened so as to increase the chances of success in the rapidly approaching attack against Menhart's forces. Although the majority at Kutná Hora were Utraquist, George could count on the support of many Catholic lords, especially from the eastern counties. The congress had no authority to bestow upon George the title of governor of the province. Confident of his strength, he began to use it, signing himself most often simply as governor. On solemn occasions he attached to his name a fuller title of "governor of the kingdom of Bohemia."[47]

Several weeks were needed to complete the diplomatic and military preparations. Rumors from George's headquarters lulled many of his foes into a false sense of security and made them believe that the target of the forthcoming expedition was Frederick, Duke of Saxony. At the end of August, George's troops totalling nine thousand were ready to strike. From a conquered position only a short distance from the Prague walls, George sent an ultimatum to the municipal council, and when no satisfactory answer came, he moved closer to the suburbs. It was too late for Menhart to mobilize his partisans. Among the masses of the townsfolk, George had more sympathizers than enemies and they were ready to help.

In the small hours of September 3, 1448, George's vanguard concentrated on Vyšehrad, one of the key positions in the system of Prague defenses, and conquered it more by ruse than by force. Another unit moved into the streets through a break in the walls and joined the columns advancing from Vyšehrad. At their head rode George with his retinue. The Prague forces offered no organized resistance, so that George easily reached the Old Town Hall and received homage from the assembled aldermen. The garrison of the castle of Hradčany capitulated when encircled by George's horsemen. Its master, Menhart, was discovered in a private home and captured, whereas some other opponents of George's policy saved themselves by flight to their country homes.

It was deemed safer to transfer Menhart from Prague to the castle of Poděbrady. He was kept there despite his son's entreaties that he be released and allowed to live in the family residence. After several weeks of detention, Menhart's physical condition deteriorated. George realized that the death of the captive could give rise to wild rumors and sought ways by which the release could be expedited without any semblance of weakness. Menhart's health was, however, so frail that while moving from Poděbrady to Karlštejn, he succumbed to his illness and died before reaching his destination. His body was carried to Jindřichův Hradec and buried there in the family crypt.

After Menhart's defeat and captivity, his party disintegrated. Only Oldřich of Rožmberk was left to challenge George's bid for the full control of Bohemia.

RELIGIOUS DIVISIONS

The political and administrative problems of Bohemia were aggravated by conflicts arising from religious divisions. The vacancy of the See of Prague was no less disturbing than the absence of an adult bearer of the royal crown. The appointment of an archbishop was a matter of grave concern for the Czech patriots of both the Utraquist and the Catholic parties.

Neither Sigismund nor Albrecht II took seriously their promises to intervene on behalf of the Archbishop-elect, John Rokycana. They did not make any effort to bring about his confirmation by the Pope, knowing well that his election by the provincial Diet was contrary to the practices of the Church. The Estates assembled in Prague after Albrecht's death to give the country provisional administration were likewise concerned about the restitution of religious unity. In the "letter of peace" they reaffirmed their devotion to the Compacts and insisted that all obligations accepted by the Council in 1436 be fulfilled. In particular, they urged that the Archbishop-elect be consecrated and confirmed. As not only the Utraquists but also the Catholics attached their seals to the "letter of peace," no other candidate could be seriously considered.[48]

The unanimous declaration for Rokycana brought into view one of the most sensitive problems to be settled in connection with the vital political issues. The Compacts were nonoperative as long as the Papacy persisted in its noncommittal attitude. As they were not brusquely rejected by Eugene IV, they could serve temporarily as a protection against the resurgence of an aggressive spirit among the Catholic neighbors of Bohemia. But practical implementation of the meager concessions wrested by the Hussites from the Council was hindered by the lack of hierarchical organization. Factional strifes, mostly of an old date, dangerously weakened the Hussite party and a firm, circumspect leadership was a prerequisite to its consolidation.

The initiators of Rokycana's election at the Diet of October, 1435, could hardly foresee the enormous complications which were bound to arise from the close linking of Rokycana's cause with the Compacts. No attempt could be made to reach a permanent agreement with the Church on the Compacts without an accompanying petition that Rokycana be recognized as the most suitable candidate for the archiepiscopal vacancy and invested with the pallium. Rokycana's followers among the nobility felt bound to adhere to the resolution of 1435; but by the insertion of articles into the "letter of peace" relating to the Compacts and Rokycana, they unwillingly precluded the settlement of either problem. Not only in 1440 but also in later years, when the Hussites reiterated their petitions, the sanction of the Compacts seemed to be feasible but the request for an approval by the highest Church authority of an election of ecclesiastical dignitaries by a Diet proved to be a stumbling block.

The endorsement of the Hussite demands by the Catholic lords, headed by Oldřich of Rožmberk, was a tactical success, but this formal manifestation of unity could not be followed by energetic steps in behalf of the Archbishop-elect. During the interregnum, there was no monarch in or outside Bohemia to espouse and earnestly promote Rokycana's cause. The matter was by no means simple, for even if Rokycana had found an advocate among the competitors for the vacant throne, a delicate question would have arisen as to whom the petition should be addressed.

Although not too closely connected with the main centers of Western Christendom, the Hussite leaders were not without information concerning the Church developments. Members of the Council who did not respond to Eugene's appeals and remained in Basel, while he and his staunch followers held sessions, first at Ferrara and later at Florence, resolved to adopt stern measures. The Estates of Bohemia most likely had heard, before inauguration of their Diet, of the deposition of Eugene IV by the depleted Basel council and the election of Felix V. Viewed from Prague, the situation looked chaotic and therefore no specific recommendation was attached to the articles in the "letter of peace" pertaining to religious matters.

The Council's breach with Eugene and Felix's election offered an ample opportunity for bargaining, but the Hussites did not seize the occasion to reap profit from the new schism. Their spokesmen possessed little ability for a successful exploitation of personal ambitions and wranglings. Only few of them were trained in intricate maneuvers or for fishing in troubled waters. Lack of contacts with the highest circles and limited acquaintance with the kaleidoscopic pattern of church life outside their home country undoubtedly acted as a brake. Both Eugene IV and Felix V made attempts to enlist adherents in Bohemia, but met with little success. Even such powerful individuals as Oldřich of Rožmberk shunned binding agreements and waited to see how the wind should blow.

Although backed by the signatories of the "letter of peace," Rokycana had to face opposition among the clergy of Bohemia. In the Hussite party, both its conservative and radical wings, each for different reasons, offered resistance to him and hindered his striving for administrative and doctrinal unification. The administrative center of the Hussites, known as the "Lower Consistory" was not a tool in his hands. The vacancy caused there by the death of Christian of Prachatice was filled in November, 1439, without previous consultation with Rokycana, and the new administrators, John of Příbram and Prokop of Plzeň, were far less compliant than the elderly Christian had been. The signatories of the "letter of peace" apparently pressed the clerics to come to an agreement about the distribution of the functions and offices, but its terms are unknown. If an accord had been reached at all, it had no immediate effects, and the conservative Hussites, obeying the administrators, paid little heed to Rokycana's appeals for conformity. Příbram's group had staunch supporters among the conservative lords and could drive Rokycana into a blind alley, should they prove successful in their repeated attempts to win the Czech Catholics for a *modus vivendi*.

Radical opposition, though tougher and more violent, presented actually a lesser threat than did Příbram's followers. The remnants of the Tábor party were legally in a precarious position, and not much effort would have been needed to coerce them into submission. Sigismund's charter of November, 1436, for the borough of Tábor, was supplemented by an agreement signed by Rokycana and the Tábor leaders, by which four Hussite theologians, Peter Payne, Martin Lupáč, Václav of Dráchov, and Buzek of Kdyně, were empowered to examine all controversial problems and to determine with the use of the "Judge of Cheb" which party held the truth.[49] Although they were expected to deliver their judgment in the Lent of 1437, they deferred it and thus saved Tábor from repressive measures. Knowing that an open attack on Rokycana could precipitate a verdict by the four arbiters against them, the Tábor leaders resorted to passive resistance and thus hindered Rokycana's endeavors to unify the Czechs *sub utraque*.

The Catholics were extremely cautious whenever the re-establishment of hierarchy in Bohemia and other administrative problems were broached. In the assemblies of the nobility, or in other public meetings, the names of Martin Lupáč and Václav of Mýto were seldom mentioned, and all attention was concentrated on Rokycana. The Hussite scheme of church organization for Bohemia, when thus simplified, was not vetoed by the Catholic lords, but their vote could not be regarded as the final word in the controversy. Not the nobility but the "Upper Consistory" held the key, as the problem was not political but primarily ecclesiastical. It was highly unlikely that the chapter of Saint Vitus Cathedral would ever become reconciled to the scheme of organization presupposed by the Compacts. The canons, headed by Dean John of Dubá, maintained that the Compacts lacked papal sanction, and, therefore, could not be accepted as legally valid. When Felix's emissaries attempted to bring the Czech Catholics over to their side, the chapter declined their offers, and although most of its members remained at heart faithful to Eugene IV, the chapter made a declaration of neutrality. This policy precluded an open action against Rokycana either in Rome or at Felix's court, but in private the canons opposed his consecration. They not only regarded his election by the Diet as uncanonical but entertained doubts concerning the validity of his ordination to priesthood. These suspicions originated in malicious rumors that Archbishop Conrad of Vechta, when performing the rites, was seriously ill and did not observe the canonical procedure.

At the time when the "letter of peace" was under discussion, Rokycana resided at Hradec Králové. For many good reasons he had cast his lot with Hynek Ptáček of Pirkštejn and his party. The clergy of eastern Bohemia looked to Rokycana as their leader and he had a following in other parts of the country, especially in the rural areas. The source of trouble was Prague, dominated partly by the Catholics of the "Upper Consistory," and partly by the conservative Hussites controlled by the "Lower Consistory." The defiance of the Compacts by the remnants of the Tábor party, though presenting no acute danger, could be at any time used as evidence of Rokycana's inability to keep all the Hussites together. No wonder that he grew impatient or even hostile in his relations with men who kept the Hussite radicalism alive!

Ptáček's attachment to the Hussite cause was, unquestionably, a valuable asset, and Rokycana used it for extending his jurisdiction wherever Ptáček's political supremacy was recognized. At the congress of the nobility from eastern Bohemia held at Čáslav in August, 1441, Rokycana was proclaimed the "supreme officer in spiritual matters," so that from then on he could count on Ptáček's personal friendship and on the sympathetic attitude of other members of Ptáček's bloc.[50] He lost no time in using this favorable circumstance for further advances toward the immediate objective—the unification of the Hussites under his banner.

Rokycana's personality was rather enigmatic, and few of his contemporaries were able to follow with unshaken confidence the meandering course of his policy. His private life and moral standards were beyond reproach: this attracted to him the masses of the Hussites, ignorant of doctrinal subtleties but desirous of having at their head an honest cleric, uncorrupted by greed or wordliness. Rokycana's search for a formula that the various factions could accept as their creed was notorious. He shunned rigid definitions and extremist opinions, endeavoring "with

God's help to strike right into the middle." His irenic disposition was misunderstood by the doctrinists who suspected him of opportunism and ideological indifference. His admonition: "Let us follow whatever promotes peace, and preserve whatever serves religious edification," indicated clearly his preference for amicable settlement as a means of allaying passions.

When with the assistance of Ptáček's partisans Rokycana extended his control over both the moderate and resolute Utraquist groups, he was confronted with a more perplexing task of determining which of the extreme wings should be approached first, Tábor or Příbram's faction. When liquidation of the radical wing came under consideration two courses were open to Rokycana's group: either a rigid application of the earlier agreements, or a public discussion of the thorny problems—a procedure very popular with the Hussite theologians since the death of John Hus.

As soon as Rokycana secured at Čáslav the position as "supreme officer in spiritual matters," he reminded the Taborites grimly that the arbitration, delayed several times, would be requested from the clerics appointed thereto late in 1436. But neither he nor Ptáček went beyond a grave admonition and gave the recalcitrants one more chance to settle their differences with the Hussite majority. Ptáček wrote letters to aldermen of Tábor and of several boroughs, traditionally allied with Tábor, and urged them to send delegates to a general assembly of the Hussite clergy scheduled to meet at Kutná Hora in October, 1441.[51]

More than three hundred and fifty clerics attended that synod and acclaimed Rokycana as their "superior." [52] Nobody was sent from Tábor or the associated boroughs to represent their views. The disregard of Ptáček's summons was not a serious matter but it was not to be forgotten. Soon after the adjournment of the synod Ptáček started preparing for a congress of the Hussite party in which the laymen were to play a more conspicuous role than the clerics. He again sent his emissaries to Tábor requesting them to appoint delegates. Realizing the weakness of their position, the Tábor leaders complied with Ptáček's call.

Recording briefly the course of the Kutná Hora synod, an anonymous chronicler stated that among those absent was a handful of priests "looking toward Prague," meaning the irreconcilable conservatives. Although Rokycana resented their intransigent attitude, he made a new attempt to convince them of the advantages that Utraquism might secure if dealing with the supreme Church authority as a unit.

In the early forties, the chances of conciliation of Rokycana's majority and Příbram's faction were indeed brighter than they had been under Bishop Philibert. The conservative clerics were disabused of their hope that by a show of moderation they could ingratiate themselves with the

"Upper Consistory." When, after the Kutná Hora synod, Rokycana made his overtures their response was favorable.

An assembly of Utraquist clerics was held in July, 1442, at Mělník, not very far from Prague. Various groups represented there reached a "full and perfect agreement," the terms of which have not been revealed by the contemporary annalist.[53] It seems very likely that doctrinal and personal differences between John of Příbram and Rokycana were bridged over by vague terms and that while Rokycana did not go too far in asserting his right to control the "Lower Consistory," Příbram's faction, in turn, recognized his spiritual leadership. His popularity among the rank and file was no secret and had to be reckoned with.

The Mělník accord and the Taborite participation in the Hussite congress were regarded as hopeful signs by Ptáček and Rokycana. Encouraged by them, they made preparations for a representative assembly of both laymen and clerics to be held again at Kutná Hora in July, 1443. To make the Taborites more amenable Rokycana hinted that the long delayed arbitration in doctrinal matters could take place if they boycotted the assembly. Afraid of the consequences of an adverse verdict, the Tábor theologians changed their tactics and prepared for an energetic defense of their doctrine.

The synod was well attended.[54] From Prague arrived the two administrators of the "Lower Consistory" along with prominent laymen. Ptáček's party sent a numerous delegation, in which clerics of Rokycana's orientation held a majority. The radical theologians, with Nicholas of Pelhřimov at their head, were accompanied by the Tábor aldermen as well as by some veterans of the Hussite wars. Thus opened the last contest among the Hussite factions. Full use was made of oratory and pens to determine the "truth of the Lord's law."

All leading theologians took an active part in these disputations at Kutná Hora and in the polemics afterwards. A bitter controversy flared up between John of Příbram and the indomitable spokesman of the radical wing, Václav Koranda. In a similar combat with Nicholas of Pelhřimov, Rokycana adopted a more moderate tone than Příbram, but refused to make concessions to the Taborite point of view. Although all differences came to the fore during the oral or written exchanges, the doctrine of the Eucharist on which the Hussites had been divided since the death of John Hus again proved to be the stumbling block. The spokesmen of Tábor tenaciously opposed Rokycana's formula, which virtually admitted transubstantiation. The views of John Příbram, identical with the doctrine of the Roman Church, aroused even more indignation among the Taborites. Drawing heavily upon the writings of John Wyclif, the Tábor leaders professed the doctrine of remanence, rejected by the Council of Constance and incompatible with the Compacts.

As public disputations at Kutná Hora yielded no satisfactory results, the assembly dissolved without adopting any declaration. A provincial Diet was called to meet in January, 1444, primarily to settle matters relating to Ladislav's succession. The conflicting parties were requested to sum up their teachings and to submit such writings to the Diet as to the supreme tribunal.

The Diet appointed a committee of "selected, wise and respectable men" to look into the controversial religious matters, seeking therefore the advice of clerics "learned in the law of God and in the doctors." The majority of the committee were apparently laymen, and the clerics functioned as advisers. The findings presented to the plenary session corresponded with the view of the moderate center. Thereupon the Diet resolved, without detailed discussion, that the views formulated by Rokycana and Příbram were "safer, better, and more reliable" than the Taborite teachings.[55]

The statement of the Hussite faith, approved by the Diet on January 31, 1444, contained five articles relating to the Eucharist. They were probably prepared by Rokycana himself and expressed his belief that in the "sacrament of the venerable body and blood of Christ is present real God and real man in his nature and in the substance of his natural existence which he had taken from the Virgin Mary and in which he sits in heaven at the right hand of God the Father." Other articles related to such problems as the seven sacraments, purgatory, the cult of saints, auricular confession, the use of vestments, and some minor points. The moderate point of view of Rokycana was endorsed summarily and the parties were urged to accept the decision.

The Diet dealt the radical wing an even heavier blow than had been the destruction of the military brotherhoods at Lipany. It deprived them of any legal protection or sympathy among the moderate Hussites. Nicholas of Pelhřimov, though depressed, did not lay down his arms. Writing in solitude, he added a third section to his *Chronicle of the Taborites,* in which he sketched the last stage of their struggle with Rokycana and Příbram.[56] Neither his book nor any other polemical tracts aroused interest among the former associates of Tábor. The party lost its appeal to the people and dwindled to the point when nothing was left of it but the walled city of Tábor, the last abode of the "little bishop," ministering without hindrance to his faithful few.

The vote of the January Diet strengthened Rokycana's position in every respect. He had nothing to fear from the left and knowing so, he once more exercised restraint and did not insist on the extermination of the "little bishop's" flock. Isolated from other communities, they did not constitute a menace to his endeavors. The differences between his bloc and the conservative wing were not ironed out. The administrators of the

"Lower Consistory" showed no willingness to surrender their office, but were too cautious either to challenge Rokycana or to plot against him. In relation to them, Rokycana took the line of least resistance, knowing well that he would not be permitted to return to Prague as long as the benevolent protector of the administrators, Menhart of Hradec, held it under his control.

After Ptáček's death, Rokycana's future depended mostly on George of Poděbrady. Their close relationship originated probably in the early years of Rokycana's stay at Hradec Králové and was cemented by their genuine attachment to the Hussite cause. While Ptáček and the Archbishop-elect were of about the same age, George was more than twenty years younger. He respected Rokycana not only for his exemplary life but also as the living witness to the rise of Hussitism under John Hus, Jacobell of Stříbro, and John Žižka. Contacts with Rokycana were not always easy and smooth, but George, convinced that the secular authority should predominate, felt safe and made little of the occasional outbursts of Rokycana's impatience. Rokycana's loyal backing in major issues, since the Hussite majority respected him, was unquestionably an asset, especially in critical moments when unanimity was the only protection against intrigues or open attacks by militant Catholics.

Shortly after his elevation to party leadership, George manifested his interest in the Compacts and in Rokycana's confirmation. At the general assembly of the Catholic and Utraquist nobility which took place at Český Brod in November 1444, George and a Catholic lord, Zbyněk Zajíc of Házmburk, were chosen to assist Rokycana in his attempts to obtain consecration. The instruction given to them was rather vague, and it was left to their discretion whether to deal with the Council of Basel, Pope Eugene IV, or the Cardinal Giuliano Cesarini.[57]

Zbyněk Zajíc evaded his obligation and did not join George when the moment for an intervention in Rokycana's behalf seemed to be favorable. The decision was easier than the assembly at Český Brod had anticipated. It was undoubtedly known in Bohemia that Cardinal Cesarini had lost his life in the battle of Varna and the choice was between the depleted Council and Rome. George was apparently informed of the growing attachment of the Czech Catholics to Eugene IV and therefore addressed his petition to him. According to some indications, the canons of Saint Vitus also appealed to the Pope to fill the vacant see. They made their step independently of George, but most likely after a previous understanding with the Rožmberk party. There is no trace of Eugene's answer to George's letter. Instead, he wrote to Oldřich claiming for himself the privilege of choosing, "according to his heart," the incumbent for the Prague archbishopric.[58]

Upon the receipt of Eugene's bull, Oldřich and his friends gathered at Plzeň and sent a messenger to Rome to convey their thanks to Eugene. In addition to that, they instructed the messenger to lodge with the Curia charges against Rokycana, consisting of a long list of overt objections, insinuations, rumors and gossip.[59] It is doubtful whether George had any inkling of the Plzeň meeting, but the Pope's failure to answer his letter was ominous and increased his caution. Rokycana also came to realize the futility of pressing the matter without an unqualified approval by the Catholics.

The two Hussite leaders had to wait long before Oldřich of Rožmberk realized the risks that would arise from his complete isolation and before he gave consent to a congress of both the Hussite and Catholic parties. When it met at Pelhřimov, the congress dealt with both the political and the eccesiastical problems. The Catholic members did not oppose a resolution concerning Rokycana.[60] In it was included a hint that the Czech emissaries who were to be elected at the forthcoming Diet would go to the Pope or "elsewhere" to obtain final decision in the long-drawn-out affair. The relevant passage was left deliberately obscure, but from the context it could be concluded that the Hussite delegates to Pelhřimov thought of the Council and not of Felix V as the next resort in case Eugene IV rejected the petition. The threat of going "elsewhere" was veiled so as not to antagonize the Catholic party.

At the Prague Diet, the Pelhřimov articles concerning the Compacts and Rokycana were put to the vote and approved.[61] The repeated endorsement of Rokycana's candidacy by a political assembly was a success, as both the Hussites and the Catholics were present. To obtain Oldřich's signature, the Hussite leaders made concessions to his point of view which reduced the importance of the Diet's resolution. The ambiguous "elsewhere" was left out of the final draft of the Diet's letter, as it was resolved to deal with the Pope only. The Hussite lords knew that in the interval between the Pelhřimov congress and the November Diet Oldřich and his party declared themselves solemnly for Eugene IV, and that they would not accept even a vague allusion to the Council. The desire to break the deadlock was so strong that only Rokycana's consecration was mentioned in the resolution, although at Pelhřimov his cause was linked, as was usual, with the Compacts. In accepting Oldřich's amendments, the Hussite leaders missed the opportunity for the sanction of the Compacts when Bohemia was about to pass overtly from neutrality to Eugene's side. The letter to him was signed on December 14, 1446, and corroborated by the seals of prominent members of the Estates.[62]

Oldřich of Rožmberk lost little time in making contacts with a prominent member of the Curia, Cardinal Juan Carvajal. No intermediaries were needed, as Oldřich knew the influential Spaniard from the time of the latter's diplomatic mission to Frederick III. As a matter of fact, Carvajal undertook, in August, 1445, a fatiguing journey from Vienna to Krumlov to enlist Oldřich's cooperation in promoting Eugene's cause in Central Europe. After his return from the Prague Diet Oldřich wrote to Carvajal a highly subjective account of the proceedings.[63] He hoped that his letter would come to the Pope's notice and therefore he revealed his innermost thoughts concerning the Diet's resolution. He recommended that the Czech emissaries be received in a friendly manner in Rome, but dismissed without a mention of Rokycana. He also urged that thereafter a high dignitary be sent to Bohemia to ascertain in how many points the Hussites differed from the order prevailing in the Church, and to convince them by concrete examples of a breach of their pledge to observe the Compacts. He went so far as to ask that an inquisitor be included among the delegates. To facilitate the procedure as outlined in his confidential message to Carvajal, Oldřich apparently induced the metropolitan chapter not to attach its seal to the intervention in behalf of Rokycana, so that the Pope would find it easier to point out the lack of universal support of the candidate for the See of Prague.

The missive reached Carvajal before the Czech delegates had left Prague. Fearing obstacles on the roads across the Alps, the Czechs departed only about the middle of March and reached the eternal city on May 1, 1447. They learned immediately of Eugene's death several weeks earlier and sought their way to the new Pope. Little understanding for the Hussite cause could, indeed, be expected from Nicholas V who, before his election, had held a prominent position among the contemporary humanists and had corresponded with some Czech Catholics, including the mighty lord of Rožmberk.

One of the Pontiff's favorites was Prokop of Rabštejn, a Czech by origin. As the Rabštejns were counted among the lesser nobility and Prokop's share in the family property was rather small, education appeared to be the safest way for him to social promotion. Prokop began his career under the protective wings of Sigismund's chancellor, Caspar Schlick, and with him he entered the service of Frederick III. Gifted and conciliatory, Prokop soon distinguished himself by great learning and diplomatic skill. While in Vienna, Carvajal perceived Prokop's sympathy for Eugene IV and used his service in paving the way for recognition of the Pope by the Estates of Bohemia. If Prokop had been less reluctant to exchange the amenities of court life for onerous pastoral duties, his appointment to the See of Prague would have been made without too much delay and without any consideration of the recent petitions from Bohemia.

Knowing, however, of Prokop's disinclination to accept a high office away from Rome, Nicholas decided to temporize rather than antagonize the moderate Hussite groups whose attachment to Rokycana could not be assessed at such a great distance. It had to be admitted that either the Council or Felix V could exploit the Czech disillusionment and stir up trouble by courting the Utraquists. To make such an alignment impossible, Nicholas V resorted to tactical maneuvers and prolonged conferences with the Czech envoys. Apart from Juan Carvajal, Cardinal Nicolas Cusa and some curial theologians participated in the discussions, emphasizing the need for an absolute submission to the Pontiff's authority.

Although enough has been said to reveal the Pope's dislike of the Compacts and of Rokycana, the final answer was not entirely negative. Nicholas V put off pronouncing a decisive word and announced his intention to send Cardinal Carvajal to Bohemia to "observe the other party, the faith of the kingdom, and the faith of the Archbishop-elect." Oldřich's suggestions apparently reached the Pope and were not disregarded, although they were not followed in every particular. The Czech envoys did not conceal their disappointment, and in their farewell speech they indicated vaguely that the Hussites, if rejected by the Pope, would seek other ways in gaining their ends, "true, good and approved by the Scriptures, though unusual and not practised at that time." [64] This could be interpreted as a reflection of the earlier deliberations whether, failing to obtain Rokycana's approval, the Hussites should not give up the idea of the apostolic succession and ordain their priests by the imposition of hands. In the solemn audience they did not go beyond a hazy statement, not revealing such details as would inculpate them.

No attempt was made from the Pope's side by pressure or threats to weaken the envoys' resistance. They did not rank high among the Hussites—no leading theologian had the courage to undertake the long journey to Rome; and if they had been detained at the papal court, no serious harm would have been caused to their party. Nicholas V dismissed them with friendly words, but turned a deaf ear to their entreaty that the Hussites be permitted to enjoy the blessings of the Compacts. His silence on this crucial point was ominous and only Carvajal's mission left a faint hope of conciliation.

Other, more urgent matters occupied the astute papal legate during the winter season of 1447–48. Nicholas V was anxious to secure universal recognition in the Empire and Carvajal spent several months in Vienna hammering out the terms of a special concordat, to which Frederick III consented in February, 1448.[65] When free of this highly complicated task and other minor duties, Carvajal, in the company of Oldřich of Rožmberk and other lords, journeyed to Prague and reached it on the first day of May.[66] His conferences with the Hussite leaders contrasted with the ceremonious reception accorded him when riding with a splendid retinue into the Bohemian metropolis. Formal conferences in the Old Town Hall were inaugurated by George of Poděbrady, who spoke with full backing of the Hussite party. The Catholic lords were also present, but their part in negotiations with the Cardinal was less conspicuous. When the speeches were over, Carvajal received a summary of the unsettled problems. In the passage concerning the Compacts, the authors of the summary emphasized that the concessions contained therein were granted to the Czechs when the Council was in accord with Eugene IV. They also maintained that in 1435 King Sigismund authorized the Diet to proceed with Rokycana's election. Carvajal's silence on the Compacts and his oblique rejection of Rokycana by a reference to the canon law portended little success in further parleys.

Carvajal did not break off the contacts and although resolved not to make any concessions or give a word of encouragement, he carried on negotiations with both the authorized representatives and private persons. He met several times with Rokycana and conferred also with John of Příbram. Under the pretext of nonfamiliarity with the text of the Compacts, he coaxed from George the solemn charter as well as some other documents and kept them in his lodgings. Pending their study, he evaded urgent demands for an open debate and made several attempts to split the Hussite party. Some conservative clerics as well as some lords, including Menhart of Hradec, abjured the Chalice, but others, noting his intransigent attitude, held fast to the Hussite tradition and aligned themselves with Rokycana and George.

Dissatisfied with his dilatory answers, the Czech leaders pressed Carvajal for an unequivocal statement. He refrained from it and declared that he had not been authorized either to sanction the Compacts or to confirm Rokycana; his only task was to restore peace. The speech roused indignation and voices of protest were raised from the audience. Peter of Mladoňovice, who in 1415 had accompanied John Hus to Constance and witnessed his martyr death, rose from his seat and spoke boldly to the cardinal: "Lord legate, if you do not confirm to us the communion in both kinds and Rokycana as archbishop, you will hear of strange developments in this kingdom before you reach Rome." [67]

Carvajal realized that there was no more hope of splitting the Hussites and that he would make his position even more awkward by appeals for succor to Oldřich and other Catholic lords. To avoid defeat and hostile demonstrations, he decided to leave the city of Prague clandestinely. His plan miscarried, for even at daybreak of the chosen day there were enough people in the streets to recognize him and to alert the security organs. The Hussite leaders were primarily concerned for the original copy of the Compacts. A squad of horsemen dispatched from the capital overtook the cardinal and his escort before they reached the city of Benešov, and forced him to give back the precious charter.

An anonymous chronicler wrote a postscript to Carvajal's mission, saying tersely that "the legate did not accomplish anything but caused an even more virulent strife." [68] Instead of disposing the Hussites to moderation, Carvajal contributed to the consolidation of their ranks. The wave of indignation, aroused by his stealthy departure from Prague, was so strong that even the most moderate elements both among the clerics and laymen were affected and cast their lot with Rokycana and George. The hero of the day was a Utraquist cleric who rode with the municipal squad and returned to Prague with a rare trophy—the tail cut off the cardinal's mule.

Carvajal did not take easily the failure of his mission and never forgot the personal humiliation to which he had been exposed. The goal, which in the days following immediately after his arrival seemed to be near at hand, was again lost in a haze of uncertainty. The Compacts were not sanctioned and Rokycana had even less chance of success now than before the Cardinal's visit. No serious thought was given to a resumption of contacts with Nicholas V to whom Carvajal reported. A partial compensation came after George's conquest of Prague in September, 1448. In the wake of George's victorious troops, Rokycana entered Prague and took possession of his former parish of the Holy Virgin of Týn which he had left in June, 1437, fearing persecution.

Soon thereafter, with George's direct participation, the Utraquist clergy reached an agreement restating their adherence to the Compacts and other documents of 1436.[69] Some controversial points were left open to be settled at a more opportune moment in accordance with the "Judge of Cheb." Rokycana was recognized without objection as "the head of priests in Prague, other boroughs and communities." The death of John of Příbram shortly before Christmas, 1448, simplified the administrative problems. His colleague in the "Lower Consistory," Prokop of Plzeň, lived for about ten more years, but was relegated to a less influential position. It is not quite clear what dispositions Rokycana made for a more effective administration of the Hussite Church. He did not fill the vacant post of administrator, but probably retained the "Lower Consistory" as a consultative body.

George's wholehearted support of Rokycana sprang not only from an attachment to the Hussite cause but also from a realistic evaluation of the grave problems with which he himself was confronted. He was convinced that monarchy was the only acceptable system of government, and wanted to restore it in harmony with Frederick III, the custodian of the boy prince. As Frederick had given ample evidence of his indifference to the request from Bohemia for the establishment of a regency, self-help proved to be the only way toward at least a provisional settlement of the political and administrative problems. Menhart's defeat and the occupation of Prague by loyal forces had, undoubtedly, more effect than any symbolic gesture from Frederick's side could bring. No matter whether respected by the Catholic lords or not, George was the virtual master of Bohemia.

Although not intensively trained in theology, George adhered to the principle of the apostolic succession. He was anxious to obtain from Rome Rokycana's confirmation. The Pope's attitude was even less encouraging than Frederick's meaningless messages. Self-help was again the only means by which to promote the consolidation of the Hussite party. George saw clearly that he was in the same boat with Rokycana, and resolved to use his power for a solid backing of Rokycana, regardless of risks and temporary complications. Rokycana's position as "the head of priests in Prague, other boroughs and communities" was far less satisfactory than the long-coveted archbishopric, but with George's support he exercised spiritual control at least over the Hussite party, leaving the Catholics under the administration of the "Upper Consistory."

A GOVERNOR FOR BOHEMIA

George's entry into Prague heralded brighter days for the Hussites and, indeed, for all the inhabitants of the kingdom of Bohemia. The conquest had been so well prepared that little blood was shed either before the city gates or in the streets leading from the Vyšehrad bastion to the Old Town Hall. Similarly, Rokycana took over the leadership of the Hussite Church without the application of harsh methods to neutralize the ultra-conservative groups among the metropolitan clergy.

The timing and the swift execution of George's designs threw the opposing camp into confusion. Many of his adversaries jumped on the bandwagon to share in the new opportunities. When the excitement subsided, George and his lieutenants were able to examine the situation closely and to devise means for consolidating their recent gains. Nothing but hostility could be expected of Menhart's son and of the other members of that house; to keep them in check, George resorted to political maneuvering instead of striking hard. In this manner he gained time and was better prepared for the intricate and tedious struggle which he had to undertake to hold in check his most powerful opponent, Oldřich of Rožmberk. Oldřich's antipathy was deep-rooted and its intensity was surpassed probably only by the aversion to Rokycana displayed on many occasions by the canons of the metropolitan chapter of Saint Vitus. Dreading molestation, the chapter moved from Prague to Plzeň and from that stronghold of Catholicism they maintained contacts with Oldřich and other lords.

Menhart's death early in February, 1449, was a signal for George's opponents to close their ranks and to make ready for an open fight. Headed by Oldřich and his son Henry, some wealthy magnates from southern and southwestern Bohemia met at Strakonice and formed a league to protect that area against George's expansion.[70] Political animosities were at that moment stronger than religious differences, so that the Rožmberks considered even the last surviving members of the Tábor

51

party as potential allies. In letters sent abroad, the Catholic character of the Strakonice league was emphasized and George's attachment to the Chalice was presented as a source of danger not only for Bohemia but for its neighbors as well.

Attempts to enlist the help of foreign princes met with disappointing results. Emperor Frederick's procrastinating attitude, which before 1448 had caused George a good deal of trouble, at this juncture proved to be beneficial, as it removed the danger from Austria and southern Bohemia of a concerted action against the Poděbrady party. Both the Strakonice league and George turned their eyes toward the northwestern border of Bohemia, knowing of the rivalry of the Saxon princes. While Oldřich cherished the hope of an alliance with the Elector Frederick, George could expect some support from Frederick's younger brother, William. George also turned to his benefit the contest between Frederick of Saxony and Frederick, the Elector of Brandenburg, who were striving with each other for some territories. Trusting that the Strakonice league would not be able to build up a solid front, George did not attack it, leaving the initiative to his foes.

Both parties spent the year of 1449 in assembling forces, and only in the spring of 1450, after some local clashes, did Oldřich's troops open hostilities on a large scale. At about the same time Frederick of Saxony decided upon an invasion of Bohemia, in the hope that the moment for the extension of his previously acquired domains within the Bohemian boundary had come. Apprehensive that an open alignment with Frederick, well known among the Czechs for his lust for conquest, would arouse indignation among both the Hussites and the moderate Catholics, Oldřich hesitated to appeal to him openly, so that the preparations for a campaign against the Hussite bloc were not coordinated. The forces of the Strakonice league and George's party spent several weeks in preliminary maneuvering and only late in May, 1450, were ready for battle. George knew at that time that a clash was imminent, and therefore seized the initiative. He issued a proclamation from his camp to both the allies and the foes, aimed primarily at Oldřich.[71] The move was well calculated and the impressive list of Oldřich's perfidies had the desired effect upon the population of Bohemia. Oldřich's half-hearted defense [72] got little publicity outside his intimate circle and its faint echo was soon lost in the din of the armored wagons and artillery.

On June 4, 1450, George launched a concentrated attack on the league's positions near the borough of Rokycany and shattered their ranks so decisively that they found safety only in a hasty and disorganized retreat. A few days after the catastrophe, the Saxon vanguard descended from the mountainous border areas into the fertile plain, but upon learning of Oldřich's change of fortune, Frederick abstained from sending reinforcements to Bohemia. Although defeated, the forces of the Strakonice league were not annihilated. George had no intention of dissipating his strength in local warfare against individual members of the league and did not spurn overtures made by the opposing party shortly after the Rokycany battle. An armistice agreement to be based on the Compacts, the "letter of peace" of 1440, and some supplementary documents, prepared the ground for more detailed negotiations.[73] Shielded by this temporary accord, George made a daring raid into the territory of Frederick of Saxony to incline him toward a peaceful settlement of problems that had been aggravating the relations between the two neighboring countries for some time past.

With prestige enhanced by the successful expedition across the border, and with strong forces at his disposal, George appeared as the dominant figure at the provincial Diet which opened its deliberations in Prague late in November, 1450, and remained in session until January, 1451.[74] Oldřich did not attend it, feeling discredited by George's manifesto as well as by his treacherous contacts with the Elector of Saxony. Representing the most powerful aristocratic family, Oldřich's son Henry acted as the leader of the Catholic lords. His more conciliatory attitude facilitated contacts between his party and the Hussites.

The Diet was not stormy, and it soon degenerated into tedious discussions of particular claims and grievances. Petty squabbles and personal jealousies obscured the chief purpose in which George was vitally interested—the need of a stable government. No serious leader could at this stage entertain illusions concerning Emperor Frederick's policy. Since 1444 he had given ample evidence of his reluctance to act as regent of Bohemia and to reside there even temporarily. There was no alternative to a regency other than an appointment of a prominent nobleman as governor.

The recent victory had given the Poděbrady party the long-coveted opportunity to have their leader endorsed not only by a party congress, but by a provincial Diet as well, as the most competent candidate for governorship. George sensed that he would antagonize even the lords of his own faith if he furthered his aspirations openly, and if he endeavored to ally himself with the lower Estates, the lesser nobility, and the spokesmen of the royal boroughs, among whom he had had many ardent followers from the beginning of his public career. Instead of rallying around George as faithfully as they had done during the struggle with the Strakonice league, the Utraquist lords showed indecision and lack of interest in an efficient provincial administration. They did not campaign for George's recognition, but followed the attitude of their rivals. Although absent, Oldřich was elected to the delegation which had to go to Frederick's court to acquaint him with the Diet's resolutions.[75] The

envoys were not instructed to insist on George's appointment, and it was
highly unlikely that they would do so of their own initiative. Instead,
they repeated the earlier requests that Ladislav be sent to Bohemia for
training and for at least nominal rule.

When contrasted with the earlier victories, the Diet could not be hailed
as a success. Although disappointed with the lack of enthusiasm among
his peers for his ambitious scheme, George acquiesced both in the composition of the delegation to Frederick's court and its instruction. In the
depressing atmosphere prevailing in the Diet it would have been risky
to display force or to put the loyalty of the vacillating members to the
Poděbrady party to a test. George left Prague with a realization of both
his strength and his weakness, disillusioned but not discouraged. Although not advanced significantly, his chances were not imperiled by
the half-hearted assembly. He soon engaged in patient negotiations with
the leaders of various factions to bind them more firmly to his side.

The Czech envoys reached Frederick's court late in March, 1451, and
received, as on many previous occasions, only a vague and dilatory answer to their request. The Emperor was, however, anxious to keep contacts with the Catholic lords and with the Hussite majority, and promised to send plenipotentiaries to the coming provincial Diet. The boy
prince Ladislav was little over eleven years old and to neglect him could
not only imperil his position but become detrimental to the House of
Habsburg.

Guided by a realization of such risks, Frederick III pursued a more
conciliatory policy in dealing with the Hungarian magnates, who requested Ladislav's residence in their own country with no less clamor
and assiduity than did the Bohemian nobles. In October, 1450, he granted
to John Hunyadi the much delayed formal recognition as the governor
of Hungary and received in exchange for this gesture an assurance that
no objections would be raised by the Hungarian nobles to Ladislav's stay
at the Austrian court until he should reach the age of eighteen. Hunyadi's position was, of course, less assailable than George's, as there existed in Hungary unity of religion, and thus the political problems were
not aggravated by such complications as the Compacts and Rokycana's
aspirations.

The compromise with Hunyadi proved to be satisfactory and pointed
the way toward an agreement with Bohemia. To push the matter, Frederick III sent to Bohemia a delegation headed by Enea Silvio Piccolomini, Bishop of Siena, who was in his service and had become fairly well
acquainted with the complex problems of Central Europe.[76] The Bishop
was accompanied by Prokop of Rabštejn, who acted as interpreter, and
by two Austrian nobles. The royal envoys were joined at Hradec by

Henry of Rožmberk and on July 18, 1451, they reached Benešov, a royal borough to the south of Prague, where the Diet was held.

The Bishop-diplomat was at a disadvantage when introduced to members of the Diet, as he was unable to address them in Czech. Prokop's translation, though undoubtedly accurate, was less effective in delivery than the envoy's Latin speech.[77] An even more serious handicap was the royal instruction according to which his main task was to dissuade the Czechs from attempts to get Ladislav under their control. Enea impressed the assembled representatives by his exquisite oratory and dexterity, but his performance would have been less effective if the Czechs had earnestly insisted on an immediate transfer of Ladislav to Bohemia. To find out how far they were prepared to go, Enea conferred with individual leaders. It did not take him long to ascertain that they were more bent upon the establishment of an administrative system after the Hungarian pattern than on Ladislav's coming to Prague. Apart from short intervals toward the end of Sigismund's life and then under Albrecht II, Bohemia had existed without a king for more than thirty years. The Czech leaders were astute enough to realize that with the boy prince would come Austrian nobles as advisers and this was a discouraging prospect. Enea was not far from the truth when, on a later occasion, he remarked that his mission was agreeable to the Czechs, especially to those who felt that it was their duty to ask for the King, although their true intentions were different from their public statements.

Enea was either instructed by Frederick III or advised by Prokop to seek a personal contact with the head of the Hussite majority. So many contradictory reports had reached Frederick's court about George that the Emperor was interested in getting a report of his personality and qualifications from such a keen observer as the Bishop of Siena. A journey to Bohemia was not an everyday occurrence, and Enea rightly assumed that the leading prelates at the papal court would appreciate no less than Frederick III an account of his impressions.[78] He was, therefore, anxious to use every opportunity to learn as much as possible about both the past and the current problems.

He saw George in the sessions of the Diet and noticed that he was somewhat handicapped by his physical appearance. He was of short stature, sturdy and heavy, of pale complexion, but these less attractive features were redeemed by his bright eyes and suave manners.[79] George was probably just as eager to discuss, in a private session, the matters at issue as was Enea. Prokop, who acted as interpreter, had no difficulty in keeping the dialogue moving and animated. Enea was aware of George's strength, as he could learn from other sources that the lord of Poděbrady was not only solidly backed by the Utraquists but also had many allies among the Catholics. Even before the long talk had opened, Enea sensed that his mission would be crowned with success if he could dispose George sympathetically toward the idea that both the welfare of Bohemia and his personal advancement depended on a lasting cooperation with the spiritual and secular authorities,—the papal and the imperial courts. He was, therefore, attentive and moderate, avoiding errors which in the spring of 1448 had brought Cardinal Carvajal's mission to naught.

Although George was a layman, the conversation soon turned from worldly affairs to religious problems. Enea directed George's attention to three points on which Bohemia's future relationship with other countries of the Roman obedience hinged: the Compacts, the restitution of church property, and the appointment of an archbishop. Without committing himself to an authoritative statement, Enea conveyed to George his hope that the communion in both kinds could be tolerated, if the Hussite clergy observed the Compacts meticulously and gave up rites and practices not included in the agreement with the Council of Basel. Enea found especially objectionable the administration of the Eucharist to infants, which many Hussite priests practiced, despite earlier condemnations by the Fathers of the Council and other persons of authority. He also made no secret of his aversion to liturgical innovations, observed during his visit or reported by his Catholic informants. Both George and Enea recognized the enormous difficulties which were bound to arise if restitution of church domains should be attempted. Catholic lords, who had a share in the spoils, were just as reluctant to give back their recent acquisitions as were the Utraquists: in a letter to Cardinal de Cusa, Enea frankly admitted that no one was more strongly opposed to a reparation of the injury than Oldřich of Rožmberk.

The conversation got over that difficult point rather quickly, and most of the remaining time was spent in the search for a compromise relative to the third point—the vacancy of the See of Prague. Enea stated rather hastily that he had no hope for Rokycana, but he instantly made a tactical retreat to calm his interlocutor. The conversation passed from concrete points to subtle problems of canon law, but soon Rokycana's qualification came up again for discussion. Enea changed his tone slightly, but in other words he conveyed the same meaning, namely, that the Pontiff would never take the decisive step if the Czechs presented Rokycana to him as the sole candidate for the archbishopric. George seemed to be impressed by the envoy's firmness and listened attentively to a suggestion that several clerics be recommended to the Pope so that he could choose one of them as the most competent and desirable. Rokycana's voluntary resignation was also mentioned as a means of breaking the deadlock. Although no formal agreement was reached, Enea was hope-

ful and left the city of Benešov with favorable impressions of George's
statesmanlike qualities.

As the Bishop of Siena had been sent to Bohemia by a secular prince
and not by the Pontiff, he could pass in silence over matters in which
on previous occasions Cardinal Carvajal and other prelates had been involved. Pestilence was raging in Prague, and Enea did not express a desire to meet Rokycana at another and safer place. He could not, however, resist the temptation of seeing with his own eyes an even more
notorious center than Prague—the royal borough of Tábor. He could
easily reach it on the way from Hradec to Benešov, and when journeying from the Diet to Krumlov, he had to make only a short detour to
reach Tábor again. On both occasions he was accompanied by a group
of Rožmberk horsemen.

A Roman Catholic bishop was, indeed, an unexpected guest among
the former warriors and the handful of theologians who resided at Tábor, embittered as they were by their dealings with Rokycana, but unbroken in their attachment to radical tenets. Not without a thrill did
Enea pass through the gate, decorated with two shields, on one an angel
holding the Chalice, on the other a likeness of elderly and blind Žižka.
A story came to his mind according to which Žižka, sensing that death
was not far, instructed his lieutenants to make a drum of his skin and
scare away the enemies by such a strange instrument. The Bishop was
not molested and he inspected the system of fortifications as well as the
city inside the walls. He lodged at a private home recommended to him
by Rožmberk's people, and tried in vain to dissuade his host from adherence to the Taborite faith.

Encouraged by his first visit and polite reception by a group of aldermen, Enea, when riding from Benešov to Krumlov, made a midday stop
in the last bastion of Hussite radicalism. The two remaining spokesmen
of the once powerful Tábor party, the "little bishop" Nicholas, and Václav Koranda the Elder, quickly heard the news of Enea's second arrival.
Accompanied by John Gałka, a Polish refugee for faith, they met the
Italian prelate and greeted him in Latin, less elegant than his own, but
nevertheless fluent. The disputation, which opened after a brief exchange
of courtesies, was long and animated, as the three theologians welcomed
the opportunity to deal with controversial problems. In defending his
radical views, John Gałka proved to be more aggressive than the senior
Tábor leaders and for most of the time the disputation was but a duel
between the Bishop and the Polish critic of the Church. A wide range
of topics was covered and Enea, single-handed, defended the Pope's
primacy, communion in one kind, transubstantiation, and in general the
official doctrine of the seven sacraments. The lively exchange of ideas
apparently attracted many onlookers, from whose ranks Enea was at-

tacked even more brutally than from the trained debaters. He was relieved of embarrassment by Lord Henry and other lay members of the retinue, who had left him for several hours alone with the theologians and took meals in somebody's home. Escorted by them, Enea left the Taborite stronghold without incident.

Enea's sojourn in Bohemia was rather short but it made an indelible impression on him. As, in the years to come, he rose to prominence in the highest ecclesiastical circles, he could draw upon his own experiences in matters concerning Bohemia instead of relying on other peoples' reports. He was not altogether pessimistic about the Bohemian situation and did not conceal his admiration for some Hussite practices—as his often quoted remark that the Taborite women knew the Bible better than Italian priests would indicate.[80] He looked with sympathetic understanding at the veterans of the Hussite wars, some half blind, others with scars or amputated limbs, and spoke highly of the thirst for learning prevalent among the Taborite clerics. When, however, he realized in how many points even the moderate Utraquists differed from the rites and usages observed in other countries of the Roman obedience, he became sceptical of the chances of a lasting conciliation on the basis of the Compacts. His two visits to Tábor satisfied his curiosity, but filled him with abhorrence and pessimism. He was shocked by the variety of ideas among both the priests and the laymen, by the boldness with which Gałka and the other theologians presented their views, smacking of all the heresies that ever had threatened the Roman Church, as well as by their opposition to the Papacy. He deeply regretted that Emperor Sigismund had, for opportunistic reasons, made peace with Tábor instead of levelling it with the ground or at least condemning its inhabitants to hardest labors.[81]

It was of no small importance for the events to come that during his sojourn in Bohemia Enea saw not only George but also his implacable foe. Oldřich invited the Bishop and Prokop of Rabštejn to Krumlov and entertained them lavishly. There is no record of Enea's conversations with his gracious host, and after his return to Vienna he reported orally, so little is known of his recommendations to Frederick III. No matter how vivid and impressive the envoy's account was, the King did not see reasons for haste.

Since no letter came from Frederick before the date fixed at Benešov, the Estates resolved to send a delegation to him with an urgent request for action. The leading nobles apparently knew that Frederick was preparing for a journey to Rome to receive the imperial crown from Nicholas V, and they wanted at that juncture to get from him a satisfying solution to their two problems. The delegates representing several factions were not of the same political orientation, but they did not mention any other name than that of George as the most competent candidate for the governorship. As such was most likely the tenor of Enea's report, Frederick needed little time to make his choice. The delegates also demanded that Frederick, when in Rome, make an intervention in behalf of Rokycana.

The Emperor-elect realized that at least a temporary appointment of a governor for Bohemia was necessary in order to avert the danger of anti-Habsburg agitation during his journey to Rome. He granted the Czechs the minimum, appointing George for an indefinite period. He also promised to plead with the Pope in behalf of Rokycana's confirmation, but as he was undoubtedly well informed of the attitude of the Czech Catholics, he added to his statement an ambiguous clause. It could be concluded from those additional words that he expected that a special delegation would be sent to Rome during his sojourn there to manifest unanimity in their support of Rokycana.[82]

The temporary appointment, the extension of which depended entirely on Frederick's pleasure, was only a bit more encouraging than had been the resolution of the Prague Diet a year earlier. Although George's prestige was at stake, he decided once more for a middle-course policy. Analyzing the events soberly, he could not deny that compared with the earlier dilatory answers, a short-term appointment represented a forward step. It indicated that Frederick had finally recognized George's powerful position and had no intention of playing Oldřich of Rožmberk or any other Bohemian magnate against him.

It is doubtful whether Frederick revealed to anyone his innermost thought concerning Rokycana's confirmation. In the absence of explicit testimony, only conjectures can be attempted concerning this perplexing problem. He could know from Enea and from other sources of the aversion of the leading Czech Catholics to Rokycana's promotion, and of the Pope's resolution not to approve directly or indirectly the manner in which Rokycana had been designated as the incumbent of the vacant See of Prague. It is also very likely that when receiving the Czech delegates, Frederick was informed of actions already in progress, by which the leading curial circles intended to break the Hussite resistance. Nothing would have been more inopportune than a display of sympathies with the Czechs, and Frederick felt no compunction in giving promises which he was not willing to fulfill.

Since 1449 the position of Nicholas V had been improving steadily. In April of that year Felix V abdicated and shortly afterwards the group of members of the Council, who in 1448 had gone over from Basel to Lausanne, dissolved silently. Free of rivals and recognized by secular princes, the Pope authorized actions aimed at liquidation of the Hussite opposition and restoration of unity among his flock. His intentions, though not trumpeted to the world, could not remain secret in such a lively and well-informed center as Frederick's court.

In July, 1451, at about the same time as when Enea sojourned in Bohemia, his countryman, Giovanni Capistrano, reached Moravia, ready to attack the Hussites in that province, and to cause confusion in their ranks. His most powerful weapons were fiery sermons which, however, lost some of their effect as they had to be translated into the vernacular. He also made direct appeals to prominent personalities and brought about some defections from the Hussite party. Finally, he opened literary polemics with the spiritual leaders of Utraquism and involved even Rokycana in the passionate skirmishes.[83]

Nicholas V did not put all his hopes in Capistrano's militant preaching, but dispatched one of his chief advisers, Nicholas Cusa, Cardinal of Saint Peter *ad vincula,* to use his learning and diplomatic skill to persuade the Czechs that submission to the papal authority was the only escape from the blind alley.[84] Cusa's mission originated in the circle of the Pope's most trusted advisers, and apparently more was expected from him than from Capistrano's campaign.

It could not be denied that this crusading monk scored some successes among the conservative Hussites, weary of the long-drawn-out opposition to the Papacy. But mass conversions did not follow, and when Capistrano passed from exhortations to invectives against the Chalice, instead of softening the Hussite resistance he aroused their passionate resentment. Whereas in Moravia he was shielded by some noblemen and municipal councils, his sole sponsor in Bohemia was the lord of Rožmberk. Apart from Krumlov, Capistrano nowhere felt it safe to mount the pulpit. Slowly but surely he recognized the failure of his mission and moved from the Rožmberk residence to Bavaria.

In the meantime, Nicholas of Cusa, the learned papal legate, proceeded cautiously and secured diplomatic help from princes in the countries adjacent to Bohemia. Some of them took their task seriously and were willing to mediate. Cusa, however, considerably reduced his chances of success by his reluctance to enter Bohemia and to meet the Hussite spokesmen in their homeland. At one point, an agreement on the place of conference seemed to be near at hand, but the Cardinal once more created an impasse by harsh statements that reminded the Hussites of Carvajal's uncompromising attitude. The theologian in Cusa triumphed over the diplomat, and the results were damaging. Neither at Regensburg nor at Vienna could a formula be found to narrow down the chasm separating the parties and to open prospects of durable reconciliation.

Cardinal Cusa's return to Rome from Central Europe was not as dramatic as that of Cardinal Carvajal's had been, but the effects as far as the papal policy was concerned were about the same. In the inner circle of the Pope's advisers, no one could be found to whom advocates of a conciliatory policy toward the Hussites could turn with new proposals. Under such circumstances, even Frederick's unequivocal declaration for Rokycana could not have turned the scale in the latter's favor. The intervention promised to the Czechs in the fall of 1451 apparently never took place, as there exists no direct evidence of it. Frederick had no reason to fear that the Czechs would ever learn what he had actually done or not done. He could soon notice, when in Rome, that no contacts existed between the Utraquist leaders and the papal court. There really was no highly placed person at the Curia to inform the Czechs whether Frederick, before or after his coronation as Emperor, had really explored the chances of an accord or dropped the matter as soon as the envoys from Prague left his Austrian residence.

Although the Hussites did not expect effective help from either Felix V or the dwindling Council, the collapse of organized opposition to Nicholas V dimmed their hope that at an opportune moment they could find allies within Roman circles. Their position, which since the death of John Hus had been awkward, showed unmistakable signs of deterioration when the Roman pontiff reasserted his claims to supremacy. The prospect of continued isolation was depressing, as some vital problems on whose solution the future of Hussitism depended could not be tackled.

The most serious of them was the ordination of the Utraquist priests. The ranks of the clergy had been depleted by defections, physical disabilities, or death, and the question arose how to fill the gaps. Contrary to Tábor, the Utraquists adhered to the principle of the apostolic succession and insisted that their candidates for priesthood be consecrated by bishops. There existed in the Czech-speaking areas of the kingdom only one bishop, that of Olomouc, appointed in accordance with the canon law. The Compacts stipulated that the priests observing them and administering the Eucharist in both kinds be regarded as equal to the clerics *sub una*.

The bishops of Olomouc looked more to the Papacy than to the Council, and did not feel bound by the Compacts. Consequently, they were reluctant to ordain candidates of known attachment to the tenet of *sub utraque*. Other bishops living within the realm of Bohemia administered the German-speaking areas, and it was useless to expect co-operation from them. The Utraquist candidates were as a rule more successful in securing ordination in some remote areas, especially in small Italian bishoprics; but when Nicholas V consolidated his position, the number of prelates daring to disregard the canonical rules dwindled rapidly. The rigorous elements among the Utraquists objected to ordination obtained in devious ways and pressed for a remedy to protect their party from moral decay. The solution which in their view would have been both

legitimate and beneficial—the confirmation of Rokycana by the Pope—
was, after the failure of the missions of Capistrano and Cusa, more than
doubtful. Yet something had to be done to prevent a catastrophe.

The veiled threats made by the Utraquist delegates in Rome in 1447,[85]
although not meant at that moment too seriously, recurred in the early
fifties with greater urgency—at least among the more resolute Utraquists.
The confirmation of Rokycana by senior Hussite priests appeared to be
the only alternative to the recognition denied by the Pope. The advocates
of such an ordination pointed to practices observed by the apostles, and
felt that their position was defensible after so many rejections by the
Pope of pleas in Rokycana's behalf. Capistrano's invectives apparently
deepened the impression that Rome would never yield in that matter
and that the only choice was between capitulation and decision for steps
not sanctioned by long tradition.

The Archbishop-elect was apparently never won over for the idea of
ordination by senior priests, as by its acceptance he would have automatically abandoned the concept of the apostolic succession—one of
the cornerstones of his faith. Rokycana's cautious views concurred with
George's untiring search for the means and ways by which the kingdom
of Bohemia could be restored to its former position among the nations
of the Roman obedience. A decision to build up the Hussite hierarchy
without a papal sanction would have ruined George's persistent efforts
to achieve conciliation on the basis both of the Compacts and of the
supplementary agreements with Emperor Sigismund.

A revival of the early Christian concepts and practices was not the
only plan studied by the leading Hussite theologians. Some consideration was also given to a scheme which, though bold, presented less danger than a separation from the historic Church. The Hussites were not
very well informed about the conditions in other parts of the Christian
orbit, but they had some notion of the Greek Orthodoxy flourishing in
the Balkans and among Eastern Slavs. They knew that apart from some
dogmatic points, the Orthodox Christians differed from Rome in that they
observed communion in both kinds and in the use of leavened bread—
the practice also introduced at Tábor.

It was of some importance for the rise of Hussitism that one of Hus's
close friends, Jerome of Prague, had in 1413 visited the Grand Duchy
of Lithuania, where the Orthodox believers of Slavic race lived along
with the Lithuanians converted to the Latin form of Christianity. Jerome's observations of the Orthodox rites, when reported in Prague,
could be compared by Jacobell of Stříbro and other defenders of the
Chalice with the earlier usage in Western Christendom. In their letters
and manifestoes sent abroad, the Hussites often referred to the Greek
Church and its adherence to the communion in both kinds.[86] Attempts

to bring about a reunion of Rome with Constantinople, made at the time of the Council of Basel as well as at Ferrara-Florence, were carefully noted by the Hussite leaders, especially those who were entrusted with missions abroad and had a broader view of the European scene than the average clerics.

A matter so delicate as the establishment of contacts with the Eastern Church was apparently discussed and finally approved by a small group among the Hussite leaders. It cannot be ascertained whether the initiative came from Rokycana himself or from the same clerics who had explored the more radical solution for which they had been unable to get Rokycana's sanction. Even if Rokycana was not the originator of the idea, he was most likely soon informed of it. He did not oppose the dispatch of an envoy to the Orthodox countries, whose chief duty it was to observe the rites of the eastern Christians and to report on them. The envoy's departure was kept secret so well that it has never been possible to establish his identity. The Byzantine sources relating to his mission report a rather puzzling name of Constantine Platris Anglikos, which does not occur in any Czech document from the mid-fifteenth century.[87] It has been suggested by some modern scholars that the envoy was of English origin and that Platris is a corrupted form of his family name. These scholars also believed that the envoy changed his given name in Constantinople and accepted one which was very popular among the Greeks. Other students of this problem maintain that the envoy was a Czech by birth but nicknamed English because of his previous sojourn in England. This interpretation seems plausible as two Hussite clerics really were called "Engliš" on account of their studies either at Cambridge or Oxford. Be it as it may, the envoy left Prague without companions of equal rank, probably in a humble pilgrim's garb.

According to some allusions in the Byzantine sources, Anglikos had visited the Rumanian principalities of Moldavia and Wallachia on an earlier occasion and became there acquainted with the Eastern rite. He was handicapped by his ignorance of the Greek language, but after his arrival in Constantinople late in the fall of 1451 he found his way into the circles hostile to the Union of Florence. Their stronghold was the convent of the Pantokrator, the residence of Gennadios, the leader of the opposition. In discussions with Gennadios and his associates, Anglikos dispelled their doubts and fears—even in Constantinople the Hussites were regarded as heretics—and in a short time created an atmosphere of mutual trust. To this end Anglikos contributed his share as he raised no objections to the Greek tenets and one day announced his desire to join the Orthodox Church.

The sources relating to his sojourn at the imperial residence on the Golden Horn are so scanty that it is impossible to find out what Gennadios actually had in mind when lending an ear to the Hussite envoy. The idea of a closer union with the Hussites came unexpectedly and its realization promised little advantage to Gennadios' party. He nevertheless did not reject it brusquely, but decided to use the zealous convert for his own purposes. Anglikos was invited to a church controlled by Gennadios' associates, ostensibly to announce publicly the Hussite project and his own conversion. The solemn session soon turned into a stormy demonstration against the promoters of the Union of Florence. Anglikos readily obliged his sponsors by attacking the Papacy in a Latin speech which was promptly translated into Greek and met with wild applause. Gennadios' supporters saw to it that the protest was transferred from the church to the streets. Demonstrations attracted a large section of the population and Constantinople resounded with loud protests against the Roman pontiff.

Anglikos did not leave the Orthodox metropolis empty handed. He carried with him a written confession of the Orthodox faith and a letter dated on January 18, 1452, and signed by four metropolitans as well as three other dignitaries, including Gennadios.[88] The missive contained an invitation to the Czechs to enter into a union with Constantinople. In view of the split among the Greek leaders, the letter was not endorsed by the Patriarch and its validity is questionable.

Anglikos reached Prague probably in May, 1452. In reporting to the Hussite leaders, he misrepresented—deliberately or out of ignorance—the situation in Constantinople. He created the impression that Gennadios was the actual head of the Greek Church and that Emperor Constantine XI was sympathetic to the Czech scheme. The Hussite leaders showed no enthusiasm for the Greek teachings or usages in matters over which the West and the East had been separated. They had no interest in the controversy concerning the procession of the Holy Spirit (*filioque*), and were most likely reluctant to approve the use of leavened bread in the communion. The differences in the baptismal rite probably also caused some difficulty. As conferences with Anglikos were not public, it is impossible to say who participated and what questions or objections were raised.

Although the Hussite leaders were aware of the adverse circumstances, they decided to continue the exchanges with Gennadios. Early in the fall of 1452, a letter was composed in the name of the administrators of the Archbishopric of Prague and all the clergy under their jurisdiction.[89] It was addressed to Emperor Constantine XI and to Gennadios, whom the Czechs styled the patriarch of the Greek Church. Couched in general terms, the document stressed the communion in both kinds and opposition to the Pope but contained nothing concrete concerning a close union of the two parties, the Hussites and the Greek Orthodoxy.

The circumstances under which the letter was drafted are so mysterious as to give rise to lively controversies. No other source from that period refers to the administrators of the Prague archbishopric, and, therefore, critical scholars are inclined to believe that the title in plural was put in to avoid Rokycana's direct commitment. One of the extant copies of the letter bears the date of September 29, 1452; the other was completed as late as November 14.[90] It has been established by meticulous examination of the two texts that in the earlier copy the Emperor's title does not agree with the official form as known from other contemporary documents. These observations led to a tentative conclusion that the letter was not dispatched on September 29, but carefully revised and entrusted to the envoy only on November 14. In addition to the written message, the envoy received oral instructions concerning the new mission which he was about to undertake. It was expected that he would accurately present the Czech point of view to the Greeks.

It is not known whether or not the envoy ever reached his destination and whether he delivered the letter to Gennadios, one of the two addressees for whom it was primarily intended. If he really reached Constantinople, his arrival would have coincided with the mission of Cardinal Isidore empowered by Nicholas V to proclaim solemnly the Union. The atmosphere in Constantinople was by no means favorable to a close study of messages from the Hussite capital as polemics and demonstrations precipitated by the arrival of Cardinal Isidore only added to the confusion and mass fear engendered by Turkish onslaughts on the city walls.

It seems unlikely that the Hussite leaders presenting themselves as administrators of the vacant archbishopric contemplated a close union with Orthodoxy. Such an idea would have encountered enormous difficulties even in more propitious times, in view of the separation of Bohemia from the Orthodox orbit by Poland and Hungary, traditionally attached by the Holy See. It can, however, be admitted that Rokycana, disappointed by repeated setbacks, agreed to an exploration of chances which would arise for him and the Hussite clergy from friendly contacts with the traditional center of Orthodoxy. His consecration by Orthodox bishops would have brought about an open conflict with the Papacy, but the principle of apostolic succession, dear to him and to the Utraquists in general, would have been upheld. It can hardly be doubted that even though embittered, Rokycana preferred the papal approval to any other solution and that even when giving approval to Anglikos' trip, he pressed for cautious proceedings so as not to block forever the path to Rome.

The secular leaders were even more reserved than the high clerics. Their goal seemed to be nearer at hand than ever before. Frederick's declaration for George, although not straightforward, pointed the way toward the stabilization of public administration in Bohemia. George's partisans took the matter energetically into their hands and arranged for a provincial Diet to have Frederick's decision corroborated. The assembly opened in April, 1452, and was attended by both Utraquists and moderate Catholics.[91] The seat usually occupied by Oldřich of Rožmberk remained vacant. Although nominally he still represented the family, Oldřich transferred, in November 1451, the administration of his vast domains to his three sons, Henry, John, and Jošt, and moved from the central part of the Krumlov castle to a more quiet wing to spend the last decade of his life in dignified retirement. Some of his close friends also decided not to attend the Diet as they were too weak to obstruct George's promotion and had no desire passively to witness his triumph. Negotiations between the Utraquist and Catholic parties at the Diet proceeded smoothly, and on April 27, 1452, George was unanimously approved as governor of the country for two years.[92] An advisory committee was elected to assist him in the discharge of his manifold duties. In it the lords were to hold five seats, the lesser nobility also five, and the royal boroughs two. The Utraquists had a majority in that small body corresponding to their strength in Bohemia. In the resolution adopted in the closing session, a hope was expressed that the restoration of order and unity would facilitate the final steps—the coming to Bohemia of the boy prince and the confirmation of the Archbishop-elect. An appeal was made to the absent members of the national community to accede, not later than the middle of August, to the resolution and to abide by it unreservedly.

George's opponents were not numerous and did not control a compact territory. Their strongest position lay in southern Bohemia and from there one could move westward toward Plzeň and beyond. They were at this time not well organized, and a wide gap separated the surviving members of the Tábor party from the Rožmberk coterie. An alliance of Tábor with their former foes could not be excluded and, indeed, some hotheads at Tábor spoke in its favor. When the term fixed by the April Diet had expired, George moved with full force into southern Bohemia. The majority at Tábor resolved not to resist and sent, on September 1, 1452, a delegation to George's headquarters to offer submission. George's terms were mild and were to be extended to other boroughs allied traditionally with Tábor. Religious differences were to be settled by a special commission headed by Rokycana himself. Its findings were promulgated late in the fall of 1452, and were accepted, though not without reluctance, by the majority of the Taborite clerics.[93] Two veteran theologians, Nicholas of Pelhřimov and Václav Koranda, supported by a handful of obdurate clerics, even at this time refused to yield and thus sealed their doom. From the city jail of Prague they were moved to George's castles; Nicholas, the "little bishop," to Poděbrady, and Koranda to Litice, to end their lives in sorrow and obscurity.

Tábor's unexpected capitulation made a deep impression on the Catholic opposition, especially on the owners of land in southern Bohemia. Some of them approached George for terms before he had moved his forces to the confines of the Rožmberk domains, and thus averted an invasion of their property. The Rožmberks realized that a speedy accord with George was the only alternative to war. Protected by a safe-conduct, Oldřich himself rode from Krumlov to George's headquarters in the vicinity of Budějovice. George did not impose harsh conditions on his foremost opponent and simply accepted Oldřich's pledge to attend the forthcoming Diet and to attach his seal to the April resolution.[94] In this agreement Oldřich's son Henry, the administrator of the Rožmberk domains, was included, as well as the walled city of Budějovice, one of the strongholds of Catholicism in the southern tip of Bohemia. George's advance through southwestern and western Bohemia was nowhere obstructed by organized opposition and was completed before the end of September. On the last day of that month George made a triumphant entry into Prague.

The provincial Diet opened in Prague about the middle of October.[95] The principal point on its agenda was the formal approval of the particular agreements made in the course of George's campaign in the Catholic areas of Bohemia. Along with them, the Diet apparently sanctioned the terms imposed early in September on Tábor and its associates. Oldřich and Henry of Rožmberk came to the Diet protected by a safe-conduct which the city of Prague issued to them with George's approval. Other Catholic lords of Rožmberk's alliance were also included in the document so that the Diet was truly representative.

Scholars investigating the contacts with Constantinople are inclined to believe that George was fully informed of them. Indeed, no Hussite cleric, not even Rokycana, would have dared to send a letter addressed to Emperor Constantine XI and Gennadius without George's knowledge and at least tacit consent. Some authors go beyond these simple facts and attribute the revision of the letter on September 20, and the completion of its new version, dated November 14, 1452, to George's intervention.[96] There is no contemporary evidence to support this hypothesis. On the other hand, it seems likely that Oldřich of Rožmberk got an inkling of the discussions in Rokycana's circle and that he obtained through his agents a copy of the letter for the Byzantine dignitaries. In this manner the negotiations came to the notice of Rokycana's Catholic foes and stiffened their opposition to his confirmation.

The Diet was a veritable triumph for George. Four years after the seizure of Prague from Menhart's hands he obtained universal recognition of his primacy. With his hand thus strengthened, he was able to open negotiations with Ladislav's guardian to get the boy prince sent to Prague for his better acquaintance with current affairs and eventually for his coronation.

UNDER THE "BEARDLESS KING"

Frederick's visit to Italy was not unusually long although by no means hurried. He left his Styrian residence, Graz, with the boy Ladislav and a retinue on December 20, 1451, and returned on June 20, 1452; after a short interval he was followed by his consort, Eleonore, a Portuguese princess to whom he had been married before his coronation.

The decision for the journey was not easy, but Frederick's desire to obtain the imperial crown from the Pontiff's hands was so everwhelming that it outweighed other considerations. The elaborate coronation ceremony exerted a fascination both on those who were privileged to participate in it directly, and on the inhabitants of the Empire when they learned of it from eyewitnesses or by other means.

Considerable risks were involved in Frederick's absence from the native lands. As the senior member of the House of Habsburg, he was bound by obligations exceeding his capacity. His portion of the Habsburg patrimony was made up of three provinces—Styria, Carinthia, and Carniola—while his brother Albrecht VI had to content himself with smaller territories in the upper Rhineland. As Ladislav's custodian, Frederick administered Austria proper on both sides of the middle Danube. Some of Frederick's acts gave rise to a suspicion that he was contemplating a permanent extension of his power to include even Tyrol. The minority of Prince Sigismund, who inherited that province in 1439, occasionally served as an excuse for Frederick's interventions and these, in turn, lent credence to rumors that the help afforded to Sigismund was not unselfish. The guardianship of Ladislav involved Frederick in the disputed successions in Bohemia and Hungary. Frederick had no ambition to exercise a genuine leadership in the Empire. He seldom journeyed there to attend the Imperial Diet, although the princes occasionally urged him to take a more active part in settling private disputes and feuds.

By appointment of George as governor and by a deceptive promise of intervention in Rokycana's behalf Frederick allayed agitation in Bohemia.

True, the Estates of their own initiative extended George's term for two years, but they did not undertake anything contrary to their earlier agreements concerning Ladislav's claims to the throne. Even when temporarily absent, Frederick was respected by them as the prince's legitimate custodian.

The nobility in Austria proper proved to be less dependable than the Czechs. One of the Austrians, Ulrich Eizinger, started a campaign against Frederick while the latter was fully occupied with preparations for his journey to Rome. Eizinger could not boast a distinguished family background, but he was at the time probably the wealthiest man in Austria. He had administered the Crown domains under Albrecht V and derived substantial gains from that and other public functions. Frederick did not act wisely when by an untoward intervention he thwarted Eizinger's purchase of a domain in Hungary adjacent to the Austrian border. Out of a loyal servant he made an enemy, to whom other nobles dissatisfied with Frederick's incompetent administration of Austria soon flocked. Frederick still resided at Graz when Eizinger's faction held a congress in Vienna. To forestall kidnapping of Ladislav, Frederick took him to Italy but did not take any action against the seditious nobles.

As soon as Frederick had crossed the Alps, the opposition gained momentum and spread from Austria to the neighboring countries. A faction of the Hungarian aristocracy sent emissaries to Vienna to negotiate an agreement with Eizinger. In Bohemia, Oldřich of Rožmberk grasped at the opportunity to vent his anger at Frederick's endorsement of George's aspirations. The Moravian nobility split and while the majority remained indifferent, some groups sympathized with the Austrian opposition. Eizinger gladly united with Frederick's sworn enemies, the Counts of Cilli. Their participation in the conflict was particularly welcomed as they could boast of their relationship with the boy prince. In fact, they were nephews of Empress Barbara, Ladislav's grandmother.

When Frederick returned from Italy, the forces of the opposition were so strong that he could not crush them without assistance from abroad. Neither Hunyadi nor George was personally involved in hostile activities, but they hoped to gain more from neutrality than from an alliance with the distressed Emperor. With troops levied in his own provinces, Frederick averted a humiliating defeat, but he felt too weak to counterattack. Late in August, 1452, he recognized the limits of his resources and indicated his willingness to make concessions to the opposing party. A preliminary agreement was concluded near Frederick's temporary residence at Wiener Neustadt,[97] and another, more representative, conference was scheduled for November, 1452.

Although reluctantly, Frederick released Ladislav from his custody and handed him over to Ulrich of Cilli. Eizinger consented to this arrangement, trusting Ulrich as a faithful ally. At Ulrich's side, Ladislav rode on horseback in the direction of the Austrian capital. He wore a scarlet tunic, bordered with gold, and a beaver hat. When he passed the city gate, he exchanged the hat for a shining headgear made of pearls and precious stones. Moving slowly under a sumptuous canopy, the prince first reached the Saint Stephen's Cathedral and thence the castle. The reception by the metropolitan population was as enthusiastic as if he had been released from captivity.

Ulrich of Cilli played his cards with great skill for several months. He acted as if Ladislav were mature enough to exercise his prerogatives. The prince's appearance facilitated Ulrich's machinations. Although in his early teens, Ladislav was passing from boyhood to adolescence. A handsome thin lad with curly golden hair, he reminded the court visitors of his grandfather, Sigismund. He liked to wear a white coat with broad flying sleeves and a sumptuous brown tunic of Burgundian fashion. Ulrich flattered his ward by treating him as an adult. Ladislav was allowed to live in luxury, surrounded by courtiers, jesters, minstrels, and dancers. Dinner seldom had less than twelve courses and lasted for several hours. Occasionally Ulrich or some courtier took the prince to the less reputable district—far too soon for his age! Ladislav's education was neglected and his future was seriously in jeopardy.

Endeavoring to exclude Frederick III from participation, Ulrich arranged, in the fall of 1452, for a gathering of delegates from all the lands over which Ladislav was expected, sooner or later, to rule. Acting as the prince's custodian, Ulrich actually was preparing the ground for his own advancement, dreaming of his rise to the position once held by Albrecht V. He endeavored to gain control of Austria so that he could immediately take over in case Ladislav came to an untimely end. The Vienna assembly in November, 1452, failed to bridge over differences among the delegates [98] and Ulrich found it advisable to open separate negotiations with leaders of aristocratic coteries to ascertain from which he could expect the maximum of profit.

Keeping in general the same course as at the time of Frederick's guardianship, George pressed for Ladislav's transfer to Prague. He did not attend the November assembly, but met with Ulrich in April, 1453, at Znojmo, not far from the Austro-Moravian border, and from there they journeyed to Vienna. There George was introduced to the youthful heir to the throne. The first contacts augured well for their future relationship, as George's friendly sentiments were reciprocated by Ladislav. According to contemporary reports,[99] they brushed aside the court etiquette and addressed each other as "my father" and "my son." In conferences, three documents were prepared and issued in Ladislav's name.[100] The most important was Ladislav's confirmation, with slight modifications, of the articles presented to him by George on behalf of the Estates of Bohemia. The charter covered a wide range of problems, including the Compacts and Rokycana's confirmation. Two charters were intended for George: one, to be promulgated immediately, approved him as governor for the term fixed by the provincial assembly in April, 1452; and the other, secret, extended the term for six more years, making George less dependent on the provincial Estates.

From the legal point of view the two charters were far more satisfactory than Frederick's decision of 1451, but George had in mind more than a personal promotion and insisted that Ladislav be moved from Vienna to Prague. It could not escape his notice that Ulrich's tutelage was undesirable and that the boy prince could be ruined morally before he could act independently. Ladislav as king had an important role in George's schemes and to play it successfully he had to be emancipated from his self-seeking relatives and prepared well for his duties. Some events in Hungary and simultaneous changes in Ulrich's circle led George to the conclusion that he must get Ladislav to Bohemia as soon as possible. Especially alarming were Ulrich's maneuvers by which he hoped to obtain easier terms for Ladislav than those embodied in his confirmation of George's articles.

Like Frederick III, Ulrich of Cilli was aware of the frictions between Bohemia, since 1452 solidly controlled by George, and the incorporated provinces. Interpreted strictly, Ladislav's charters of early May, 1453, sanctioned George's position in Bohemia only, leaving out the other parts of the Kingdom. The provincial Estates of Moravia, Silesia, and of both Lusatias showed far more respect for the hereditary principle than did the nobles of Bohemia. In this position they were confirmed by the repeated disregard of their wishes of which the Czech leaders were guilty. Thus a gap existed which Ulrich wished to utilize for his machinations to keep George in check.

Ulrich's dealings with Moravia, which because of its proximity to Vienna was approached first, were neither short nor easy, but they reached visible results that disquieted George. Early in July, 1453, Ladislav, in Ulrich's company, arrived in Brno and received homage as the legitimate ruler from the assembled Estates. Nobody was invited to represent Bohemia at this ceremony, and the omission was resented by the Hussites as well as the Catholic leaders as an intrusion from Vienna, the Czech position being that the coronation in Prague should precede symbolic acts of recognition in the incorporated provinces.

Ulrich's attempts to strengthen Ladislav's position, coupled with his machinations both in Hungary and Austria, paved the way for a closer union of three influential leaders, George, Hunyadi, and Eizinger. Sensing that Ulrich's ambition, if not curbed promptly, could endanger any one or all of them, they drew together at first for protective measures. It soon fell to Eizinger to launch the offensive and to drive a wedge between Ulrich and his ward. Ladislav proved to be more tractable than had been expected and dismissed his guardian without any previous warning. George was initiated into the plot, and immediately after Ulrich's fall from grace sent for the prince. Neither Hunyadi nor Eizinger opposed this move believing that a lesser threat would come to them from Ladislav's sojourn in Bohemia than from his rather shaky position among the court coteries in Vienna or Styria.

Cogent reasons could be found for George's insistence that the heir to the throne be brought into closer contacts with his subjects. At Frederick's court Ladislav received instruction in the fundamentals of the Roman Catholic faith. His tutors inculcated in his receptive mind a strong dislike of heretics, in which category they included the Hussites. This aversion, coupled with a fervid devotion to Rome, could cause troubles in Bohemia, and it was advisable to modify it while the prince was flexible. It was regarded as a matter of course that Ladislav would not only respect the Compacts, but also use his influence with the Papacy to obtain Rokycana's confirmation.

His presence in Prague had political significance as well. He was fluent in German, and not only the language but also his manners were bound to impress the inhabitants of the German-speaking portions of the kingdom. As Ladislav's guardian, George had a better chance of acceptance in those areas than if he attempted to assert his authority merely as a governor of Bohemia. George's prestige would have been impaired if homage to Ladislav were to be sworn by the Estates of the incorporated provinces in his absence, as it happened at Brno in July, 1453.

During the welcome ceremony at the border of Bohemia and in the ensuing solemn acts in Prague, no omission occurred that could be exploited by George's adversaries or anybody else. Ladislav's right to the throne was not expressly denied, but the role of the Estates of Bohemia in duly electing him was stressed.[101] The coronation took place in Saint Vitus Cathedral soon after his entry into Prague. It was attended by several friendly princes as well as by Hunyadi and Eizinger. The Bishop of Olomouc, assisted by the Bishop of Breslau and other prelates, performed the rite in accordance with the *Ordo coronationis* of Charles IV. The sources make no mention of the Utraquist clergy, but some of them report the arrival of the metropolitan chapter from Plzeň so that its members were able to attend the services. The oath formula stressed the elective principle to the satisfaction of both the Catholic and the Utraquist nobles.[102]

Steps were taken immediately to provide accommodations for the youthful king. The castle at Hradčany could not be quickly adapted for that purpose, as it was badly damaged. For several months Ladislav enjoyed George's hospitality and only in the spring of 1454 was he able to move into his own quarters in one part of the royal court in the Old Town. Along with these measures, arrangements were made for Ladislav's education. His Austrian courtiers were replaced by natives of Bohemia, among whom was included a tutor in the Czech language, who compiled for his august disciple a Latin-German-Czech dictionary to facilitate his instruction.[103]

Contemporary observers were surprised at how quickly George gained Ladislav's affection. There was between them a difference of twenty years and in contacts with other people Ladislav usually was reserved and diffident. An orphan, he craved a friendly atmosphere and he instinctively trusted George more than his relatives. Not enough is known of other members of the Poděbrady family. George was married for the second time in 1450, amidst struggles for recognition as governor, to Johanna of Rožmitál, a Utraquist with relatives of the Catholic creed. Two children of his first marriage died before their mother, but five survived: three boys, Boček, Victorin, and Henry, and two girls, Catherine and Zdeňka. Johanna gave birth, between 1452 and 1458, to three children. Of the second one, Agnes, little besides the name is known, but the other two, the boy Hynek and his sister Ludmila, were destined to play an active part in the public life of their country. Intimate relationship apparently existed only between George and Ladislav, while in contacts with the other members of the family conventional rules were observed. Ladislav's rank and his attachment to the Roman Church precluded any cordiality where it could be naturally expected, that is, in relation to those of George's children who were of about the same age.

Ladislav's religious education and his attendance at divine services presented the most delicate problems, with which only a statesman so tolerant and tactful as George could cope. Being steeped in Hussite principles, he had full understanding of the Utraquist sensibilities. But he could not satisfy them fully, since he could not disregard the Catholic population of the kingdom. He also had to pay attention to public opinion in the Catholic orbit, especially among Bohemia's neighbors. Any attempt to exert pressure on Ladislav to change his religious ties was bound to provoke protests, or even attempts to take him away from George's tutelage.

Some incidents which took place soon after the coronation revealed the depth of Ladislav's antipathy to the Utraquist party. Knowing of it, George, in the interest of peace in his kingdom, did not insist that Ladislav attend Utraquist ceremonies—not even on special occasions. All that George could accomplish was a careful preparation of the King's public appearances, so that there would be no clash or stormy scenes. Ladislav learned little, indeed, from his guardian and persisted in his unfriendly attitude toward the Utraquists. He never entered a Utraquist church, and it was George's duty to allay the Utraquist displeasure by participation, with other members of the family, in their processions on Corpus Christi day and other ceremonies.

It was to be expected that the Estates of Austria and Hungary would strongly object to Ladislav's permanent residence in Prague. Therefore, George gave the King but little time for his orientation and attempted to settle within a short period the political and constitutional problems that had accumulated during the interregnum. It was the King's duty to restore order in all parts of his kingdom and to strengthen the ties between Bohemia and the incorporated provinces in the spirit of Charles's charters.[104] As Ladislav could not act on his own because of age and ignorance of the intricacies of both the written documents and the traditional usages, power was left virtually in George's hands, and he used it shrewdly, sensing that any delay or omission would, sooner or later, be turned against him.

Two provincial Diets were held in Prague in quick succession, one soon after the coronation, the other in the Lent of 1454.[105] A wide range of problems pertaining primarily to Bohemia came up for discussion. Many agreements made between the parties since Albrecht's death automatically lost their validity, as the country had again its legitimate ruler. George was primarily interested in the formal sanction of his position, as the danger of Ladislav's alignment with the Catholic lords of the league of Strakonice could not be excluded. According to the secret Vienna agreement, George was to assist Ladislav for six more years.[106] The royal charter of March 14, 1454, soon afterwards endorsed by the provincial Diet, fixed the term of governorship for three years only, but it was understood that it could be extended.[107] Vacancies in the supreme offices of Bohemia and in the provincial tribunal were filled and most of those posts went to the Catholics, such as Prokop of Rabštejn, who was appointed the chancellor.

A good deal of time was devoted to financial and economic problems. Apart from the traditional measures, such as the tax to be levied upon the inhabitants of Bohemia to defray the coronation and other extraordinary expenses, the Diets approved in principle a thorough revision of the recent transfers of property, a step to which only the royal authority could give sufficient weight. Owners of domains belonging prior to 1419 either to the Crown or the Church were requested to present documents legalizing such acquisitions or else risk their loss. Estates seized arbitrarily during the Hussite wars and the interregnum after Albrecht's death were to be returned to the Crown, and it was left to the King's discretion to determine to what purpose the former ecclesiastical domains should be put. Sources pertaining to the large-scale revision are insufficient, so that it is impossible to ascertain how much of Crown and Church domains had been regained and in which cases the royal edicts were sabotaged by the new owners.[108] Even a partial restitution marked some progress toward the consolidation of the Crown property, that at one time had been in danger of dissipation.

Resolutions of the two Diets, although not popular, were sanctioned without opposition, as it would have been foolhardy at that time to defy the monarch. The Czech-speaking population trusted George and adopted a benevolent attitude toward Ladislav. The resolute Hussites were alarmed by his bigotry, but they toned down their objections in the hope that in those matters, too, George would not tolerate excesses or flagrant violation of the Compacts.

Stabilization of relations between Bohemia and the incorporated provinces required a good deal more time and ingenuity than the local affairs of Bohemia. The start was difficult, as the long-pending divisions were accentuated by recent constitutional problems. The Estates of the incorporated provinces resented their exclusion from conferences preceding the King's coming to Bohemia and looked for an opportunity to retaliate. George regarded as urgent the harmonization of the conflicting points of view and approached at first the Moravians, success with whom seemed to be reasonably within sight. But even there he was unable to accomplish more than a tactical compromise.[109] The road to an agreement with the Estates of Silesia was more difficult, as their antagonism had deep roots, and exceptional skill was needed to find concrete issues on which the parties could reach an accord.

Although Silesia lacked the geographical and administrative homogeneity with which Bohemia was blessed, opposition there to the Hussites was resolute and widespread. As this antagonism was accentuated by ethnic differences, it could not be neutralized by a formal treaty, whether freely negotiated or signed under duress. More widely ramified and permanent ties had to be created in order to strengthen in Silesia as well as in the Lusatias the elements favoring their continued attachment to the Crown of Bohemia. Some steps in that direction had been made before Ladislav's coronation, but their effects could not be discerned immediately.

Ladislav alone would have been acceptable to these provinces, but as on every public occasion George appeared at his side, the unsettled problems could easily be reopened. Since February, 1453, Breslau had served Giovanni Capistrano as headquarters and from him George could hardly expect a conciliatory attitude. Although the Hussites were not Capistrano's only target—he helped the local authorities in investigating accusations of blasphemy leveled against the Jews [110]—his anti-Czech bias caused serious complications. While some Silesian princes, following the ancient custom, came to Prague to swear fealty to their liege lord in his residence, Breslau and its associates paid no heed to appeals from Prague, and insisted that Ladislav visit Silesia and receive homage there. Coupled with this obstinacy was the desire to make the Silesian metropolis the second capital of the kingdom, to which the German-speaking areas would gravitate.

Realizing the gravity of the situation, George was ready to meet the recalcitrants halfway. A delegation of four Catholic nobles was sent to Silesia to receive the oath of allegiance in the name of the King. They succeeded in breaking the opposition in most cities allied with Breslau, but the capital itself, controlled by fanatical preachers, remained adamant. Its aldermen persisted in their defiance, at the risk of an armed conflict, even after Capistrano's departure early in the summer. Fortunately, George did not lose balance of mind and by some skillful moves on the diplomatic chessboard contributed to the isolation of Breslau. The Estates of Upper Lusatia obeyed Ladislav's summons and came to Prague in the middle of November. Steps were taken to release Lower Lusatia from temporary control by Frederick of Brandenburg, but the scheme could not be carried out, as the sum needed for the redemption of the old debts was not available. Late in November, 1454, the opposition of Breslau became critical and the kingdom's peace hung by a slender thread.

In the eleventh hour George overcame his instinctive dislike of the recalcitrants and worked out a more realistic plan. This sudden decision to journey to Breslau proved to be sound. Escorted by a strong and well-armed retinue, Ladislav and George left Prague in the last week of November and on December 6, 1454, they entered the defiant city. Five days later, representatives of the municipal council bent their knees before their "born and hereditary" lord.[111] They accepted, not without murmur, a heavy fine of fifteen thousand ducats to redeem their disobedience and promised to defray royal expenses. Soon afterwards the Bishop and the chapter followed suit and paid homage to their sovereign.[112]

These symbolic acts, which terminated Ladislav's striving for recognition by all parts of the kingdom were followed by conferences with the Silesian and German princes and elaborate religious ceremonies. Thereafter, the King and his illustrious companions plunged into a round of games and amusements.[113] As the weather was cold and snow covered the ground, the King and his friends often used sleighs for rides through the city or for excursions into the surrounding countryside. It did not pass unnoticed that one day when returning from a ride, the King gave orders that his sumptuous sleighs turn in the direction of the notorious district of Breslau. Nobody seemed to be scandalized by the King's conduct. Breslau had paid heavily for its refusal to send delegates to Prague, and as the inhabitants' wrath could not turn against the King, it was rumored that George deliberately prolonged the royal visit and caused them heavy expenditure. Ladislav's decision to cede to George one third of the penalty inflamed their passions and gave rise to speculation as to the purpose for which George wanted to use the money.

More familiar with the intricate constitutional problems than Ladislav, George endeavored to buttress the legal structure by concrete provisions, some of which were clearly intended for his own enhancement. In 1454 he greatly enlarged his family possessions by a purchase of the Častolovice domain consisting of areas in Bohemia, Kladsko, and Münsterberg. The latter two portions were particularly valuable, as they formed a link between Bohemia and Silesia which enabled George to claim a seat among the Estates of that province. He kept an eye also on the principality of Legnica and made steps toward its acquisition for his family. In Breslau his enemies believed that the money exacted from them was to finance these operations.

By the purchase of Častolovice and some other minor acquisitions, George's wealth increased and he ranked second after the Rožmberks. He realized that his advancement could engender ill-will among other members of the nobility and reverse the progress of consolidation which with Ladislav's coronation reached one of its main goals. George did not have to fear that any of the Utraquist lords would capture Ladislav's favor and force him out of the commanding position at the royal court; but an alliance between the Catholic king and the lords of the same faith could not be dismissed from the mind as unlikely. By his retirement from administrative duties, Oldřich of Rožmberk did not relinquish his personal ambitions; but in his advanced age he was even less qualified for actual leadership of the Catholic party than at the time of George's rise to power. Oldřich's sons had a better chance, and apart from them members of other families aspired to political career and coveted lucrative offices in the public administration.

While it would have been foolish to increase their influence in the King's entourage, appointments to high dignities in other parts of the kingdom served a double purpose: they satisfied personal ambitions and tightened the ties between Bohemia and the German-speaking and Catholic provinces. With Ladislav's consent, George appointed Henry of Rožmberk captain of Silesia. In this function he represented the King in the royal domain, but he could also be employed in contacts with the princes ruling in their inherited territories as vassals. The Rožmberks enjoyed unquestioned reputation far beyond the confines of their domains, and Duke Henry of Głogów gladly gave Oldřich's second son John his daughter Anne in marriage. The third son, Jošt, chose the church career and won favors from Nicholas V. In 1456, not without the intervention of his brother Henry, Jošt was elected Bishop of Breslau and was confirmed by Calixtus III, although he had not reached the prescribed age of thirty.

Reorganization of the public administration in the two neighboring provinces of Silesia was also overdue. Problems of Upper Lusatia were neither intricate nor troublesome, and the appointment of Henry of Rožmberk as the *voigt* of the league of the six royal boroughs again proved to be a skillful move. The remotest part of the kingdom, Lower Lusatia, was plagued by local feuds and by the aggressive designs of its neighbor, Frederick of Brandenburg. Any attempt to move there with armed forces would have increased the danger of an international conflict, which George attempted to avoid. He decided upon a less irritating measure and used the Lords of Šternberk as his protagonists.

The older of them, Aleš, could be trusted, as he had once adhered to Hynek Ptáček and afterwards held a prominent position among George's partisans. Aleš' nephew, Zdeněk, started his political career in cooperation with the Rožmberks, but in 1448 changed his party alignment and joined George in the expedition against Menhart of Hradec. Although seemingly on the best terms, the two leaders were not bound by sincere friendship. They were apparently not too far apart in age and tacitly recognized that in alliance they could reap larger benefits than if divided or at odds. With George's connivance, Zdeněk filled the vacancy caused by Menhart's death, and as the supreme burgrave played a significant role in the Czech political and social life.[114] Some chroniclers accuse Zdeněk not only of unbounded ambition but also of inordinate vanity. According to one of them Zdeněk introduced an effeminate fashion by wearing a bonnet to cover his prematurely greying hair.[115]

The Lower Lusatia grant was not too generous, but the Šternberks did not decline it, as they wished to gain a foothold in that province. On George's recommendation, Ladislav transferred to them some of his claims to properties at Choćebuz;[116] by accepting them, the Šternberks were instantly involved in disputes with the Elector of Brandenburg.

The new appointments or awards were not received without murmur, as both the Rožmberks and Šternberks had family possessions in Bohemia and received positions coveted by the local nobility either in Silesia or in the Lusatias. Their allegiance to Catholicism mitigated the initial resentment, and they were able to retain the grants and extend their personal contacts.

Religious issues on which the Czechs and the Germans were divided were touched upon in the preliminary negotiations with Ladislav, as well as in the documents issued either at his coronation or soon thereafter. One of the most perplexing problems was Rokycana's confirmation, which was no nearer to its realization than on the eve of Frederick's journey to Italy. Urged by the Czechs, Ladislav dispatched envoys to Rome before his departure from Vienna, but they were apparently not too zealous in pressing the matter and failed to accomplish anything. The problem was temporarily eclipsed by political events, but it appeared on the horizon again late in the spring of 1454. Urged from many sides, Ladislav ordered the Catholic and the Utraquist clerics to assemble in Prague and to settle their controversies amicably. Two synods were held simultaneously, one under the presidency of Václav of Krumlov, the administrator of the "Upper Consistory," and the other with Rokycana in the chair. The Utraquist clergy unanimously reaffirmed their adherence to the Archbishop-elect. Informed of the vote, George hastened to obtain for it the royal sanction. Not realizing perhaps all the implications of this act, Ladislav gave his consent before any Catholic representative could dissuade him.[117]

Ladislav's declaration could not be used for an extension of Rokycana's jurisdiction over the Catholics, but it enhanced his prestige among the Utraquists. Acting as their spiritual head, he performed the administrative functions reserved for bishops, with the exception of the ordination of priests. His chief concern was the organization of the Utraquist party and improvement of the moral standards among the clergy. His actions ran parallel with the program of the Catholic administrator and conformed to the instructions issued by Ladislav for all clergy of Bohemia.[118]

Although the King's name was used in relevant documents, their author was undoubtedly George himself, who was guided by the desire to achieve religious unity in Bohemia in the spirit of the Compacts. The immediate cause of his concern was the rise of separatist tendencies on both sides, which could mostly be ascribed to the flat denial of the petitions in behalf of Rokycana on the part of the Pope. To nip in the bud the danger of a complete split, George rebuked Václav of Krumlov when he had learned that the metropolitan chapter through its own channels communicated to Rome the name of their candidate for the archbishopric. In George's opinion, Rokycana's claims were valid and his confirmation should not have been endangered by unilateral dealings with the papal court. Ladislav instructed the Utraquists to stay within the limits of the Compacts and enjoined them to observe the teachings and ceremonies approved by the Church in order to avoid altercations and mutual accusations with the Catholics. There was little hope that both parties would loyally support George's enlightened policy, but a statement issued in the name of the young king could not be couched in other than conciliatory terms.

The royal instructions for the clergy were not followed by a new mission to Rome. Unsatisfactory results obtained on previous occasions induced George to refrain from taking a new direct step, and Rokycana, too, preferred to wait for a more opportune moment rather than suffer another rebuff. Shielded at least nominally by Ladislav's authority, he was free from personal danger and could afford to wait for the sanction by the Pope.

Early in 1455, hopeful signs appeared on the horizon and gave rise to delusive hopes that the Czech conflict with the Papacy might be settled along with the major issues of European policy. At the time of George's exclusive occupation with Ladislav's transfer to Prague, Constantinople fell into the hands of the Turks and its conquest not only portended their further advance across the Balkans into the Danubian plain, but an extension of their power in the Mediterranean as well. Along with other European rulers, Ladislav was regarded as an important figure in the planned campaigns, since Hungary was one of his kingdoms. As soon as the idea of an anti-Turkish crusade, shielded by the papal authority, assumed a distinct shape, the potential roles of Ladislav's other domains were explored, as without their assistance Hungary could not be built up into a mighty bulwark to stem the Turkish expansion.

A delegation from Bohemia, including Prokop of Rabštejn, attended the imperial Diet held early in the fall of 1454 at Frankfurt and announced Ladislav's decision to participate in any further deliberations.[119] At a congress convened by Emperor Frederick III at Wiener Neustadt, George represented Bohemia, while John Hunyadi spoke in the name of the Hungarians. In a public session on March 19, 1455, George assured the Emperor of his willingness to help as soon as Bohemia could achieve durable peace with other countries.[120] As only minor issues relating to the boundary with Saxony and to the Duchy of Luxemburg remained unsettled, it could be conjectured that George also thought of the differences hindering the final act of conciliation with the Papacy.

Enea Silvio energetically performed his duties as Frederick's chief diplomat at the imperial Diets in 1454 and at the congress at Wiener Neustadt. In that city he re-established personal contacts with George and used Prokop of Rabštejn again as interpreter. In private meetings the governor and the bishop-diplomat took up the matters debated four years earlier at Benešov, and the two men apparently reached a closer understanding. In 1455 Enea was less communicative than after his departure from Benešov, and neither he nor George disclosed to friends the contents of their confidential talks. Only later documents contain some indirect hints as to the questions debated at Wiener Neustadt.[121]

While the congress was in session, the news came from Italy that Nicholas V died. Hopes arose that the new pope, Calixtus III, would have a livelier interest in the expedition against the Turks as well as to the problems directly or indirectly affecting the defense of Christendom. As was customary, the rulers of countries under the Roman obedience sent envoys to Rome to congratulate the Pontiff on his election and to pledge him their allegiance. Frederick III appointed the Bishop of Siena as the spokesman of the imperial delegation. His solemn audience with the Pope took place early in September, 1455.[122]

Soon thereafter Enea Silvio was again received by Calixtus III and submitted him a detailed plan for dealings with the Czechs. He did not invoke Frederick's direct authorization for his plan, although he indicated clearly enough that both his master and George were informed of it. The long and well-prepared speech addressed to Calixtus III was, in fact, a plea for an amicable settlement of the Hussite affair in view of the imperative necessity of consolidating Western Christendom.[123] Enea attempted to convince the Pope that the rift could not be healed by forcible methods, and hinted obliquely that the prestige of the Holy See would not be lowered if concessions previously made by the Council of Basel were endorsed.

In order to impress the Pope agreeably, Enea drew a distinct line between the Compacts, including the communion in both kinds, and Rokycana's confirmation, and treated each point on its own merits. He recalled not only the Czech petitions to the Pope's predecessors for a sanction of the Compacts, but also the disheartening results of the diplomatic interventions by Cardinals Carvajal and Cusa. Enea's comment on Capistrano's mission was appreciative but nonetheless negative. It was summed up in a terse statement that after his preaching Bohemia remained what it had been before. Enea also disavowed as delusive Menhart's and Oldřich's suggestions that the Compacts not be approved, and supported the positive recommendations of Prokop of Rabštejn and the moderate Catholic lords, in whose opinion the Compacts were the only way to peace with the Hussites. He also made reference to the measures adopted recently under Ladislav's and George's authority, by which it became a public offence to accuse either of the existing parties among the Czechs of heresy. Coming to the subtlest point, Enea maintained that the Compacts did not declare the communion in both kinds obligatory, but granted it only to those laymen who had practiced it prior to the agreement reached with the Council of Basel. This plea for a papal sanction culminated in an emphatic statement that it would be easier to turn back the course of a river than to deprive the Czechs of the communion in both kinds.

In introducing the other topic, Enea was less discreet in accentuating the contrast between them. He used harsh words concerning Rokycana, calling him "black and pestilent soul," "a lamb" when officiating at the altar, "a lion" when preaching from the pulpit. He assured the Pope that

Rokycana's appointment to the See of Prague should not be regarded as the only means of breaking the deadlock. In this connection the bishop-diplomat revealed pertinent details of his talks with George. If he rendered them accurately, then George, too, clung firmly to the Compacts and desired that the Czechs be cleared of the taint of heresy, but showed more flexibility in the Utraquist administrative problems. With reference to George, Enea developed ideas corresponding more accurately to his own versatility than to George's past honest endeavors to obtain Rokycana's confirmation. Enea held out the hope that when assured on the communion in both kinds, the Czechs would not obstinately demand Rokycana's confirmation, but would present ten or twelve candidates, including Rokycana, among whom the Pope would be free to choose. To dispel Calixtus' suspicion, Enea extolled the Czech respect for the given word or the freely accepted obligations. They could not drop Rokycana from their list, he said, as he had been designated by the provincial assembly and approved by Sigismund, Albrecht, and recently by Ladislav. If the Czechs could be induced to present him along with other candidates, it could be expected that they would respect the papal decision, even if another cleric from their list were chosen.

Viewed in historical perspective, Enea's elaborate speech was the most challenging appeal for the papal sanction of the Compacts ever made by the Roman side. If the communion in both kinds had been approved for those who were already practicing it, after fifty years—so Enea hoped —only few laymen would live who had been permitted to partake of the consecrated wine at the Lord's table. As far as the other point was concerned, the right to choose the incumbent of the Prague See from a large number of submitted names would have sufficiently protected the papal prerogatives in making appointment. It is very difficult, indeed, to ascertain how far George actually yielded in his hints at possible concessions, and to what extent Enea enlarged on the governor's general statements to make his scheme more plausible.

References made to George in relevant passages of the speech were complimentary and optimistic. Enea presented him to the Pope as a man of high spirit and mental power and of even higher prudence. He lauded George's stability, persistence, and fairness, and concluded that all Czechs looked to him with respect. Enea regarded the presence in Bohemia of a king of Catholic faith as a hopeful sign. He also called the Pope's attention to the predominance of the Catholics among the nobility and expressed the conviction that the royal boroughs, although mostly Utraquist, would abide by the laws imposed on them by the King and the lords.

The vista which opened before the ailing Pope while Enea enumerated the benefits to come from an agreement with the Czechs, was broad and enticing: a large kingdom and a warlike people would be brought back into the fold of the Church; unity among the peoples inhabiting the country would be restored; Ladislav would possess a quiet patrimony; the Germans in the vicinity would enjoy peace; Christendom would have at its disposal forces equipped against the Turks; and above all, an accord with the Church would open the gates of paradise to innumerable souls.

While making it clear that George as the governor and recognized leader of the Utraquists would be the chief agent in promoting the settlement, Enea also indicated that the Pope would have to appoint a legate to conduct the negotiations on the spot, consecrate the designated incumbent, and supervise the restoration of traditional rites and practices, so that "what had been deformed could be reformed." His recommendations were couched in general terms, but of whom else could he think as the most competent representative of the Holy See if not of himself? The red hat would have been, indeed, an appropriate compensation not only for the thoughtful analysis of the Czech situation, but also for a successful implementation of the papal decision to adopt the plan of action.

Calixtus' reply to Enea's proposals has not been found and probably was never put into writing. According to some indications, the Pope did not flatly reject the idea of conciliation but decided on its further exploration. A matter of such great importance could not remain secret for a long time. Rumors emanating from Rome flew on the wings of the wind and were magnified in the passage. Giovanni Capistrano, crusading in Hungary, was greatly disturbed when he heard that not only the confirmation of the Compacts was in the offing, but that even the promotion of Rokycana to the cardinalate was talked about, if he proved as tractable as some Greek prelates were in negotiating for the union of Florence. Capistrano's stern warning against such concessions was followed by Carvajal's steps and possibly by other interventions, which the Pope could not disregard.[124] Enea was too weak to press his scheme and he himself abandoned it when other, more feasible, tasks were entrusted to him in the winter and spring of 1456.

While the Czech cause lay in abeyance, spectacular events transpired which supplanted the diplomatic preparations of an anti-Turkish league. The Turkish invasion campaign, expected with fears since the fall of Constantinople, opened in June, 1456, and was aimed at the fortress of Belgrade, guarding the northward passage over the rivers Danube and Sava. The Hungarian forces stemmed the tide of the Turkish advance, but their leader, John Hunyadi, soon after his victory over Mohamed II, succumbed to the plague ravaging the Christian camp. Giovanni Capistrano, another prominent figure distinguished in the heroic defense of Belgrade, died in southern Hungary several months later.

The victory over the Turks gave Hungary no more than temporary relief. Ladislav was no wiser than the other Christian rulers of that time and instead of consolidating his international position, he allowed himself to be drawn into rivalries and intrigues, some of which were long pending, while others were engendered by the more recent developments in Austria and Hungary. Bohemia was not affected directly, but George could not stand aloof from them, as he had commitments not only to the King but also to the leaders of the various factions in those countries. His obligations were not too clearly defined and a good deal of freedom was left him for bargaining and tactical maneuvers.

The King, sixteen years old at that time, was too young to rule without circumspect guidance, and this George had given him while in Prague and Breslau. Soon after his return to Vienna, early in 1455, Ladislav again came under the pernicious influence of Ulrich of Cilli, who pushed him against Emperor Frederick III, and later against John Hunyadi. Plotting with the latter's rivals brought Ulrich some immediate gains, but eventually led to his ruin. In November, 1456, he was lured by John's older son, Ladislav, into the Belgrade fortress and there was slain before anyone could come to his rescue. The King, experienced in dissimulation, masked his ire and lulled Ladislav Hunyadi into a false sense of security, promoting him to the captaincy of the Hungarian kingdom. During the winter season of 1456–57, the King consolidated the ranks of his followers and in March, 1457, he decided to strike. Resorting to the same stratagem as that of Ulrich's foes, the King one day invited Ladislav Hunyadi and his brother, Matthias, to his apartments in the Buda Castle and with the help of loyal nobles took them captive. Proclaimed guilty of Ulrich's assassination, Ladislav was beheaded on March 15, 1457. Matthias was imprisoned and carried away in chains to Vienna, when the King moved there to avoid involvements in the conflicts between the rival parties in Hungary.

Viewed from Prague, the King's return to Austria appeared to be a lesser evil than his Hungarian entanglements, but it gave rise to other problems no less menacing than the former alliances with Ulrich of Cilli. Although Ladislav, in the dark hours following Ulrich's assassination, proclaimed himself of full age, he needed assistance to discharge his many onerous duties. Eizinger's position was not too strong, and Ladislav's financial adviser, Conrad Hölzler, won the King's favor. The new alignment was inconsistent with the King's manifold obligations, as Hölzler lacked political acumen and pushed Ladislav into dangerous experiments. George was particularly alarmed when he discovered Hölzler's

contacts with some Catholic lords in Bohemia, which apparently were
established with the King's connivance so as to lessen his dependence
on the Hussite leader.

To foil the intrigues before they could take a dangerous turn, George
entered Austria late in July, 1457, not as an invader but nevertheless with
a strong body of horsemen, and allied himself with Eizinger and other
rivals of Hölzler. He by-passed the latter, and established direct contacts
with the King. In closed sessions, the two men discussed urgent problems and obligations, including the royal marriage. Reluctantly the King
yielded to George's argument and consented to a transfer of his residence from Vienna to Prague. Without undue delay, Ladislav prepared
for the journey and on September 29, 1457, he entered the city accompanied by a splendid retinue in which one could see both Hölzler and
Eizinger. Matthias Hunyadi was brought under a strong escort as the
King's prisoner. No less conspicuous than Hölzler's presence was the attendance of Oldřich of Rožmberk as well as that of his son John, who
after the premature death of his older brother Henry, administered the
family domains.

The three years during which Ladislav lived elsewhere were not a
long period when measured in time elapsed, but they meant much to
him and to his subjects. The absence, though contrary to George's original ideas, was not detrimental to the welfare of the people. With Breslau's submission to the royal authority the long period of internal struggles finally ended and the country soon began to reap the fruits of pacification. More quickly than other classes, the merchants in the surrounding countries recognized the change and their wagons laden with a
variety of merchandise appeared again on the roads leading to Bohemia.
Prices of agricultural products and of goods manufactured in the country went down, and according to one chronicler "all was cheap." [125]

Nothing but a hypothetical answer can be given to the question
whether the "beardless" and emotionally unstable King, if he had remained permanently among the Czechs, would have really become one
of them. More was needed for complete assimilation than to learn the
Czech language and to drink beer, which in Enea's opinion were the
prerequisites of popularity. Religious orientation was really the touchstone, and Ladislav's dislike of the Hussite rites seemed to be insur-
mountable. [126] George attempted to mitigate it, but the results of his tu-
torship were far from satisfactory. After Ladislav's departure for Vienna,
Czech influences were superseded by Austrian customs and waned rapidly. When he returned to Prague in the fall of 1457, the King was again
a stranger, different from the Czechs in apparel and manners. He was
surrounded by Austrian nobles and used their language, as his Czech
was halting. More alarming than the King's external appearance was his

intolerant spirit, which George again attempted to curb as soon as it came to his notice. The King was still very young and looked innocent, but Prague was not too far from Budapest. Enough had been heard in the Czech capital concerning Hunyadi's execution and of Ladislav's part in it to make people cautious.

There was not much time for domestic problems. The King's mind was occupied with the preparation for his marriage, which was to be celebrated in Prague as the most attractive of Ladislav's three residences. The prospective bride was Magdalen, the fifteen-year-old daughter of the French king, Charles VII. In the preliminary exchanges not only the family union was taken into consideration, but also political problems, including Ladislav's desire to reassert his claims to Luxemburg. Late in the summer of 1457 the negotiations with the court of Paris entered the final stage and a solemn embassy was to be sent to France to bring back the bride. Austria, Bohemia, and Hungary were to be equally represented and two delegates were added to the delegation to symbolize Ladislav's claims to the Luxemburg patrimony. Zdeněk of Šternberk headed the Czech group. As Ladislav wanted to have the entourage as impressive as possible, a good deal of money was needed. Hölzler was slow in supplying it and therefore incurred the King's wrath and lost his office. George ingratiated himself with the King by procuring the sum and thus facilitating the departure of the royal envoys.

The embassy traveled slowly and, as communications were inadequate, while en route they did not receive the bad news from Prague. When they were leaving, the King seemed to be in perfect health and good spirits. In the second half of November, the atmosphere in Prague suddenly deteriorated. An ominous sign disturbed the preparations for the royal wedding: a new comet appeared in the sky. At about the same time, lions in the royal menagerie began to roar and became so ferocious that nobody dared to approach the cage. On Sunday, November 20, 1457, Ladislav, accompanied by George, attended the baptismal ceremony of the new-born son of Zdeněk of Šternberk, acting as the infant's godfather. He had a restless night and in the morning two swellings appeared in the King's pubic region, of which he for shame said nothing to his attendants. Not properly diagnosed and treated, the disease advanced rapidly. On Wednesday, Ladislav himself felt that the end was coming. He called in George, thanked him for the services rendered and entreated him to protect peace not only in Bohemia but in other parts of his patrimony as well. Priests were called to administer the last rites. Thereupon, the King recited the Lord's prayer, but paused before "deliver us from evil" and expired.[127]

For fear of contagion, the funeral was held on the third day. As the royal court was situated in the Old Town, Rokycana opened the funeral rites in his parish church at Týn, and surrounded by the Utraquist clergy escorted the hearse to the Cathedral of Saint Vitus. The burial ceremony was long and elaborate, including such symbolic acts as breaking of the royal seal, the scepter, and the sword, and the destruction by George of the royal standard and the flags of the various portions of the kingdom of Bohemia. Couriers dispatched to France reached Charles's court at Tours on Christmas Eve and only after some days could they break the news to the French king, who was himself ill.

Symptoms seen by trustworthy witnesses indicated that Ladislav succumbed to the bubonic plague that had spread to Hungary from the camp at Belgrade and had some victims in Prague. Realistic accounts of Ladislav's death could not satisfy excited and over-suspicious minds. In centers hostile to the Czechs, especially Vienna and in Breslau, rumors cropped up that Ladislav's end was caused by poisoning. Czech courtiers were suspected of complicity in it. As the time went on, scurrilous details linked with the names of George, his wife Johanna, Rokycana, and Ulrich Eizinger, were woven into the descriptions of Ladislav's death. Thoroughly re-examined by modern scholars, the explicit accusations or innuendos inculpating the prominent personalities of Ladislav's entourage proved to be malevolous inventions and propaganda tools fabricated in anti-Hussite circles.

The youthful king died a natural death. As a contemporary chronicler put it, "he was extinguished like a candle illuminating the darkness, and as if someone had lost an oar from a boat plying in high waters, or as if someone had taken the staff from a cripple." [128]

ELECTION, CORONATION, AND RECOGNITION

Ladislav's death caused consternation among his subjects and reopened the perplexing question of succession. The ties with Austria, Bohemia, and Hungary, established by his father, Albrecht V, were not too strong, and as the King had died before he could marry, the hereditary principle could not be invoked in the same way as after Albrecht's demise. It was not very likely that the three countries would remain united under the same ruler. Their separation loomed on the horizon as a hard but inevitable political reality.

The House of Habsburg at that time was not too widely ramified. Its three male members, Frederick III, Albrecht VI, and their nephew Sigismund of Tyrol, quarreled among themselves and by personal rivalries spoiled the chances of their acceptance as Ladislav's successors in either Bohemia or Hungary. Ladislav's older sisters had been married before his death: Anne to William of Saxony, and Elizabeth to Casimir IV of Poland-Lithuania. Their claims to the vacant thrones were disputable and neither in Bohemia nor in Hungary were taken too seriously. Soon after the King's burial, these two countries entered upon separate roads, following their national traditions.

The process of consolidation, which had been going on in the kingdom of Bohemia since Ladislav's coronation, was still far from its final stage. The results accomplished in settling political and constitutional problems were far more satisfactory than those achieved in the efforts at religious conciliation; but a sudden change in the situation could not be excluded in case the throne were to remain vacant again for a considerable length of time. Only three years had gone by since Ladislav's sojourn in the Silesian capital, and the spirit of defiance lingered there as well as in some other centers. A speedy decision in regard to the future king appeared to be the best protection against the revival of separatist tendencies and internecine strife.

The basic document regulating succession in Bohemia, Charles's charter of April 7, 1348, if taken literally, granted hereditary rights to both male and female descendants.[129] With respect to it, a case could be made for Anne, and indirectly for her husband, William of Saxony. Those among the Estates who thought of either Frederick III or Albrecht VI as candidates for the crown of Bohemia could invoke the treaties never formally abrogated between the Luxemburgs and Habsburgs from 1364 and 1366.[130] The principle of legitimacy was, however, not fully admitted by the Utraquists or the Catholics, and a free election was accepted as the most appropriate means of solving the problem.

Knowing of these trends, William of Saxony did not support his campaign merely by references to the ancient charters, but used other means as well to improve his chances. Two other candidates were considered at least temporarily: the Estates of Lower Lusatia interceded in favor of Albrecht (Achilles) of Brandenburg who administered their province, and some Catholic Czechs, grouped around Zdeněk of Šternberk, favored Charles, the second son of King Charles VII of France and the brother of Ladislav's intended bride. A clause in the charter of April 7, 1348, if adhered to rigidly, would have demanded that in the election of a new sovereign the Estates from the incorporated provinces be granted an active part along with those of Bohemia.[131] This would have made a timely and unanimous agreement on the candidate highly unlikely and there was, in fact, among the Czech nobles no inclination to grant equal partnership in the election to the other groups. Traditions, coupled with ethnic antagonism, proved stronger than solidarity in matters of faith.

The Utraquist party in Bohemia was indifferent to charters and agreements from the pre-Hussite period, and to promises held out by foreign princes. The French candidate would have had the best chance if the campaign in his behalf had been pushed more energetically. France, adhering to the Pragmatic Sanction of Bourges, could be considered by the Hussites as their potential ally in their efforts to obtain fair terms from the Papacy, whereas the princes of German blood were instinctively distrusted. The time was too short for the French envoys to display their diplomatic skill and to counter the strong movement in favor of a national king.

It would have been very difficult, indeed, to leave entirely out of consideration the governor of Bohemia, who for fourteen years, since the death of his mentor, Hynek Ptáček of Pirkštejn, had headed the Utraquists. Standing loyally on Ladislav's side, George had gained the confidence of moderate Catholics so that a resolute opposition to him could come only from the irreconcilable elements, stronger in Silesia than in any other region. Sensing that an open bid for the royal crown could affect unfavorably the uncommitted elements, George proceeded cautiously, his main concern being the shortening of the interregnum.

The provincial Diet of December, 1457, extended George's term as governor to the election of the new king, and set the date of the next session for February 22, 1458.[132] Although the vote was not spectacular, it left George in the key position during the period of the search for the most suitable candidate. To dispel some objections and prejudices, George agreed to release from his custody Matthias Hunyadi, known thenceforth also as Corvinus. A strong faction of the Hungarian nobility fostered Matthias' election as king of Hungary, and his presence at Buda was needed to make sure of victory over the coterie of the former allies of King Ladislav, who maintained friendly relations with Frederick III. George facilitated Matthias' return and betrothed to him his nine-year-old daughter Catherine. Being in great need of cash, George exacted a handsome sum of money from Matthias' partisans. Matthias' election as king on January 24, 1458, aroused wide attention and prefigured sooner or later a similar turn of events in Bohemia.

George was sure of solid backing by the Utraquists, laymen as well as the clerics. It was not necessary to campaign among them and a danger would less likely result from moderation than from excessive zeal. The best service the Utraquist leaders could render George was to fan the deep-rooted resentments and fears against a prince of German blood. "Deliver us, O Lord, from all German kings and governors," wrote an anonymous author of a *Succinct Compilation from Old Czech Chronicles*, circulated probably during the winter of 1457–58.[133]

The danger of foreign rule was the main theme of Rokycana's fiery sermons. According to Enea Silvio, he took a firm stand on that question and declared from the pulpit at Týn that "it would be better, following the example of the judges of Israel, to transform Bohemia into a republic," than to elect a foreigner in case there were no native worthy of bearing the royal crown.[134] Other reports express Rokycana's feelings more accurately. He had no doubts of George's competence and worked for him not only in Prague but in other Utraquist centers. Emissaries dispatched from the capital visited many royal boroughs and country residences of the Utraquist nobles to enlist their support of George's candidature. Most likely from the pen of another ranking cleric, Martin Lupáč, came an impassionate appeal in the form of a letter to the Prague aldermen, extolling George's experience in governing, his sense of justice, and his attachment to the Czech faith.[135]

Although the Utraquist lords were favorably disposed toward George's bid for the royal crown, his most ardent supporters came from the gentry and the royal boroughs, Hussite in their majority and traditionally allied with Prague. Their position in the provincial Diet was a knotty point and a good deal of harm to George could have come if his opponents had succeeded in fanning up among the lords their traditional resentment of the lower ranks. A sober and realistic survey of the situation made it clear that the Czech Catholic lords held the key position, and that serious difficulties could arise either from their decision for a foreign prince or from their alignment with the German Catholic Estates in the incorporated provinces.

Leaving to his ardent partisans the consolidation of the Utraquist ranks, George applied himself to the most delicate task of using means and tactics to which the spokesmen for foreign candidates were also ready to resort. In addition to the money supplied by Matthias' partisans, George could use other funds—one source, for instance, alludes transparently to the Prague Jewry.[136] George had still another advantage over the foreign candidates to which the mighty lords did not close their eyes even if they did not talk about it openly. The possession of the former church estates by many Catholic lords, including the Rožmberks and the Šternberks, was a cause of great concern. It could not be excluded from consideration that a foreign ruler, once established, might yield to pressure from Rome and insist on their restitution, whereas George could be trusted not to do so. When Zdeněk of Šternberk was personally assured of continued holding of the former archiepiscopal domain of Roudnice, the pro-French party fell apart. A group of rigidly Catholic lords, headed by John of Rožmberk, continued opposition to the last moment but it was too weak numerically to become a real menace.

When the sounding of the leading personalities and bargaining with them had passed the preliminary stage, time became the most important factor. Nothing would have been more inopportune than to bring up for discussion such vexatious problems as the rights of the Estates of the incorporated provinces or the relationship between the lords and the lower ranks. Fortunately for George, nobody reopened such controversies and the provincial Diet, scheduled for February 22, 1458, convened in the Old Town Hall only five days later. The delegates from two Upper Lusatian cities withdrew, finding themselves isolated, so that only the Estates of Bohemia attended. The spokesmen of foreign princes attempted to prepare the ground for their respective masters, but only the Saxons were admitted to the assembly hall to present William's claims. To counteract the effects of their insistence on Anne's rights, George sent to the castle of Karlštejn for the ancient charters. The Saxons were misled into believing that a serious study would follow and relaxed somewhat in their campaigning among the assembled nobles.

The decisive session opened on March 2, 1458.[137] Better aware of its importance than were William's envoys, George's partisans attended in large numbers. The metropolitan populace was alerted and the large square between the Town Hall and Rokycana's church at Týn was filled to capacity. The city judge with his assistants, including the executioner, and a strong armed unit, were prepared to deal with any emergency. The scrutiny of the ancient parchments increased the tension, but resulted in the conclusion that the assembled lords, knights, and representatives of the royal boroughs were entitled to proceed to an election.

Thereupon, the Catholic lords retreated to the adjacent chamber where those favoring George succeeded in breaking the resistance of John of Rožmberk. When they reentered the great hall, no formal vote was necessary. Zdeněk of Šternberk moved closer to George and announced: "May the Lord Governor be our King." While he knelt before George, the assembled electors signified their approval by acclamation which was instantly echoed by the masses milling in the large square. Bells were rung and the elected king, surrounded by high officers of the realm, marched through the jubilant crowd into the Týn church. There he was greeted by Rokycana, who concluded the ceremony with a solemn *Te Deum* sung by the clergy and the students. Then the procession, headed by George, moved to the temporary royal residence, not far from the Powder Tower, all singing the ancient hymn in honor of Saint Wenceslas.

Cooperation of the two groups of the Estates of Bohemia, Catholic and Utraquist, gave George a strong position, enhancing the chances of his recognition in the incorporated provinces, and reducing the danger of an alliance of the rebels with any of the defeated competitors for the royal crown. The king of France made no hostile move, but William of Saxony did not take the setback calmly and had to be watched. His brother Frederick harbored vindictive feelings against George for quite a long time, not forgetting the latter's daring dash into the Saxon Misnia in the Fall of 1450. He would have given active support to William if it came to war. An alignment of the Saxon Wettins with the Hohenzollerns of Brandenburg had to be borne in mind as a remote possibility. A more serious complication would have arisen if Frederick III had been prevailed upon not to recognize George as king and bar his admission to the college of electors. On the other hand, the Pope's full preoccupation with Italian affairs, as well as his expectation that the new kings of Hungary and Bohemia would participate actively in his long-cherished scheme, the anti-Turkish league, proved to be the most favorable circumstance.

As a Catholic, King Matthias was in a better position than George and could operate more freely in circles closed to the Hussites. His good will and the benevolent neutrality of Casimir IV of Poland-Lithuania were valuable assets to George, outweighing the Saxon machinations. In fact, Matthias stood by George and helped him to steer his bark safely between Scylla and Charybdis when arrangements for the coronation were to be made. It was George's firm decision to observe strictly the *Ordo coronationis* [138] set up for the kings of Bohemia by Charles IV, thus to dispel any doubts as to the validity of the solemn act. According to the *Ordo*, the Archbishop of Prague had the privilege of crowning the king. Rokycana, whom the Hussites would have liked to see on George's right, had not been recognized by the Pope, and no Catholic prelate had been appointed to the See of Prague. There were two Catholic bishops on the territory of the kingdom of Bohemia at that time: but Tas, Bishop of Olomouc, had not yet been consecrated and Jošt of Rožmberk, Bishop of Breslau, was in opposition to George. Matthias was willing to help and promised to send two bishops, Augustine of Györ (Raab) and Vincent of Vácz to Bohemia to perform the ceremony.

The bishops realized that they would run into a conflict with their sovereign if they did not comply with his wishes. To protect themselves against charges of simony or a rebuke from Rome, they laid the matter before Cardinal Carvajal who sojourned in Hungary as the papal legate. He neither forbade the journey nor authorized it, but had a long conference with them and gained the impression that "he was not telling the story to deaf ones." [139] Protected by about six hundred horsemen under the command of a Hungarian magnate, Nicholas Ujlaki, the bishops arrived in Prague early in May and went immediately into consultation with George's advisers.

The *Ordo* prescribed the coronation oath in such general terms that the King could have taken it without qualms. But George's attachment to the Chalice posed problems which the bishops endeavored to smooth by a special formula amounting to an abjuration of errors. George declined their request, maintaining that he was a layman, not trained in letters, brought up by priests of his faith, and that by renunciation he would admit implicitly that he had been guilty of heresy. Seeing that they would not break his resistance the bishops devised another procedure. They permitted George to take an oath in a secret session to which no Utraquists and only four Catholics were admitted. Two of them were laymen, Zbyněk Zajíc of Házmburk, the supreme judge, and Prokop of Rabštejn, the royal chancellor; the hierarchy was represented by Bishop Tas of Olomouc and Přibyslav, Abbot of the Premonstratensian convent at Louka.

The formula agreed upon had no reference to the Compacts.[140] George pledged obedience to the Roman and Catholic Church as well as to Calixtus III and his successors. He also promised to observe, protect, and defend the true faith, professed by the Church, and to lead his people from errors, sects, and heresies into conformity and unity with the Church. As the Compacts were not named, George was able to accept the text of the oath, for since the promulgation of the agreement with the Council of Basel in 1436, the Utraquists had considered themselves not heretics but true sons of the Church. The bishops were also satisfied, because it was possible to see in George's oath an indication of his will to preserve peace with the Papacy. There is no doubt that there was a *reservatio mentalis* on both sides and that, in the final reckoning, George paid a very high price for the presence of the Hungarian bishops at his coronation.

The solemn act took place on May 7, 1458, in the Saint Vitus Cathedral which, even during the Hussite period, remained in Catholic hands. Catholic lords performed the duties reserved by the *Ordo* for the representatives of the Estates. Although according to one of its clauses the Archbishop and the assisting prelates had to crown the King, an alteration was made because of the foreign origin of the two bishops. Not the prelates, but the Catholic lords placed the ancient crown of Saint Wenceslas on George's head. One article of the *Ordo* served to allay the anxiety of the Utraquists, who followed distrustfully both the previous negotiations and the ceremony itself. At the coronation mass George received the Sacrament in both kinds as had been stipulated by Charles IV, the author of the *Ordo*. The Utraquists were little concerned with the details of the *Ordo,* and accepted George's communion not as in conformity with Charles's directives, but as an evidence of the King's fidelity to the Chalice.

Encouraged by the coronation, George pressed forward to gain recognition by the Estates in the incorporated provinces and by other princes. He made a successful start in Moravia, profiting from the benevolent attitude of Bishop Tas, a scion of an aristocratic Moravian family. Municipal councils in some royal boroughs representing the German speaking patriciate were somewhat reluctant in pledging allegiance, but only one of them, Jihlava, persisted in its defiance and sought support at the court of Duke Albrecht VI of Austria. Instead of mustering forces for a swift descent on the rebel center, George laid a siege to Jihlava and prepared for an expedition into Austria, so as to disperse the hostile elements there before they could form a league.

A good deal of restraint and tact were needed to deploy the invading forces that they might cause damage to Albrecht VI and his allies without touching the domains held by Frederick III and his party. Although the august brothers were at odds with each other, George's intrusion into their family affairs at that point would nevertheless have been resented. George's position became really delicate when Albrecht VI consented, on August 21, 1458, to leave Lower Austria to Frederick III in exchange for a compensation elsewhere. A meeting with Frederick III appeared to be the safest protection against intrigues and suspicions and George seized the first opportunity that presented itself to do so. Impressed by George's military preparedness and his desire for friendship, Frederick III indirectly recognized George's coronation, pledging that as the Roman Emperor he would regard George "as king of Bohemia and the leading elector." [141] As George was careful not to overstep the proper bounds, he did not press for a more spectacular act and concluded agreements with the other Habsburg princes, Albrecht VI and Sigismund of Tyrol. Thereupon he withdrew his forces from Austria and did not impose hard terms on Jihlava when, in November, 1458, the city recognized the futility of continued resistance. [142]

George's decision not to inflict heavy punishment on the Jihlava citizens indicated that in other, more serious cases, he would use moderation rather than the iron fist. Silesia presented more perplexing problems than did Moravia and demanded a higher degree of sagacity and skill to be dealt with. While the princes ruling over the various portions of Upper Silesia were prepared to swear the oath of allegiance, the city of Breslau stood firm in its defiance and served as the rallying point of the anti-Czech elements in other areas. George could not close his eyes to the alignment of his Silesian opponents with William of Saxony, from which more serious troubles could arise than from the comparatively weak link between Jihlava and Albrecht VI of Austria. The method which George had used in 1454 was adapted to the more serious situation in 1458, and again patience and prudence triumphed over the temptation of a merciless crushing of the resistance. George's progress in Austria could not fail to make an impression on the less resolute elements in Silesia and Upper Lusatia. Before the end of 1458, the league of the six Upper Lusatian boroughs passed over to George and the number of Breslau's allies in Silesia dwindled markedly.

The course of events in Central Europe was so rapid that the papal court was unable to keep pace with it and give fresh instructions to the legates sojourning in those countries. Much depended on their initiative and sagacity, which did not always guide them safely. Even a diplomat of such stature as Carvajal was unable to direct the activities of local leaders in such a manner that the traditional claims of the Curia would not be impaired. Calixtus III rebuked him mildly for his neglect of papal interests at the time when new rulers were elected to the vacant thrones of Hungary and Bohemia. [143]

Nobody in Rome intended seriously to question the validity of Matthias' election; but matters were somewhat different in Bohemia. The first reaction to George's election, though not enthusiastic, was not negative. Calixtus III was, in the spring of 1458, interested in consolidating the area from which an expedition on land against the Turks could be launched and supported. On May 13, he sent to Carvajal letters addressed to Matthias and Casimir IV, urging them to maintain friendly relations between themselves and with the neighboring princes so that local discords would not hinder the preparations of a campaign against the enemy of the Cross.[144] A letter to George was also prepared, but it was not dispatched to his court, as in the meantime the Pope and the cardinals received protests from Duke William and resolved to await the arrival of the Saxon envoys.

Written about a week after George's coronation, the papal letter to Carvajal was of no great import. Calixtus III maintained a complacent attitude for some time thereafter. He did not reject flatly the Saxon request for assistance, but warned Duke William against an armed conflict with his rival fearing that even a local war would be detrimental to the common cause—the defense of Christian Europe against the Infidel.[145]

Whether aware of the Saxon intervention or not, George acted promptly and sent a messenger to Rome with a copy of the coronation oath. Before the emissary could return from the long journey, George instructed Prokop of Rabštejn to go to the papal court to counteract adverse propaganda and to assure the Pope of George's loyalty. Prokop apparently succeeded in his mission and obtained for his master a letter addressed to "George, the king of Bohemia, the most beloved son." The episode is rather puzzling, as no trace could be found of this letter in the extant papal registers; but there is a reference to it in the continuation of the Commentaries of Enea Silvio from the pen of Jacob of Pavia.[146] In the absence of an authentic text, it is impossible to say whether or not the letter given for transmission to Prokop agreed with the missive referred to in the papal correspondence with Carvajal. Be it as it may, there is no indication in the sources that the Curia gave any encouragement to Duke William.

The atmosphere at the papal court was on the whole favorable to George. Both Enea Silvio and Carvajal held out the hope that, when firmly established in his position, he would seek a lasting conciliation with the Church. George was anxious to cultivate Carvajal's good will and to use him as an intermediary. In view of the Pope's intense preoccupation with the Turkish menace it was of great advantage to George that the king of Hungary joined with Carvajal in assuring the Pope of George's honest intentions. Matthias' letter along with another copy of the coronation oath was attached to Carvajal's report to the Pope, inquiring whether the oath should be regarded as satisfactory, or whether more pressure should be put to bear on George to get from him a more solemn profession of faith.[147]

Written at Buda on August 9, 1458, the letter could not reach the ad-

dressee, since Calixtus III died three days before that date and was succeeded by Enea Silvio, known henceforth as Pius II. The new Pope was
more familiar with central European affairs than any of his predecessors.
Shortly before his election, while taking the waters at Viterbo, he completed writing his outline, *Historia Bohemica,* and he had vivid memories of his two conferences with George. In the early part of his pontificate, Pius II coordinated his steps with the policy of his former master, Frederick III. His dependence at that time on Frederick's judgment
was well known and elicited in Bohemia a sarcastic comment that "the
Emperor keeps the Pope in check as effectively as four hounds the
hare."[148] It could hardly escape the Pope's notice that Frederick's attitude toward George was sympathetic and that any unfriendly gesture
toward Prague would cause displeasure at the imperial court.

Pius II harmonized his policy with his former master and regarded
the coronation oath as a hopeful sign. He did not insist that it be immediately followed by a public profession of faith, hoping that George
would make it when freed from exclusive dependence upon the Utraquists. The Pope's preoccupation after the election and coronation was
with the consolidation of Western Christendom so that the crusade
against the Turks would have the maximum support. He resolved to
hold a congress of Christian princes at Mantua and included George
among those to be invited.

The matter was rather delicate, as the invitation, to be effective, had
to be addressed properly. Calixtus' letter created a precedent in that it
gave George the royal title and its use by the new Pope could be explained as a mere continuation in the established practice. Nevertheless,
Pius II acted cautiously and did not dispatch the invitation directly to
Prague but to the imperial court, so that Frederick III would be able
to decide whether the royal title was appropriate. Another letter requesting George's presence at Mantua, dated January 20, 1459, was sent to
Carvajal. As Frederick had delayed the sending of the first invitation, George received the two missives at about the same time, in March,
1459.[149]

Viewing current events from a different angle than Pius II, George
acted with circumspection so that he would neither hurt the Pope's sen-
sitivity nor move too far ahead. He did not appoint envoys to the papal
court to represent the kingdom and its population, but sent Prokop's
brother, John of Rabštejn, to Italy. Attached to him was the new royal
procurator, Fantino de Valle, a doctor of law of Dalmatian origin, who
probably soon acquired a working knowledge of the Czech language
and could converse with George without an interpreter. The two clerics
met Pius II early in March, 1459, at Siena, where he made a stop on
his way from Rome to Mantua. Although disappointed, the Pope granted

John an audience and accepted the pledge of loyalty in the name of George and his family, not on behalf of the entire country.[150] This distinction corresponded to George's intention of striking a middle line between studied indifference and unconditional submission to the Pope's point of view.

Although George's contacts with the highest ecclesiastical circles were neither extensive nor intimate, he could conclude from fragmentary reports that his opponents inside and outside the kingdom hoped to find better understanding for their complaints at the Curia than at the imperial court. The most significant evidence of this tendency was the attitude of Breslau. Its envoys, when they arrived in Siena to pay obeisance to Pius II, declared that they would not accept as king anyone suspected of heresy, and complained that George was styled king in papal letters.[151] These and other statements, whether known to George from reliable sources or from hearsay, indicated that papal diplomacy would be of great help in the dealings with Breslau or other Catholic opponents. On the other hand, no effective contribution could be expected from the Emperor, as his means were limited and he instinctively avoided interventions in the affairs of other countries.

Leaving temporarily the conflict with Breslau unsettled, George devoted his skill and energy to his dispute with William of Saxony. The Duke persisted in his claim to the crown of Bohemia, but he soon proved to be less formidable than his initial steps had indicated. He was not too energetic in exploring the prospects of an anti-Czech coalition and allowed several months to pass without taking any resolute steps. Some of his potential allies lost interest in his cause, while others fell away from him and sought to join the master of Bohemia.

The state of affairs in Germany turned out to be of immense advantage to George's effort to consolidate the kingdom and gain the same rank as had been customarily reserved for the rulers of royal blood. The Empire had a nominal head, but Frederick III had no ambition to restore the imperial dignity to its pristine splendor. As he was reluctant to leave, at least temporarily, his hereditary lands and take part in the pressing affairs of the Empire, the leading princes organized themselves into leagues to promote particular interests. Some of the alignments corresponded to deep-rooted traditions and were loyally supported by their members, while others arose out of the chaotic conditions and broke up quickly.

George was not involved personally, as he had no ties with other princely families, but with the election to the royal office he acquired a legal claim to membership in the college of electors. As a matter of fact, the king of Bohemia held the highest position among the secular electors, while the electors of the Palatinate, Saxony and Brandenburg,

ranked after him. In the first year after his election George's orientation
in the imperial affairs was determined primarily by his relations with
Frederick III, but that path was not entirely free, as the Emperor's partisans were headed by George's foes, the Wettin princes of Saxony. In
the opposite camp stood the Wittelsbach princes, one branch of them
ruling in the Palatinate while the other possessed Bavaria. Saxon policy,
supported by Elector Frederick of Brandenburg, precluded George's immediate attachment to the imperial party, but he did not throw himself
into the arms of the Wittelsbachs for fear of straining his relations with
Frederick III. For some time nothing was left him to do but to mark
time and make good use of his none too strong contacts with both the
Pope and the Emperor.

A passive role which afforded some benefits did not agree too well
with George's temperament. It also could not remove the danger of an
alliance of Breslau with the princes in the vicinity of Silesia and the
Lusatias. Without radically changing his policy, George began to explore the situation in both directions and established contacts first with
the Wittelsbachs and soon thereafter with the Wettin-Hohenzollern coalition. The Elector Frederick of the Palatinate was more responsive than
Lewis of Bavaria, George's neighbor. On the opposite side, George found
a congenial partner in Albrecht of Hohenzollern, dubbed Achilles by
that keen student of German affairs, Enea Silvio. Ruling over a small
domain in Franconia, not far from the western boundary of Bohemia,
Albrecht assessed George's position more realistically than the other members of the Wettin-Hohenzollern alliance had done, and undertook to
hammer out an amicable settlement of the outstanding differences among
them.

George welcomed Albrecht's initiative, but moved ahead slowly, not
severing his contacts with the Wittelsbachs. After a preliminary conference at Wunsiedel, a more representative gathering was held at Cheb
(Eger) in April, 1459. George attended it personally and his position
was strengthened by Frederick of the Palatinate, who arrived at Cheb
to the great surprise of the Wettin-Hohenzollern group. William's claims
to the crown of Bohemia became naturally the principal subject of consultation and were given a good deal of attention. The princes also canvassed other problems arising partly from local frictions, partly from the
appalling decline of imperial authority.[152]

A good deal of resentment had been engendered in the past by persistent efforts of Charles IV to acquire enclaves in the imperial territories adjacent to Bohemia either by ownership or at least by recognition
of him as their liege lord. He succeeded in creating a network of crown
properties and dependencies which only a firm hand could keep together.
Under his less eminent successor, Wenceslas IV, and even more during the

Hussite wars, the ties by which Bohemia held scattered enclaves were loosened considerably, but the original charters did not lose their validity and could be invoked, if an energetic king vindicated the rights and titles once acquired by Charles IV. Similarly, the Wettin house held castles and lands in northern Bohemia under its king as sovereign. They had been either granted to the Saxon dukes for services and loans or seized by force. It seemed to be of mutual benefit not to examine the various claims and counterclaims individually, but to seek a broad formula which could serve as a basis for cooperation between George and the Wettin-Hohenzollern coalition. The final agreement comprised clauses regulating the legal position of the Bohemian enclaves "beyond the forest," and the transfer to the crown of Bohemia of the Wettin possessions south of the mountain ridge. William gave up his claim to that crown, and betrothed his daughter Catherine to George's son Hynek. Preparations were also made for a marriage of Prince Albrecht, the younger son of Frederick of Saxony, to George's daughter Zdeňka. George's simultaneous treaty with the Hohenzollern princes was couched in more general terms and did not touch upon the delicate question of Lower Lusatia held by the elector of Brandenburg for sums that had never been paid.[153]

The Cheb agreement caused consternation among the Saxon people and loud protests were raised by Breslau, abandoned diplomatically by both the Wettins and the Hohenzollerns. The city elders appealed to Pius II, warning him against "the cunning of that fox," meaning George, and his "siren luring." [154] These warnings and remonstrances had but faint results; in fact, a few weeks after the Cheb parley, William broke ties with the Silesian rebels. Some of the vassal princes and cities in Silesia sought contacts with George to avert punitive expeditions, and in the end Breslau could count on only one ally, Prince Balthasar of Sagan.

It was George's ambition to appear at Cheb with a strong escort to show his wealth and strength. Among the German delegations were not only the princes but also their councillors. One of them was Martin Mair, known among his countrymen for his training in law and for his earnest occupation with a scheme of imperial reform. He journeyed to Cheb with his master, the Elector of the Palatinate, and apart from current duties he explored the chances of an agreement among at least the leading princes on the most effective measures by which the Empire could be saved from chaos and disintegration.[155]

Martin Mair was not a radical and did not advocate deposition of Frederick III and a new imperial election. He recommended a revival of the ancient dignity of the *rex Romanorum* which would be separated from the imperial title and accorded to another prince so that Germany

would have two leading figures at the top. Mair was less concerned with
the reaction that might come from Frederick III than with the search
for a competent candidate for the new function. In the early fifties he
approached several princes, including Duke Philip of Burgundy and Albrecht VI, but he failed to arouse their interest.

While at Cheb, Mair observed George's activities and his easy contacts with the German princes whose language he did not command. He
soon reached the conclusion that at last a candidate had appeared on
the scene on whom he could pin his hopes. With the tacit consent of
Elector Frederick, Mair sounded King George on the need of reorganization of the Empire. He obtained a reserved answer, as George felt that
from the envisaged reform "no profit but rather a good deal of ill-will
could come." [156] Although sceptical and cautious, George did not close
the door, and as he was apparently impressed by Mair's ability, he took
him into his service. The new position did not exclude Mair's employment by his former master, and later also by Lewis of Bavaria.

Neither Mair's letters nor related documents from that time give a
clear answer as to the motives which induced George to show at least
mild interest in the plans of imperial reform. Apart from personal ambition, many good reasons could be given for his decision to use Mair's
services. George apparently sensed that even after the Cheb congress his
position in relation to the German princes was rather awkward, depending on many incalculable factors. Mair's offer concurred with George's
natural desire to reduce the differences of birth and to give his family
a permanent position among the ruling houses in Europe. Some concrete
tasks, especially the pacification of Breslau, lost much of their weight
when confronted with such an impressive project as the restoration of
peace and order all over the Empire. In the spring and early summer
George did not spend much time in analyzing Mair's ideas but he
watched more carefully the activities of the two principal figures in
European affairs, Pius II and Frederick III.

The Pope's chief occupation was with the Mantua congress and he
proceeded there from Siena, though many of his friends tried to dissuade him from that venture. When he reached Mantua, he found there
only few insignificant delegates; but so great was his enthusiasm that
he decided to open the congress formally. Among the missives dispatched
to royal and princely courts, was a letter to George, sent on June 8,
in which he urged him to appear personally.[157] To make the bid more
attractive, the Pope wrote that Breslau also had been asked to send a
delegation to Mantua. He expressed the hope that through personal
mediation the feud could be settled so that the two parties would be
free to participate in the crusade. The Pope wrote four days later to

Prokop of Rabštejn and requested him to prevail on George to take an active part in the congress.[158]

Neither the personal letter, addressed again to the "king of Bohemia," nor Prokop's intervention produced the desired effect. Developments in areas much closer to Bohemia claimed George's vigilance. A group of Hungarian magnates, who early in 1458 acquiesced in Matthias' election, began to conspire against him as early as July, 1458, and sought contacts with other rulers, especially George. When they realized that George had no desire to get involved in their conspiracy, they pinned their hope on Frederick III and elected him their king. He accepted their offer of the crown of Saint Stephen and began to use the Hungarian royal title, and, to support his claims, mustered forces for an expedition into Hungary. He had a successful start, but soon Matthias counterattacked and scored a splendid victory. The rebel faction disintegrated and left Frederick in an unenviable position.

Frederick's resources were inadequate for a protracted conflict. Pius II, from whom moral and diplomatic support could be expected, turned a deaf ear to his appeals, as a war would have made Hungary useless in the contemplated campaign against the Turks. As little help could come from the Wettin-Hohenzollern coalition, the king of Bohemia seemed to be the only potential ally against the angered and bellicose rival. Frederick's plenipotentiaries were soon able to report George's friendly reaction to their preliminary soundings and recommended further negotiations. As the Emperor feared a new defeat and needed immediate help, George's position was strong and he raised the price of his service accordingly. In addition to vague promises relating to George's increased influence in the imperial affairs, Frederick III offered an immediate compensation. He notified George of his willingness to confirm him in the possession of the kingdom of Bohemia.

Arrangements for a solemn visit by Frederick were made quickly, and on July 30, 1459, he, accompanied by a splendid retinue, entered Moravia. He was received at Brno by George and the assembly of nobles from Bohemia and Moravia. Sitting next day on an improvised throne in the main square of the city, the Emperor handed over to George the symbols of royal dignity and the banners of the incorporated provinces. Thereupon, he invited George to sit at his right "as the true and undoubtful king and as the most venerable elector." [159] George in turn swore fealty to Frederick III as was customary on such occasions.[160] In another ceremony George's son Victorin was elevated to the rank of an imperial prince, Count of Kladsko and Duke of Münsterberg.

Medieval charters regulating the relations of the king of Bohemia to the Emperor, revised by Charles IV, were still valid but it is doubtful whether Frederick would have insisted on their observance had not the ceremony promised palpable advantages to him. The solemn act was witnessed by the imperial escort and George's subjects, and by Matthias' envoys empowered to negotiate with Frederick III under George's mediation. Frederick III was not prepared to renounce the Hungarian title, and promised George an ample compensation for any help rendered him if the war actually reopened. Although tempted by the large sums pledged, George directed the parleys in such a way that the danger of an armed conflict would be minimized. Both Matthias and Frederick III consented to an armistice to last till June, 1460, during which negotiations for a final settlement were to be resumed.

With his hands again free, George pursued the policy adopted in the early part of that year. Knowing that pending mediation the Emperor would not undertake any harmful action, George moved closer to the Wittelsbachs to settle the differences with Lewis of Bavaria along the lines similar to his earlier dealings with the Wettin princes. Using the good offices of the Elector of the Palatinate, George opened negotiations with Lewis relating to the fiefs of the crown of Bohemia which since the reign of Charles IV had dotted the Bavarian lands and had been increasingly resented as obstacles to administrative unification. Also in dispute were some sections of the political boundary, which differed from the natural boundaries of that area and hindered transport. After a preliminary conference, the parties met in mid-October at Plzeň and arrived at a compromise, not too advantageous, but still acceptable as a means of avoiding further altercations.[161]

In less than a month from the Plzeň conference, George, accompanied by Queen Johanna and some of their children, proceeded from Prague to the westernmost part of Bohemia. Escorted by many nobles and about three thousand horsemen, the royal family passed through the gates of the city of Cheb to meet with the Wettins. There they celebrated the wedding of their ten-year-old daughter, Zdeňka, to Prince Albrecht of Saxony, then aged sixteen. As had been agreed in April, 1459, the other much younger children, Hynek of Poděbrady and Catherine of Saxony, were married *per procurationem* only. Archbishop Frederick of Magdeburg performed the solemn rites in the presence of many guests. The Hohenzollern princes attended personally, whereas the Wittelsbachs found it more appropriate to send only their envoys.[162]

According to all indications, George found negotiations with the German princes more attractive than his other task, the pacification of Silesia. But the matter was too urgent to be left entirely to its own course. George sensed that it would not be too wise to await passively what the papal diplomacy would be able to accomplish and resolved to resort to arms.

About the middle of July, 1459, he gave orders to his captains to open operations on a limited scale against Breslau, so that the door was still open for intermediaries. He was apparently well informed of divisions among the people and hoped to accomplish more by alternate display of force and good will than by an all-out attack. In the city council moderate elements were gaining ground, and there existed among the clergy a faction favoring a reasonable compromise. The majority of the clerics, however, followed George's inveterate foe, Canon Nicholas Tempelfeld of Brzeg, and other implacable preachers. Having campaigned in vain in 1454, when George was shielded by a Catholic king, they doubled their efforts after Ladislav's death, proclaiming George's election and coronation invalid. It can hardly be doubted that vitriolic letters sent from Breslau to Pius II or to other powerful addressees on behalf of the city senate had been inspired by fanatical clerics rejecting George on account of his Czech origin and his adherence to Hussitism.[163] Tempelfeld and his associates did not relax their efforts even when the aldermen saw the city's isolation and were inclined to sheathe the sword. The masses responded more impulsively to fiery sermons than to cautious tactics of the moderate leaders and the guilds pressed for changes in the municipal council. The city moved rapidly to the brink of civil war.

Late in August, 1459, George joined his forces and marched as their head through the Silesian territory, accepting oaths of allegiance from loyal elements. In the last week of September, 1459, he stopped at no great distance from the Breslau city walls. Skirmishes in the suburbs did not develop into large-scale operations, as George decided not to attack but to let the negotiators attempt a settlement.

The Pope had no chance to close the rift by personal mediation, as neither George nor Breslau heeded his appeals for participation at the Mantua congress. The King did not send his delegates to that meeting, as he did not feel quite certain whether they would be received in the same manner as envoys of other kings. The municipal council of Breslau assured the pope of their attachment, but expressed fears that their plenipotentiaries, if sent, would be captured by George's forces. Though disappointed in his expectations, the Pope was determined to use other means to gain his ends, as he wanted to have both the King and the wealthy Silesian capital as his allies in the planned crusade.

Since the fall of 1458 Bishop Jošt had sojourned in Italy and made many contacts in the highest ecclesiastical circles. He did not come to Italy as George's partisan, but while there he changed his original, rather negative, attitude. It could not escape his notice that Pius II had no intention of accepting the rebel's point of view and proceeding against George rigorously. Jošt's reorientation was neither easy nor quick but it was sufficiently advanced before he had his final conference at Mantua with the Pope. He accepted without hesitation his new assignment, and after his return to Silesia he attempted to convince the bellicose elements among both the clergy and the laymen that by accepting George they would concur with the Pope's desire to have all local conflicts terminated.

Jošt's initiative yielded no positive results. Tempelfeld and other fanatical preachers did not disobey him when he acted as their ordinary, but were by no means prepared to follow his lead in political matters. In their eyes he was an intruder, a representative of the Czech people in their midst. The session to which the bishop invited them was stormy and broke up in mutual accusations. Carried away by emotion, Jošt told the aldermen bluntly that they were not concerned for the faith but that they resisted George on account of his Czech origin.

The Pope probably sensed that Jošt could not do more than prepare the ground for more experienced diplomats. Soon after the Bishop's departure from Mantua, two clerics were selected as papal delegates to Bohemia and to Breslau. One of them, Girolamo Lando, was a Venetian by birth and had the title of Archbishop of Crete; the other, Francisco of Toledo, was a Spaniard in papal service, bearing the title of Archdeacon of Ecija. They received their credentials on September 20,[164] but left Mantua only after the public session of the congress in which Pius II and Cardinal Bessarion depicted the Turkish aggression and outlined the tasks before the rulers of Christian Europe.

Although George would have preferred citizens of his kingdom as intermediaries, he accommodated himself to the Pope's decision and granted the legates a solemn audience. Nothing in the long and elaborate speech by the senior legate could be construed as an allusion to the King's exceptional position.[165] The Archbishop spoke as if George had fulfilled all obligations, and dwelt mostly on the Turkish advance. He requested strongly a generous and immediate help, echoing the Pope's and Bessarion's general appeals as delivered recently at Mantua. Turning to the King directly, he extolled his high spirit and experience in warfare. Discreet references to the Breslau imbroglio were followed by an offer of help and by a request for a royal sanction of their mission.

Escorted by the King's loyal vassal, Duke Conrad the Black of Oleśnica (Oels), the legates covered the distance between Prague and Breslau without incident, and entered the walled city on the Odra river on November 11. They were received by the council, clergy, guilds, and the population with pomp and acclamation. The King's determined opponents made sure that the legates would be assured not only of the city's attachment to the Holy See but also of its military preparedness in case the mediation did not yield the expected results.

To soften the ground for an agreement, the envoys touched lightly on the core of the controversy, the Chalice and other Hussite tenets, and emphasized the Turkish menace.[166] Negotiations proceeded slowly, as the clerical opponents of the Hussite king were more tenacious than some of the aldermen. Among the guilds, the spirit of opposition was not abating and the company of butchers was prepared to unleash violence. The envoys were reluctant to drive matters to an extremity and to put the populous city under interdict. Their authority was not too extensive and they realized how difficult it would be to enforce the rigid sentence. A formula was hammered out by Peter Eschenloer, the city secretary, and other representatives of the city, to mask a retreat from the positions originally held by the negotiating parties.[167] In this manner peace was saved. The proud city consented to obey George and to render an oath of allegiance to him as "the right and undisputable Catholic and Christian king of Bohemia," although not immediately, but only after a lapse of three years.[168]

It would have been hazardous for George to reject the submitted formula even if he had realized its full implication. Hostilities, if reopened, would undoubtedly have ended in his military victory, but by an attack on the defiant city he would have antagonized the Pope and alienated some of his Silesian followers. The analogy between the coronation and the capitulation of Breslau was apparent. In both cases the Papacy helped to overcome the obstacles without insisting on a formal renunciation of the Chalice. But both the coronation oath and the Breslau formula could be interpreted broadly or rigidly according to circumstances.

A delegation representing the Breslau Chapter and the city government left for Prague early in January, 1460, carying among other presents four fur coats for George and four for the Queen. The envoys were received by the King in a friendly manner and bent their knees before him acknowledging him as their ruler. Twelve heralds by the blare of trumpets announced the end of the rebellion in Silesia, and bells rang in the churches of Prague on Rokycana's orders. The envoys encountered no hostility among the Czechs and were treated courteously wherever they went. George sent to their quarters food and wine, game, large pikes and carps, so that they could hold a banquet. The last rebel, Balthazar of Sagan, failed to reach Prague, hoping to get milder terms through Saxon mediation.

It was undoubtedly of considerable advantage to the papal legates that during their negotiations with the Breslau leaders George was far away from Silesia and refrained from actions which the radicals could use as an excuse for breaking off the contacts. Conferences with German princes, culminating in the Cheb ceremonies, claimed part of his time late in 1459, and when he returned from Cheb to Prague he had many domestic problems to deal with. He was in his residence late in December to receive preliminary reports from Breslau and give instructions for the final settlement.

It seems very likely that the successful meetings with the Wittelsbachs and the Wettin-Hohenzollern faction increased George's interest in the imperial reform as outlined by Martin Mair. He was no longer a stranger among the imperial Estates and he could expect help from some prominent figures among them. The papal interest in the Breslau pacification did not remain a secret and helped to dispel suspicions as to George's religious convictions. Why should the Catholic princes hesitate to maintain friendly relations with the ruler of Bohemia whom the Pope in his letters addressed as "the most beloved son"?

In the summer of 1459, Duke Francesco Sforza approached George to find out whether he could use the King to speed up his negotiations with Frederick III.[169] Even since his victory over the Ambrosian republic, Sforza sought an imperial confirmation of his ducal title, but Frederick's answers were evasive and dilatory. Having heard of George's close connections with Vienna, Sforza sounded him on conditions under which he would be willing to break the Emperor's reluctance. George's reaction was favorable, but only late in 1459 did he give Sforza's request a more serious consideration. At this stage he did not treat it as an isolated case, but connected it with Mair's scheme. Both the King and Mair anticipated a good deal of expenditure, once their diplomatic offensive would be launched, and who else could supply the much needed funds as promptly as the Duke of Milan?

Empowered by George to deal with Sforza directly, Mair proceeded to Lombardy in January, 1460. He had two audiences with the Duke, one public, the other limited to the Duke and his three trusted advisers. Finally, he was received by the Duchess Bianca Maria, and in between he had several conferences with the court councillors. He used every occasion to convince the Milanese that George would be a worthy partner in their political combinations not only as the king of Bohemia but also in his high position in the Empire which Mair, of course, regarded as assured.

The first point mentioned by the Duke was the investiture, and he spoke of sixty thousand ducats as a reward to all those who would expedite the matter. In further discussions he raised the sum by ten thousand and to that figure Mair, after some hesitation, assented. In addition to the investiture as the immediate objective, the Duke and the other negotiators hinted at means and ways by which a more permanent alliance between the two rulers could be achieved. Mair obtained not only tentative texts of the treaties of friendship but also the names of unmarried Sforza children, one of whom could be married into the Poděbrady family. The councillors, when alone with Mair, raised questions transcending concrete problems which the Duke originally had in mind. They inquired whether George would be willing to promote an alliance between Milan and Hungary (aiming at Venice), and whether in case of his own promotion in the Empire, he would be willing to grant their duke special powers in some parts of the peninsula, meaning those undoubtedly which in earlier times had been regarded as imperial fiefs.

The envoy left Milan with high hopes but with no formal agreement on any of the discussed problems. The Duke was noncommittal and promised to send at an opportune moment his plenipotentiaries to Prague for further negotiations. He was realistic enough to see that George's promotion in the Empire was by no means assured and that it would be foolish to pledge even a fraction of the mentioned sum before he could get a more concrete evidence of George's ability to secure the Emperor's consent to the investiture. George's good offices were not to be accepted as the only way to the much desired goal. Sforza knew from his sources of information that the Pope, interested in any ruler whose cooperation in the crusade could be expected, would be quite willing to approach the Emperor directly or through Bessarion and to dispose him favorably.

Taking place at about the same time, the liquidation of the Breslau opposition and Mair's mission to Milan gave evidence of George's success in his struggle for recognition. By January, 1460, the entire kingdom obeyed his will and his international reputation was established.

A KING OF TWO PEOPLES

Surveying the diplomatic contacts between the Curia and Prague in 1458 and 1459, one could reasonably conclude that more good came from them to the king of Bohemia than to the Roman pontiff. The latter's effort to organize the Western rulers against the Infidel bore little fruit and revealed a lamentable lack of enthusiasm on their part for the common Christian cause. Disappointed in his expectations, Pius II resolved to leave Mantua and risk the discomfort of travel in winter to reach his beloved Siena soon, and from there Rome. Before he departed, he issued two bulls, dated on January 14 and 18, 1460.[170] In the first of them, *Ecclesiam Christi,* he announced the opening of the struggle with the Turks, to be supported by the Christian countries for three years. In the second bull, *Execrabilis,* he forbade appeals from Papal verdicts to a future council. The Pope declared them unlawful, and to give more weight to his condemnation, he branded them as heretical and detestable. He declared anyone as *ipso facto* excommunicated who would attempt to evade the judgment of the Apostolic See by an appeal to the general Church assembly.

The bull *Ecclesiam Christi* was issued after conferences with imperial envoys and representatives of some German princes. Their statements gave Pius II a hope that campaigning for the crusade in Germany would have a fair chance of success. To stress the importance of the matter, he appointed Cardinal Bessarion as his plenipotentiary. It was concluded in those conferences that two assemblies of the princes of the Empire would be held, one at Nurnberg early in March, 1460, the other at the imperial residence toward the end of that month. According to the Pope's interpretation, the assemblies were not to be regarded as a new venture but as a continuation of the earlier efforts to raise subsidies in the Empire for the anti-Turkish expedition in which he, the Pope, had formerly played an active role as Frederick's chief diplomat.

Pius II expected that the princes of the Empire would organize a large army—thirty-two thousand infantry and ten thousand cavalry—as promised at Frankfurt in 1454. A financial contribution, a tenth of all regular incomes, was expected from the clergy, with only those exempted who would participate directly in the expedition. As the Pope was anxious to have the Emperor entirely on his side, he promised him a share in the collected money and offered him the supreme command of the assembled forces. Thought was given also to the appointment of the commander's deputy, and the name of Duke Albrecht Achilles was mentioned in that connection. He enjoyed the Pope's full confidence and received from him, while at Mantua, a gift of high distinction, a sword and a cap adorned with pearls.

In his farewell speech to the remaining members of the congress, Pius II mentioned expressly the number of troops to be supplied by the Germans. His reference to Bohemia was less specific. He indicated that men could be hired there, although the Czechs would not fight outside their country at their own expense.[171] By a letter dated on January 8, the Pope notified George of the two forthcoming assemblies and urged him to attend personally and thus to fulfill the duties which were expected from every Catholic king.[172]

Another recommendation that George appear at Nurnberg came from Martin Mair, who lay bedridden there of an illness contracted during his return journey from Milan.[173] Mair expected that the Diet would debate really vital matters and requested George to grant him full powers in case the king found it impossible to attend. Mair mentioned not only the tenth from the clergy, but also the thirtieth to be levied upon the laity for three consecutive years. He also hinted that George should secure for himself an appropriate share of the monies collected in his domains. Furthermore, he held out a hope that George could obtain the appointment as supreme commander, or at least to have a friendly prince designated for that function. Finally, Mair believed that the Diet would sanction the appointment of a *conservator* whose chief duty would be to protect peace in the Empire, and recommended that George make an earnest attempt to obtain that office.

The Diet was not too well attended and George was among those princes who were absent. He was to some extent protected against a papal reproach of nonobedience by his efforts to heal the rift between the Emperor and the king of Hungary. He presided at Olomouc over a conference of envoys from the two courts, but he accomplished very little and scheduled another meeting to take place early in May in Prague. Technically, it would have been possible to reach Nurnberg after his return to Prague, but George apparently learned from agents other than Mair that many of his friends in the Empire were reluctant to lend Bessarion help and thus to incur burdensome obligations.

Papal diplomacy highly assessed George's role as mediator and refrained temporarily from interference with his steps. The task was not
enviable, as it was in the interest of the crusade that both Matthias and
Frederick III take active part in its preparation. It was really difficult to
devise a formula that would satisfy one of the rivals without painfully
affecting the other. George duly reported the meager results of the
Olomouc parley to Pius II and was, in turn, admonished to continue
his efforts.[174]

The Pope, sojourning in Siena, transmitted copies of this correspondence
to Bessarion and asked him to make direct contact with George.[175] The
papal instructions were rather vague, leaving it to the cardinal's discretion
whether he should attend the Prague conference or send his representative. It may be gathered both from the full powers granted to Bessarion
and from the covering letter that the Pope did not want to leave the
mediation between the Emperor and Matthias entirely in George's hands,
but that he wanted to grant papal sanction to the accord, accomplished
by the Czech king, provided that its terms were favorable to Frederick
III. The latter's friendly disposition was of paramount importance for
the success of Bessarion's mission.

Unsettled conditions in Germany caused the papal legate far more
trouble than he had anticipated when accepting his onerous assignment.
He could not obtain at Nurnberg any concrete results, and found it necessary to postpone the second assembly to a later date, scheduled originally
for late March. Only toward the end of April was he able to extricate
himself from the mesh of petty conflicts ravaging Germany and to hasten
to Vienna. On April 26, he wrote to George from Regensburg,[176] sug-
gesting that he either conduct the negotiations with the Hungarians in
his own name, or adjourn the Prague conference and come to Vienna
to attend the opening session of the Diet.

Bessarion's knowledge of Central European affairs was rather limited,
and at each stage of his mission he encountered, if not opposition, then
at least indifference to the grandiose project conceived by the Pope.
Frederick III received him in Vienna with all the honors traditionally
accorded to cardinal-legates, but he showed little enthusiasm for the
task which had been assigned to him in the general plan of the papal
offensive. The Diet could not be held, as the number of delegates present
in Vienna was pathetically inadequate. Nothing was left for Bessarion
to do but to acquiesce in another date, September 1, 1460; and in the
meantime to second the Emperor's appeals for a more impressive attendance.

Frederick made a reference, in his letter to George of May 25, to the
delegation from Prague to the Diet.[177] The names of its members are
not mentioned in the letter, and as more detailed information is lacking,

it is impossible to say whether they went to Vienna merely as observers or as plenipotentiaries. George apparently wanted to show good will to, and continue his contacts with, Bessarion. Whoever the envoys were, their report could not be satisfactory, as in Vienna they did not meet with any important delegation. To correct this situation, both Bessarion and the Emperor wrote to George, asking him to enhance the authority of the September Diet by his personal attendance.[178]

Bessarion's correspondence with George was carried on in cordial terms, but it probably was suspended after the dispatch to Prague of the new invitation to the Diet. Not much could be done in matters relating to the crusade, and the chances of successful mediation between Frederick III and Matthias decreased markedly. Matthias had Hungary under his control and nothing but a decisive defeat could undermine his position there. On the other hand, Frederick III clung to the Hungarian title but was in no position to back his claims. Consequently, in the late spring or in the summer of 1460 no one of the parties insisted that George renew his efforts to bring about a settlement more satisfactory to them.

Contacts with Bessarion by letters or messengers protected George against charges of indifference to the papal designs. He did not go beyond general promises of participation in the crusade, as other matters occupied him more intensively. In the early part of 1460 several conflicts raged in the imperial territory and the alignments of the princes were changing with the progress of the military operations. George had nothing to fear from the Wettin princes to the north of Bohemia; he therefore directed his attention to the southwestern boundary to strengthen the ties established in the fall of 1459 with Lewis of Bavaria. To supplement a treaty of mutual support, the two rulers agreed on a bethrothal of Ludmila of Poděbrady to Lewis' son George, with the proviso that the marriage would be concluded eight years later. With Lewis' consent, King George undertook efforts at mediation between the Wittelsbachs and Albrecht Achilles, by which their bloody conflict was brought to an end.[179]

George's diplomatic activities since his coronation are rather perplexing. In a short time he concluded so many oral agreements and treaties that only a political genius could have harmonized and kept them. Although it can be easily perceived that peace among Bohemia's neighbors was the cornerstone of his policy, other motives were also present, but they are not always clear. Of considerable help in unraveling his intentions is the assumption that since Mair's return from Lombardy, George, not discouraged by Sforza's hesitation to supply money, worked assiduously for his own promotion in the Empire. He was apparently not too much concerned about the Emperor's attitude, provided it would not be resolutely hostile. More important than the Emperor's declaration was undoubtedly the Pope's good will, as any unfriendly gesture from Rome would have brought the King's religious orientation into a sharper focus. As it was, the family agreements with the Wettins and the Wittelsbachs blurred the dividing line and helped to create the impression among the Germans that there was no irreconcilable difference between the Poděbrady family and any other respectable princely house. Consequently, late in September, 1460, another link was forged by the betrothal of Duke Albrecht Achilles' beloved daughter Ursula and George's son Henry.[180]

From frequent contacts with the German princes or their councillors George gathered sufficient information concerning their reaction to Bessarion's endeavors to become more cautious. He did not appoint a delegation to the Vienna Diet, which instead of opening on September 1, as scheduled, was begun more than a fortnight later. He assured Bessarion in general terms of his interest in the crusade. At about the same time he wrote to Pius II promising to send his representatives to Rome not later than February, 1461, to pledge allegiance.[181]

When the Diet settled down to work, the delegates of the imperial cities displayed more initiative than did the petty princes and caused Bessarion a good deal of inconvenience. Trained in law and administrative matters, they insisted that not only the principal articles but also the technical details be formulated precisely and then debated thoroughly. From such an assembly Bessarion could not obtain definite assurances of help and consented to an adjournment of the Diet. The Emperor promised to use his influences with the princes and to make arrangements for a more representative assembly to be held in 1461, not in Vienna, but again at Nurnberg.

While Frederick III was occupied with Bessarion's endeavors, George resumed contacts with Lewis of Bavaria. This alignment, when first attempted, caused resentment at the imperial court; but George by his diplomacy succeeded in bringing about Frederick's acquiescence. As a matter of fact, George harbored no aggressive designs against Frederick, but wanted to enlist Lewis' aid for imperial reform in a more coordinated and vigorous campaign along the lines drawn by Martin Mair. On October 8, 1460, George concluded three treaties with Lewis supplementing each other.[182] It is rather puzzling why in one of them the two rulers allied themselves against King Matthias. To explain this unexpected step, one has to give attention to the peculiar developments in the northern counties of Hungary, in which George had become involved. That mountainous area, inhabited predominantly by the Slovak people, was infiltrated by Czech warriors after the Hussite wars. They served various masters and were not always too well disciplined. In the summer

of 1460 their leader, John Jiskra, ran afoul of Matthias and appealed
to George for help. A gesture against Matthias, who did not always
respond enthusiastically to George's calls for cooperation, was one of
those quick moves that George liked to make to show his strength
and to get a stronger position for further bargaining.

The other two treaties were of a more direct practical importance.
One of them supplemented the earlier agreement concerning the transfer
of certain scattered enclaves, while the other represented Lewis' promise
to assist George in his effort to obtain the rank of King of the Romans.
Clauses attached to the principal article of the third treaty specified what
compensation the Duke expected from George for his favorable attitude
toward Mair's scheme.

Lewis' formal pledge of support was an important step forward, as
it could be quoted in dealings with other less favorable princes. This
was primarily Mair's task and he dedicated himself to it with both
George's and Lewis' blessing. His first destination was the Palatinate and
from there he moved to Mainz. Both Elector Frederick and Archbishop
Diether declared themselves for the project and stated in detail conditions under which they would be willing to cast their vote for George.[183]
One of the prerequisites of their own action was the active participation
of the Electors of Saxony and Brandenburg.

While it was chiefly Mair's duty to secure prospective supporters among
the German princes, prominent Czech noblemen were sent on a similar
mission to the eastern neighbors. George's most intimate councillor,
Zdeněk Kostka of Postupice, a Utraquist by faith, went to Hungary,
ostensibly to restore good relations between Matthias and the captains
of the Czech brotherhoods. One of the October agreements with Lewis
of Bavaria thus automatically lost its value. Another message delivered
by Kostka was George's promise to send his daughter Catherine to
Hungary, so that her marriage with Matthias could be formally celebrated.[184] It actually took place at a somewhat later date, in May, 1461.
It cannot be ascertained whether the Czech envoy hinted at the expected
promotion of his master or contented himself with a renewal, after a
temporary cooling off, of friendship between the two courts. By Kostka's
mission George virtually gave up his role as a neutral mediator, but did
not make the fact public so as not to arouse the Emperor's indignation.

The mission to Poland was unquestionably easier, for apart from minor
incidents nothing troubled the contacts between Cracow and Prague.
George appointed Zdeněk of Šternberk as his envoy, to gratify the latter's
ambition. Zdeněk returned to Prague with an agreement that the two
kings should hold a conference not later May, 1462, at Greater Głogów
in Silesia, and review there problems of common interest.[185]

True to his methods, George, even after his treaty with Lewis, did not openly declare himself for Mair's plan, but wanted to learn first the reaction to it on the part of the leading princes of the Empire. When he received encouraging reports, he invited his friends and many neutral princes to Cheb, despite the Emperor's warning against such unauthorized conferences. Although rather hazy, Mair's project took such a firm hold of George's mind that the risk of the Emperor's indignation seemed to be worth taking.

The congress opened early in February, 1461, and was well attended.[186] William of Saxony, Lewis of Bavaria, and Albrecht Achilles were often seen there in George's company, whereas Albrecht's brother, Elector Frederick, chose a more reserved attitude. From Austria arrived Albrecht VI, ostensibly at peace with his brother, Frederick III, but not entirely free from bitterness and thoughts of revenge. The Elector of the Palatinate and the three spiritual electors sent their representatives. Several minor princes attended personally along with a handful of bishops and delegates from the imperial cities. George left the initiative to Martin Mair, who soon established contacts with Gregory of Heimburg, a publicist of great experience, acting at Cheb as an observer for Prince Sigismund of Tyrol.

When the opening ceremonies were over and serious discussions got under way, it became evident that not all the members of the congress would support Mair's scheme. Some princes were secretly reluctant to grant such a high position to their host, the king of Bohemia, as that envisaged by Mair, for George's connection with the Empire was rather loose. Others hesitated to commit themselves to a far-reaching program for which its initiators failed to secure the Emperor's approval. The Elector of Brandenburg spoke in the name of this group when he raised objections and recommended further exploration of the ways and means by which peace in the Empire could be safeguarded.

Mair obtained little help from a group of princes who journeyed to Cheb with intentions differing from those of George's close friends, and who regarded the congress as a forum for discussion of current problems. Instead of taking up Mair's proposals, they aired their grievances arising from Bessarion's activities. They expressed fears lest the Cardinal's requests for contributions by the clergy and the laymen reopen the era of papal interference with imperial affairs. It was not too difficult to realize that the critics of the papal fiscal policy were in one or another way connected with the Archbishop-Elector of Mainz, Diether of Isenburg, whose conflict with the Pope produced vigorous agitation in clerical circles. Gregory of Heimburg, too, was far less interested in Mair's project of political and administrative reform than in combating the papal claims. For he had incurred the sentence of excommunication for his service to Sigismund, involved at that time in a bitter feud with

Cardinal Cusa; [187] he (Heimburg) showed no intention of deserting his master and submitting to the Church authority. The presence at Cheb of men of Heimburg's orientation was somewhat embarrassing, as in an atmosphere filled with suspicions it could be interpreted as evidence of George's association with the anticlerical faction in Germany. Its German members were free from any stigma of disobedience in matters of doctrine, whereas he could be easily reproached for his attachment to Utraquism and his failure to implement his coronation oath.

Judged by the number of princes and delegates, the Cheb congress was far more impressive than many regular Diets. But the results were meager and in clear contrast with Mair expectations. No formal vote was taken on either Mair's scheme or the other issues mentioned in the discussions. All these matters were delegated to a Diet scheduled to meet in March at Nurnberg. In this respect there was no difference between the congress and the other assemblies of princes, which usually reached agreement only on the time and place of the next meeting.

After George's return from Cheb to Prague he sent his delegates to Nurnberg, in order not to lose contacts with his allies.[188] In the King's absence, little attention was given by members of the Diet to Mair's project. Instead, the papal policy came up for criticism in public sessions and even more often in conferences behind the scenes. Reports from Nurnberg showed George that apart from a handful of trusted friends, the princes were indifferent to Mair's solicitation. Seeing that no good would come of continued campaigning, George dissociated himself without much ado from Mair's activities which, in addition to other inconveniences, laid heavy claims on the royal treasury.

George had cooperated with Mair for a little less than two years, including the exploratory period. The balance sheet of all these labors was far from favorable, but the losses did not outweigh the gains. It was to George's enduring advantage that by his intense occupation with the imperial affairs he averted the formation, around William of Saxony or any other prince, of a coalition in the vicinity of Bohemia which could give help to the German-speaking opposition in Silesia. In view of the perennial tension between the Teuton and the Slav, such a situation could have easily arisen and it would have been extremely difficult to cope with it. Both the ethnic antagonism and the religious division affected the contacts in politics, commerce, and education. A king of distinctly Czech origin and devoted to the communion in both kinds risked rejection of his claims to membership in the College of Electors more seriously than either his Habsburg or Luxemburg predecessors.

In all these designs and calculations the Emperor's amicable disposition figured as one of the fundamental points. Frederick III was neither strong nor aggressive enough to contemplate an invasion of Bohemia from his family domains. He was not too dangerous, but could become useful especially for his friendly relation with the Holy See. As long as Pius II was satisfied with the coronation oath, no intermediary was needed; but it could not be excluded that one day he would insist sternly on George's open disavowal of the Compacts.[189] At such a conjunction who else could be approached with more confidence than Frederick III?

George's sanguine temperament could not always be brought into harmony with the Emperor's mood. Whenever Frederick showed an inclination to treat the King as a vassal, the latter recoiled and sought opportunity to retaliate. A threatening gesture, whenever he made it, instead of clearing up the misunderstanding increased the Emperor's irritation. He then accused George of ingratitude for services rendered and sought allies among his inveterate enemies. Complaints against George were publicized among the German princes and the imperial cities and also in clerical circles, instinctively prepared to take the Emperor's side whenever he was at odds with the Hussite king.

It could not be denied that in the period following Frederick's visit to Brno, George strained the mutual relationship by several impulsive acts. Although his identification with Mair's scheme could have been regarded by other people as the most serious departure from the former relationship, Frederick himself felt more acutely hurt when he was informed of George's contacts with a faction of the Austrian nobility who took ill his domination of the lands which had belonged to the Albertine line, and into which he had moved after Ladislav's death. Although George was sensitive to foreign meddling with the affairs of Bohemia, he did not exercise restraint when Frederick's foes, with Eizinger in their ranks, sought his help. They did not receive from Prague more than assurance of sympathy, but in the tense atmosphere of the autumn of 1460, even mere contacts incensed the Emperor with indignation. Whether or not Frederick poured out his heart to Bessarion or to a less prominent cleric, the Pope learned of his grievance and resolved to give him another proof of solidarity.

The papal chancellery issued on November 27, 1460, two letters, one addressed to George,[190] the other to his chancellor, Prokop of Rabštejn.[191] The Pope expressed his displeasure with George's contacts with Frederick's opponents in Austria and stated emphatically that he would not look with indifference at injuries inflicted by anybody upon the Catholic Emperor. He admonished George sternly to remain satisfied with whatever God had granted him in his own kingdom and to refrain from intereference with the affairs of other sovereigns. Although identical in content, the letter to George differed somewhat in style from that addressed to Prokop and was couched in stronger expressions.

As connections between Prague and Rome were irregular, even papal correspondence was often delayed. In the absence of concrete evidence, it is difficult to say when the two letters reached their addressees. Their contents were apparently known to the princes assembled in March, 1461, at Nurnberg; [192] it can, therefore, be assumed that they arrived while George was at Cheb or soon after his return to Prague. The tone was not menacing, but the purport could not be dismissed as merely a stereotyped admonition to obedience.

In fact, the letters had lost some of their importance before they reached Bohemia. Late in 1460, George on his own initiative loosened his ties with Frederick's opponents. The death of Eizinger deprived him of a trusted ally and other members of the faction pinned their hopes on Albrecht VI rather than on the Czech king. The dissociation from Mair's scheme also contributed to the lessening of the tension between Vienna and Prague. George did not seek reconciliation ostentatiously, but waited for a situation in which Frederick again would run into distress. It arose late in the summer of 1461, when Albrecht VI, Lewis of Bavaria, and Matthias combined their forces and were closing the ring on Frederick's position. George did not join them, but rather sent Prokop and some other of his councillors to Austria with instructions to achieve peace between the feuding neighbors.[193]

George, at certain conjunctions broadminded and magnanimous, was slow in swallowing anger caused by duplicity of his bona fide allies or betrayal by the princes in whom he had put confidence. Since the Cheb congress, he eyed the Elector of Brandenburg sternly, waiting for an opportunity to punish him for the wrecking of Mair's scheme. Frederick's acrimonious remarks uttered at Cheb, when coupled with the earlier conflicts in Lower Lusatia, gave sufficient evidence of his unfriendliness and justified in George's opinion an energetic action. In a calmer atmosphere, the King would have perhaps accepted the good offices of William of Saxony or another ally interested in peace in his vicinity; but the example of so many German princes who went to war with their rivals on any slight excuse was contagious. When George reached the conclusion that neither the Emperor nor any other mighty prince would succor the Elector, he instructed Zdeněk of Šternberk to launch an offensive. The primary targets were those places in Lower Lusatia that Frederick had been able to keep since his accession to the throne.

Brandenburg was poorly prepared for a defensive campaign against superior forces advancing from Lusatia northward. Frederick did not capitulate, but appealed to Saxony for mediation. George welcomed that step as he did not want to get embroiled in a long war. He had no designs on the Hohenzollern patrimony and had no intention of making the Elector his permanent enemy. Despite the Saxon efforts to bring the warring parties together, negotiations were neither short nor easy and only in June, 1462, did the two rulers agree on a formula that was more favorable to the Elector than he could have hoped for in the fall of 1461, when he was hardly pressed by George's forces.[194] The King reasserted his sovereignty over Lower Lusatia, but returned Choćebuz and some other castles to Frederick, not, however, in full possession, but as fiefs. Soon after the signing of the treaty, George appointed Albrecht Kostka of Postupice as the *voigt* of Lower Lusatia and found in him a trustworthy representative of the royal authority in that province, which never was too securely connected with the Czech-speaking area of the kingdom.

Limited in scope, the Brandenburg campaign did not absorb much of George's time and passed without any detrimental repercussions among the population of either the Lusatias or of Silesia. Other disturbing forces were set in motion after George's sojourn at Cheb in February, 1461. This time it was not the German-speaking Catholics, but the Czech Utraquists who showed discontent and insisted that the King give more attention to their concerns. Since the death of King Ladislav, George had been intensively occupied with political affairs at home and abroad, and he relegated the unsolved religious problems to a second rank. Often they were left entirely to their erratic course and rendered illusory the hope that Bohemia could be brought back into the fold of the Roman Church by a mere sanction of the Compacts.

Sources of that period are reticent on such matters as the Utraquist reaction to George's coronation oath. It seems very likely that neither Rokycana nor the Utraquist laymen knew its text or at least suspected that the King had accepted obligations which one day could affect his attachment to the Chalice. Enthusiasm with which the King was received in the Utraquist towns when he visited them after his coronation, as well as the virulent opposition of Breslau and of other strongholds of Germandom, created the impression that no startling change had occurred in either politics or religion. It was to George's temporary advantage that Calixtus III died soon after the Prague coronation and that his successor observed in general the line which clearly separated political issues from the Church affairs. This policy prolonged the interim for about three years, from March, 1458, to approximately the same date in 1461.

The first step taken by Pius II to assert his authority in spiritual matters boded ill for Rokycana. In September, 1458, Václav of Krumlov was appointed as administrator of the Prague Archdiocese.[195] From the purely formal point of view hardly any objection could be raised to this act.

Václav had served for many years past as the dean of the metropolitan chapter, and since 1451, as the administrator of the "Upper Consistory." But when examined more closely, his appointment indicated that Pius II had no intention to fill the Prague vacancy after consultation with both the Catholics and the Utraquists. After his return from Rome, Václav endeavored to gain full recognition in Bohemia, but met with resolute opposition from the Utraquists. His tactics, whether authorized by Rome or spontaneous, gave rise to fears that the final act, Václav's elevation to the archbishopric, would follow. George found it advisable to exercise his prerogatives and admonished both parties to moderation. As Pius II refrained from Václav's promotion to the archbishopric, the excitement subsided, but a durable peace was not achieved.

Despite occasional clashes, the two parties existed side by side, respecting the royal decrees of 1454.[196] The ranking clerics on both sides knew that they would risk the King's displeasure if they reopened the doctrinal polemics or attempted to proselyte. In the course of almost fifty years since the death of John Hus, Utraquism had lost much of its original impetus and had become stabilized on a rather moderate basis, formulated mostly by Rokycana. Foreign prelates like Juan Carvajal had been profoundly shocked when they observed that in addition to the communion in both kinds the Utraquist rites differed in many points from the approved pattern. The "Lower Consistory" did not introduce absolute uniformity in liturgy even when it had come, after 1448, under Rokycana's control. Much depended on local sentiments, and those were undoubtedly more outspoken in the boroughs formerly allied with Tábor than among the traditionally conservative elements.

The clerics who, like Rokycana, got their training in the dynamic period of Hussitism, preserved not only the ideas of the pioneers but also the determination to keep alive the yearning for reform, so that even after the expected sanction of the Compacts by the Pope, Utraquism would not dissolve itself without leavening the universal Church. In contrast, the younger generation remembered hardly more than the stagnant atmosphere prevailing in the country after Sigismund's restoration. The absence of a sympathetic bishop caused enormous difficulties in providing competent candidates to fill benefices vacated by defection or by death. Clerics from Poland afforded some help, attracted as they were by better living standards; they ministered to the Utraquist congregations in conformity with the local traditions. In his speech to Calixtus III in 1455, Enea Silvio referred to his conversations with Polish priests in Bohemia who rejected his admonitions by a simple excuse that they must earn a living.[197] It could not be expected from priests thus motivated that they would attempt to restore to their flock the vigor which had animated Hussitism in its creative period. Most of them simply conformed to the pattern that prevailed in the community they had joined.

Critics from the Utraquist ranks seldom aimed their arrows at the radicals when exposing defects or evil. More often the lack of moral rigorism or too ready an assimilation to the Catholic pattern were the sources of the complaints leveled at individual clerics or the "Lower Consistory" in general. At the time, when the knowledge of writing and reading was a privilege of a tiny minority, most of the dissatisfaction was expressed orally and a written protest was an exceptional occurrence.

Not many people in Bohemia had much opportunity to watch the Utraquist clergy so closely as did Vaněk Valečovský of Kněžmost, and few among the keen observers had such a strong position as he, thanks largely to George's benevolence. Serving as royal subchamberlain, Vaněk had under his jurisdiction the royal boroughs, which were, but for few exceptions, attached to the Utraquist party. Vaněk, a moderate Utraquist, abstained from interference with spiritual affairs and insisted that the priests exercise the same restraint in matters relating to municipal administration and in secular affairs generally. It probably occurred more than once that the local clerics influenced the selection of aldermen or of other functionaries, and endeavored to govern, rule and issue orders more effectively than the King himself or his officers. Vaněk extended his criticism from the particular issues affecting him directly to a wide range of problems which he had pondered for some time. He drew a rather grim picture of the clerical life among the Utraquists, confronting the current practices with the Four Articles and pointing out the gross violations of their spirit.

His treatise was completed most likely in 1457, and it was not intended for Ladislav or George exclusively, but also for a wider circulation.[198] It appealed particularly to those laymen who, like the author, resented the meddling of clerics in political concerns; it also had echoes among the earnest Utraquist elements who were worried by the increasing worldliness and indifference to the outcome of the strife for the ultimate recognition of their status. Even more effective than the booklet was the allegorical painting with which Vaněk decorated the wall of his residence in the Old Town. Executed by an imaginative artist, it represented the militant Church as a wagon full of people seeking salvation. The vehicle was so constructed that horses could be attached to it at both ends; whipped by the coachmen—the clerics heading in opposite directions— the horses were unable to pull forward or backward. Frustrated in their attempts to get anywhere, the passengers, leaving the coachmen alone, started to quarrel and fight among themselves "like madmen."[199]

Vaněk's town house was situated not far from the Týn church in which Rokycana had preached regularly ever since his return to Prague in 1448.

In his long career, the periods of occupation with routine tasks were occasionally interrupted by crises in which the accomplished work seemed to be in danger of complete ruin. Sudden changes for the worse were reflected in his sermons more faithfully than in his written works. In the first decade following his resumption of the living at Týn, Rokycana had twice passed through grim interludes, first after Ladislav's arrival in Prague and then again after his return in 1457. In both instances the "beardless king" had failed to conceal his dislike of Rokycana and by his conduct had strengthened the latter's fears that his confirmation by the Pope would never be achieved. Indeed, no progress had been made toward that goal under the pontificate of Calixtus III, and Rokycana's patience was wearing thin.

Irked by unfriendly gestures and by endless delays, Rokycana professed his adherence to the Hussite faith more positively than in the former, brighter days. His sermons from the Týn pulpit revealed his concern not only for the outcome of the repeated attempts to reach an understanding with the Papacy, but also for the future of Hussitism in general. He appealed to his audience for perseverance and for high moral standards, thus answering indirectly some critics of the Utraquist practices. Extolling the purity and simplicity of the early Church, he spoke in transparent terms of the contemporary evils corrupting Christian society. Some of his invectives could be interpreted as attacks on the papal court, and if they were so reported to Rome by his foes in the "Upper Consistory," they blackened his record and reduced to nil the chances of his confirmation.

Rokycana's effort to combat indifference and laxity met with sympathetic response not only among his parishioners but also among groups in various parts of the country who obtained copies of his sermons or oral accounts of his fierce invectives. Shielded by their formal adherence to the "Lower Consistory" the nonconformist elements professed ideas transcending the Compacts and listened sympathetically to any preacher who assailed indifference or laxity. As the origins and backgrounds of the groups of zealots were different, they seldom cooperated among themselves, even if they knew of one another. Their most characteristic mark was their dislike of concessions to the Roman Church, so that Rokycana's prestige among them was low whenever he toned down his exhortations and seemed to be ready to accept a lean compromise. He recaptured much of their good will whenever he ceased maneuvering and renewed his fervent appeals to his flock.

Under Ladislav's reign, Rokycana's pulpit served as the rallying point for earnest believers living in Prague or visiting it frequently. One of the most devoted auditors of his sermons was Gregory, a son of Rokycana's sister, and of a squire whose family name has nowhere been recorded. Gregory and his friends were particularly impressed by sermons preached during Ladislav's sojourn in Bohemia in 1453–54 and turned to Rokycana for advice whenever a thorny problem arose.

Rokycana fostered these contacts and called Gregory's attention to the writings of Peter of Chelčice, of which he had copies. Apart from attachment to the idea of reform, Peter Chelčický had little in common with the Archbishop-elect as he loathed any compromise with Rome and adhered to radical tenets for which many parallels could be found in the writings of the Taborite theologians. Peter never completed higher studies and had but scant knowledge of Latin, so that he could draw only limited amounts from the treasury of medieval learning, including the writings of John Wyclif. He apparently divided his time between the management of a small estate in southern Bohemia and literary activities, using for that purpose exclusively his native Czech. A reunion with Rome, to which Rokycana was committed, had no appeal to the sage of Chelčice, whose sole model was the apostolic Church and who in matters of faith and conscience bowed before no other authority than that of the Holy Writ.

From Gregory's acquaintance with Peter's books arose his desire to meet their author and the latter's faithful followers, living either at Chelčice or in its vicinity. The visit to Peter's home did not lead to an amalgamation of Gregory's circle with the group known as the Brethren of Chelčice. The search for a safe way out of the spiritual barrenness could not end at one oasis only, but extended to other religious communities, existing nominally within the Utraquist party. Agitated by fear of corruption, Gregory and some of his intimate associates traversed Bohemia and Moravia, seeking priests of exemplary life, and kindred souls with whom they could affiliate. These contacts, though at first inspiring, proved in many instances to be deluding. The bands of seekers visited by Gregory suffered from isolation and some of them professed views no less objectionable than the current Utraquist doctrine. In the end it became evident that the Týn circle had a more solid basis of doctrine than the other groups, and that it should retain the initiative in kindling a new reform.

Life in a large and busy city gave little satisfaction to the sensitive souls in Gregory's following, and they decided therefore to retreat into a rural area, where conflicts between civic duties and conscience might be minimized. Some time in the winter of 1457–58 the group left Prague for the village of Kunvald in northeastern Bohemia. Good reasons supported that decision. Kunvald was situated on the estate of Litice, owned by George of Poděbrady. Rokycana, to whom the idea had been presented, had obtained from George permission for their transfer to what then apparently was a thinly populated area. The new settlers soon established connection with priest Michael from the nearby town of Žamberk, who was sympathetic to their program. Priest Michael was of the Roman ordination, but inspired confidence as "he had given up some papistic precepts, contrary and detrimental to the truth, and administered sacraments in close harmony with the truth and the examples of Jesus Christ and of the apostles." Members of the community called each other brother and sister. Thus came into existence a new religious body, the Unity of Brethren. The names of the provinces from which they were recruited, Bohemia and Moravia, were also used to distinguish the Kunvald foundation from other groups. The renewed Unity assumed the name of Moravians because of members who came to Herrnhut in 1722 from that province.

The exact time of the journey to Kunvald cannot be established, as the contemporary sources are vague on that point. According to a late tradition, March 1, 1457, was the date when the Kunvald community was organized. References in the narrative sources, closer to the origin of the Unity, indicate that the date was later, some time between the death of King Ladislav in November, 1457, and George's election in March, 1458. One history of the Unity, from the pen of Jan Blahoslav,[200] mentions the year 1457, but according to its well-informed author the decisive conversations between Rokycana and Gregory took place after Ladislav's death, that is, late in 1457.

Gregory's zeal was not extinguished by the establishment of the Kunvald community. He resumed his journeys to bring new settlers to Kunvald and to link congenial circles in the more distant parts of Bohemia and Moravia with the Unity. Gregory's tireless efforts bore fruit. Kunvald proved to be solidly supported by its founding members and the ties connecting it with other communities could not be easily destroyed by the coercive measures to which the authorities resorted, as soon as they realized that in less than a decade since the suppression of Tábor another threat arose to the unity of the Czech Church.

The part the two leaders of Utraquism played in the early history of the Unity cannot be assessed accurately, as they left no document revealing their intentions. Testimonies of the Brethren are not dispassionate and some of their writings are clearly distorted by later developments. In 1457, Rokycana manifested an understanding of Gregory's aspirations and refrained from pressure. The Brethren appreciated his benevolent disposition, but they expected more than an intervention in their behalf with the King. Gregory on more than one occasion urged his uncle to step down from the Týn pulpit and withdraw from the corrupted world altogether. They were not too far apart when they talked of current problems, but Rokycana was deeply involved in public affairs and felt no inclination for a life of seclusion. Not only Gregory but also later historians of the Unity expressed regrets at Rokycana's reluctance to separate himself from "the Antichrist" and to share "with God's people vilification, ignominy and danger." [201]

George's role was more passive but no less perplexing. At the time when he was ascending from governorship to the highest position in the nation, he was requested to deal with a minor problem in his own religious party. He consented to Rokycana's recommendation that Gregory's group be permitted to settle at Litice; [202] but who knows whether he thought of this episode when he accepted from the Hungarian bishops the text of his secret oath including a pledge to suppress sects in his kingdom? [203] In May, 1458, the plant which sprung up from the "mustard seed" was rather tender and not even Rokycana, more familiar with Gregory's intentions than the King, was able to foresee how fast it would grow.

The three years of George's exclusive occupation with political affairs were not barren ones for the Brethren. Gregory had an opportunity to solidify the fluid forms and to prepare the Brethren for dangers that were soon bound to come. The Unity struck roots in the Czech soil and possessed enough vigor to endure adversity.

During those three years George was frequently absent and could not attend to problems not transcending local limits. Thus he considerably loosened his contacts with the members of his own social class, upon which his political career largely depended. He usually journeyed to his conferences with the Emperor or lesser princes with some of his councillors or personal friends, but when intricate international questions were to be debated, men with better linguistic equipment and wider experience joined the royal retinue. Czech lords like Zdeněk of Šternberk or Zdeněk Kostka served appropriately when sent to Poland or Hungary, but George preferred professional agents when the mission related to a court in Western Europe. Besides Martin Mair, he used the talents of a former French diplomat, Antonio Marini, a native of Grenoble. Like Fantino de Valle, who was destined to protect the King's interests in Rome, [204] Marini acquired a working knowledge of Czech and was able to converse with the King on various topics, practical as well as theoretical. While Mair combined services to George with employment by other rulers, Marini resided for some time in Prague and enjoyed George's full confidence. Other men who distinguished themselves as diplomats or pamphleteers were hired for specific duties whenever the need arose.

No serious objection could be raised to the King's practice of sending Catholic noblemen to rigid Catholic courts where a Utraquist would have been given a cold shoulder. To avoid frictions and rivalries, George distributed the roles proportionately between the two religious groups.

But even his ingenuity had its limits. Frequent dealings with German princes in 1460 and early 1461 were viewed by Utraquists with growing dissatisfaction, as they could not play in them more than a subordinate role. George valued highly the loyalty of Bishop Tas of Olomouc and facilitated the political reorientation of his former opponent, Bishop Jošt of Rožmberk. More aggressive than Tas, Jošt tried the patience of the Utraquist leaders when he virtually moved from his residence at Breslau to Bohemia and was accepted into the King's inner circle.

According to many indications, the splendid congress at Cheb in February, 1461, marked the highest point that George attained in the pursuit of his political ambitions. The challenge offered to Mair's scheme by the Elector of Brandenburg cured the King of overconfidence in the strength of his connections with the German princely courts. When back in Prague, he found there a situation not alarming but serious enough to require cautious action. As at the end of the Cheb parley, he did shelve but not entirely abandon his striving for promotion in the Empire, he found it advisable to give palpable proof of his determination not to tolerate in Bohemia transgressions of the Compacts. Even normal contacts with the Catholic princes would have been hindered by suspicions of duplicity. Besides, more than the secular princes, the Pope had to be placated, as messages reached Prague of how displeased he had been with George's failure to send to Rome a delegation representing the entire kingdom.[205] Influenced by these considerations, George resolved soon after his return from Cheb to reissue the decrees against heretics dating from the reign of Charles IV.[206] There existed, of course, no unanimity between the Catholics and the Hussites in the definition of heresy, and George himself always maintained that by the Compacts the Utraquists had been cleansed of any suspicion of heresy. Nobody among his officers thought of invoking Charles' decrees for an attack upon Rokycana's flock, but local interventions could be made under that guise against dissidents whose ideas or practices exceeded the narrow framework of the Compacts.

Although it would have been possible to use the last remnants of the Tábor party or sectarians of radical views as scapegoats, the search turned in another direction. Restrictions introduced some time in the winter of 1460–61 by the steward of Litice against the Brethren brought Gregory and his followers to the King's mind. Charles' decrees could easily be invoked to justify drastic measures against members of the Unity outside the Litice property, whenever it was found advisable to apply them. About the middle of March, 1461, the municipal judge of the New Town of Prague apprehended Gregory and some students at a clandestine service and put them in jail. Some of the prisoners were tortured, others induced by threats or persuasions to renounce their views.[207] They were regarded as Utraquists, and it was left to Rokycana to compose the text of abjuration and to present it to the group at a special service in his church at Týn.[208] Gregory was released from prison without torture or formal recantation, but soon afterwards he ran into other troubles from which he extricated himself only with the help of mighty protectors.

Although the number of victims was not large, their persecution aroused ill feelings among the Utraquists. They accepted it as a factual confirmation of the rumors that some German princes expected George's abjuration of the Chalice as the price of his election as the King of the Romans, or at least for an admission to a greater share in the conduct of imperial affairs.

Reactions to the new course varied, as some Utraquists suspected the King of putting his political concerns above an unswerving loyalty to the Compacts, whereas others ascribed the initiative to Queen Johanna. It was rumored that she was elated by the connections established with the Wettins, Wittelsbachs, and Hohenzollerns, and wished to extend them to other ruling houses. Some court dignitaries who during the King's absences had to consult with the Queen and were regarded as her partisans were also suspected of insidious machinations, not only against the Brethren, but against any faction among the Utraquists that professed fervently its adherence to the Four Articles of Prague.

The most conspicuous target of the Utraquist displeasure was Bishop Jošt who was with the King at Cheb and then found Prague more attractive than his residence in Silesia. His frequent appearances at the royal court aroused suspicions as to his designs. The concern expressed by some Utraquists seemed to be amply confirmed by Jošt's ill-conceived intervention at a time when restraint would have been more appropriate. Preaching on Maundy Thursday, 1461, in the Saint Vitus Cathedral, the Bishop inveighed against the communion in both kinds. A contemporary chronicler described laconically but eloquently the effects of Jošt's aggressive sermon: "There was a great storm in the city of Prague against that fat bishop." [209]

The King was absent, spending the Easter week, probably intentionally, at Kutná Hora, as in that city he could attend the Utraquist ceremonies with less publicity than in Prague. When informed of Jošt's sermon and the demonstrations it had engendered, George could not pretend that the reopened controversy was none of his concern. The eyes of his partisans were turned in his direction and a firm gesture from him was expected either to confirm or repudiate the rumors of his readiness to abjure the Chalice.

The provincial Diet, which opened several weeks after Easter, was apparently held in a tense atmosphere. To ease this tension, George issued on May 15, 1461, a charter confirming the ancient privileges of the kingdom.[210] In normal circumstances, such a document was expected from a new ruler immediately after his coronation. George at that time most likely had calmed the Utraquist leaders by oral assurances, so that they had not insisted on a written document. This was one of the concessions to which they had agreed in view of George's rather delicate position. But now, alarmed by rumors and by Jošt's challenge, from the pulpit at Saint Vitus, to their faith, they lost the sense of security, and instead of words, insisted on a parchment with the royal seal and signature. George's pledges did not exceed those that had been granted by his predecessors, Sigismund, Albrecht, and Ladislav. He merely reiterated their assurances in the two points dear to the Utraquists—the Compacts and the confirmation of Rokycana. What mattered was not the text of the pertinent clauses, but the circumstances in which the charter was issued. The last act occurred on June 4, 1461, which was Corpus Christi Day. George and his consort stayed in Prague, attended the Utraquist service, and walked at the head of a procession led by the Archbishop-elect. The gesture was understood by both sides and quickly reported to Rome by the vigilant "Upper Consistory." [211]

None of these acts was followed by any unfriendly steps against the Catholics. Simultaneous liquidation of repressive measures against the Brethren could be interpreted as another evidence of George's intention to pour oil on the troubled waters. His occupation with external affairs, including the conflict with Frederick of Brandenburg, helped to divert public attention from religious issues and to keep foreign countries aware of Bohemia's strength.

George's policy met with only partial success. He calmed his Utraquist subjects without losing the confidence of loyal Catholics. Their contacts in everyday life went on undisturbed, but an enduring peace in the country could be achieved only by papal sanction of the Compacts. In order to get it George would have to make a step which for reasons fully known only to himself he had put off several times: that is, to send envoys to Rome who would first pledge obedience on behalf of the kingdom and its entire population, and then present a petition for the approval of the Compacts.[212] This he at last decided to do. But it can be assumed that the composition of the royal embassy proved to be a most delicate problem and that several consultations with both Catholic and Utraquist lords preceded the final decision. The matter would have been infinitely simpler had it been a secular ruler to be approached for cooperation in a secular affair. A delegation to the papal court had a twofold mission to perform and it would have failed to achieve its purpose had it not acted in perfect unison.

Looking at the matter from Rome, both Fantino de Valle and Antonio

Marini saw only one of its facets. They had little understanding of the internal problems of the kingdom but knew from their sources of information that the Pope's patience was wearing thin and that George's foes had an easier access to him than ever before. Sensing the danger, they urged their master to counteract adverse publicity by assuaging the Pope's irritation with an immediate dispatch of envoys to Rome.[213]

Early in January, 1462, George cast the die, accepting all risks involved in his decision. He selected for the task four men, all Czechs from Bohemia, thus reducing the danger of disharmony. They left Prague in the middle of the winter season in order to reach the papal court as soon as possible. One of the four, Prokop of Rabštejn, represented the Czech Catholics, and as he knew personally not only Pius II but also some cardinals, he was eminently qualified for the role assigned to him by the King. His colleague, Zdeněk Kostka of Postupice, was well known for his close relationship to the royal family. Two clerics in the embassy, Václav Koranda the Younger and Václav Vrbenský, ranked high among the Utraquist spiritual leaders. The embassy was not broadly representative. When they spoke in public, they referred usually to Bohemia and Moravia only, passing in silence over the three incorporated provinces of the Catholic faith—Silesia and the two Lusatias. Their purpose was not to announce solemnly George's submission, personally and in the name of the kingdom, to the papal authority, but to present calmly the Utraquist cause and to plead for a papal sanction of the Compacts. The background of George's action cannot be reconstructed for lack of contemporary evidence, but the decision was neither easy nor quickly taken. Who else than George had enough power and prudence to disjoin the two cardinal requirements—the Compacts and the appointment of Rokycana—and to stress only the sanction of the Compacts? Traditionally, they were linked together and in the charter of May 15, 1461, George obligated himself to foster Rokycana's cause.[214] Did the Archbishop-elect give his consent to the omission of his candidacy, or was the instruction to the envoys drafted without a previous consultation with him?

George was anxious to obtain from Pius II a positive answer. To make success more likely, he turned to Frederick III for assistance. Although their former friendship was not fully re-established, Frederick III did not reject George's request, and he attached to the Czech embassy his own diplomatic agent, who proved to be helpful in both the technical arrangements and the mediation.[215] They all arrived in Rome on March 10, 1462, and made contacts with Fantino de Valle and Antonio Marini. Václav Koranda acted as the secretary of the mission and compiled for George an account of its proceedings.[216]

The envoys did not enjoy an auspicious start. Shortly after their arrival, a large embassy from France reached Rome to inform Pius II that

Louis XI had abolished the Pragmatic Sanction and was ready to enter into a closer relationship with the Holy See.[217] Several days were filled with solemn gatherings and festivities to mark the restitution of friendly relations between the two courts. Pius II thus found time only for a formal reception of the leading Czech envoys, Prokop of Rabštejn and Zdeněk Kostka. As he learned that they had come not simply to pledge obedience but also to ask for the confirmation of the Compacts, he appointed four cardinals, Bessarion, Carvajal, Cusa, and d'Estouville, thoroughly to examine the complex problem.

At a meeting in Bessarion's home on March 16, 1462, Prokop of Rabštejn attempted to invalidate the charge that George had broken his coronation oath by joining the Utraquist procession on Corpus Christi Day, 1461. He praised George for his impartiality, emphasizing "that George rules, in fact, over two peoples inhabiting the kingdom of Bohemia, the Catholics and the Utraquists, and that he regards it as his foremost duty not to antagonize one section of the population by a manifestation of sympathy for the other; that therefore, he participates on some occasions in divine services with Rokycana, and on other festive days he attends the ceremonies conducted in the cathedral by the canons of Saint Vitus chapter." [218] The learned cardinal did not comment on this point, but lauded the decision of Louis XI to come to terms with the Holy See, and urged Prokop to recommend to his sovereign the same policy.

Other conferences were held in the residences of the leading cardinals to prepare for a public session on March 20. On that day, twenty-four cardinals accompanied the Pontiff to the audience hall, which was filled to capacity. The two Czech lords were introduced by the imperial agent and pledged obedience on behalf of their king.[219] The formula read by Prokop in Latin did not satisfy the Pope and he somewhat angrily asked why the pledge was made in George's name only and not on behalf of the entire kingdom. After a brief consultation, the envoys assuring Pius II of the loyalty of their respective parties, the original course of the session was resumed.[220]

Václav Koranda made his plea for confirmation of the Compacts.[221] He addressed the Pope as the vicar of Christ and the successor of Saint Peter, and adorned his long speech with quotations from Aristotle, Seneca, and Cato, in deference to the Pope's familiarity with the classics. He did not argue theologically the merits of the communion in both kinds, but reconstructed the historical background of the issue, recalling its rejection by the Council of Constance, the horrors of Sigismund's crusades, Hussite victories, the Cheb parley of 1431, and the negotiations with the Council of Basel. He pointed to the Compacts as an instrument of conciliation, their solemn promulgation and successive confirmation by Sigismund, Albrecht, Ladislav, and finally by George. He extolled the blessing of peace promoted by George in the kingdom of Bohemia and in the neighboring countries, and warned discreetly against reopening of hostilities. In his survey of the past, Koranda referred repeatedly to Bohemia and Moravia and, without stating it expressly, he spoke in the name of the ethnic body of the Czechs, inhabiting those two provinces, as united on the basis of the Compacts. He deplored the resurgence of a bellicose spirit among some neighbors of his country and beseeched the Pope to calm their passions by the confirmation of the Compacts. A hint that the King would express his gratitude by a substantial contribution to the anti-Turkish crusade linked the Hussite cause with the Pope's long-cherished scheme.

The pontiff's reply to the Hussite cleric was long and passionate, lasting almost two hours; [222] in it he revealed his familiarity with both the earlier developments and the current issues. He sketched the history of Bohemia from its dawn to the reign of Wenceslas IV and passed over to religious controversies engendered by avid readers of the works of John Wyclif. He pointed out some articles from Wyclif's works propagated by John Hus. More time than to Hus was reserved for Jacobell of Stříbro, the foremost champion of the communion in both kinds. In the Pope's rapid survey of the Hussite period, the names of John Žižka, Prokop the Bald, and Prokop the Lesser were mentioned, along with that of Václav Koranda Senior with whom he had debated the Hussite tenets at Tábor in 1451. (It was a coincidence that the name of the Czech envoy was identical with that of the veteran Tábor leader.) Pius II referred to the Czech delegates at Basel, mentioning Rokycana only by name but calling Peter Payne archheretic. According to the testimony of Václav Koranda the Younger, Pius II recited the four articles agreed upon at Basel for the benefit of the audience, and invoked the decree of the Council of Basel of December 23, 1437, by which the communion in one kind was declared a law and the Chalice permitted only under certain circumstances. [223]

But it soon became apparent that the Czech position would not be considered favorably. The Pope viewed the Compacts as a temporary measure to facilitate the gradual conciliation of the Hussites with the Roman Church and denied their unlimited validity. His reference to George's coronation oath was even more ominous, and it was followed by transparent threats that the King's assurances of loyalty would not be accepted if not accompanied by deeds.

Two days later, on March 22, 1462, Zdeněk Kostka and the theologians met in Bessarion's home with Cardinal Carvajal, Cusa, and d'Estouville of Rouen. Opening the conference, Carvajal urged Zdeněk to prevail upon his master to implement the oath by suppressing all differences in religion. Cusa accentuated the evils of disunion and recommended an unequivocal acceptance of the Pope's supremacy. But his words made little impression on the Hussite envoys. Prokop of Rabštejn was apparently not present, as the purpose of the meeting was to change the mind of the chief Utraquist envoy.

In the last private session in Bessarion's home, Zdeněk was flanked by Prokop and the imperial agent.[224] He persisted in his reluctance to make commitments exceeding his instructions, despite Carvajal's appeals. Tactfully but firmly, he cautioned the cardinals that a rejection of the Compacts would not hasten unification but reopen the struggle in Bohemia. Neither Prokop nor the imperial agent joined the cardinals in their attempt to break Zdeněk's resistance.

As the private conferences yielded no palpable results, Pius II took matters again into his own hands. A plenary session of the consistory was called for March 31, 1462, and was attended by over four thousand persons. In his speech,[225] the Pope reiterated some points formulated in his reply to Koranda, but gave more time to the doctrinal aspects of the controversy. To justify more convincingly his negative attitude, he spoke not only of the moderate Hussites but also of the Tábor party, making it clear that he found the variety of ceremonies more alarming than the Compacts. His treatment of the Compacts was more exhaustive than in the preliminary session, as it dealt with both the Constance and Basel councils and their decrees. He rejected emphatically Jacobell's teaching that the communion in both kinds is necessary for salvation. It was accepted by the Basel Council as a temporary concession only to those who had practiced it previously and their number was dwindling with the progress of time. This passage could be interpreted as an indication of the Pope's willingness to tolerate the Chalice until the old generation would die out, but not permanently. He also condemned such practices as the administration of the consecrated bread and wine to infants, adhered to by some Hussite priests.

The speech culminated in a resolute rejection of the request for the papal sanction of the Chalice, as that would be offensive to other rulers and nations, with the exception of the Greeks. A danger of heresies would arise from its approval, and the Germans, Hungarians, and Poles would be antagonized by a privileged treatment of the Czechs. The Pope was determined to uphold his authority so that nobody would be able to interpret his connivance as an admission of vacillation.

The papal procurator, Antonio di Eugubio, made a statement that the Pontiff would not accept George's pledge of allegiance if not corroborated by a sincere endeavor to exterminate errors among the Czechs. He then proclaimed the Compacts null and void.[226]

On April 1, 1462, the envoys were received in the papal garden by Pius II and six cardinals. The Pope strenuously urged Zdeněk Kostka to use his influence to turn the King's thought in the right direction. Koranda's account of the conversation, written for George's information, makes it sufficiently clear that Pius II was not shaken in his conviction that George's authority among the Hussites was supreme, and that his firm action would avert wavering among the rank and file.[227] He believed that the clerics, too, would follow the King's lead. He recalled the Diet at Benešov, and his prognostication at that time that George would accomplish great things if he renounced the Chalice. Turning to the envoys personally, he pointed out the merits of the King's voluntary submission. He dismissed them with a political message for George to remain in friendly contacts with the Emperor.

The Utraquist envoys left Rome soon after the farewell audience, and were followed by Prokop of Rabštejn and Fantino de Valle. The latter went to Prague as a papal envoy to acquaint George accurately with the Pontiff's decision. The contacts were not broken off. Pius II most likely expected that after his flat rejection of the Compacts George would see the futility of clinging to them. As Fantino knew George intimately, he seemed to be a more suitable mediator than some other Roman prelate in whom George might not have confidence.

ROMA LOCUTA . . .

No available source contains information concerning George's thoughts and hopes at the time when his envoys were leaving Prague for Rome. It can be surmised that he expected a favorable answer and planned his foreign policy accordingly. The separation of the two basic demands, which on other occasions had been presented as prerequisites for the integration of Utraquism with the Roman Church, the sanction of the Compacts and Rokycana's confirmation, was undoubtedly a concession to the Pope's point of view. No document reveals whether Rokycana consented to it or was not consulted when the instruction of the envoys was under discussion.

The place among the envoys assigned to Prokop of Rabštejn was prominent but not enviable. He was personally known to Pius II and had other contacts at the Curia. It would have been highly embarrassing for him to participate in a mission which would have been expected to plead for both the Compacts and Rokycana. He knew better than anybody else at George's court that the Pope would never approve the election of a church dignitary by an assembly of laymen, in this instance the provincial Diet of 1435.[228] It is quite likely that the two demands were separated on his insistence, and the envoys were instructed to petition only for the sanction of the Compacts. George and his councillors, Catholic and Utraquist, probably expected that in this matter the Pope would be benevolent and regard the approval as a political concession. Contacts between Prague and Rome were not extensive and neither George nor Prokop was fully aware of the Pope's effort to suppress any reminder of the conciliar era. They had known him when he was in the Emperor's service and they probably were unable to think of him in any other terms.

Knowing that several months would be needed for the envoys to reach Rome, acquit themselves of their delicate mission, and return, George did not put off political tasks which, if left unsolved, could threaten him

in the rear. Apart from conclusion of peace with Frederick of Brandenburg, he spent a good deal of time in negotiations with Casimir IV.
According to a previous agreement, a conference was held at Greater
Głogów in Silesia with George as the host.[229] To this rather remote place
George's agent, Antonio Marini, apparently hastened from Rome, while
the Czech members of the delegation remained in Prague. There was
no danger that Casimir IV, if informed of Pius' negative answer, would
break off discussions with George. Relations between the Polish court
and Holy See were strained at that time, as the vacant See of Cracow
had been filled by a papal provision without regard to the King's wishes.
Casimir IV wanted to have George on his side, as for some time he had
expected Czech mediation in the struggle with the Teutonic knights.
The Order did not accept the offer, for they feared that the Czech verdict would be favorable to the Poles. The struggle dragged on, and the
part that Czech professional soldiers played in some battles was significant. As no serious problem stood between the two rulers, minor claims
and counterclaims were either adjusted on the spot or shelved. Before
parting, the two kings renewed their pledge, made through their plenipotentiaries at Bytom in 1460, to live in sincere and perpetual friendship.[230]

As the Hussite cause was discussed not only in cardinals' homes, but
also in open sessions, the Pope's decision to repudiate the Compacts received a good deal of publicity. The Wittelsbach princes kept an eye on
these developments and offered their good offices to the King to avert
a deterioration of his relations with the Papacy. George was apparently
not ready to accept their services, regarding the matter as so serious
that it could not be settled by an intervention of two minor princes. He
began to contemplate a more ambitious scheme that would create a basis
for a durable order in the Western Christian orbit. He also resolved to
consolidate without delay the ranks of loyal citizens, so that the kingdom would be protected against disruptive forces if the threatening rift
with the highest Church authority could not be healed quickly.

Sources relating to the spring and early summer of 1462 are scarce,
so it is impossible to trace accurately the King's steps. When he returned
to Prague in mid-June, he probably requested Prokop and other members of the delegation to give him a detailed account of the public sessions and the conferences in the cardinals' homes. The dealings with
Fantino de Valle were less satisfactory than in the earlier stages of his
service. The versatile Dalmatian, disregarding the biblical adage, attempted to "serve two masters," since he consented, before his departure from Rome, to act in Prague as both the royal procurator and the
papal envoy.[231] When he reached Bohemia, he established contacts with
Czech Catholics and also with prominent persons in Breslau.[232] In audi-

ences and in written documents, Fantino urged the King that he and his family abandon the communion in both kinds, and communicate at the Lord's table in Saint Vitus Cathedral in company with prominent members of the nobility. George was reminded that the decision of the king of France to renounce the Pragmatic Sanction pointed the way for him to follow. In addition to attending a solemn communion in the Cathedral, George was urged to dismiss Utraquist priests from his household and to fulfill in every point the coronation oath.

An answer to these demands came sooner than the legate expected. Instead of taking the sacrament at the castle, George with the Queen and children marched on Corpus Christi Day (June 17) in the procession led by Rokycana, thus dispelling suspicions as to his steadfastness in the faith. Coming after Fantino's appeal, George's ostentatious participation in a Utraquist ceremony could not but be viewed as an indication of his policy. In protest, Fantino was ready to leave the city, but George prevailed on him to stay and attend a court assembly, scheduled for Saint Lawrence's Day (August 10), 1462.

The intervening time was not used for quiet exchanges of views or a search for a compromise. Fantino did not wait passively for the opening of the assembly, but turned to the King again and submitted to him a detailed proposal for the ultimate settlement of the conflict.[233] Had his advice been accepted and acted upon, a solemn renunciation of the Chalice would have been only the first step, to be followed by a systematic suppression of all Hussite peculiarities and a complete assimilation of church life in Bohemia to the general pattern. The legate's thoughts and activities could not pass unnoticed; consequently, an anticurial sentiment was rising among the Utraquists. When Fantino urged George to suppress Czech songs defaming the Roman Church and the Pontiff, he apparently was well informed by his Catholic friends concerning their contents.

In that atmosphere the court assembly opened on August 12, 1462, two days later than scheduled.[234] It was well attended by delegates from Bohemia and the incorporated provinces. The Utraquist party had a strong representation, whereas many Catholics abstained to avoid embarrassment. The King, having his consort on the right and his sons on the left, opened the session and asked the envoys to report on their mission to Rome. As soon as they concluded their detailed description, the King addressed the assembly again. Speaking at length, he recapitulated the story of the Compacts and refuted the charge that he failed to abide by his coronation oath. He read its text, of which but few of the assembled dignitaries had a clear idea, and he rejected as inappropriate any attempt to treat the Utraquists as sectarians or heretics. To leave no doubt of his personal convictions, he professed his attachment to the communion in both kinds, which he had practiced as a lord of family domains, as governor, and as king. Pointing to the Queen and his children, he declared that they would remain faithful until death to the communion of bread and wine, in the spirit of the Compacts, being ready to give for it not only the crown but life as well.[235]

The accounts of the session compiled by various reporters followed in general the same line, but differed at this point. The municipal council of Breslau received the information from their agent that George supported his reassertion of attachment to the Chalice by a declaration that he saw no other way to salvation than the communion in both kinds as instituted by the Savior. They included this declaration in their letter to Pius II dated August 28, 1462, which probably was the first description of the assembly to reach the Curia. Later the declaration touching upon the Church doctrine was resolutely disclaimed by the King and his advisers and attributed as a malicious distortion to Zdeněk of Šternberk.[236]

The King's firm statement threw the assembly into a commotion, and its Utraquist members burst into tears. When the excitement subsided, the King took up the matter and analyzed the political aspects of the Pope's verdict. A question arose whether the Compacts after their formal rejection should be left on the books of statutes as one of the basic laws of the kingdom. Without waiting for an answer from the audience, George ordered a secretary to read the reports concerning the negotiations with the Council of Basel and the text of the Compacts. As soon as this was done, the charters of Kings Sigismund, Albrecht, and Ladislav were read to show that ever since the proclamation at Jihlava the Compacts had been regarded by the rulers of the country as valid. George expressed surprise that he, a Utraquist, should be denied the privilege which the Catholic kings were allowed to enjoy, and thus answered his own rhetorical question. He then assured members of the assembly that he would continue to shield by his royal authority both Catholics and Utraquists.

Having made his position clear, George appealed to those present to state unequivocally whether they were ready to defend the Compacts, if the kingdom were threatened by an invasion on their account. The position of the Utraquists was clear, and on their behalf Zdeněk Kostka pledged readiness to stand unswervingly behind the King. The replies from the Catholic ranks were reserved. Zdeněk of Šternberk disclaimed any responsibility for the Compacts and pledged help only in defense of the honor and rights of the Crown. Bishop Tas assured George of cooperation in all matters not contrary to the faith and obedience of the Roman Church. Bishop Jošt made a similar statement, offering help in restoring harmonious relations with the Apostolic See. The discrepancy between the Utraquists and the Catholics was obvious, and the King's attempt to get from the Catholic side a more explicit promise yielded no positive results.

In the next session the King accepted a general assurance of loyalty from the Catholic representatives and bade Fantino de Valle to speak in the name of the Pontiff. John of Rabštejn served as interpreter. Following his instruction, Fantino accused the Hussites of nonobservance of the Compacts and of violating them by various excesses. He concluded that by notorious transgressions of the approved limits they forfeited the right to invoke the Jihlava agreement.[237]

Fantino's speech revealed vividly the differences of opinion in regard to the Compacts. The Hussites believed that no defect impaired their validity. Whenever objections were raised, they referred not only to the Council but also to Eugene IV, meaning in particular his bulls of March 11, 1436, and September 18, 1437.[238] Neither of these documents contained an express confirmation of the Council's agreement with the Czechs. In this subtle but pivotal point, the spokesmen of the Curia would not yield, maintaining that Eugene's acquiescence could not be interpreted as a sanction. By this interpretation Eugene's successors claimed complete freedom to pass judgment on the validity of the Compacts.

The concession which Pius II was at one time willing to make was partial and limited to the older generation.[239] If granted, it would have excluded from the communion of both kinds all members of the Hussite Church who did not practice it at the time of the Basel Council. Fantino spoke in an imperative tone, holding out no hope that the Pope would not insist on strict obedience to his sentence. Turning his face to the throne, Fantino urged the King to honor his coronation oath. To add weight to his appeal, he repeated the specific demands that the King had heard during the previous meetings with the legate: that he communicate at the Lord's table in the cathedral, and that he expel from his court all disreputable chaplains, disseminators of errors, and originators of damnation. A heated controversy flared up when the legate defended the Pope's right to interpret the meaning and import of the coronation oath. He finished his speech amidst protests and excitement, and hurriedly left the assembly hall.

His Catholic friends urged Fantino to leave Prague at once, but he disregarded their warning and attended a secret session of the royal council to give at the King's request an account of his activities as his procurator. Emboldened by the echoes of his public speech among the Catholics, he declared that he had given up the royal service when he became convinced that it was not his master's intention really to implement his oath. Rumors gained ground in Prague and spread quickly beyond its limits that the legate's words aroused George's anger to the extent of unsheathing his sword, but that he recovered himself in time.[240] He gave an order that documentary evidence be brought in to convince the former procurator of a breach of faith. On the King's instruction, Fantino was imprisoned in the Old Town Hall and from there sent to jail at the Poděbrady castle. A milder verdict was issued against Prokop of Rabštejn because of suspicion that he did not discharge his duties effectively. Perplexed by the King's outburst, both Zdeněk of Šternberk and Bishop Jošt quickly left the city, to avoid getting involved in any complication.

Some of the King's actions, like the arrest of Fantino, were taken on the spur of the moment. But the basic decision to adhere to the Hussite faith resulted from a calm analysis of the situation at home and abroad. As the sources do not assign any prominence to Rokycana, either in preparation of the assembly or in its conduct, it may be assumed that in that fateful hour George had turned for advice to such distinguished laymen as Zdeněk Kostka, and that the political aspects of the conflict were deliberately accentuated. George hoped to keep on his side not only the moderate Catholics in the kingdom but foreign princes, who for one or another reason resented papal interference in politics. Guided by this intention, George resolved to put pressure on the clergy of both parties, so that they would not disturb peace by polemics. The administrators of the two consistories received orders to arrange for a convocation of the clergy to be held in the King's presence in mid-September, 1462.[241] Instructions given by royal officers were rigid and the attendance was impressive. The Catholic priests gathered in the Cathedral and marched from there in a procession headed by the dean of the chapter, Hilarius of Litoměřice. They were joined in the royal court by the Utraquists, who came with Rokycana, most likely from the Týn church. The King spoke firmly and reprimanded the clerics for marring his efforts to safeguard peace by their incessant wrangling and moral laxity. His threat of intervention, if vigilance were not intensified, reminded the audience of the fourth Prague article, assigning to those "whose office it is to prohibit and punish all mortal sins, especially those that are public." Finally, he enjoined the assembled clerics to regard the Compacts as a basis for coexistence, reaffirming his readiness to uphold them by all possible means. Dean Hilarius assured the King of his willingness to respect the Compacts, though they were not binding on his own party, and Rokycana also made a declaration of loyalty. The King's stern admonitions produced the desired effect and averted, at least temporarily, a public discussion of the controversial issues. In this manner George asserted his sovereign right to enforce the laws, and left no doubt in anybody's mind that the Compacts were as valid as they had been since Sigismund's restoration.

Some documents from the spring and summer of 1462 indicate that soon after the return of the royal envoys from Rome, a campaign was planned by George to create a broader basis of defense against the impending papal attack. His resolution not to accept the Pope's unilateral decision concerning the Compacts called not only for tightening of the existing ties with friendly courts, but for extension of the network of treaties to reduce the danger of a rearguard action. Although the primary task of George's diplomacy was protection against a hostile grouping of Bohemia's neighbors, he kept in sight the major issues of a wider range, especially those in which he had been involved either as governor or as king.

George knew well enough how seriously Pius II was occupied with the Turkish menace. Such urgent appeals as Bessarion's two requests that the King personally attend the imperial assembly at Vienna could not easily be forgotten.[242] Suggestions that George would amply compensate Pius II for concessions in the matter of Compacts were not empty gestures, and had they been accepted, George would have been in a position to implement them. Trained warriors, some remembering the Hussite campaigns, could be mustered in Bohemia and Moravia without too much difficulty, and used for a crusade against the enemies of the Cross. Czech soldiers had a good reputation and George himself had a wide experience in warfare.

Those who knew George intimately did not expect his meek submission to the papal authority, and endeavored to devise a settlement in which both the Pope and the King could participate without a loss of prestige. Antonio Marini speculated on what service his master should render to achieve concord with the Papacy without an abjuration of the Chalice. While waiting in Rome for the arrival of George's envoys, Marini hit on an idea which, if pursued energetically, could clear the path toward conciliation. In his report to George [243] he inserted a transparent allusion to Godefroy de Bouillon and promised to work out a scheme in which the kings of Bohemia, Hungary, and Poland would share. He urged George to express his opinion in the near future, as he wanted to reveal his thought to the Pope. It can hardly be doubted that Marini envisioned a powerful coalition, which would put into execution the Pope's calls for a crusade.

There is no evidence that Marini had a chance to talk to Pius II concerning the crusade prior to the arrival of George's envoys in March, 1462. After the repudiation of the Compacts, his scheme could no more serve as a means of bringing Prague and Rome together. Marini did not drop it, but reoriented it so that its chief supporters would be secular rulers. Not much pondering was needed to conclude that the start should be made with the Poles. Not having found George in Prague, Marini hastened to reach him at Greater Głogów. There he gave him a report on the Pope's rejection of the Compacts and called his attention to the anti-Turkish scheme.

Separated from the sultan's domains by Hungary, the kingdom of Bohemia was in less danger than the Polish-Lithuanian state, which was open to raids from the southeast. Thinking not only of his own country, but of general problems affecting Christendom, George assented to a treaty which obliged him and Casimir to watch the Turkish designs and movements. The alliance was conceived as defensive and the contracting parties pledged mutual help in case of a Turkish attack.[244]

It seems very likely that Marini had some opportunity to talk to the Poles about his scheme. He was apparently encouraged by their response and drafted, soon after his return to Prague, a memorandum embodying the results of his deliberations. With the meager outcome of the Mantua congress in mind, Marini endeavored to build the Christian bloc on more solid foundations than that of reliance on either the Emperor, the Pope, or the general council. He reckoned with active participation of the secular princes as well as that of the wealthy cities, Venice in particular. He did not want to exclude the supreme spiritual authority from his consideration, as a crusade without the Pope's blessing seemed inconceivable; but he suggested that the anti-Turkish forces be supplied by five "nations," the Greeks, the Germans, the French, the Italians, and the Spaniards. He recommended that the Pope appoint to each "nation," for a more effective co-ordination of common efforts, not only a cardinal legate but also a captain. Marini inserted in his memorandum respectful references to the Emperor, but indicated clearly enough that the more energetic rulers of national states should take the matter in hand. In the first stage of preparations, he thought primarily of the partners of the Greater Głogów defensive alliance, but soon he added to them the kings of Hungary and France, the dukes of Burgundy and Bavaria, as well as Venice.

Marini intended his memorandum primarily for George, but transmitted it also to Casimir IV to follow up the Głogów soundings.[245] Early in July, 1462, George sent the versatile diplomat to Venice. On August 9, 1462, Marini was admitted before the senate and laid before them his scheme. The official reaction was mild and hesitating, and private conversations were most likely held in the same tone. The leaders of the Republic were potentially interested in a coalition of so many powerful rulers, but were apparently reluctant to endorse publicly a scheme not attributing to the Pontiff the dominant role.[246]

Marini realized that it would be inopportune to insist on a public endorsement of his scheme and left the city. No source sheds light on his whereabouts in the late summer of 1462, when the princely courts maintaining contacts with Prague were disturbed by international repercussions of the Fantino affair. It is possible that he traveled back to Prague via Hungary to inform Matthias of his activities. An alternative to this assumption is a visit to Bavaria. If he really proceeded from Venice in that direction, he could see the effects of his master's dramatic gesture. Both Duke Lewis and Elector Frederick of the Palatinate regarded it as their duty to assist in averting an irreparable rift between Rome and Prague.

Fantino's imprisonment was not the first instance in which George showed little interest in traditional forms of legal niceties; but as Fantino had come to Prague with papal credentials, the action against him could not be hushed up as a trifling incident. A question arose why the King, knowing of Fantino's new function as a papal legate, did not insist that he acquit himself formally of his service as royal procurator. Even mild critics of George's conduct entertained suspicions that he put off a drastic action against Fantino until the Prague assembly to heighten its effect on the public.

Some of the royal councillors doubtless exercised a moderating influence on George, and convinced him that amends had to be made without much delay. George followed this lead and, in addition to a written account,[247] he sent to Rome the Vyšehrad provost, John of Rabštejn, who could gain access to Pius II through his many contacts. George also complied with the recommendations from Bavaria and the Palatinate and released Fantino from captivity.[248] Before the end of October, 1462, the legate was able to leave Bohemia. At the same time Prokop of Rabštejn was rehabilitated and resumed his office as royal chancellor.

Following the Wittelsbach mediation, a welcome relief came from Austria. The Habsburg princes played unwittingly into George's hands by reopening their grim feud and thus diverting public attention from Bohemia to their homeland. Frederick III was hard pressed by leagues of nobles who sided with his brother Albrecht. Moreover, in Vienna the inimical elements staged a coup in which the city government was changed in Frederick's disfavor. His partisans in the capital and elsewhere were in the minority and could not resist superior forces without help from abroad. In October, 1462, the imperial residence in Vienna was encircled by the rebels and the loyal garrison was too weak to attempt a successful sortie. An emissary was sent to Prague with an urgent request for immediate help.[249]

From George's point of view, the moment was most favorable for an armed expedition into Austria that would be bound to increase the Emperor's indebtedness to him and to show others how well George was prepared for any conflict. A Czech vanguard under Prince Victorin and Zdeněk of Šternberk moved quickly toward the Danube and was followed by stronger columns headed by George himself. Skirmishes between the Czech forces and the rebels before the walls of Vienna indicated that the struggle would be bitter. The assault did not take place, as neither party was prepared to give the signal for an attack on enemy positions. Instead, contacts were established through intermediaries both with the rebels and with Archduke Albrecht. The result of the laborious negotiations was a compromise by which Frederick III transferred to Albrecht the government of Lower Austria.[250]

George's attempt to restore mutual confidence between the Habsburg princes met with little success. Frederick III was embittered by his brother's alignment with the rebels, and ruminated over the personal humiliation to which he had been subjected while his residence was besieged. Although he was promised reasonable compensation for concessions to his brother, the Emperor showed no desire to let the wound heal. The strained relationship between the two brothers hindered the pacification of Austria, and only Albrecht's death in December, 1463, opened a brighter prospect for the Habsburg subjects.

Frederick's sense of obligation to George seemed to have no limits. He promised a generous compensation to the King personally, and to the other Czech warriors. As George was intensely interested in liquidating long-standing feuds wherever they existed, he offered his help in reconciling Lewis of Bavaria with the Emperor, and vice versa. He also accepted the latter's good offices in restoring friendship with Albrecht Achilles.[251] The kingdom of Bohemia profited by this occasion, as the Emperor revised the Golden Bull of 1212 and reduced by half the King's traditional obligations. Added to this was a pledge of noninterference with the internal affairs of Bohemia.[252] By another charter, Frederick III renounced the treaty of mutual succession, concluded in 1364 by Charles IV and Rudolph IV.[253] George and his family valued the promotion of their two sons, Henry and Hynek, to the rank of imperial princes.[254] One charter designated George as the guardian of Prince Maximilian in case of Frederick's death.[255] Of immediate importance, however, was the Emperor's willingness to use his influence with Pius II for a more moderate policy.[256]

George's promptness in relieving the Emperor's dire straits could hardly have been compensated more generously. The traditional links of Bohemia with the Empire were preserved in such a manner that no danger could come to the kingdom from its more powerful partner. On the contrary, the King's membership in the College of Electors facilitated his contacts with other princes of the Empire, which George had made one of the main objectives of his foreign policy. He also could believe that his family's aspirations took a more concrete shape. The renunciation of the treaty of 1364 reduced the danger of the Habsburgs pressing their claims to the crown of Bohemia in case of George's death. Elevation of George's sons to princely rank tended in the same direction, making more likely an election of the first-born, a scheme probably seriously considered by the royal couple but kept secret, for obvious reasons, even from the members of the most intimate circle. A stipulation that in case of the unexpected death of the boy prince Maximilian, his possessions should pass on to George, had a more symbolic than practical significance. The situation in which it could be implemented never did arise, but at the time of its signature, it manifested the harmony existing between the two rulers.

The Austrian imbroglio not only gave George an appreciable respite, but also enhanced his prestige. As soon as it had been allayed, he turned to his own worries. The release of Fantino liquidated an irritating episode, but the broad issues of the conflict could not be settled by a mere intercession of friends and allies. More effective methods had to be devised to bring about a durable settlement.

Documents which originated in the papal chancellery, if examined carefully, indicate that after the rejection of the Compacts, Pius II contemplated an elaborate maneuver to force George into submission. Fantino's mission to Bohemia was the first move and the Pope apparently entertained a hope that George would listen attentively to his former procurator so well versed in the curial affairs. George's vigorous reaction dispelled the Pope's optimism and induced him to resort to harsher methods.

It was known in both Rome and Prague that the most sensitive spot in George's system of security was the interim accord with Breslau.[257] It was in its third year, and the date on which the city was expected to swear the solemn oath of allegiance was approaching. The senate and the King were well aware of the Pope's lively interest in the matter and admitted that the final settlement could hardly be achieved without the latter's participation. Elements in Breslau hostile to the Czech king maintained relations with his resolute opponents at the papal court, and were encouraged by the rejection of the Compacts. The senate was informed by one of its secretaries, John Kitzing, of the public sessions and the conferences in the cardinals' homes.[258] Kitzing prolonged his stay in Rome and worked zealously among the cardinals and other influential clerics. As after Marini's departure George had no official representative in Rome, Kitzing encountered no opposition and achieved considerable success. Guided by his reports and by information from other circles, the senate widened contacts with prominent prelates either residing in Rome or active in diplomatic missions, missing no opportunity to present the Czech developments unfavorably.[259] In this manner, the ground was prepared for the Pope's spectacular gesture—his suspension of the interim accord of January, 1460.[260]

The papal missive had no immediate effect because, owing to Kitzing's death, it reached Breslau only late in November, 1462. At that time George was fully occupied with Austrian affairs. As Pius II had made harmony with the Emperor the cornerstone of his policy, he could not embarrass by stern measures the man on whose assistance depended the eventual outcome of the Austrian struggles. In the meantime, Archbishop Jerome fulfilled his various assignments and moved to Breslau to establish closer contacts with the Silesian princes and cities.[261] Encouraged by his arrival and by the papal missive, the senate resolved not to make preparations for the solemn oath which they were to swear not later than February, 1463.[262]

George was probably not fully informed of the extent of the correspondence emanating from, or reaching, Breslau, but sensed the danger of complications. In the late fall and early winter of 1462 he had a trusted representative, John of Rabštejn, in Rome and the imperial agents also worked in his behalf. When Rabštejn returned from Italy, George decided to break his silence and to protect the failure of Breslau to abide by the accord of January, 1460. He invited Pius II to resume his mediation by putting pressure on the senate.[263]

The King's appeal to the Pope produced adverse effects. His foes at the papal court, whose power Rabštejn apparently underestimated, were firm in their resolution to use Breslau as a base for offensive operations. The matter could be presented to Frederick III and Lewis of Bavaria as an internal affair, in which the Pope had been involved with the King's knowledge and the senate's acquiescence. This interpretation enabled the papal diplomacy to resume the initiative without risking the Emperor's displeasure.

The offensive started before George's appeal for mediation had reached the Curia. The senate's new procurator, Canon Nicholas Marboth, worked hand in hand with Fantino de Valle and other high clerics. The time was opportune, as George again had no representative in Rome and the expected imperial envoy had not yet arrived. The letters to Breslau, one by Fantino and the other by the Archdeacon of Toledo, presaged the bull of March 29, 1463, by which Pius II took the rebel city under his protection.[264] Shorter letters were sent on the same day to Archbishop Jerome and to the Archbishop of Gniezno, to whose jurisdiction Silesia belonged even after its political union with Bohemia.[265] The Pope urged them to give the widest publicity to the bull and to insure its execution. A special order was sent to Breslau on April 1, 1463, forbidding its leaders to swear the oath of allegiance to George which they were not ready to do anyhow.[266] Several weeks elapsed before Pius II found it expedient to explain his policy to Frederick III. The breve, severe in tone, left a faint hope of reconciliation, the condition being George's surrender to papal authority.[267]

The March bull reached Breslau early in May, and Archbishop Jerome saw to it that it was widely disseminated in the Catholic areas of the kingdom as well as in the neighboring countries. Both parties realized that the papal actions imperiled chances of a peaceful settlement. Among the clerics and the aldermen of Breslau a bellicose spirit prevailed. In their reply to the bull, dispatched to Rome on May 24, 1463, they pleaded for a more energetic policy.[268] They recommended that another candidate for the crown be designated. Coupled with this was a suggestion that the Pope send a legate *a latere* to Germany with wider powers than that possessed by the Archbishop of Crete. The legate's chief duty would be to give a more effective protection to all Catholic subjects of the Czech king and to prepare for a crusade. The letter reflected the agitated atmosphere in the capital, as well as fears that in the more moderate circles there would not be enough fervor for an open defiance of the King. Large sections of the Silesian population were aware of the blessings of peace and prosperity under George's scepter.

When informed of the Pope's resolute step, George resumed the initiative by mobilizing his loyal forces. On May 15, 1463, he met at Kladsko with the Bishops of Olomouc and Breslau and urged them to work for the preservation of peace along with the Catholic lords and boroughs. The conference was fruitful and ended in a decision that a general assembly be held at Brno on July 13. Although only Bishop Jošt's letter has been preserved, it can hardly be doubted that Tas of Olomouc, too, concurred with George's request and used his influence to calm peoples' minds.[269]

Jošt's position at that juncture was awkward and painful. He was loyal to the King and feared a civil strife which could result in distressing consequences. But as a bishop he was exposed to an increasing pressure from the Catholics and risked unhappy complications for his continued cooperation with the Hussite king. His position in Breslau was never rosy, and after he had gone over to George in 1459, he was suspected by fanatical preachers and monks of indifference and softness in dealing with the Hussites. He felt safer in his summer residence at Nisa and seldom stayed in the crowded capital. In the spring of 1463, the Pope himself rebuked Jošt for a prolonged absence from Breslau, released him from any obligation to George, and urged him to return to Breslau promptly.[270]

Informed of this papal admonition, Archbishop Jerome requested Jošt to come and assist him in the publication of the papal bull as well as in the actions connected therewith. The Bishop heeded the summons and appeared in Breslau. His conference with Jerome was neither short nor pleasant. Shocked by the Bishop's hesitancy to turn against the King, the Archbishop of Crete resorted to stronger language. Jošt replied promptly in the same vein, not sparing Jerome the odious scriptural testimony: "Cretans are always liars, dangerous animals, idle gluttons . . ." Two princes accompanying Jošt to the conference had a hard time trying to separate the two temperamental prelates, but with their help the unsavory episode was terminated.[271]

The mediators found it difficult to accomplish more than a personal reconciliation. Bishop Jošt was determined to honor his obligations to the King and to attempt an amicable settlement. He left for Prague to join hands with other Catholic leaders in preparation for the Brno assembly. With the exception of a handful of irreconcilable individuals, the Catholics of Bohemia and Moravia had no desire to get involved in a conflict with their recognized king. Their contacts with the German-speaking nobles of Silesia and of the two Lusatias were not strong enough to facilitate the formation of a solid bloc. Even less co-operation could be expected from the Breslau patricians, as Jošt himself recalling his experiences could tell. The Czech nobles had no desire to have a rival for the throne designated by the Pope. It could be anticipated that the papal candidate would be of foreign blood, and aversion to such a solution was just as strong in 1463 as it had been in 1458. Charges leveled against Jošt by the Breslau senate indicated that the Czech Catholic lords were still beset by fears that a Catholic monarch would insist on the return to the Church of its former properties. No great pressure needed to be exerted by George to keep the Czech Catholics together and to have the support of the two bishops and the leading lords.

The counteroffensive of the loyal Catholics opened on June 10, 1463. On that date four letters were executed, signed, and sealed by a large number of lords, knights, and delegates from the Catholic boroughs. They were destined for Pius II, Frederick III, for the papal legate at the latter's court, Dominico de Torcello, and for Archbishop Jerome.[272] In all of them the forthcoming assembly at Brno was mentioned as the most appropriate overture to a general pacification. When Jošt reached Prague, he acceded to the action of the bloc and wrote personal letters to de Torcello and to the Pope himself in order to obtain suspension of any disciplinary measures against George, so that the general assembly would not be disturbed in its deliberations.[273] Soon afterwards he hastened to Breslau to attend the assembly of Silesian princes and boroughs, called by Jerome for June 29, 1463. The attendance at this assembly was disheartening for the papal envoy, and nothing was accomplished, as the delegates wanted to await the outcome of the Brno congress.[274]

A detail of the Zátoň altar (1440) showing Salome and her mother offering the head of St. John the Baptist to King Herodes. Center figure is traditionally supposed to represent King George.

National Gallery, Prague

Portraits of King George, in heavy armor, and his first wife, Cunegonde.

Poděbrady Castle at the present time.

Emperor Frederick III.

Öster. National Bibliothek, Vienna

yerbook given by Queen Johanna to King
rge on Christmas, 1462. Figure at right is
ight to represent King George, at left an
unidentified cardinal.

The Church at Týn at the
present time.

King Matthias of Hungary.
(*right*)

Pope Pius II at Ancona,
shortly before his death.
Original painting by Pintu-
ricchio in the Piccolomini
Library at Siena Cathedral.
(*left*)

PAVLVS . II . PAPA . VENETVS.

Pope Paul II.

Frontispiece and title page of the first edition (1522) of a book of sermons by Peter Chelčický, who is represented as talking to a group of Utraquist clergy.

George's suggestion that the general assembly be held in Brno was a concession to the Catholic lords. The upper classes there were predominantly German and Catholic, and the danger of external pressure on the delegates was far less than in Prague. It was the King's intention to present his cause in political terms and to request from both parties loyal support in his endeavor to save peace. While the Bishops of Olomouc and Breslau played a prominent part in the sessions, no Utraquist cleric was allowed to defend his faith. The chief speaker from that side was the King himself, who presented the Compacts in their historical and political context.[275] Maintaining that the agreement was duly approved by the Council of Basel, accepted factually by Eugene IV, and confirmed by Kings Sigismund, Albrecht, and Ladislav, he re-emphasized his conviction that the continued observation of the Compacts would enhance chances of peace inside and outside the kingdom. There were in his speech, apparently, vague allusions to a general council at which the controversy could be reopened and settled; these were most likely inspired by the King's secular advisers, not by the Hussite clergy.

Rumors circulating before the opening of the congress ascribed to George an intention to obtain from all delegates a binding assurance of unlimited support in the defense of the Compacts. Although he virtually controlled the assembly, he wisely abstained from a step that might have driven the Catholic party into open opposition. Sensing that even the moderate elements would not be willing to risk the Pope's indignation, he did not press for a declaration in favor of the Compacts. He contented himself with the promise that the Catholics would use their influence with the Pope, the Emperor, the cardinals, and the papal legates at the imperial court, Dominico de Torcello and Bishop Rudolf of Rüdesheim, to avert a harsh and irrevocable verdict. Fulfilling this pledge, the Catholic leaders sent short letters to the Pope and the Emperor imploring them to achieve an accord.[276]

George's effort to preserve unity was motivated by his concern for peace and order as well as by his confidence in the Emperor's mediation. It was widely believed that Frederick III was willing to send envoys to Rome and to confer with Pius II personally, if the envoys should run into difficulties. From his side, George declared his intention to reveal fully his thought to the Emperor and to submit to his judgment.[277] Chances of success seemed to be brighter than in the early part of 1463.

Since the middle of July, 1463, Frederick III had had a new agent in Rome, Hartung von Capell, who apparently was more energetic and successful than his predecessor, Wolfgang Forchtenauer. Hartung scored a notable success before any report from Brno could reach the papal court. On July 18, 1463, Pius II suspended his proceedings against the Hussite king to facilitate imperial mediation.[278] When letters from Brno and other pleas for moderation reached Rome, the atmosphere was balmy and hopes of success were rising rapidly. The Pope did not insist on an immediate action, making possible exchanges of letters and personal messages between Prague, the imperial residence at Wiener Neustadt, and Rome.

The hopes kindled by the Pope's benevolence flickered for several weeks following the Brno assembly and then waned. Even the optimists came to realize that the matters were more complicated than they first appeared. The Pope's commitments to Breslau had gone too far and the city was virtually exempted from the King's jurisdiction. Hostility against George was so intense there that even after his submission to the Pope there would have remained vestiges of the high-running passions. The Breslau senate and other irreconcilable elements were alarmed by reports from Rome indicating the possibility of a compromise. They redoubled their efforts, advocating vigorously drastic measures by which the King would be coerced into capitulation. In this policy they were supported by the Archbishop of Crete and in Rome by George's implacable foes among the cardinals and in the lower ranks. In the fall and winter of 1463, the senate endeavored to intensify the feeling against the Hussite king by widespread correspondence and other means and to weaken the effects of Frederick's interventions.[279] The King unwittingly supplied the material for new accusations, as he felt that it was his duty to proceed energetically against disobedient elements and to assert his authority. In letters to the Pope and the leading cardinals, George and his partisans were presented as incorrigible heretics and intriguers, who hindered commerce between Breslau and other countries and under cover of negotiations actually prepared for war.

As the winter advanced, these complaints grew louder and the request for a cardinal legate was expressed in more urgent terms. To add more weight to this petition, the senate accused Jošt of leniency and hinted discreetly that the Archbishop of Crete did not enjoy enough prestige among the perturbed population.[280] His departure in February, 1464, for other destinations, left a vacancy and increased fears that in the crucial moment the city might be sacrificed in the interest of a general pacification.

The moderate endorsement accorded to George by the Catholics at Brno could not be trumpeted to the world as an outstanding achievement, but George's diplomacy could point to it in dealings with the Emperor and other more distant princes. Frederick III pursued his conciliatory policy, but awaiting George's envoys, he did not throw his personal prestige into the scale. Although appreciative of Frederick's good will, George did not seize the opportunity immediately, but allowed several months to pass before he entrusted two of his most distinguished advisers with the delicate mission to the imperial court.[281]

George's tactics in the latter part of 1463 resembled his dilatory policy from 1460 and 1461. At that time, instead of sending a truly representative group to Rome, he became involved in German affairs and fostered Mair's scheme of imperial reform. Similarly, in August, 1463, he held a congress of German princes in Prague and arbitrated in various controversies that had accumulated in the Empire during the past six years. Among them was the long-standing feud between the Wittelsbachs and Frederick III, which George helped to close. He also succeeded in healing the breach between the Emperor and Sigismund of Tyrol and in re-establishing contacts between Lewis of Bavaria and Albrecht Achilles.[282]

Encouraged by successes in individual cases, George lent his authority to a more comprehensive plan of alignments among the leading princes of the Empire, by which conditions there could be improved and put on a solid basis.[283] The initiator, Martin Mair, attended to George's concerns and assigned to the Emperor the role of mediator in several controversies between the secular and spiritual authorities. George's lively interest in Mair's renewed activities sprang from the desire to have his cause linked with other unsolved problems, such as the feud between Sigismund of Tyrol and Cardinal Cusa, or the competition of Diether of Isenburg and Adolf of Nassau for the See of Mainz. A cumulative deal seemed to offer brighter chances of success than a strict separation of the Hussite cause from the other current issues and its classification as a heresy. The outcome of Mair's explorations was meager, as some princes raised embarrassing objections that could not be smoothed out easily. It was highly unlikely that the Pope would await the outcome of such negotiations, whose anticlerical character could hardly be disguised.

Time, instead of mitigating the tension, worked steadily against George. Letters arriving from Breslau at short intervals kept alive the flame. More fuel was added to it by complaints from some Catholic nobles who had boycotted the Brno assembly and thus incurred the King's wrath. Punitive expeditions against them were promptly reported to Rome as evidences of George's truculence, and produced unfavorable effects there.

The papal diplomats working at various princely courts had special reasons for suspicions and vigilance. Marini's preliminary explorations in Venice had no immediate effect, but he continued to pursue his designs, not paying too much attention to the internal developments in Bohemia or its vicinity. At the time of the agitation over Fantino's imprisonment, he abstained from travel and redrafted his memorandum, adding new articles to the original text.[284] Even after the revision, the project remained rather hazy, as Marini probably thought it advisable not to be precise pending further negotiations. The version available to modern scholars is not arranged methodically.[285] It cannot be excluded that suggestions received at the different courts were inserted into the original draft or that passages found objectionable by the statesmen consulted, were either modified or left out.

The cardinal point of the project with which Marini left Prague late in 1462 was the Turkish menace and its international significance. Nothing but a close and effective cooperation of the Christian rulers could stop and ultimately roll back the aggressive enemy, under whose tyranny had successively passed many flourishing areas of Africa and Asia, and lately the Greek Empire. Instead of analyzing the causes of the ineffective countermeasures in the past, the document opened with passionate laments and general charges of indolence. Thus the relevant passage sounded more like a sermon to propagate a crusade than a preamble to a diplomatic document. In the merciless criticism of the past, there was no harsh reference to the established authorities in Christendom, the Papacy, the Empire, and the general council, but the silence also had its meaning, as the reader could guess what roles would be assigned to those traditional institutions in the future.

The burden of defense was to be borne by the rulers of the countries that had not fallen under the Infidel's yoke. Marini did not mechanically include in his calculations all sovereign states of Europe—England, Scotland, the Scandinavian nations, and Muscovy were not considered at all, and some other countries were mentioned only in general terms. He did not intend to subordinate them to either the papal or the imperial supremacy, but envisioned a league in which the sovereign members would enjoy equal rights and accept equal duties. This was, undoubtedly, a momentous departure from the traditional concepts of unity, achieved in spiritual matters by the Papacy, and in worldly affairs by the Empire.

As the projected organization could become unwieldy and even paralyzed by potential divergences of particular interests, Marini recommended a subdivision of the participants into "nations," following in this matter the practices at general councils, universities, and other international bodies. The "nations" were to be grouped as follows: France with the adjacent kingdoms and principalities; Germany (in which Bohemia, Hungary and Poland were tacitly included); and Venice with other Italian principalities and cities. He left it to the King of Castile and other princes in the Iberian peninsula to decide for or against membership in the league.

As the danger of another Turkish onslaught was imminent, Marini insisted that no time be lost in preparatory negotiations. He recommended that all rulers concerned send their representatives to a congress in Basel in the German nation, which should open not later than February, 1464.

The delegates should not return home after the constitution of the league but remain in Basel for five years and function as an assembly (parlement) of the league. One delegate should be elected as the "presiding father." Marini's reference to a special council within the assembly is not clear enough to permit more than speculation. Did he think of a steering committee while the assembly would deliberate, or of a small circle consisting of the delegates from the leading countries and associated with the president? After five years, the assembly was to move to France and thereafter to Italy. The rotation was to prevent an identification with any one ruler or any one people.

The assembly was designed to function as an international institution. A special coat of arms and seal were to distinguish it from other powers. It should administer its own treasury and public archives with the help of its staff. The leading officers were to be chosen from the "nation" in which the assembly would reside in a given quinquennium to avoid conflicts with local laws.

Few people among George's advisers were so keenly aware of the diversity of the legal systems in Europe as was the widely traveled Marini. Anticipating difficulties from that source, Marini recommended that a "general consistory" be established in the headquarters of the assembly from which "like from the fountain of justice the streams would flow in all directions." He left it to the assembly to determine the number and qualifications of the members of the "consistory." Its president and the assessors were to be obliged to conduct the proceedings simply and plainly, without the practices prevailing in the existing courts. To the "consistory" should be submitted quarrels and dissensions among the member countries, to be settled there according to the statutes and norms set up by the assembly.

As the supreme organ of the league, the assembly was assigned far-reaching powers. Not individual countries or "nations," but only the assembly would have the right to admit new members into the league. Guided by the principal concern, the consolidation of the Christian orbit for a successful campaign against the Turks, Marini devised ways and means by which the harmony and peace once established could be perpetuated. The members were expected to renounce solemnly any hostile designs against each other, and refuse to support initiators of private feuds or grant shelter to troublemakers from other countries. In case of an act of aggression by a nonmember of a nation adhering to the league, the assembly was expected to take immediate action and dispatch delegates to the aggressor's capital to bring about cessation of hostilities; should he spurn mediation, the assembly would resort to arms. If a war opened somewhere among nonmember rulers, it would be again the assembly's duty to attempt pacification, first by a diplomatic intervention, and in case of its failure, by an expedition against the aggressor or the power sabotaging negotiations.

Since the primary purpose of the league was the struggle with the Turks, Marini imposed on the assembly the full responsibility for its preparation and conduct. It was to be its duty to fix either unanimously or by the majority its beginning, assign the roles to the ground and naval forces, appoint commanders, decide on weapons, and designate the place at which the armed contingents would assemble. He also suggested that the assembly control the supplies, establish hospitals, introduce common currency, and transfer conquered territories in accordance with the general interests of Christendom. The struggle was to go on to its ultimate goal, the expulsion of the Infidels from Christian territories.

The funds of the league were to be made out of contributions by the member countries. One source of income was traditional, the tithes to be granted by the clergy, both secular and regular. The sums thus collected were to be augmented by contributions by the rulers and their lay subjects, amounting to an income for three days yearly.

Marini realized, either when he himself contemplated his scheme or when he dealt with some of its prospective sponsors, that the Papacy could not be left entirely out of consideration. It was universally recognized that the right to launch a crusade belonged to the spiritual father of the Christian family, and that financial contributions from the clergy should be sanctioned by him. A lengthy article concerning the relations between the assembly and the Holy See was included in Marini's scheme. Its position toward the end indicates that it was inserted into the original draft at some later occasion, perhaps when some of the courts approached found inopportune the total silence on the part of both the Empire and the Papacy. The relevant article presupposed a diplomatic mission from the assembly to the papal court to reach a perfect agreement on the tithes and on the papal mediation in conflicts between the spiritual princes and nations not adhering to the league. To this passage was attached a stipulation that the Pope call the Italian princes and cities to a congress and urge them to assemble a fleet, since they were closer to the Turkish-dominated area than other nations.

Marini did not entertain excessive hopes for his scheme, but reckoned with a long period of the preparations and of the warfare. He wanted to protect the league against decline and defections. Therefore, he concluded his draft with an article regulating succession to the throne in the member countries. The heir or the pretender was obliged to accede to the covenant or else his rights would not be recognized by the member nations.

With hardly more than a preliminary sketch, Marini left Prague late in 1462 for Burgundy and France. Neither he nor the Burgundians left at their court a record of the negotiations. Co-ordination of the roles and interests of Burgundy and France would have been among the knottiest problems in Marini's scheme, had it been accepted by the friendly courts, as a concrete project. Marini did not devise a solution which both rivals would find acceptable, but turned away from the embarrassing point and simply assigned the leading position in the French "nation" to France. In the absence of contemporary evidence, it can only be assumed that Duke Philip was not acquainted with all details, but was informed of it only in general terms so that he would not be driven into opposition if by-passed.

The French were reserved in talking about Marini's project, but as he spent more time there than in Burgundy and disclosed to them some delicate matters, the papal diplomats and their secular colleagues picked up bits of information and reported them to their masters. Marini was suspected of campaigning in France against the Pope and of attempting to secure the King's interest in a coalition of princes who advocated both church reforms and defense of the faith. This may have been echoes of Marini's hints that the eastern monarchs would support the French bid for primacy in the league if Louis XI took the matter seriously. The King was noncommittal in his answers, but apparently so graciously disposed to the scheme that Marini left Paris convinced of success.

His destination was not Prague but Venice. He reached it in the early part of March, 1463, and found the atmosphere less congenial than in August, 1462. The message from France that the King would not have hesitated to join with the King of Bohemia and other princes in the proposed league if Marini had possessed full powers intensified instead of dispelling the Senate's distrust. In their reply to Louis XI of March 17, 1463, the Venetians did not belittle the need for the concentration of forces, but pointed out that the invasion of Hungary was imminent.[286] The reigning doge, Christoforo Moro, was of the opinion that effective help from Bohemia and Poland should be sent to Matthias at once instead of building up reserves for the chimeric league.

Reports that had reached Rome concerning Marini's activities were not too precise or trustworthy, but they prompted Pius II to a counter-offensive. About the middle of May a papal emissary to Burgundy and France left Rome and a letter to Duke Philip followed after several weeks.[287] But the center of gravity was in Venice, in view of both its geographical position and its direct contacts with the Hungarian court. No less a figure than Cardinal Bessarion journeyed there in July, 1463, to dissuade the Republic from diplomatic actions not co-ordinated with papal policy.[288] Other papal envoys, Dominico de Torcello and Rudolf of Rüdesheim, used their talents in bringing about the reconciliation of Frederick III and Matthias, which George had abandoned after the fruitless attempts in 1460. An agreement was reached on July 19, 1463, and it eased markedly the tension between the two rulers.[289] Less than two months later the papal diplomacy witnessed the signing on September 12 of a treaty between Hungary and Venice.[290]

Pius II took up in earnest the idea of a congress of the Italian states not, of course, to facilitate the formation of a league of secular princes, but to prepare a crusade under his own aegis. More important than dealings with petty princes on the Apennine peninsula was an alliance in which the Pope's partners were to be Burgundy and Venice. Duke Philip reassured the Pontiff that he would send auxiliary troops, as promised at Mantua, not later than May 1, 1464.[291]

Heartened by these diplomatic successes, Pius II declared the crusade on October 22, 1463, and endeavored to bring other princes into the alliance.[292] His legate, Theodore de Lelli, Bishop of Feltre, tried hard to dissuade Louis XI from contacts with George, presenting the latter as a defender of inveterate heresies. Lelli's speeches did not bring about a complete reorientation of French foreign policy.[293] But his mission fitted in with other countermaneuvers which reduced to the minimum the chances of Marini's success. Not even the most enthusiastic supporters of his scheme could entertain a hope that the assembly of Christian princes would open at Basel in February, 1464.

Along with these countermeasures, efforts were made to loosen the ties between George and Frederick III in order to relieve the Pope of any insistence by the Emperor on milder terms for George. Frederick's renunciation of his claims on Hungary reduced the value of George's friendship. The death of Archduke Albrecht VI simplified matters in Austria. The Emperor now felt less dependent on help from Bohemia, and could act more freely when in the middle of March, 1464, George's envoys reached Wiener Neustadt.[294] By choosing Prokop of Rabštejn and Beneš of Veitmil as the negotiators, George underscored the importance of the mission. They ranked very high among the royal advisers and made a good impression in social contacts. They were, however, handicapped, as they were not empowered to announce their master's unconditional submission to the papal authority. Instead, they requested Frederick III to intercede with the Pope that a cardinal legate be sent to Bohemia to restore unity.[295]

Papal legates at the imperial court were invited to join the negotiations and to offer their opinion on the feasibility of an agreement. They responded gladly to Frederick's call and saw the Czech envoys. In talking to them they used a more austere language than did Frederick III and his councillors, maintaining that no purpose would be served by the dispatch of a cardinal legate before George had fulfilled his oath and the other obligations.[296]

Rudolf of Rüdesheim was apparently more interested in the Czech problem than was his Italian colleague. A scion of a noble German family, he earned considerable distinction in the service of the Curia, and in 1461 represented the Pope at the Diet of Mainz. When Pius II decided to call Bessarion back to Rome, the appointment of a new legate became a serious matter. Although Rudolf did not hold a high office at that time, he was selected, most likely for his familiarity with German affairs. Late in July, 1462, Pius II issued credentials for his "angel of peace" and gave him specific instructions on dealing with the unsettled problems.[297] It is not quite clear how long Rudolf stayed in Germany and other parts of Central Europe. Early in November, 1463, Pius II assigned to him as a special duty the dissemination of reports relating to the plight of the Christians enslaved by the Turks, which the Curia received from its sources of information. Another letter issued simultaneously pertained to the conflicts raging incessantly among the German princes.[298] At about the same time Rudolf was promoted to the bishopric of Lavant. As this diocese was situated in the Habsburg patrimony, Rudolf came to be closely attached to Frederick III and gained his confidence.

In private talks concerning George's problems Frederick III modified the attitude of the legates. On his request, Rudolf consented to depart for Rome and lay the matter before the Pontiff. An Austrian envoy, Hans Rohrbacher, accompanied the Czech nobles on their journey home and supplemented their report to George by his account of Frederick's willingness to pursue the mediating policy.

Prokop of Rabštejn loyally performed his duties, and apart from the official conferences, he met with the papal legates and other clerics. Impressions gained from these contacts were gloomier than those gleaned from the public statements. Prokop realized that the King's declaration for the Chalice and Fantino's imprisonment had produced a deep resentment at the papal court, and that his humble submission was the only way to conciliation. In a private letter attached to the official report, Prokop entreated George to bow before the papal supremacy and thus to save his work from ruin.[299]

George apparently took the official reports more seriously than he did Prokop's impassionate appeal. He had a high opinion of Frederick III, and expected a good deal from his intervention in Rome. In the meantime, the envoys in Czech service developed intense activities in an effort to strengthen the ties between Prague and foreign courts. After the premature death of his eldest daughter, Catherine, George believed it advisable to have the relations with his son-in-law bolstered by a written agreement. Negotiations in Buda were not easy, as Matthias was hardened by both the outcome of his invasion of Bosnia and the dip-

lomatic successes scored in 1463. Nevertheless, he not only contracted a
treaty with George, but consented to continuation of Marini's endeavors.
According to some indications, the royal advisers were divided on that
matter; Marini complained later that some Hungarian bishops threatened
him with excommunication.[300]

As Casimir IV was not directly affected by the diplomatic offensive
directed from Rome, Marini gained his permission to speak also on behalf of Poland.[301] He could therefore start on his second journey to
France soon after his return from Buda. To give more prestige to the
mission, George, instead of sending Marini alone, appointed as his personal representative Albrecht Kostka, lord of Postupice, the *voigt* of
Lower Lusatia.[302] The envoys reached Louis XI in the country near Abbéville late in June, 1464. On the last day of that month they were received in a public audience. Lord Kostka explained the purpose of his
journey in a Latin speech. Marini greeted Louis XI in Latin on behaf
of Casimir IV and in French in Matthias' name. In conferences which
opened after the ceremony the King was represented by both the clerics
and laymen and, most likely he received the Czech envoys also in a secret audience. The French prelates were opposed to a treaty with the
Hussite king and pointed to the defects in Kostka's credentials. Negotiations dragged on and were saved from a final rupture by the King's
energetic intervention. Leaving aside the project of the league, Louis XI
decided for a bilateral treaty of friendship. Its text was agreed upon at
Dieppe on July 16, 1464, but the seals were appended four days later
at Rouen.[303] Further discussions concerning the league were put off until the arrival of the French envoys to Prague in November, 1464. Realistic observers could hardly be deceived by the delay, which only veiled
the failure of the Czech mission in that vital point. Among those who
realized that the league of princes would never come into existence was
its originator, Antonio Marini. He left George's service and retired to
Venice to engage in more lucrative pursuits than diplomacy.

George's attempt, with the French and Polish help, to hasten the formation of the league foundered both because of the hesitation of some
courts to join a multilateral alliance and of fears of papal displeasure.
Representatives of Pius II found enough support for their countermaneuvers among the conservative elements in many countries, loathing any
contact with the Hussite king. The latter's diplomat was on the whole
poorly equipped for such widely ramified negotiations, and got little aid
from the representatives of friendly courts. Neither Matthias of Hungary
nor Casimir of Poland was prepared for a closer co-operation than the
permission to Marini to speak at the French court in their names. As this
envoy was known for his anticlerical sentiments, he antagonized many

clerics in high positions and jeopardized his project instead of facilitating its realization.

Bishop Rudolf's intercession on George's behalf at the papal court, as promised to Frederick III, could not be taken seriously even by those who had given the impulse for it. He was not in George's service, and he accepted the delicate assignment only to preserve the Emperor's good will. How could it be expected that a papal diplomat would earnestly espouse George's cause and hinder effectively the campaign aiming at the King's ruin? The Pope's animosity to the latter was no secret, and enough could be heard at the imperial court of the letters from many parts of Europe to Rome, pressing for a decisive act. The Breslau senate was more persistent than the other enemies, fearing that out of deference to Frederick III the Pope might postpone his verdict.[304] Indeed, in the spring of 1464, Pius II had no intention of closing the door to imperial envoys, and late in April, 1464, he calmed the Breslau senate by the appointment of two cardinals for the study of the charges and complaints received from that city.[305] One of them, Nicholas of Cusa, was well known for his dislike of the Hussites, while the other, Beraldo Erolo of Spoleto, was not fully familiar with the causes of the conflict. Thus Cusa's idea and recommendation were to dominate whatever was to be done.

When late in May, 1464, the Archbishop of Crete returned to Rome, the matter hung by a thread. The Pope was anxious to visit the assembled crusaders at their gathering place and prepared for a journey to Ancona. The Breslau agents and their allies in the highest clerical circles did all in their power to obtain a decision before his departure. Cardinal Cusa supported them vigorously, and prevailed on the Pope not to wait any longer for messages from the imperial court but to declare his decision. The concerted efforts of George's foes were crowned with success. Early in June, 1464, the Pope appealed to Silesia's neighbors—King Casimir and the Markgrave of Brandenburg—to aid Breslau in case of attack of it by the Hussite troops. A few days later he took the commander of the Breslau forces under his protection.[306]

In the meantime, the papal legal experts prepared a formal indictment of the recalcitrant king. On June 15, 1464, the Pope held a public consistory attended by numerous clerics and also by the envoys of Louis XI and the Duke of Burgundy. After its solemn opening, the senior advocate of the Curia presented the charges against George, making special reference to a stone statue of George with a gilded chalice in one hand and the sword in the other, erected on Rokycana's order in front of the Týn church. The list of complaints was long indeed, and ended in an appeal to the Pope not to neglect, on account of the preoccupation with the crusade, another no less serious threat to the Church. In his reply, the

Pope recalled significant events which had caused George's estrangement from the Roman Church and rejected the petition for a dispatch to Bohemia of a legate *a latere*. The period of exploration and mediation was over, and the Pope announced his decision to summon George to Rome. The term of one hundred and eighty days was granted to give the sentence wide publicity in countries neighboring on Bohemia. It was to be expected that in his own kingdom, the King would not permit the reading of the bull. It appears very likely that the papal chancellery prepared the text, but that Pius II found no time to attach his seal and signature to the parchment.[307]

Four days after the consistory, he took the Cross at a ceremony in Saint Peter's basilica and then left Rome for the Adriatic coast. The papal party travelled slowly, owing to the Pope's weakness and many mishaps. They reached Ancona on July 18, 1464. Nothing more could be seen in that port and its vicinity than badly organized, undisciplined bands of crusaders from various parts of Europe. Although depressed by the meager effects of his appeals to friendly princes, Pius II did not give up his cherished project and attempted to mobilize other forces. He sent Cusa to Livorno to stir up interest in the crusade on the western coast of the peninsula. That mission was never fulfilled, as the ailing cardinal, having fallen ill, interrupted his journey and died at Todi.

Report of this loss reached the Pope's sickroom in the bishop's palace at Ancona at about the same time as his hopes were lifted by the arrival of the Venetian fleet commanded by the doge. Exhilarated by the thrilling tidings, the Pope asked to be brought to the window so that he could watch the procession of the Venetian galleys. This was his last consolation, for two days later he succumbed to the illness at about equal distance from Rome and from his beloved Siena, thus closing his brilliant career.

ANATHEMA . . .

The new pope, Paul II, a member of the wealthy Venetian family Barbo, was far less versed in political affairs than his predecessor had been, and as before his elevation he had not taken an active part in designing the campaign against George, he was not committed to Pius' policy. The King's position in the opening stage of Paul's pontificate was, therefore, not hopeless. It was of some advantage to him that his most resolute foe, Cardinal Carvajal, did not have the Pontiff's ear at the time of discord over Paul's centralistic policy. A Czech cleric named Thomas, whom Bishop Jošt had sent to Italy in the late summer of 1464, defended George and obtained from the Pope a promise that Pius' citation would not be published pending further investigation.

The King himself did not contribute to an improvement of his chances. Instead of sending personal representatives to Rome to congratulate Paul II, George requested the envoys of Frederick III to speak also in his name. The head of the imperial embassy, John Rohrbacher, took his mission seriously and obtained from the Pope a similar assurance to that given Jošt's agent. Rohrbacher also requested that a cardinal legate be sent to Bohemia, but at this point he met with tough resistance. The cardinals into whose hands the Pope had put George's cause opposed the petition, maintaining that no sincere conversion could be expected from the Hussite king.[308]

The situation was complicated by the activities of the Breslau secretary, Fabian Hanko, who had dwelt in Rome since the spring of 1464. He insisted that a cardinal legate be sent not to Prague for negotiations but to Breslau for a more effective protection of that city against George's designs. The Pope and the leading cardinals were reluctant to designate one from their midst for such a mission. Hanko also soon realized that it would be fruitless to recommend that the Archbishop of Crete be reappointed to his former post in Silesia. He did not press the matter and acquiesced in a compromise solution.[309] In the desire to preserve Frederick's good will, the Pope decided to make the imperial residence the headquarters of future negotiations. Before the end of December, 1464, he instructed Bishop Rudolf of Lavant to go once more to Frederick's court as a special envoy.[310] It was expected that from there the Bishop would establish contacts with both Breslau and Bohemia and explore, in harmony with Frederick III, the prospects of a general settlement.

An intervention from the opposite side jeopardized Rohrbacher's mission no less disturbingly than did Hanko's activities. While he was trying hard to soften the cardinals' resistance to his request for a cardinal legate, one of George's staunchest opponents, Hynek Bítovský of Lichtenburg, arrived in Rome to air his grievances. His feud dated from the time of George's efforts, in 1458, to gain full recognition in Moravia, and was aggravated by Hynek's refusal to abide by the resolutions of the Brno assembly of July, 1463. His defiance, combined with disobedience of some other lords, was regarded as a violation of the provincial laws; several Moravian magnates, including Bishop Tas, joined George in a punitive expedition against Hynek's stronghold, Cornštejn, not far from the borders of Moravia and Austria. Hynek escaped from the besieged castle and reached Rome shortly before Christmas.[311] He immediately got in touch with Hanko and was introduced by him to Cardinal Carvajal. The Bishop of Lavant also lent Hynek his aid and obtained for him an audience with Paul II. The Pope was apparently favorably impressed and resolved that Hynek should be given more than verbal consolation. In this manner a private feud was linked with Breslau and other grievances and given wide circulation as a striking example of George's vindictive policy in relation to his Catholic subjects.

When choosing Bishop Rudolf as his envoy, Paul II was not yet determined to treat George as an incorrigible rebel. Frederick III was once more to be granted an opportunity to bring George to his senses. Not Breslau but the campaign against Hynek Bítovský was selected as the means. Paul II instructed Bishop Rudolf to obtain from George a promise to stop it without delay. The envoy, in fact, needed no prodding, as he had espoused Hynek's cause even before the Pope became interested in it. Strengthened by the Pope's authority, Bishop Rudolf, though busy with the preparation for his journey to Austria, admonished by short letters Bishop Tas of Olomouc and the leading Catholic lords in Bohemia and Moravia to dissociate themselves from the King and withdraw their forces from the Cornštejn expedition.[312]

Assured by the Pope that no drastic action against George was imminent, John Rohrbacher left Rome early in the New Year of 1465, not waiting for Bishop Rudolf's departure. Shortly after his arrival in Wiener Neustadt, Rohrbacher sent a comprehensive account of his mission to Prokop of Rabštejn, recommending that a delegation, with prominent

Utraquists among its members, be sent to the imperial court to confer with the papal envoy whose coming was daily expected.[313] Not to lose time, George followed Rohrbacher's other suggestion and in a letter dispatched by a safe messenger to Rome, he first explained why no personal representative had been sent to Rome in the fall of 1464, and then recapitulated the causes of his conflict with Hynek, explaining it as a purely internal affair with no religious implications.[314]

Lack of direct contacts with Rome hindered George's attempts to ease the tension. Without accurate information concerning the Pope's intentions, the King gave less time to problems of foreign policy than to domestic affairs, feeling that an accord between the two religious parties should precede a diplomatic offensive. To reduce the chasm between the Utraquists and the Catholics, he resorted to methods which had been tried on earlier occasions, though without much success. Early in 1465 he gave impulse to a convocation of clergy and prominent laymen from both sides. An agreement, if it could be reached or at least initiated, would have invalidated objections to religious dualism in Bohemia; hence the matter seemed to be worth trying.

The results were contrary to the King's hopes. In giving initiative to a joint meeting, George took a dangerous step and unwittingly rekindled religious disputes. Given opportunity for reaffirming his adherence to the Chalice, Rokycana spoke vigorously for it and elicited from the opposite side a resolute condemnation of the Hussite faith. The spokesmen of the Catholic clergy, Dean Hilarius of the metropolitan chapter, and his assistant, Václav Křižanovský, a doctor in theology, were soon joined by prominent lords of that communion.

In turn, Zdeněk Kostka and some of his friends seconded Rokycana. After five days of hot disputes, George saw that neither party was willing to yield an inch to facilitate a compromise. On February 11, 1465, the convocation was adjourned and a public discussion of religious controversies was never repeated.[315]

Strangely enough, religious polemics aroused at this juncture less attention in high ecclesiastical circles than the expedition against Hynek Bítovský. Convinced of the righteousness of his cause, George disregarded warnings, and when the spring was somewhat advanced, he moved energetically toward Cornštejn to force its surrender. The castle was well protected by its position above a river and its conquest soon proved too risky. Instead of attempting an open attack, the success of which could not be guaranteed, the commander of the royal troops placed Cornštejn under siege, thus prolonging the campaign. Hynek's sponsors gained time for diplomatic maneuvering, which caused George nothing but embarrassment.

The Pope's decision to obtain favorable terms for the lord of Cornštejn unavoidably complicated Bishop Rudolf's mission. Frederick III, when approached, showed little interest in Hynek's fate and remained cool to requests for an intervention on his behalf. The city of Breslau, disappointed by the Pope's decision to send to the imperial court an envoy of comparatively low rank, instead of appointing a cardinal legate with full powers, jealously followed the shift of emphasis from their grievances to Hynek's affair, and several times requested Bishop Rudolf to visit Silesia at least for a short time.[316] Bishop Tas showed no inclination to subordinate his policy to Rudolf's instructions, and instead of withdrawing his armed units from the camp near Cornštejn, he attempted to dissuade the envoy, and through him the Pope, from furtherance of Hynek's interests.[317]

Mindful of Rohrbacher's friendly hint, George sent to Wiener Neustadt one of his ablest diplomats, Beneš of Veitmil, as soon as he heard of the papal envoy's arrival.[318] Beneš' instructions were simple but rigid. It was his duty to explain to the Emperor and to Bishop Rudolf that both the laws of the country and George's personal honor made impossible a retreat from Cornštejn or any compromise. He was not authorized to broach other problems unless the papal envoy called off his threats to the participation of loyal Catholics in the Cornštejn expedition. As, on the other hand, the legate insisted that he was instructed by the Pontiff to give Hynek priority over other problems, a deadlock was reached which even the Emperor would have found difficult to break.

An unexpected complication destroyed the last chance of an agreement. One day a sealed letter was delivered to Bishop Rudolf by a messenger from Bohemia for transmission to the Emperor.[319] Its contents were shocking, as its originator, Zdeněk of Šternberk, along with thirty-six other noblemen, accused Frederick III of neglect in paying arrears owed by him for their expedition to Austria in the fall of 1462. It was hastily concluded in the court circles that such an affront could not have been made without at least the tacit consent of King George, and there was nobody in the Emperor's entourage to dispel his annoyance. In fact, Zdeněk's relations with the King, since the February religious disputation, grew worse and it seems likely that he chose this time for his daring step so as to spoil the effects of Beneš' mission.

The papal envoy was experienced enough in public affairs to realize that with the parties so firmly entrenched in other positions, his endeavors had no chance of success. Instead of journeying to Breslau, as its senate repeatedly requested, he prepared for a more attractive assignment—visits to German princely courts in the vicinity of Bohemia to deflect them from contacts with George. His long account of the futile attempts to compel respect for the Pope's will ended in the recommendation that sterner measures against the Hussite king be taken promptly.

He advocated a solemn declaration of George as heretic. The ban should be followed by an appeal to George's subjects and allies to sever their ties with him. As the final step, a crusade should be launched against Bohemia to settle the conflict forever.[320]

The Pope's decision in December, 1464, not to send a highranking prelate to Silesia but to give Frederick III another opportunity for mediation reduced temporarily the danger of war. George's implacable foes among both the Breslau aldermen and clergy could not clamorously oppose Bishop Rudolf's activities, but they found it difficult to conceal their disappointment. His travels in southern Germany seemed to be a poor excuse for his reluctance to make a public visit to their city and to win the moderate elements to his side. Disquieted by evasive answers and dilatory proceedings, the radical leaders of Breslau poured out their hearts to the Archbishop of Crete, then residing at the royal court in Buda, in the hope that he would transmit the message to Rome. They openly accused their own bishop and Tas of Olomouc of complicity with their archenemy, the King.[321]

Bishop Jošt, indeed, became vulnerable to an attack from the radical wing. Comforted by reports brought by his diplomatic agent from Rome, he did not regard George's cause as lost and was ready to use his contacts for further negotiations. In this policy he was supported by moderate elements among the city dwellers and among the princes of Silesia, who wanted to remain faithful to George as their liege lord. Jošt was impervious to arguments and protests emanating from the radical circles, so that a strong reprimand either directly from Rome or through Bishop Rudolf seemed to be the only means of bringing about his reorientation.

In April, 1465, Jošt added one more item to the list of grievances. On Maundy Thursday he left Breslau and betook himself most likely to his residence at Nisa. It was believed among the radicals that he had more in mind than a retreat from the busy capital to a less troubled region. They feared that Jošt would journey to Prague and resume his attempts at mediation. Not knowing enough of his intentions, they wrote at once to the papal envoy, repeating their earlier complaints.[322] Admitting the possibility that Jošt would not stay in Prague but proceed from there to Wiener Neustadt to get in touch with Frederick III and Bishop Rudolf, they warned against his activities, maintaining that under no circumstances could they accept Jošt as their spokesman. He was in their eyes compromised by friendly contacts with George, and as he regarded their feud with the King as a political rebellion, he obscured the religious issues standing between fervent Catholics and the Hussite king.

The Breslau radicals were correct in assuming that Jošt would soon appear in Prague, but otherwise their fears proved exaggerated. Soon after his arrival in Bohemia, Jošt became involved in internal affairs of that country and did not accomplish anything worth reporting either to Frederick III or to the papal envoy. Jošt found that the Hussite leaders were alarmed by the reopening of religious polemics which the King had unwittingly started by the February convocation. Aggressive sermons preached after its failure by Václav Křižanovský caused much displeasure in the highest circles, including Queen Johanna. As George was averse to harsh means, there seemed to be no better way of silencing the fiery preacher than Jošt's personal intervention.

Křižanovský's sermons and the attitude of the metropolitan chapter and some Catholic lords elicited complaints from the Utraquist leaders. Jošt was not prepared to throw his prestige on the scale or use pressure in enforcing restraint. The Prague canons were not under his jurisdiction, and it could be expected that if treated harshly they would turn to Rome for protection. Jošt practiced prudence in making social contacts. He was not seen too often at the royal court but he undoubtedly held many sessions with the clerics and laymen of his faith to inform himself as to the cause of the mounting tension in Bohemia.

In their conversations, one topic was probably often mentioned. The Catholic nobles viewed with distrust the favors bestowed by the King on the members of his party. Guided by the desire to strengthen his position, George had filled several vacancies by the appointment of resolute Utraquists and made all kinds of grants to individuals known for their fervent attachment to the Hussite cause. Jošt decided to call the growing resentment to the King's attention, but instead of approaching him directly, he compiled a statement in Czech and addressed it to Queen Johanna.[323] Some other documents from the same time indicate that George was suspected among the Catholics of attempts to reduce his dependence upon the mighty lords and to establish a strong personal regime. Efforts to reduce the power of the aristocracy would have been resented even if initiated by a ruler of royal blood. In George's case they were more irritating, as both he and the Queen had risen to the royal dignity from the aristocratic ranks, and it was presumably their duty to safeguard the privileges of that class. Their search for family contacts with the ruling houses in Germany was also resented. Each agreement on the betrothal or marriage of one of their children to a person of princely rank was suspected as being a steppingstone to the establishment of a hereditary monarchy. As a Catholic prelate and scion of the leading aristocratic family, Jošt was susceptible to the charges and rumors concerning the royal couple that he heard in meetings with his equals.

Records of the spring of 1465 are so scanty that it is impossible to find out how effective were Jošt's contacts with the King or the Queen. While mixing with Catholic nobles, he discovered the incipient opposition to George and his regime, but instead of counteracting it, he moved himself in that direction. As he neither went to Wiener Neustadt nor returned to his diocese, he widened the circle of his Czech friends and became increasingly involved in their political activities. His usefulness as a mediator in Bohemia and Silesia decreased rapidly, and before the end of the summer of 1465 he could no longer be counted among the King's partisans but rather among his opponents.

In the spring and early summer of 1465 there existed little coordination between the centers of opposition, so that George did not see any serious reason for effective countermeasures. He regarded as his foremost task the preservation of peace on the home front against the Breslau machinations as well as any other challenge to his authority. As he felt protected against a charge of persistent disobedience by his March letter to Paul II,[324] he insisted that the Cornštejn expedition be carried on to its bitter end. The commander of the castle's garrison realized after several weeks of siege that since no replenishment of the dwindling reserves of food and amunition could be expected, he must surrender. He therefore capitulated on June 9, 1465.

If the campaign had been conducted under more favorable circumstances, the surrender would have closed it without too much publicity or ominous repercussions. Hynek Bítovský did not belong to any influential faction and even those lords who were veering away from the King were too cautious to link their cause with an outlaw. Bishop Tas's reluctance to heed the papal envoy's admonition indicated the prevailing opinion more accurately than any other barometer.

As Paul II was far less familiar with conditions north of the Alps than his predecessor had been, he paid little attention to the concrete facts on which Bishop Tas based his conduct in that matter. Once he had taken a firm position in Hynek's behalf, he was not responsive to suggestions of a compromise and insisted that George's expedition be liquidated. He did not reply to George's explanatory letter, but wrote on May 13, 1465, to the Catholic lords in a last attempt to drive a wedge between them and their Utraquist partners in the Cornštejn expedition.[325] It was of little importance whether the papal missive reached George's kingdom before or after the surrender of Cornštejn: Hynek's material ruin was not averted and he was for the time being unable to return to his homeland.

George's refusal to refrain from drastic measures against Hynek strengthened the position of his foes at the Curia. The reasons for the Cornštejn expedition were not analyzed and a local incident was so inflated that the papal authority seemed to be at stake. When confronted with a choice between meek submission to the Pope's order and protec-

tion of his sovereign rights, George decided for the latter, caring little
for the eventual consequences.

His position at that juncture was rather awkward, as his connection
with Frederick III was temporarily blocked. Bishop Rudolf, and, after
his departure, some anti-Czech courtiers, fanned the Emperor's indignation. Knowing how deeply he was hurt by the request for payment of
the arrears, George's foes kept harping on that subject as if the King
and not Zdeněk of Šternberk had reopened the painful story.[326] Frederick III never liked to be reminded of the dismal periods when he had
depended on help from other countries; when he felt safe again and
could rely on his own resources, such recollections were humbling and
irritating. In 1465, he faced no troubles in his lands and risked nothing
when he assumed aloofness in relation to his former ally.

Reports coming to Rome from Wiener Neustadt indicated that the
Emperor would not resent it too much if the Pope passed from correspondence, warnings, and admonitions to an energetic action. No further
evidence of George's recalcitrance was needed to set the complicated
machinery in motion. On June 28, 1465, Paul II held a public consistory,
attended by all the cardinals, numerous bishops, ambassadors of the
Kings of Aragon and Cyprus, and an envoy from Savoy. In that solemn
gathering the Pope bade Cardinals Bessarion, Carvajal, and Berardo Erolo
of Spoleto to carry out the citation sanctioned almost a year ago by Pius
II and left in abeyance after his death. Carvajal was instructed to write
to Frederick III, to all the electors, and to the kings of Hungary, Poland,
and Denmark, requesting them to abstain from any contact with the king
of Bohemia. Letters were to be sent also to Breslau, to the prelates and
Catholic lords in Bohemia, and to the Bishop of Lavant, informing them
of the Pope's resolute step.[327]

The array of documents mentioned by the Pope in the consistory was
formidable, and they were undoubtedly prepared for execution without
too much delay. In addition to all the measures concerning the Hussite
king personally, Paul II formally confirmed Pius's bull of March 29, 1463,
and took the city of Breslau under his protection.[328] In doing so he indicated clearly his intention not to keep religion and politics apart but
to interfere actively in the internal affairs of the kingdom. To increase
George's worries, Paul II sent a breve to Markgrave Albrecht Achilles,
urging him to annul the bethrothal of Princess Ursula to George's second
son Henry.[329] Although presented in stern words, the Pope's request remained unheeded both at that time and early in 1467, when it was repeated.

The three cardinals worked quickly despite the advanced season, and
issued, on August 2, 1465, a lengthy document in which they reviewed
the earlier stages of George's conflict with the Papacy, and enumerated

the instances of his refractory conduct in the first year of Paul's pontificate. A reference was made to the Cornštejn expedition and to the appointment of resolute Utraquists to public offices. George was expressly accused of a relapse into heresies and summoned before the papal court. A period of one hundred and eighty days was granted him to prepare for the journey and to complete it.[330]

The citation, signed by the three cardinals, was followed by a papal bull, issued on August 6, 1465, and addressed to the Bishop of Lavant.[331] He was instructed not to negotiate but to proceed against George with the utmost severity. The Pope directed the legate's attention to both the King and his allies, especially those who had participated in the hostile designs against the city of Breslau and against Hynek Bítovský. He instructed him also to assist those Catholics who intended to defect from the King, and to rescind any agreements or obligations into which they had entered. To isolate George and coerce him into submission, the legate was asked to work among the princes of the Empire and promise to anyone willing to take up arms against the King the same papal favors as had been granted to the crusaders operating against the Turks or against the Moslems in the Holy Land.

There is no evidence that in the summer of 1465 George had a trusted man in Rome who could at least inform him of the changing mood of the Pope and of the successive steps being taken against him. His former ally, Zdeněk of Šternberk, was more vigilant, and had employed the services of a Czech Premonstratensian, Eliáš, dwelling at that time in Rome. Zdeněk received news from Rome at an earlier date than the King himself, so that he saw which way the wind was blowing and oriented his policy accordingly.[332]

While it is likely that George was not fully aware of the growing influence of his adversaries with Paul II, he sensed intuitively the increased oscillation in the Czech circles and sharpened his vigilance. A man of his cunning and shrewdness could not have failed to notice the changes in personal relationships, no matter how carefully they were masked. His efforts to reduce his dependence on Zdeněk of Šternberk and other members of his group were not motivated by unwarranted suspicions, but by an unmistakable evidence of their attitude. Replacements of unreliable advisers by more loyal men either from the Hussite party or from the ranks of the lesser nobility only added fuel to the flame and were given to the world as examples of religious intolerance. In this uneasy atmosphere, local episodes like the Cornštejn expedition grew into monstrous proportions and threw into the shade the cardinal points on which depended peace in the country and the welfare of its people. Bishop Tas soberly assessed its weight when, in the spring of 1465, he warned the papal envoy against unreserved endorsement of Hynek's grievances and pointed out how ridiculous it would be to begin the tremendous task of conciliation from that small castle.[333]

The lords of the Šternberk circle realized that individual attempts at resistance had no chance of success and late in the spring and in the summer of 1465 spent several weeks in conferences. Their meetings could not remain a secret, as George had many allies outside his own party. In the middle of August, probably after some advance information concerning the Pope's steps reached him, George decided to call the general Diet of the kingdom.[334] Between its announcement and opening the lords intensified their activities and prepared a list of demands. It was presented in the first session of the Diet on behalf of Bishop Jošt, his brother John of Rožmberk, Zdeněk of Šternberk, and their associates.[335] Although carefully worded, it amounted to a declaration of hostility to the King's policy. George reacted impulsively and gave a detailed answer, discussing it point by point and missing no opportunity to remind the Diet of his untiring efforts to enhance the prestige of the kingdom.[336] The authors of the accusations failed in enlisting support for their position, and the Diet by an overwhelming majority professed loyalty to the King.

With the exception of one article mentioning Rokycana and some priests as instigators of the disputes, religious differences were not broached by the Catholic faction so that the political issues dominated the conflict in its initial stage. The most important among them was the changing relationship between the sovereign and the lords. George was accused of autocratic leanings and of a desire to lessen the dependence of his family on the lords by aiming at the establishment of a hereditary monarchy. The lords complained that they were not consulted in important matters and that the King discussed public affairs only with his favorites. The composition of the royal council was an age-old problem and the grievances expressed in 1465 were identical with the charges that had been leveled by the Czech magnates against King Wenceslas IV prior to the Hussite movement. The lords reminded George of his solemn pledge not to curtail the rights and privileges of the estates and urged him, in the concluding paragraph, rather to enlarge than diminish the freedoms of the realm.

Several articles referred to concrete points that emerged from the specific atmosphere of the time. The lords warned the King not to hire military brotherhoods operating lawlessly in various parts of Central Europe for an expedition against Breslau. They insisted that no general tax be imposed on the inhabitants of the kingdom, as such a request by King Ladislav had been granted only to facilitate payment of accumulated debts and should not be repeated arbitrarily. Other articles related to the participation of the lords in military expeditions outside the national boundary, excessive claims of the royal chamber on devolutions, depreciation of currency, and other problems of that kind. In this manner the incipient rebellion was cloaked with seemingly fair and justifiable exposure of defects in the public administration.

The King, in turn, resolutely defended his policy, pointing out his fairness in selecting his councillors. He refuted charges that the hereditary principle was one of his objectives. Not without pride he listed the benefits reaped by the kingdom during his governorship and reign. He explained the problems from his own angle to show that the lords' grievances were ill-founded. He gave a good deal of attention to the diplomatic gains, mentioning specifically his friendly contacts with the Emperor, which had resulted in significant concessions and pledges beneficial to the Crown of Bohemia. It was George's conviction that under him Bohemia enjoyed more freedom from foreign interference than it had possessed since the reign of Charles IV.

George's reference to Charles IV, whose name symbolized peace, security, and prosperity, was not a display of vainglory but an indication of his thoughtful analysis of the perpetual problems of Bohemia. In a historical perspective, the reign of the "Father of the Country" appeared to have been the last period of undisturbed relations between the sovereign and his subjects as well as of unprecedented prestige in relations to other powers. Nothing could be more ambitious than to emulate Charles IV, both in domestic affairs and in contacts abroad, and George, indeed, followed that guiding star with remarkable success. There existed, however, obstacles that proved to be more formidable than George was willing to admit. While Charles had been able to maintain smooth and friendly relations with the Papacy, George in this regard faced perplexing complications. He was aware of them, but he was not seriously troubled by them as long as he was assured of the loyalty of his subjects. Breslau was a thorny problem, but even a populous and wealthy city, if left to its own resources, could not defy its sovereign indefinitely.

Thereafter attention must be given to George's optimistic disposition, when reasons are sought for the course of his policy in the fall of 1465. As on many previous occasions, he was inclined to view his position with more confidence than was warranted by the grim realities. The emergence of an organized aristocratic opposition was a shock, but George soon recovered from it and was comforted by his victory in the Diet. Only a handful of Catholic lords dared to endorse the list of grievances, whereas other members of the first Estate, Utraquist and Catholic alike, joined with the lesser nobility and the royal boroughs in the manifestation of loyal sentiments.[337] The King closed the Diet with a sense of success and indulged in the hope that the rebel faction would lose importance and dissolve.

Zdeněk of Šternberk and his associates upset the king's calculation.

They retreated tactically, but soon thereafter they acted with more zest than before to recover from the setback suffered in the first round. Contacts were resumed and widened with some hitherto noncommitted lords, who now joined Zdeněk's circle. A more impressive document than the original list of grievances was compiled in the castle of Zelená Hora and was signed on November 28, 1465, by sixteen magnates, mostly from southern and southwestern Bohemia, a predominantly Catholic region.[338] An organization known henceforth as the League of Zelená Hora (Green Mountain) came into being to threaten George from the flank.

Bishop Jošt, whose name headed the list, and other members of the League, were agreed that matters pertaining to religion should be left out of their charter. The impression was to be created among neutral elements that the lords rose to uphold the traditional liberties against royal usurpation and to protect all classes against hardships imposed on them arbitrarily by the King. Charges leveled against George in the September Diet were repeated, and some new points were inserted into the charter. The lords pledged their solidarity with one another for five years, and invited other landowners to join the League. An appeal was addressed to the King not to exact from the nobility public services exceeding the current norms.

There was not in the lords' charter even a passing reference to the Breslau imbroglio. George's conflict with the Papacy was also not mentioned, as if a report of it had never come to either Jošt's or Zdeněk's attention. Silence on these points could not be regarded as a mere omission. It indicated that the leaders of the League were not yet ready to burn their bridges and openly join other hostile elements. From George's side, an attempt was made to avert the rift. According to some indirect evidence, Bishop Tas visited Zelená Hora, not with an intention to join the League, but rather to exercise a moderating influence upon it.[339]

Although ostensibly motivated by internal problems, the lords' opposition, along with other unsettled problems, added to George's worries. News from Rome concerning the citation reached Prague and the King realized that energetic steps must be taken to counteract the papal offensive. In former times, Frederick III would have been the first to whom he would turn for good offices. After the estrangement, caused in the spring by Zdeněk's haughty letter,[340] the King could not expect much from that quarter. In this matter, too, Zdeněk proved to be more agile than George; he cleared himself of all suspicion and ingratiated himself with the Emperor. Zdeněk's visit to Frederick's court gave rise to wild rumors, which sooner or later were bound to come to George's notice. Even when taking them with a grain of salt, the King could not condone the undercover contacts of his subjects with foreign rulers. In this case he was more susceptible, because Zdeněk had first poisoned the atmosphere and then turned the Emperor's indignation to his profit.

With Frederick III sulky, George moved in other directions, first to Hungary and then to Bavaria. He hoped that with the help of their rulers he would be able to communicate with Rome, notwithstanding the citation. It was concluded in court circles that a new approach was to be attempted instead of merely repeating the demands formulated in 1462. Ideas and proposals transmitted to Hungary were not identical with those destined for Lewis of Bavaria, as the Bavarian help was to serve other purposes than Matthias' expected intervention.

The intermediaries who acted between George and Matthias were two prelates, Tas of Olomouc and John Vitéz, the Archbishop of Esztergom and the primate of Hungary. As Matthias was occupied with preparations for an anti-Turkish drive in Bosnia, correspondence relating to Bohemia was concentrated in the Archbishop's hands. He met with Tas in Trnava and listened attentively to his report of the Prague developments. When the conversation turned from the recent events to the conditions under which mediation between the Pope and the King should be attempted, Tas neither repeated the request for a sanction of the Compacts nor did he mention the name of Rokycana in this connection. The Hungarian mediators were given to understand that George and the Utraquist leaders would acquiesce in an appointment of a candidate more acceptable to the Holy See. A vague reference to a cleric born either in Bohemia or Moravia admits the assumption that Tas's promotion would have been regarded in Prague as the best way out of the blind alley. A partial restitution of church property was hinted in general terms to make the offer more attractive.[341] When informed of the Trnava conference, Matthias showed no interest in the mission which George wanted to confide to him. Instead of helping, the Hungarian king, in fact, passed into the enemy camp. In a confidential letter to Paul II, dated October 2, 1465, he promised the Pope his help in any military expedition, whether it be against the Czechs or the Turks.[342] His offer forestalled the events, as the Pope at that juncture did not have a detailed plan for a punitive expedition and wanted to get moral support from friendly courts for disciplinary measures against the king of Bohemia. Shaken in his attitude partly by the reports from Rome and partly by Matthias' reaction, Archbishop Vitéz did not exert himself to alleviate George's plight and simply sent to Carvajal a report of his Trnava talks with Tas.[343] In this manner Hungary was lost as a potential ally and soon passed openly to the enemy side.

The Duke of Bavaria was approached with a more concrete proposal. George and his councillors realized that it would be hazardous simply to ignore the citation of the three cardinals, as none of the Prague courtiers possessed adequate training in canon law or sufficient experience in dealings with the Curia. As it would have been futile to expect help from anyone obeying the "Upper Consistory," it seemed to be necessary to invite an expert from abroad. Duke Lewis was responsive to inquiries from a befriended court and released Martin Mair temporarily from his service, so that he could advise George on the steps to be taken to avoid a charge of disobedience. The learned jurist compiled a letter to Paul II explaining in legal terms why George found it impossible to heed the summons to Rome.[344] Instead, a conference was suggested either in Bohemia or not far from its border, with several cardinals and envoys of Christian rulers as principal members. To such a representative body George was prepared to give an account of his reign for its evaluation and final decision. Letters of the same tenor as that to Rome were sent to the Emperor, to the king of France, to Albrecht Achilles, to William of Saxony, and to other princes and imperial cities whose good will George was anxious to preserve.[345]

Apart from the centers with which Prague had a direct connection, there existed in Western Europe numerous courts to which a messenger was seldom dispatched. No effective help could be expected from them, as they were either too remote or prejudiced against Hussitism. Feeling that they should not be left entirely out of consideration, George received sympathetically the offer of his brother-in-law to travel abroad. The journey on which Lev of Rožmitál set out late in November, 1465, was not planned as a diplomatic mission and apparently no concrete tasks were imposed on the Queen's brother. It was expected that he would make social contacts and observations, and then report his findings.

Accompanied by a retinue of some forty persons, Lord Lev made his first stop at the residence of Markgrave Albrecht Achilles at Ansbach and from there he proceeded to more distant cities. He visited the court of Philip the Good at Brussels, crossed from Calais to England and was entertained by Edward IV at Westminster. After his return to the Continent he traveled to the court of Duke Francis II of Brittany and from there to Angers, the residence of René of Anjou. It was not necessary to go to Paris, as Louis XI could be reached at his hunting lodge near Tours.

Lord Lev's travels in southern France and south of the Pyrenees were hazardous and fatiguing. He visited several princely courts and places of interest in Castile, Portugal, and Aragon. The friendliest reception accorded him in those countries was at the Portuguese court. He carried with him letters for King Alfonso V written by Eleonore, the King's sister and wife of Frederick III. Little could be accomplished in the Iberian Peninsula that could bring profit to Bohemia, so that both Lord Lev and his companions had ample time to observe the life and dress of the people, inspect relics and historical monuments, jousting and games. A side trip to Santiago de Compostella and Finisterre afforded them a thrilling experience. When the party reached the plains of northern Italy through southern France and the high mountains, involvements in the current affairs were hard to avoid. Both Milan and Venice had a place in George's calculations and even a mere observation of the trends of public life there was of some value. The audience with Frederick III was formal and rather disappointing, showing the effects of the Emperor's estrangement from George in the spring of 1465.

Two members of Lord Lev's retinue wrote accounts of his travels and impressions but none of them hinted at political negotiations.[346] It was probably deemed advisable to tone down the political implications of the journey so that it would not give rise to suspicions of countermeasures.

A question arises why a person of such a distinction as the Queen's brother was not used for a mission to the center of pressure, the papal court. His loyalty to George was beyond doubt and his attachment to the Roman Church was likewise firm. No available source sheds light on his decision to travel leisurely at the time when his talents could have been more judiciously invested. It can be surmised that the King drew a lesson from his earlier attempts to use the Czech Catholics as intermediaries, and wanted to avoid another humiliating setback. A less conspicuous figure was selected to go to Rome with a royal letter for the Pope. Known as Jaroslav, he had some experience in diplomacy, as he had accompanied the royal envoy, Albrecht Kostka, on his mission in 1464 to the French court.[347]

Jaroslav belonged to the lesser nobility and nothing was expected of him but the safe delivery of George's letter. The burden of negotiations was taken over by Valentin Bernbeck, a councillor of the Duke of Bavaria. He carried with him to Rome an elaborate proposal for a settlement of all outstanding issues. It was prepared, most likely, by Martin Mair after consultation with George and his most trusted advisers, and it was much bolder in its principal points than the scheme on which Bishop Tas and Archbishop Vitéz had agreed at Trnava.[348]

No record has been preserved of the conferences preceding Bernbeck's appointment as envoy. It is therefore impossible to analyze in detail the instructions given to him orally and in writing. It can be assumed, however, that Lewis of Bavaria in general accepted the suggestions made by the Prague court, but added to them his own recommendations to ward off flat rejection of his overture by the Curia. Bernbeck was apparently authorized to go beyond the limits observed heretofore and to hint at George's willingness to return, with his family, into the fold of the Church. Personal submission to the papal authority was offered as a guarantee that the Utraquist party would gradually be amalgamated with the body of true believers. Such questions as an express sanction of the Compacts were passed over in silence. More attention was given to problems of church administration, and in this connection one of George's sons was mentioned as a candidate for the archiepiscopal dignity. To make such a bold idea more acceptable, it was suggested that the papal court send to Bohemia a high-ranking cleric accompanied by an inquisitor to investigate and suppress views and practices exceeding the Compacts. Once established in the highest position, the archbishop would have full jurisdiction in spiritual matters and priests approved by him would have freedom to preach the word of God.

Those who talked with Mair probably had in mind George's eldest son Victorin as the candidate for the archbishopric, and thought of the second son, Henry, as the heir to the throne. In Prague and in the Duke's residence at Landshut, however, broader issues were connected with George's cause. The perplexing problem of the defense of Christendom against the Turks, so often debated in imperial Diets or private conferences of German princes, was included in a startling form. It was suggested that George be granted the title of Byzantine emperor and appointed the supreme head of all Christian forces. This was very likely Mair's idea, but George took it seriously and spoke of a substantial contribution to the crusade, indicating that every fortieth man could be recruited for the contingents from Bohemia.[349]

The chronology of George's steps and of the activities of his opponents is somewhat obscure. Since distances between Rome and various other centers presented serious problems, co-ordination was faulty and often an important decision was doomed to failure because it was made too late and without adequate knowledge of the opposing party's intentions.

Since the summer of 1465, the Pope had felt himself obliged to pursue the line to which the citation pointed. Accordingly, he invested the Bishop of Lavant with full powers and instructed him not to reside at the imperial court but to proceed, at an opportune moment, to the most sensitive spot, the city of Breslau.[350] He arrived there on November 9, 1465, and set out immediately to organize a systematic campaign against George within the kingdom and among the German princes. He opened it by a long letter, dated November 19, 1465, and addressed broadly to both the Catholic inhabitants of Bohemia and their neighbors, naming expressly the Bishop of Misnia.[351] He recapitulated George's conflict with the Holy See and enjoined the Catholic subjects as well as foreign princes to withdraw any support from the recalcitrant king. Couched in stern terms, the letter encouraged their rejection of allegiance and put the Catholic population under the papal protection pending election of a new ruler. Another letter went to Zelená Hora and reached that center of opposition before the lords signed their charter.[352]

The anti-Hussite circles in Breslau and elsewhere were exhilarated by the legate's arrival, believing that the period of waiting for George's recantation was over. Bishop Jošt pledged his co-operation and acted as an intermediary between the legate and the League of Zelená Hora. George reacted quickly but discreetly and instead of moving against Breslau with force, he circulated among the princes of Silesia and other loyal elements copies of his letter to the Pontiff which had been entrusted to Jaroslav.[353] In this manner he hoped to calm their minds and show them that contacts with Rome had not been definitely broken.

Acting upon earlier reports and informed of the emergence of aristocratic opposition at the September Diet, Paul II took a step which was not in strict conformity with the legal precepts and practices. On December 8, 1465, he issued a bull in which he branded George as a notorious heretic, guilty of broken faith and of a relapse into abjured errors.[354] He referred to the recent developments in the lands of Bohemia, and without waiting for expiration of the period of one hundred and eighty days specified in the citation, he immediately released George's subjects from their oaths, obligations, or services and hinted in conclusion at an election of a new king. So severe was the tenor of the bull that no title was prefixed to George's name, which was followed by the ominous phrase, "the son of perdition . . ."

The two envoys, Valentin Bernbeck and Jaroslav, reached Rome apparently just at the moment when the threatening bull was being prepared. According to an oblique evidence, the Bavarian envoy made a good impression on the Pope, who did not brusquely reject the idea of a re-examination of the causes of the conflict. Two days before the publication of the bull, Paul II wrote to Bishop Rudolf requesting his return to Rome for consultation.[355] The sequence of the Pope's steps is obscure and confusing, but it is clear enough that his interest in resuming the negotiations was momentary, and that it gave way to the earlier firmness as soon as he got an inkling of the nature and contents of Bernbeck's instructions.

The Pope deemed it advisable to treat the Bavarian spokesman courteously, but vented his indignation on Jaroslav when the Czech envoy attempted to reach him. As it was impossible to get an audience, Jaroslav waited on the Pope in the sacristy of Saint Peter's basilica and put into his hands the royal missive. The Pope without opening it threw it away. Somebody lifted the letter from the floor and handed it over to Carvajal. No answer came either orally or in writing, and on Christmas Day Jaroslav was, at the Pope's bidding, expelled from the basilica of Santa Maria Maggiore. Boiling with anger, he left Rome at once and it needed no effort to convince George of the futility of further attempts to communicate directly with the papal court.[356]

After Jaroslav's hasty departure, the Bavarian envoy was the only person to further George's cause. Not too well acquainted with the conditions at the papal court and without adequate funds to distribute presents among its personnel, he stood helpless against George's foes. They were joined early in 1466 by an emissary of the Zelená Hora League, Dobrohost of Ronšperk, who supplied more information concerning the aristocratic rebels than could be done by letters. Pressed by persons interested in the observance of conventional practices, Paul II gave on January 12, 1466, his answer to George's letter.[357] It was negative and imperious and focused on one point, the assembly before which George wanted to defend his policy. The Pope rejected the idea and admonished the King gravely to appear before the cardinals appointed as his judges.

The Duke of Bavaria received an answer to his own message on February 6, 1466.[358] The letter to him was long, stern, and negative, and it was probably drafted by the same man who rejected George's idea, Cardinal Carvajal. Point by point, the Pope repudiated the ambitious scheme elaborated at Mair's conferences in Prague and in Landshut. No thought was given to Victorin's promotion to a high office in the Church. The other part of the proposal concerning the crusade was also dismissed as inappropriate. It must have been known at the papal court that George's physical condition was growing worse and doubts were expressed whether he would be able to participate in a military expedition. The Pope regarded as preposterous the idea of compensating George by the grant of an imperial title and pointed out that the older of two nephews of the last Byzantine emperor, Constantin XI, would be in the line of succession, if Constantinople once more came into Christian hands. In conclusion, the Duke was urged to break off contacts with Prague and join the group of princes loyal to the Holy See.

The other resolutions pointed in the same direction as the papal letters. The three cardinals extended the period of one hundred and eighty days, which had expired early in February, for six more months. Toward the end of February, the Pope instructed the legate Rudolf to disregard the earlier command to return, and instead to pursue his activities in Breslau.[359] Further attempts at mediation in Rome were precluded and the center of gravity shifted again to George's domains.

By his continued residence in Breslau, the legate symbolized the Pope's intention to reduce George to submission. To obtain victory, he needed allies willing to move against Prague, with force if necessary. The results of letters from Rome and Breslau were meager and mostly disheartening. Duke Lewis took seriously the papal warning in that he gave up his attempts at mediation. He showed no intention to move beyond that point and adopt a hostile attitude toward his northern neighbor. Princes ruling in the more remote parts of Germany sank into apathy and none of them responded to the legate's appeals for a resolute action against George. It would not have been difficult to take up Matthias' offer as contained in his letter of October 2, 1465,[360] but his zeal at this juncture was more embarrassing than comforting, as the rebels contemplated offering the royal crown not to him but to Casimir IV of Poland.

The trends of public life in Bohemia caused the legate more concern than joy. The League of Zelená Hora was not prepared to rise against the King without an assurance of effective help from abroad. Misled by the grandiloquence of the messages from Rome, they expected financial assistance from the papal treasury. Their request, when transmitted to Cardinal Carvajal, elicited only a caustic comment, which one of his interlocutors, Fabian Hanko, promptly reported to his masters in Breslau.[361] The prelates familiar with the affair missed in the rebels' program reference to religious issues, and regarded the League as a purely political body. Hanko himself fared no better when soliciting a subsidy of twenty-five thousand florins for his city and had to learn the painful lesson that only on rare occasions did money flow freely from Rome to Germany.[362]

Instead of closing its ranks and enlisting new members, the League showed, in the spring of 1466, signs of wavering and indecision. While Zdeněk of Šternberk headed the intransigent group, John of Rožmberk favored a settlement by mediation and severed his ties with the League.[363] George, informed of the failure of the Bavarian mission, did not move against either Breslau or the treacherous lords, and by his authority he also held both the clerics and laymen of his own party under firm control, so that no act of aggression was committed by zealots. Toward the end of April, 1466, the two parties reached an agreement to observe peace until the middle of October. The period was extended before its expiration to last until Saint George's Day (April 23) of 1467.[364] With such local exception as an abortive revolt of the city of Plzeň, peace reigned in Bohemia despite fulminations from Rome and the legate's exhortations.

Nobody at the papal court seriously questioned the legate's fervor, and his failure to enlist support was ascribed more to his rank than to lack of energy. To strengthen his plenipotentiary's hand, the Pope addressed, on May 16, 1466, a breve to Frederick III. Letters of the same content went to the king of Poland, Duke Lewis, Albrecht Achilles and Frederick of Brandenburg, to the Bishops of Bamberg and Regensburg, and to the senate of the free city of Nurnberg. Repeating the customary invectives against George, the Pope endeavored to secure help for the lords' League.[365] Contemporary letters to the dukes of Saxony broached specific grievances, but their purpose was identical—to drive a wedge between George and the princes either indifferent or friendly to him.[366]

It is not very likely that the Saxon princes had known of the papal correspondence when they started with their own scheme. One of them, Albrecht, had personal reason for a friendly intervention, as he was married to George's daughter; his brother Ernest, as well as their uncle William, acted in solidarity. Knowing that George was in control of his kingdom, they contemplated an action that could be initiated in the legate's residence at Breslau and transferred in due time to Rome. After the retreat of Duke Lewis from active participation, the Wettin princes were indeed predestined for a reopening of negotiations.

About the middle of June, 1466, Saxon delegates arrived in Breslau and treated with both the legate and the senate.[367] It can be surmised that the step was taken after preliminary exchanges between the Saxon princely residences and George's court, for the delegates disclosed to both the clerics and the city fathers the idea of mediation on a truly international basis. It was the princes' intention first to secure support from the Emperor and other prominent princes, and with such backing turn to the Pope. In this manner a new action was initiated to break the deadlock caused by the Pope's rejection of the Bavarian proposal.

On Duke Albrecht's recommendation, George took into his service Gregory of Heimburg, whom he might have met at the Cheb congress in February, 1461.[368] Gregory's principal duty was to devise a strategy for a vigorous campaign to be conducted by both conventional diplomatic methods and appeals to the learned circles in Europe. His qualifications for a new assignment were eminent and they were recognized equally by his admirers and staunch opponents. Close association with this brilliant pamphleteer gave George an advantageous position in the war of ideas, but it also had its drawbacks. Princes whom Heimburg had served in his earlier years had a tarnished record at the Curia and he himself had incurred the sentence of excommunication.[369] He showed no interest in craving the Pope's forgiveness or in changing his attitude. Several weeks before accepting the new appointment, Heimburg exchanged letters with Cardinal Carvajal in which a good deal of space was devoted to the papal proceedings against Bohemia.[370] Heimburg's name had formerly been included in the gloomy list of heretics and other enemies of the Holy See, promulgated yearly on Maundy Thursday, and it, indeed, symbolized fight, not peace.[371]

Gregory's foremost duty was to attack the citation [372] and to convince the princes and their advisers of the dangers that might arise to secular authorities from unrestrained clerical interventions. From his conferences with George and the royal councillors emerged a plan based essentially on the same idea as that of Mair's earlier proposals, but destined primarily for the secular circles whose support seemed to be a prerequisite of any diplomatic intervention in Rome.[373] Taking up the thread which had fallen from Mair's hands, Gregory worked out a scheme of general pacification by a congress attended by both papal legates and plenipotentiaries of secular princes. Participation of distinguished laymen was to counterbalance the clerical influences in problems of such magnitude as the citations and fulminations against a legitimate and annointed ruler.

Although the Saxon princes gladly assisted George in the preparation of his action, their prestige was not high enough to assure its success. If Frederick III had persisted in his benevolence, he would have been the first ruler to whom to turn. For some reasons which apparently were carefully weighed in George's intimate circle, the king of Poland was left out of consideration. Instead, Matthias was chosen as the addressee of a long letter prepared by Gregory and signed by George on July 28, 1466, less than a week before the expiration of the extended period of the citation.[374] George could hardly have had any illusions concerning Matthias' firmness and loyalty, especially since the death of Queen Catherine in February 1464, but he thought it wiser to disregard the Hungarian king's wavering and to bring him in as a partner, rather than to leave him out of the far-flung scheme and thus risk his enmity.

In drafting the appeal to Matthias, Gregory observed the proper external forms; but his text often read more like a polemical treatise than a royal letter to another sovereign. It was prefaced by an enumeration of George's deeds which had saved the kingdom of Bohemia from the dangers of anarchy and re-established monarchical order. A fairly long passage was devoted to the citation of the King by the cardinals and its consequences. The author endeavored to bring to light the legal and factual defects of the citation and of the bull of December 8, 1465.[375] As the Prague chancellery intended to give the letter wide publicity, Gregory stressed points that would appeal to other rulers more effectively than could the tactical deviations from the prescribed legal order. It was pointed out that in both the citation and the bull George was denied the royal title and that he would have tacitly admitted its loss if he had obeyed the summons. The bull of December 8, 1465, was represented as a premature step, promulgated before the expiration of the period specified in the citation. By his condemnation and by the appeal to the citizens over the King's head, the Pope tied the cardinals' hands and, in fact, pronounced the verdict. Following Gregory's advice, George demanded that the documents issued against him by the Pope and the cardinals be revoked and that he be granted an opportunity to defend freely his conduct before an assembly of papal representatives and of secular delegates.

There were in George's letter impressive passages, destined not only for Matthias but also for the other august addressees to whom copies were sent simultaneously. Not without pride did the King list the contributions of Bohemia to the protection of Christian territories against the advancing

Turks. He referred expressly to the campaigns fought under Matthias'
father. The Turkish menace was a matter of common interest, and it
seemed appropriate to hint discreetly that time and energy spent in
proceedings against a Christian ruler would be more conveniently invested
in a co-ordinated defense of Christendom against the aggressor.

George's letter gave rise to an extensive correspondence, which was
concentrated in Heimburg's hands. Copies of the letter to Matthias
were sent to Christian courts with which Prague had direct contacts,
along with suggestions as to how letters to the Pope supporting the idea
of a general assembly should be composed. Gregory also approached
the vassal princes in Silesia, imperial cities in the vicinity of Bohemia,
and the municipal councils in loyal boroughs in Silesia and Moravia, to
enlist their active cooperation in his scheme.[376] The immediate effects
of his offensive were meager. Five Silesian princes friendly to their liege
lord wrote to the Pope on September 1, 1466, but they used a milder
and less effective formula than that suggested by Gregory of Heimburg.
Their intervention was flatly rejected by the Curia as inopportune.[377]
Foreign princes were moving even more slowly than the Silesian vassals.
With a few exceptions, they were just as reluctant to join the pleas for
a general assembly as they had been when urged from Rome to move
against Bohemia.

In his Prague conferences, Gregory of Heimburg learned of many
factors relating to the conflict with the Papacy and to the change in the
Emperor's policy. Derived partly from reliable sources, partly from court
gossip, most of these details were derogatory and therefore unfit for
insertion into a letter which was to bear the King's signature and seal.
Heimburg included them in another document which was not intended
for crowned heads only but for wide circles of educated readers, whose
anticlerical sentiments the author hoped to use for the advancement of
the idea of an assembly. Heimburg's writing, often referred to as *Apologia*,
was probably not composed at once but in intervals between his official
correspondence.[378]

The paths originating in Prague and in Rome were not destined to
meet. The Pope and the cardinals showed no intention to consider the
idea of a general assembly. Its championship by Gregory of Heimburg
was irritating and instead of producing the desired effect, it worsened
George's prospects. The Pope was determined not to deal with George's
cause before any other tribunal than his own. This decision was made
early in the summer of 1466, before the high-ranking clerics had exchanged the suffocating atmosphere of the eternal city for the amenities
of their summer resorts.[379]

When the fall season set in, the Pope launched an offensive in two
directions, legal and diplomatic. He gave instructions that legal proceed-

ings be pursued to the extreme point so as not to leave a gap which some princes could use as a justification for their continued contacts with Prague.[380] No lesser figure than Cardinal Carvajal undertook the refutation of George's letter to Matthias. Carvajal's reply was to serve a double purpose: to counteract Heimburg's diplomacy and to prepare the ground for the Pope's final sentence.[381]

The diplomatic offensive was aimed at three targets: the courts of Frederick III, of Poland, and of Hungary. No more was expected at this juncture from the Emperor than his benevolent disposition; a renewal of the former contacts between his residence and Prague would be precluded. Of the two neighbors of Bohemia, the king of Poland was expected to play a more active role than Matthias. As the Pope did not give up the plan of an expedition against the Turks in which a prominent place was assigned to the Hungarians, he did not want to impair the chances of its success by requesting Matthias to participate in the coercive campaign against the Hussite king.

The Polish combination was not quite smooth; but complications there seemed to be less embarrassing than in Hungary. Poland had been engaged in an expensive war with the Teutonic knights, and it was the tradition of the papal diplomacy to support the Order. To improve relations with Casimir IV, the Pope ordered his legate to leave Breslau and to attempt mediation between the belligerents.[382] At a peace conference at Toruń, an agreement was reached which was highly favorable to Poland. Fearing a reversal, Casimir insisted that the treaty be sanctioned by the Pope. The legate suggested that helping against George could be the best compensation for papal favors. Casimir found it difficult to reject the legate's offers and requests and put off his final answer until the next Diet to be held at Piotrków in May 1467. To neutralize rumors and suspicions, Casimir ordered his emissaries to Rome to make a stop in Prague and to assure George of his continued sympathies.[383]

George's foes regarded Casimir IV as the ideal candidate for the throne of Bohemia and thought of Matthias merely as an ally. They probably knew of the role for which Gregory of Heimburg had selected him, but they soon found that Matthias had no intention of assisting George by promoting the idea of an assembly. On the contrary, he lost no time in stirring up trouble. In his complaint to Prague, Matthias pointed to the military brotherhoods, mostly of Czech origin, operating in the borderlands of Moravia and of his kingdom and held George or his captains responsible for the unrest. An exchange of letters between the courts of Prague and Buda, which followed after local clashes between the regular Hungarian forces and the unruly elements, portended an open rift between the former allies and relatives.[384] Turning in another direction, Matthias endeavored to ingratiate himself with George's enemies in Rome and overcome their reluctance to choose him, rather than Casimir, as the protagonist in any punitive action against the Hussite king. On November 10, 1466, he submitted to Paul II an authentic copy of George's coronation oath, the original of which had been in his possession since the return of the two Hungarian bishops from Prague in the spring of 1458.[385]

The Pope, indeed, had valid reasons for keeping Matthias free of involvements in Bohemia. After a temporary lull, the Turks reopened hostilities in the Balkans in the close vicinity of Hungary. Matthias sounded an alarm several times and requested help for his army from other parts of Christendom. It would have been an arduous task for the papal diplomacy to support these appeals, if instead of resisting the Turks vigorously he split his forces and used some of them to harass his Christian neighbor. In the late summer of 1466, the Pope extended sponsorship to an assembly of princes from Germany and elsewhere for which Frederick III set the middle of November as the opening date. The Turkish menace was strongly emphasized so that the attendance would hit a high mark.[386]

When the Diet opened its sessions, the German princes present could be counted on the fingers of one's hands. Frederick III was represented by one of his councillors, Count Grafeneck, who always enjoyed Matthias' confidence and was designated as the commander of the Christian army. This selection indicated that George's opponents were determined to forestall any attempt to promote the king of Bohemia to the highest position among the crusaders. And even more ominous was the Pope's appointment of Fantino de Valle as legate. George sent to Nurnberg two of his most skilful negotiators, the lords Albrecht Kostka and Beneš of Veitmil, to further his cause.[387] It was no wonder that the Diet accomplished nothing worth recording. The papal legate soon turned away from the main purpose of his mission and endeavored to change the assembly into an instrument of papal policy against the king of Bohemia.[388] The two Czechs retaliated and in their speeches re-emphasized their master's readiness to give substantial support to the contemplated expedition against the Turks.[389]

Annoyed by the legate's obduracy, Markgrave Albrecht Achilles made an agreement with several princes and with plenipotentiaries of the absentees that a new intervention at the papal court be made in George's behalf so that all Christian forces could be used to stem the Turkish advance. It was suggested that the delegates meet in Venice before the carnival of 1467 and proceed from there to Rome.[390] Some of them really came to Prague around Christmas and were prepared to undertake the delicate mission. Before they left, George furnished them with a letter for the Venetian senate asking that august body to join the princes of the Empire and promote conciliation.[391] It is very likely that the step was suggested by Heimburg, who tried to salvage his far-flung scheme in its most concrete part. Those delegates who left Prague early in January, 1467, arrived in Venice in February only to learn of the unfavorable turn of George's fortunes. Thanks to its contacts, the city on the lagoons was soon fully informed of the decision to close the negotiations which the Pope had made before Christmas, 1466.

This decision had been under consideration since the summer, when the period of six months expired. Carvajal's refutation of George's letter to Matthias of July 28 was a polemical prelude to the formal act.[392] In the public consistory on December 23, 1466, the procurator of faith recapitulated the preliminary investigation of George's guilt. In accordance with the canon law, George or his plenipotentiary was called into the assembly hall. As no one presented himself, Paul II made a long and passionate allocution and thus introduced his sentence, the text of which was recited by the cardinal-vicechancellor.[393] George was branded as an obstinate heretic, patron and defender of condemned heresies. In a transparent allusion to the Prague assembly of August, 1462, he was also accused of fostering erroneous views concerning the communion in both kinds, rejected by the Council of Constance. Another charge leveled against him was the persecution of his Catholic subjects. As by his disobedience of previous summonses he had put himself outside the law, he and his descendants were stripped of their possessions and his subjects were declared free of any duty or obligation toward him.

Attached to the sentence was a bull, addressed to the archbishops and bishops in Bohemia and in the adjacent territories.[394] They were instructed to take energetic steps to give the sentence of excommunication widest publicity and to dissuade the inhabitants of the kingdom from obedience, service, or even contact with George. Thus a signal was given for rebellion against the legitimate and crowned king.

Far away from Rome, George and his family were preparing to observe Christmas in the traditional manner. The continued friendship of Markgrave Albrecht Achilles and some other princes brightened the outlook. Queen Johanna surprised her husband with a handsome present, an illustrated book of Psalms and prayers in the Czech language. An anonymous artist attempted to insert George's portrait into the several initials, but neither his eye nor his hand was sufficiently trained to produce more than a rudimentary likeness of his illustrious patron.

As George had no personal representative in Rome, he was unaware of the Pope's action. His foes received from their own sources advance notices of the meeting of the consistory, accompanied by an abridged version of the sentence. The first among them was the legate Rudolf who, with the help of the Breslau senate, immediately launched a vigorous campaign against George.[395] Not only the countries bordering on Silesia but also the more remote territories seethed with rumors that a crusade against the Hussite king was imminent. Among the Czech lords, the sentence was received with mixed feelings. Those who did not want to rise against their sovereign felt that a resolute step must be taken to break the deadlock. They assembled at Jindřichův Hradec, but reached no unanimous decision. Zdeněk of Šternberk hindered the search for a compromise by excessive demands, but as at that advanced date he did not have detailed instructions from either Rome or the imperial court, he hesitated to pronounce himself openly for a rebellion.[396]

The failure of the moderate elements among the Catholic nobility to find a formula which the King could accept increased the importance of the provincial Diet scheduled for the last week of February. Supported by the loyal elements, George made his last attempt to settle internal problems by an agreement.[397] He successfully refuted Zdeněk's exaggerated interpretation of some legal problems and traditions, and announced concessions to the dissatisfied faction of such concrete demands as the quality of currency, taxation, the transfer of royal castles into private holding, and requests for assistance in military expeditions abroad. He was very cautious whenever a reference to his conflict with the Papacy was made, and used no harsh words which could be reported to Rome. To allay their fears, he discreetly assured the Utraquists of his attachment to the Compacts. Lev of Rožmitál exercised a moderating influence on the lords of his faith, and was supported in this policy by John of Rožmberk, so that Zdeněk of Šternberk with his small group remained in the minority. To protect the agreement against disturbing influences, the Catholic lords promised to send a messenger to Rome to explore the situation. They bound themselves to prepare a more imposing delegation, if the messenger's report indicated that Paul II would be willing to receive it.

The Breslau agent, Fabian Hanko, assessed correctly the Pope's disposition when he reported to his superiors that no further attention should be paid to diplomatic interventions and that the Pope would remain adamant even if all the electors of the Empire arrived to his court to plead for the King.[398] As had been often stated in papal letters, the axe had been put to the roots of the tree and it had to be wielded mercilessly. On March 20, 1467, Paul II issued a bull by which Zdeněk of Šternberk was confirmed as the leader of the Catholic party among the Czechs, and the faithful were admonished to follow him until the vacant throne should be occupied by a worthy candidate.[399] In less than a week afterwards, on Maundy Thursday, the Pope made another hostile gesture. As was customary, he reiterated a summary condemnation of heretics and sectarians, and added to such general designations as the Khazars,

Patarenes, the Poor of Lyons, Wyclifists, and Hussites, two personal names, those of George and of Gregory of Heimburg. Included in the anathema were other associates or followers of the excommunicated king, and any person maintaining relations with him.[400]

At George's court the opinion prevailed that such measures as the compromise between the Utraquist and Catholic nobility at the provincial Diet or the friendly disposition of the Hohenzollern and Saxon princes should be buttressed by a more intensive campaign. George's cause was to be taken out of the Pope's hands and be transferred to a representative body in which laymen would not be expected to sit as mere spectators. In the Diet, George used the good offices of his brother-in-law and other loyal lords, and the diplomatic campaign was again conducted by Gregory of Heimburg. The King, usually cautious and reluctant to give a weapon into the hands of his enemies, was gradually convinced by Heimburg that an appeal from the Pope's sentence of December 23, 1466, should be made to a general Church assembly. This decision conflicted with Pius' decree made at Mantua in 1459,[401] but the conciliar theory had so many adherents in Bohemia that the step seemed to be worth risking.

On April 14, 1467, King George opened a session at his court to which were invited prominent members of the Catholic party. Among the clerics present were Dean Hilary of Litoměřice and Václav Křižanovský; the group of the lords was headed by Lev of Rožmitál. Some Utraquist lords acted as witnesses. The King read the Czech version of his appeal, which was then translated into Latin and corroborated by public notaries, so that no doubt could arise as to its authenticity. It was a remarkable document, indeed, one of the most important decisions that George made in his life.[402]

Presuming that Paul II did not act in harmony with the valid precepts, George appealed from the Pope's person to the Holy See as an institution, sanctified by the Apostles Peter and Paul, and by Peter's worthy successors. From that sublime tribunal he first requested an appropriate action to remedy the defects in the proceedings on which Paul II had based his sentence. Second, accepting as possible that in the near future no situation would arise in which Paul II could be dissociated from the Holy See, the King appealed to a general assembly of the Church which, according to the decree adopted at Constance, was to be held every ten years.[403] Thirdly, the King appealed to Paul's successor, and in general to any Christian assembly or to any individual loving law and justice.

There was in the appeal no direct or oblique reference to the bull *Execrabilis* of 1459. According to some later references, Hilary of Litoměřice, as the highest ranking cleric, attempted to dissuade George from a reference to the general Council, anticipating grave consequences.

The King trusted his own judgment, as the distinction between the person of the existing pope and the Holy See was no more than a legal technicality. In invoking the Constance decree, George undoubtedly followed the advice of Heimburg, whose antipapal sentiment was shared by the king's Hussite advisers.

George's appeal from the Pope's sentence was not an improvisation but a well-weighed decision by which he hoped to arouse other monarchs from passivity. His advisers in international affairs knew, at least in general, which princes in and outside the Empire resented clerical interference in politics. As it was illusory to expect that any temporal lord would come to George's aid merely out of sympathy for his devotion to the communion in both kinds, the Prague leaders made preparations for a diplomatic offensive to be launched simultaneously with the King's appeal to the future council.

The chief source of information concerning these matters is a lengthy account of public and private audiences which an anonymous envoy from Prague had with Louis XI in the spring of 1467.[404] As the first of them took place on April 20, only six days after George's reading of the appeal, it must be concluded that the scheme which the Prague envoy laid before the French king had been completed some time in March. Keeping in mind the strong faction among the courtiers, who in 1464 had opposed the alliance with Bohemia, the Prague leaders instructed the envoy to play down George's conflict with Rome and emphasize current political problems. The rivalry between Louis XI and Charles the Bold figured prominently in the envoy's propositions and in the answers from the French side. In both its general outline and the details, the scheme of 1467 was more concrete than had been Marini's project of the earlier years.[405]

The chief partners in the proposed alliance were to be France and Bohemia. The Prague envoy expressed the hope that other rulers would join sooner or later. He mentioned not only the Polish king but also Matthias, as George, in the early spring of 1467, apparently still believed that it would be possible to deflect the Hungarian from his hostile orientation. In Germany the three Dukes of Saxony, Ernest, Albrecht, and William, were regarded as dependable; the same opinion prevailed concerning the two Hohenzollerns, Frederick and Albrecht Achilles. It was expected that the latter would bring into the alliance his friends among the lesser princes in the Empire. The king of Denmark was also mentioned as a potential ally. The Prague envoy left no doubt of George's willingness to render military help to France if she were threatened by her neighbor. In that connection he pointed to the claims on Luxemburg which originated in the union of the patrimony of the Luxemburg house with the kingdom of Bohemia and which were revived several times after the death of Emperor-King Sigismund. If necessary, they could be invoked to justify the use of Czech armed forces in the war with Burgundy.

The French court knew, of course, of George's excommunication, since Paul II had sent a special envoy there with a copy of the bull of December 23, 1466.[406] It would have been foolish to observe silence on that point but it was mentioned only in connection with the political issues. The envoy complained of the Pope's effort to keep in his hand both the swords, spiritual and temporal, and to bring the secular powers under his authority. In another connection, the envoy spoke of the general Council as the best means of re establishing peace and order in Christendom.

When George's appeal of April 14, 1467, is connected, as it should be, with the project of a great alliance, it cannot be lightly dismissed as an emotional gesture. Having excluded unqualified submission to the Pope's call for obedience, he sought other means and ways to avert concentration of hostile forces within Bohemia and in its vicinity. From the council he hoped to obtain an even more solemn confirmation of the Compacts than had been, in 1462, expected from Pius II. An alliance with several kings and many imperial princes was promoted as a safeguard against any monarch who might respond to the Pope's call and wage a crusade against the only country in the west that had failed to conform to papal policy.

REBELLION AND WAR

The spiritual leaders of the Catholic minority in Bohemia received George's appeal to the general Council as an indication of a more resolute policy in religious matters. They took immediate steps to avoid any involvement in the King's scheme. Dean Hilarius and Václav Křižanovský, accompanied by prominent members of the metropolitan chapter, left Prague at the first opportune moment and made the Catholic city of Plzeň their headquarters. A handful of clerics remained at Saint Vitus Cathedral to perform the rites and to minister to the Catholic segments of the Prague population.

Gladdened by their hasty retreat, Rokycana and other Utraquist priests requested from George an authorization to take over the Cathedral so that the "Upper" and "Lower" Consistories could be united under the Archbishop-elect. This seemed to be a golden opportunity for Rokycana, who for many years had been unable to promote the interests of his party. He apparently threw his personal prestige into the scale to obtain from the King substantial concessions for the Utraquists. A contemporary chronicler omitted the details, but recorded a terse sentence which illustrated George's dislike of clerical meddling with worldly affairs: "Master Rokycana, you had mastered us long enough, permit us now to be your master." The chronicler remarked laconically that since that time Rokycana's contacts with the King were less frequent than before.[407]

George had good reasons for his refusal to bestow favors upon the Utraquist clergy. He really had no ally in the world in whom he could place absolute trust. Even the Dukes of Saxony and Markgrave Albrecht Achilles kept themselves aloof when the Pontiff fulminated. The only source of comfort was the lack of organization on the enemy side. There existed no immediate threat of invasion and George could patiently await the outcome of the negotiations with Louis XI.

In the spring of 1467, opinions at the French court were no less divided than in 1464. The Bishop of Evreux, Jean de la Balue, had the King's full confidence and expected that he soon would be admitted into the college of cardinals. Louis XI showed interest in the alliance fostered by the Prague envoy and spoke of emissaries whom he would send to Prague, to Saxony, and Brandenburg for further negotiations. He posed discreetly a question whether it would be more advantageous not to give George too much prominence among the founding members of the alliance, as he would in any case be included in it through his friends. Louis' attitude in regard to the Council was even more cautious. He recommended that George seek mediators to have the ban lifted or at least suspended. Louis XI promised to intervene on George's behalf but not immediately; the month of October was mentioned as the time when French envoys would be sent to the papal court. If even after such an action the Pope and the Emperor should remain inflexible, the campaign for a council would have more supporters than at the given moment.[408]

In the absence of concrete evidence, it is impossible to fix the date of the envoy's return from France. In the meantime George's foes pushed forward with their own designs to gain advantage over George's diplomacy. Copies of the sentence of December 23, 1466, were sent not only to France,[409] but to other courts, so that the Pope's decision to strike hard would be universally known.

More sensitive than any other foe, the leaders of Breslau girded for the opening of hostilities. Even before they could receive reports from Prague concerning the King's appeal, on April 17, 1467, the chapter, the clergy, and the senate of Breslau recommended to the Pope an energetic action leading to the election of a new king.[410] They insisted that in papal plans for the defense of Christendom, the priority was to be given to the struggle with the Hussites rather than the contemplated expedition against the Turks. They maintained that no significant force could be mobilized in Central Europe until the Czech heresy had been exterminated.

Shortly afterwards, on April 21, 1467, the city reiterated its desire to enter into a closer relationship with the lords of Zelená Hora, and a formal agreement was concluded to supplant the earlier, rather loose, ties.[411] Zdeněk of Šternberk was designated captain of the antiroyal troops and both parties pledged their support to the new king as soon as he should be elected. On the next Sunday, the papal legate preached an aggressive sermon against the Hussite king, thus declaring the crusade.[412] Other clerics dispatched by the legate to various centers in Silesia and the Lusatias preached in the same bellicose spirit.

This was approximately the time at which the truce between George and the rebels, after its second extension, finally expired.[413] Neither party was interested in resuming negotiations. The King had his troops prepared, and in the week following Saint George's Day, he moved against six castles owned by his archenemy, Zdeněk of Šternberk.[414] As an attempt to conquer them by an open attack was not likely to succeed, the royal captains, after an initial demonstration, invested the walled residences and waited for the garrisons' capitulation. About the middle of May, the city of Breslau opened its campaign in Silesia, forcing George to split his armies.

Although well prepared technically and financially, George was at a disadvantage, as his opponents did not stand against him as a solid block controlling a compact territory. Castles of the rebel lords and the walled cities allied with them were scattered all over the kingdom and each of them tied down a portion of the royal army. George was assisted by his sons, Victorin and Henry, and by the loyal lords. The Utraquist leaders were aware of the problems confronting them but failed to enforce vigilance and were often confounded by the enemy strategy. In local clashes with the enemy they suffered setbacks before reinforcements could reach them. Instead of concentrating on such objectives as the city of Breslau, the King became entangled in numerous operations, initiated as a rule by his opponents. The late spring and the summer were spent in irregular warfare, and neither party scored a decisive victory. It was admitted by the opposing party that George's forces were superior and could hold out longer than the Catholic units. In some letters, fears were expressed that the Catholic party would face disintegration and defeat unless prompt aid from abroad were forthcoming.

George's evaluation of the chances of success resulted in a sober conclusion that the conflict would not be closed even if his forces succeeded in wearing out their enemies. Not expecting immediate help from Heimburg's campaign, George resorted to realistic methods to lessen the danger of an alliance of the rebels with any ruler in the vicinity of Bohemia. In studying the problems arising from the close alliance of the Zelená Hora with Breslau, George did not use Heimburg as his confidant but relied on his Czech councillors, both clerics and laymen. The number of Catholics loyal to him was greatly reduced by the hostile pressure from Rome, but George was not completely deserted and could use some Catholics in missions abroad and in collecting information concerning his foes' intentions and activities. In fact, correspondence with foreign courts concerning George's appeal to the Council was the last major task assigned to Heimburg. Its meager results diminished his prestige, for which reason the King turned to more conventional practices.

In the situation created by Frederick's animosity and Matthias' leanings toward Rome, the Polish court became the focal point of political activities. As soon as George realized that the Pope contemplated stern measures against him, he hastened to ascertain Casimir's intentions.

In February, 1467, George sent a loyal cleric, Provost Paul of Zderaz, to

Casimir's court to size up the situation. His report apparently indicated that the Polish king still valued highly George's cooperation in matters of common interest. To pursue the traditional policy, George instructed John Jičinský of Cimburk, one of his most faithful adherents among the high nobility, to proceed to Poland and to deal not only with the King but also with the Polish and Lithuanian magnates assembled in May, 1467, at Piotrków. When received by Casimir, John of Cimburk reported the recent developments and stressed George's resolution to abide by the Głogów pact of 1462. Casimir's answer was not enthusiastic and pointed out the Czech reluctance to implement some clauses of the Głogów agreement. As this reply, though guarded, was made without threat, John realized that his master had really nothing to fear from Poland. He contented himself with partial success and did not insist on a formal declaration of friendship.[415]

George's orientation toward Poland was motivated by memories of the Głogów conference and also by other and weightier considerations. Casimir's relations with the Papacy were not too cordial, owing to several disputes in the past concerning the right to fill vacant Polish sees. More recently, Casimir tried to obtain from Paul II two friendly gestures: the lifting of bans and ecclesiastical censures pronounced against the Poles and their allies during the struggle with the Teutonic Order, and even more, a papal sanction of the treaty of Toruń. The Pope was reluctant to grant Casimir's requests, as he wished to use them at an opportune moment for diplomatic bargaining.[416] Contacts with George, if kept within reasonable limits, could improve Casimir's chances of success in negotiations with the Pope. On the other hand, a close co-operation would have been rather risky in view of the Pope's efforts to isolate the Hussite king completely. Under the circumstances created by Paul's sentence, George undoubtedly derived more relief from silent sympathies than from an emphatic statement of solidarity.

At the time of Cimburk's sojourn in Poland, George's foes at the Curia redoubled their efforts to force George into submission. The fiercest of them, Cardinal Carvajal, was temporarily absent from Rome, performing a mission in Venice; but others acted offensively, using the King's appeal to the Council as another evidence of his recalcitrance. When preparations for a vigorous action passed from the preliminary stage, several appointments were made to assure an efficient execution of papal orders. The chief diplomatic post in Central Europe was assigned to Bishop Rudolf on account of his knowledge of the local conditions as well as his marked ability to deal with Frederick III. Other prelates were considered for lower ranks or for special missions.

At this junction, Lawrence Roverella, Bishop of Ferrara, moved higher and began to play an influential role in political affairs. He had at least

ten years' experience in diplomacy, having being initiated in that profession in 1457 by Cardinal Carvajal. In the early sixties, he had often
journeyed to Germany to attend assemblies of princes with the purpose
counteracting antipapal propaganda. In May, 1464, Pius II appointed
him treasurer of the crusade and issued a safe-conduct for him and his
retinue. After Pius' death, little could be achieved in that field and the
Bishop was free to accept other duties.[417]

The training of another cleric, Fra Gabriel di Verona, was in many
respects different from that of Roverella. A member of the Rangoni
family, Gabriel joined Giovanni Capistrano and in 1451 accompanied
him, along with other disciples, on his journey across the Alps northward.
While other members of that group left no imprint on religious life in
Bohemia, Rangoni contributed to reorganization of a Minorite province,
incorporating the kingdoms of Bohemia and Austria, and he had remained
in contact with leading Catholic clerics ever since. In March, 1466, Paul
II appointed Rangoni, then a professor of theology, to the post of
inquisitor for Central Europe, with a special task to hasten the eradication of Wycliffite and Hussite heresies.[418] He was instructed to work hand
in hand with bishops heading dioceses infected with such errors, and, if
necessary, seek assistance from secular powers. The sources relating to
him do not reveal whether at the time of Paul's decision he resided in
Rome or elsewhere.

Pressed from many sides for resolute steps, Paul II issued on May 15,
1467, a bull by which he reiterated George's condemnation and reaffirmed
the right of the Holy See to rescind the ties between a heretic and his
subjects or allies. Other bulls issued on the same or the following day
were addressed either to George's opponents in general or to individual
persons. Their purpose was to enlist co-operation of the Emperor and of
other princes, temporal and spiritual, in annulling the oaths and pledges
made to George since his election, and to organize a crusade.[419]

In a short letter, Paul II requested Frederick III to concur with the
ecclesiastical censures and to free by imperial authority George's Catholic
subjects, vassals, and allies from any obligation assumed by them.[420]
In another, more comprehensive, bull, Paul II declared void the treaties
or any contractual obligations between the king of Bohemia and other
princes.[421] The list was impressive, including among secular princes
the Emperor, the kings of Hungary and of Poland, Dukes Ernest, Albrecht, and William of Saxony, Ludwig, Sigismund, and Otto of Bavaria,
Sigismund of Austria, Frederick of the Rhenish Palatinate, Frederick and
Albrecht of Hohenzollern, and Lewis, Landgrave of Hesse. In the list
of the ecclesiastical dignitaries, there followed after the three spiritual
electors several archbishops and bishops, including those of Olomouc
and Breslau.

In organizing a crusade against George, a resolute step was made by the Pope in granting to Bishop Rudolf the powers of a legate *a latere* for Poland, Bohemia, Prussia, Livonia, and Misnia.[422] He was urged to set in motion a crusade by which the faithful would be liberated from George's domination and the King as well as his obdurate partisans put to rout. The bull superseded the earlier documents, the scope of which had been limited by practical considerations. In May, 1467, Paul II favored an energetic, ruthless action. He authorized Rudolf to levy a tithe upon all ecclesiastical income in the sphere of his competence for the purpose of financing the crusade. Another duty assigned to him was no less onerous, for the Bishop was urged to concentrate in his hands the money contributed after the previous appeals, but held in custody by various individuals or institutions. To make collecting easier, Rudolf was authorized to leave no more than one third of the sums in the hands of those who actually had the contributions in their possession.[423]

Two other papal bulls pertained to political matters. The legate was advised to speed up the election of a new king, and provisionally to approve the choice by the local Estates of the most suitable candidate. The Pope reserved for himself the final confirmation.[424] As a benevolent gesture to Casimir, the legate was permitted to absolve that King and his supporters from any ban or censure incurred during the war with the Teutonic Order.[425]

It cannot be ascertained when the bulls of May 15 reached their addressees. As on other occasions, an advance notice of their contents or even abstracts of their text could be brought north of the Alps by special messengers, while the original documents traveled more slowly. Acting on an advance notice, the Catholic lords met some time in June at Jihlava, the temporary headquarters of Zdeněk of Šternberk. They acted as if the throne were already vacant and resolved that it be offered to the Polish king. A messenger was sent at once to Breslau to report this to the legate Rudolf. He, in turn, consulted with Bishop Jošt and the senate in order to secure a unanimous decision. Two delegates were appointed to accompany Zdeněk's messenger, Eliáš, the titular administrator of the bishopric of Litomyšl, to Cracow. One of them represented the legate, the other the city of Breslau.[426]

The three men appeared before Casimir on July 2, 1467. They acquainted him with the situation in the kingdom of Bohemia as created by recent developments and stressed his right to claim the vacated throne. To add weight to their juridical analysis of the pertinent constitutional issues, they produced a document, signed and sealed by Catholic lords at Jihlava.[427] In it reference was made also to Casimir's son, whom the lords were willing to accept as their ruler in case Casimir found it too burdensome to rule over two countries. Casimir apparently had not at that time received the papal bulls of May 15, and gave the messengers only a vague answer.

The delegation by which he was approached was by no means impressive or representative. To obtain more positive results, legate Rudolf himself left for Cracow and reached it on July 28.[428] At some earlier date the papal messengers, Fra Gabriel Rangoni and his companion, arrived not only with the bulls of May 15, but also with detailed information concerning the situation at the papal court. They had an audience with Casimir on August 1, and offered him the crown in the name of the Pope. Again his son was mentioned as a candidate, if the King could not accept the offer for himself. The high-ranking clerics felt competent to go beyond the offer made by the three men of lesser authority. They promised Casimir aid from the Pope and from the Emperor, from the princes of Germany and of Silesia, and last but not least from the Catholic nobles of Bohemia, Moravia, and the Lusatias. Legate Rudolf believed that he could offer to Casimir more than the crown of Bohemia: he showed him the bulls by which he was empowered to lift the bans from Casimir and to confirm the treaty of Toruń. His move produced the opposite effect, as Casimir resented the linking of the Toruń peace with the Czech affair.

The ensuing negotiations were neither hurried nor easy. Casimir was reluctant to be drawn by the papal diplomacy into a conflict which in his sober estimate could not be but expensive and risky. Memories of the long and exhaustive struggle with the Teutonic Order probably guided him just as safely as his dislike of clerical interference in political affairs. On one occasion he admitted openly that he just could not believe that an annointed and crowned king could be dethroned. Endeavoring, however, to avoid an irreparable rupture with the Papacy, the King resorted to his wonted method of procrastination and pointed to the general assembly of nobility from all parts of his commonwealth as the place at which a problem of such a magnitude should be discussed and settled. To escape accusations of passivity, he signified his intention of sending his envoys to George. He promised to urge George earnestly to terminate his military operations against Zdeněk and the other lords, and to submit himself to the authority of the Pontiff. On the other hand, Casimir requested from the legate that both the ban and the preaching of the crusade against George be suspended.

Toward the end of August, the conference was broken off and legate Rudolf started immediately on his journey to Breslau. Fra Gabriel and his companion traveled back home by way of Hungary and most likely made a stop at Matthias' court to report Casimir's policy to him. It seems highly probable that the papal representatives, before leaving Cracow, tacitly wrote off Casimir as a potential ally, and that a decision was made to search elsewhere for a more pliable instrument of the papal policy in relation to the king of Bohemia.

Paul II had full confidence in legate Rudolf's dexterity, but did not want to leave the burden of the manifold activities exclusively on his shoulders. Bishop Lawrence Roverella was appointed as an additional envoy to Central Europe and his first assignment was Germany.[429] Late in July, the princes of the Empire were assembled in Nurnberg for a Diet and it seemed highly advisable to have an agile representative there to foster the Pope's favorite projects. The attendance was fairly large and some prominent rulers were among those present. George did not attend, nor did he send delegates lest they be exposed to chicanery and humiliating treatment. His foes were represented by Dean Hilarius and two noblemen whom the presiding officers admitted as the official delegates from Bohemia.[430]

The princes maintaining contacts with Prague knew of George's intentions, as he had sent them copious letters before the assembly opened.[431] In these letters he recapitulated the causes of the conflict and asked for effective support of his campaign for a general Council. Drafted apparently by Heimburg, the letters warned the princes against leniency or indifference in matters so vital as the clerical interference in worldly affairs; for if the Church under the guise of spiritual interests assumed the right to deprive the princes of secular government, no person could rule longer than he was permitted to do so by the Church authority.

Two unfinished tasks were presented by the directors of the assembly to its members: the pacification of the Empire and the expedition against the Turks. No serious discussion of them took place, because the Czech question weighed heavily on everybody's mind. The princes, whose hearts were with George, refrained from a declaration in favor of a general Council, but refused to grant subsidies for a crusade against Bohemia. Some of George's former friends, among them Duke Lewis of Bavaria, passed over to the Emperor's party; but others, headed by the Markgrave Albrecht Achilles, strenuously obstructed proposals directed against their ally.[432] The assembly broke up before the middle of August, and although it did not give George satisfaction in the matter of the Council neither did it sanction an armed expedition against him as demanded by the papal legate.

The Nurnberg assembly had a diplomatic sequel by which Duke Lewis of Bavaria and Martin Mair endeavored to mask their defection from the group of princes siding with George. Instead of a general Council, they proposed a conference, authorized by both the Pope and the Emperor, at which George would be instructed by a papal legate as to what to believe in matters separating the Hussite party from the Roman Church.[433] George was informed of these parleys and as for tactical reasons his friends attended them, he did not brusquely reject Mair's scheme. He requested, however, that as an overture to the conference, all hostile actions against him be suspended and the papal bans lifted. As no such concession could be expected from Rome, diplomatic exchanges were broken off. The Wettin and Hohenzollern princes refused to go further with Bavaria, sensing danger in Mair's new project—an alliance of the Hohenzollern, Wettin, and Wittelsbach houses with Frederick III.

Although aggravated by the persistent efforts of his enemies, George's situation in the early fall of 1467 was not hopeless. The papal diplomacy and its secular collaborators failed to forge a ring by which the Hussite domains would be surrounded. If Martin Mair's second scheme had been put into operation, the Emperor and the Wittelsbachs would have deprived George's most faithful allies among the German princes of freedom of action. A league of four ruling houses—Hohenzollern, Wettin, Wittelsbach, and Habsburg—even if not committed to an aggressive policy, would have caused a good deal of uneasiness on George's part and would have left him without a friendly soul in the imperial Diets.

On the opposite side, Casimir's tactics, if not bringing immediate relief, alleviated George's problems considerably. Casimir endeavored to preserve freedom as to the time for action to be chosen by himself and not imposed on him by any of the parties competing for his favors. Realistic elements among the Czech opposition could conclude from an observation of his doings after the Piotrków Diet that he would not accept the offered crown and join them in a campaign against George. But they realized that a sudden rupture of contacts would be extremely risky, as it would free Casimir's hands for an even closer alignment with George. Thus, by his dilatory policy, Casimir rendered George a valuable service by hindering the formation of a bloc on the eastern flank.

Although Casimir did not make clear his innermost thoughts, he was undoubtedly interested in securing the throne of Bohemia for his dynasty, but did not want to go to war with George on its account. An open support of rebels was to him just as objectionable as was the clerical influence in politics. He felt that a cessation of hostilities in Bohemia, if it could be achieved by mediation, would relieve him of embarrassing interventions either from the side of the rebels or that of the papal diplomats. A show of good will was also advisable, as the general Diet to which he referred the papal envoys was to meet in several months. Not much was done in September, but some time in October Casimir appointed his envoys to Bohemia; John Długosz, a canon of Cracow and a historian, was one of them. They reached Prague late in October and presented their credentials to the King.[434]

A keen observer, Długosz at once perceived George's dilemma. The Polish recommendation that he submit to the Church authority and suspend struggle with the rebels could not be accepted by George in its original form, as it would have amounted to capitulation. But George was anxious to maintain friendly relations with Poland, and finally resorted to a less painful formula announcing his willingness to put his cause into Casimir's hands.[435] Thereupon, the envoys journeyed to Jihlava and made contacts with Zdeněk of Šternberk. He was not opposed to an armistice, and in this way the envoys scored their first success—an agreement by which hostilities were to be suspended from the last day of November to late January, 1468.[436] George also raised no objection to a gathering of his opponents at Brzeg, Silesia, at which the Polish envoys were to be present.

If the leaders of the Catholic party had really been interested in more than a respite, Brzeg would have been a suitable place for a conference with the Polish envoys. It was quiet and free from disturbing elements. The proud capital of Silesia raised objections and prevailed on its allies to reject Brzeg and insist on Breslau as the place of meeting.[437] By this change, the conference lost even the semblance of neutrality, but neither George nor the Polish envoys found it opportune to insist that the original agreement be strictly observed.

An unexpected complication occurred shortly before the opening date. On their journey to Silesia, Zdeněk of Šternberk and his cronies learned of the serious illness by which Bishop Jošt had been incapacitated for some time. They made a stop at Nisa, the Bishop's private residence, and found him on his deathbed. Medical help was of no avail, and Jošt died during the lords' sojourn at Nisa. As he had been involved in a conflict with some powerful circles in Breslau, the senate raised objections to the transfer of his body and his burial in the Cathedral. Zdeněk found it necessary to exert his prestige to have the resolution changed. It was an odd coincidence that at the same time as Zdeněk with his escort passed through the gate in the Breslau city walls and was welcomed by the blaring of trumpets, Jošt's servants carried the casket with his mortal remains through another gate, the bells in the adjacent churches and convents pealing. In due time the Bishop's body was buried in the Cathedral with customary ceremonies.

The conference opened in the town hall immediately after Jošt's funeral. The papal legate Rudolf presided, assisted by Gabriel Rangoni, who apparently arrived from Hungary, and by Bishop Tas. The prelates were joined by Prince Nicholas of Opole and his son Lewis as well as by Prince Balthasar of Sagan who had persisted in hostility toward George since their first conflict in 1460. The group of Czech lords was quite large and among them George's inveterate enemy, Hynck Bítovský of Lichtenburg and Cornštejn, was quite conspicuous. Many royal boroughs of Moravia and the Lusatias sent representatives who were joined by the delegates from Plzeň and from some cities in Silesia, including, of course, Breslau. The Polish envoys were not admitted to secret sessions, but they were kept informed on the less delicate points under deliberation.[438]

Apart from secular political problems, the vacancy in the See of Breslau called for an instant decision. It depended in principle on the vote of the chapter, but influential members of the senate did not want to leave the matter to the discretion of the canons. They had their candidate, the legate Rudolf, and they supplicated the Pope to appoint him irrespective of the chapter's vote.[439] In the meantime, they campaigned for him in clerical circles. The chapter was assembled on January 20, 1468, and resolved to comply with the wish of the leading patricians recommending Bishop Rudolf for a papal confirmation. The senate endorsed the vote at once and, undoubtedly, with the Bishop's knowledge, wrote to the Pope asking that their new shepherd be relieved of the customary obligation of paying an annate to the papal treasury and to be permitted to keep his former dignity as the Bishop of Lavant.[440] The Pope confirmed Rudolf in his office on April 27, 1468, but the senate's petition apparently was not granted in all respects.[441] Preparations were soon made for the appointment of another cleric to the See of Lavant.

There was no discord or wavering at the rebel assembly in the cardinal point—the war with George—but even its most ardent advocates realized that no significant success could be expected immediately. Therefore, the Polish envoys were encouraged to meet with the King's representatives and to obtain extension of the truce until Saint George's Day, 1468. The conference was held at Strzelin and it was short, so that the Poles returned to Breslau before the end of December. The assembly approved without any serious objection the terms hammered out at Strzelin, and adjourned.[442]

Documents destined for the Poles and other addressees who could not be absolutely trusted were worded carefully, to give the impression that Casimir was still the only candidate for the crown of Bohemia. According to some fairly clear indications, the rebels were resolved in their hearts to turn elsewhere. In this policy they were apparently supported by Fra Gabriel, who was able to give them an account of conditions in Hungary. Bishop Tas, whose defection from George was final, was empowered to go at an opportune moment to that country and explore the chances of Matthias' alignment with the Catholic party. He was well qualified for such a mission, as he had made friends among the Hungarian hierarchy on several previous trips there on George's behalf. Through them he could reach Matthias, if other attempts to get him interested failed.

Gabriel Rangoni, accompanied by Dean Hilarius and Dobrohost of

Ronšperk, were sent to Rome with a detailed instruction to guide them in reporting to Paul II and the leading cardinals.[443] The document contained concrete facts concerning the losses the Catholic party had suffered since the outbreak of hostilities in the spring of 1467. In another section of the instruction were listed the Catholics who continued to sympathize with George despite papal sentences and admonitions. The king of Poland was not omitted, as he had sent George several hundred horses. The instruction also hinted at the need of subsidies to continue the resistance. This point was followed by a recommendation of sterner measures against disobedient or indifferent members of the Church, no matter whether they lived in the kingdom of Bohemia or outside. Of special importance was the petition to the Pope to intervene with the Emperor so that he would withdraw from George and his sons the recognition of royal dignity as well as other grants and privileges.

Of the three delegations leaving Breslau early in January, 1468, the Poles had the most arduous task. They carried with them to Prague the articles presented to them by the secular leaders of the opposition. Either from them or from another agent, George received a copy of a letter which Gabriel Rangoni had sent to the Poles while they were in Breslau.[444] When the envoys were admitted before George, they quickly noticed his dissatisfaction with the results of their work. He reproached them for leniency, rather than strict neutrality, in dealing with the rebels. If they had been less genuinely interested in achieving success with which they could return to their homeland, they would have probably left immediately after the first audience.

After his outburst of indignation, George adopted a more realistic attitude and accepted their proposals in principle. His answer was drafted carefully and the truce was presented as a gesture to Casimir, not as a concession to the disobedient nobles. The time limit was extended from St. George's Day (April 23) to the Feast of the Ascension, which was to be observed that year on May 26. In an additional document, a clause was inserted making it clear that only the King's opponents in the kingdom of Bohemia were included in the truce.[445] By this clause George reserved for himself freedom to deal with his other enemies according to his own judgment.

It appears very likely that not only the regular members of the royal council, but also Gregory of Heimburg (and possibly some Hussite clerics) were consulted concerning Gabriel Rangoni's letter. A refutation of his statements was added to a conventional letter addressed by George to Casimir. Written in Latin either by Gregory or a Hussite cleric, the refutation sounded more like a religious tract than a royal letter.[446] Its author, whoever he was, first summed up Rangoni's letter and wrote his comment on each of its four articles. In each instance he contrasted

Rangoni's assertions with George's deeds, and seasoned his incisive remarks with coarse epithets and bitter invectives against the author of the letter. It was probably expected that the refutation would not be deposited in the royal archives but would circulate in copies among Polish laymen and clerics and thus help to shape public opinion.

In all his communications, including this polemical writing, George was careful not to hurt Casimir's feelings. He fully realized the importance of Casimir's benevolence and did his best to preserve it. Even as a neutral country, Poland was of considerable help and it would have been an act of folly to antagonize Casimir personally, either by an unpremeditated remark or by a show of indifference to his attempt to stop the hostilities. Contacts between the two courts were sufficiently frequent so that George could measure fairly accurately the amount of dissatisfaction among the Poles with the Pope's reluctance to sanction the peace of Toruń without making it conditional on Casimir's acceptance of the crown of Bohemia. Discreet allusions to the papal policy were indeed more effective than would have been appeals for Casimir's public endorsement of George's point of view. Casimir met with no strong opposition when ignoring appeals from Rome for turning against George, although he would have kindled keen agitation among zealous Catholics if he had gone too far in supplying aid to the Hussites—an action categorically and repeatedly forbidden by the Pope.

George's policy in regard to Hungary lacked the candor and magnanimity by which the earlier contacts between the two courts, Prague and Buda, had been marked. It is very likely that George had at least an inkling of his foes' machinations by which Matthias was to be lured away from the relatives of his first consort, and made the leading member of the anti-Poděbrady bloc. Personal contacts between the two rulers almost ceased. Matthias was too often called from Buda to some remote area along the southern or south-eastern frontier and he gave evasive answers when sounded as to a suitable time and place for a meeting. Bishop Tas's defection was a serious loss to George, as he had served previously as a link with the Hungarian hierarchy, and through these channels confidential information could flow in both directions. There was no replacement for the Moravian bishop, as the number of Catholic clerics in George's service had dwindled. For political transactions, George relied mostly on Albrecht Kostka of Postupice, whose social rank and personal qualities were so outstanding that he could move with a good deal of success in Hungarian court circles and make friends among Matthias' councillors.

Late in 1467, an opportunity presented itself to test Matthias' feelings. When the Polish envoys made some progress in arranging for an armistice, George was left with forces that could not be instantly disbanded.

He knew that Matthias was entangled in conflicts with unruly elements in some parts of his kingdom, and it seemed advisable to promise him assistance. Prince Victorin, stationed in Moravia, apparently carried out instructions from Prague when he offered Matthias a force of from five hundred to one thousand horsemen.[447]

No reply came from Hungary to this gesture of good will, but George was not deflected from his adopted course by Matthias' silence. He used the news that Matthias had been wounded in a skirmish with insurgents as a cover for sending Prokop of Rabštejn to Hungary. The chancellor's task was to congratulate the King on his escape from danger, but it was undoubtedly expected that more would come out of such a trip than a momentary improvement in personal relations. Prokop did not execute the delicate mission, as he was taken ill and could not travel. Instead, a person of minor importance was sent to Hungary with George's letter.[448] The substitution of a messenger for a representative figure, though accidental, in fact changed the original intention as Prokop was the only man who could to some extent replace Bishop Tas.

The troops under Victorin's command indeed posed serious problems. Something had to be done quickly to prevent disorder and pillaging of those parts of Moravia in which they were stationed. To give them some satisfaction, George decided upon a hazardous operation, and without fully realizing it, he crossed his Rubicon. One of Bohemia's neighbors appeared to be incorrigible: Frederick III. In 1467 he added new instances to his earlier proofs of enmity. Some of his actions were directed against George personally, others against some Austrian noblemen known for their friendly relations with Prague. The leading figure among them was George von Stein, whose castle was in November, 1467, besieged by Frederick's forces under the command of Ulrich von Grafeneck.[449] Patient and circumspect in other maneuvres, George acted impulsively when Frederick III crossed his path. Using von Stein's appeal for help as an excuse, George instructed Victorin to invade Frederick's domains with selected troops.[450] Nominally the expedition was not directed against the Emperor but against the Duke of Austria, as if a legal nicety could change the hard facts.

Frederick III could assemble adequate forces to drive Victorin's troops back. The conduct of the Czechs stirred up excitement in Austria and the adjacent countries. George's enemies seized upon this new opportunity to stigmatize him as an aggressor, unwilling to live in peace with his Catholic neighbors.

While Victorin and his associates from Moravia and Austria harassed Frederick's party, George's foes at Breslau and elsewhere went ahead with forging a league in which the king of Hungary was destined to play the leading role. He was keen to accept it, but could not do so precipitately. A fairly strong faction of the Hungarian nobility demanded that the country's resources be used exclusively for defensive measures to keep the Turks at a reasonable distance from the Hungarian boundary. Matthias endeavored to win them over for the idea of an expedition against George, but the provincial assembly, held early in March, 1468, at Eger, ended in discord. Matthias felt that the opposition party was strong enough to organize a rebellion in his rear, and decided to go ahead by using forces in his pay and mercenaries to be hired specifically for that purpose.[451]

Late in March, King Matthias reached the royal borough of Trnava in the Slovak region, not far from the Moravian border. Both Zdeněk of Šternberk and Bishop Tas arrived there to assure him of loyalty and of effective cooperation. Out of respect to Casimir, the Czech rebels did not offer Matthias the royal crown. Matthias did not insist on a formal declaration in his favor and contented himself with the less brilliant role of protector of the Catholic population in George's domains. Tas journeyed from Trnava to Cracow to inform Casimir of Matthias' arming and to dispel doubts concerning the purpose of the prepared expedition.[452]

On March 31, 1468, the day of the momentous conference with the Czech leaders, the royal Hungarian chancellery issued a letter addressed to Victorin of Poděbrady.[453] In it Matthias pointed to the treaty of July 19, 1463, by which he was obliged to succor Frederick III whenever a need of assistance arose.[454] Within less than ten days Matthias wrote to George and openly admitted his alliance with the Catholic opposition.[455] Reference was made to the papal admonitions as well as to the intervention of legate Rudolf; the campaign, which was already in progress, was presented as no less meritorious than a war with the Turks. The relevant passages were formally addressed to George, but were intended for a wider audience, including the aristocratic opposition in Matthias' rear, which put the defense of the southern boundary of the kingdom above any other obligation.

At the time of this letter, April 8, 1468, one part of Matthias' forces was moving into Austria to join whatever force Frederick III possessed. Victorin was caught by surprise and only with the help of reinforcements rushed from Moravia was he able to extricate himself from encirclement. George was not too far from the scene, as he probably had received an advance notice of Matthias' designs. Thanks to his watchfulness, a catastrophe was averted and preparations were quickly completed for a defense of Moravia against the combined Austrian and Hungarian troops.

Intense activities at Matthias' court in the winter and early spring of 1468 had their parallel in harsher measures against the Hussite king enacted by Paul II. The distance between Rome and the Central European capitals hindered agreement on details, but in general co-ordination was well arranged. Fra Gabriel Rangoni brought to Rome letters from Breslau and reported orally on the resolutions of the December conference.[456] It is possible that initiatory measures were executed before his arrival, but he apparently participated in designing the plan for a concerted action against the Czechs.

In the absence of diaries and similar sources, it is difficult to reconstruct the situation in Rome in those months. Second to the Pope in determining the course of the papal policy was undoubtedly Cardinal Carvajal, who returned from Venice in September, 1467. As Bishop Rudolf was fully occupied in Breslau, an appointment of a legate to Hungary was to be made in the near future. Paul II did not send there a special envoy, but instructed Bishop Roverella to combine his mission to Germany with the representation of the Holy See at Matthias' court.[457]

The bull for him dated on January 25, 1468, showed that the Pope had overcome his earlier hesitation to use Matthias as the chief instrument of the punitive expedition against George, and wanted to include Hungary in the alliance supporting the anti-Hussite offensive. Bishop Lawrence was empowered to collect in Hungary contributions from both clergy and laity in the same manner as in the territories of the Empire.

The legate's responsibility was rather heavy in view of the prevailing indifference among the princes and their subjects. Subsidies for which he appealed when attending the Nurnberg Diet and afterwards were not forthcoming as generously as expected. Moreover, some collectors through whose hands the money had to pass did not deliver it to his coffers, but diverted it to other and less laudable purposes. The abuses apparently reached alarming dimensions so that late in March the Pope issued a strong declaration against the delinquents and excommunicated them.[458] The bishops of the Empire were requested to make notarized copies of the declaration and give it the widest publicity, so that nobody could plead ignorance as an excuse.

At the observance of the rites of Maundy Thursday (April 14, 1468), Paul II promulgated the traditional condemnation of heretics and other enemies of the Church.[459] Their list was headed by that "disciple of perdition," George of Poděbrady and Kunštát. After him followed Victorin for his audacity in attacking Emperor Frederick III. From among George's followers, Rokycana was singled out for a severe censure and equally strong terms were attached to the name of Gregory of Heimburg. In the general condemnation were included all clerics and laymen maintaining relations with the Wycliffites and supplying them with weapons, horses, iron, lead, timber, salt, oil, wine, clothing, and any foodstuff.

The Emperor had his own share in the widely ramified campaign against the Czechs. In a letter issued at Graz on March 14, 1468, and

intended for the princes and Estates of Silesia and Upper and Lower
Lusatias, he expressed his indignation with George and accused him
and his sons Victorin and Henry of ingratitude.[460] With reference to the
papal sentence of December 23, 1466, he admonished the addressees to
desist from any dealings with the excommunicated King. After some
weeks (April 23) he recapitulated his earlier letter and informed the
addressees of Matthias' willingness to fulfill his obligations to help in
driving out Victorin's troops from Austria. A special missive of about
the same length was dispatched to Breslau.[461]

The Emperor's letters and Matthias' declaration that he took the Catholics in George's lands under protection lifted the spirits of the Silesian
rebels.[462] Writing on their behalf, legate Rudolf assured Matthias of their
readiness to join forces with him against the common enemy.[463] The joy
caused by the glad tidings from Hungary and Austria was wild. After
several years of helpless waiting, the anti-Czech party in Silesia saw a
common front in the process of formation, and expected confidently that
military operations would start with the advent of the spring weather.

Admonitions to the faithful, appeals for generous subsidies, threats and
bans, as well as increased diplomatic activities, were conceived as the
papal contribution to the common cause. As soon as Lent was over, Paul
II plunged into passionate activities to reaffirm the earlier decisions and
to plug the holes in the elaborate scheme by which he hoped to hasten
the end of the Hussite opposition. Rome, like Breslau, was pervaded by
radiant optimism and Matthias won the affections of all advocates of
relentless proceedings against the Czechs.

Three days after Easter, on April 20, 1468, the Pope issued several
bulls, all aiming at the same goal but different in concrete provisions.
The most important item in this collection was a lengthy appeal to the
princes and people of the Empire to use for an expedition against Bohemia the forces which otherwise were intended as the German contingents for the crusade against the enemy of the Cross.[464] The Pope spoke
of twenty thousand warriors and motivated his request by a reference
to the invasion of the Austrian territory by George's troops. Their movements there were described pathetically as if they were but a prelude
to sufferings and ravages to be soon inflicted by the Hussites on other
German regions. Continuing in this agitated tone, the Pope stressed the
need for an energetic drive against "the pestilent and armed Hussite
heresy" and obsecrated "by the bowels of the mercy of Jesus Christ and
by his tremendous judgment" the entire German nation, the prelates and
the princes, the knights and nobles, the communities and universities, to
take up arms for the defence of the faith, for the safety of the father-
land, and for their own protection.

The bull was supplemented by an impressive array of charters and letters executed by the chancellery on the pontiff's order. Bishop Lawrence as the legate *a latere* was destined to bear the burden of co-ordinating and financing the large-scale preparations.[465] With reference to the Mantua congress of 1459, Paul II enjoined him to exact and collect financial obligations—the tenths, the twentieths and the thirtieths, according to each contributor's status—and to see to it that money not be diverted to purposes other than the support of the anti-Czech expedition. To strengthen the legate's position, the Pope repeated his requests for a full tenth from all ecclesiastical revenues and issued detailed instructions for its collection and delivery into the legate's hands. The pertinent bulls were addressed to the Archbishops of Salzburg, Magdeburg, Mainz, Köln, Trier, Bremen, and Riga, so as to comprise the entire territory of the Empire.[466]

One bull of April 20 corroborated that passage of the pronouncement on Maundy Thursday which referred to George's allies or benevolent supporters.[467] Expanded and conformed in words to the style of the papal charters, the text had the same meaning and purpose as the previous condemnation: to isolate the loyal areas of the kingdom of Bohemia from the rebel-controlled territory as well as from the neighboring countries, so that George's subjects would be cut off from any imports or subsidies and thus throttled. Specific causes provided for the confiscation of goods and properties owned anywhere by the Czech heretics, for the dissolution of bonds and ties of any kind, for an automatic extension of the interdict over the places in which the heretics had been given shelter. Briefly, all contacts with them were to be severed and any violation of the papal orders in these matters was to be punished by excommunication.

Another bull of the same date enumerated indulgences reserved by the Holy See for all the faithful who would support the campaign either by personal participation or by donations.[468] In an attempt to secure the largest amount, the Pope granted full powers to confessors in the Empire to commute penances and vows, such as the pilgrimage to the Holy Land or to a renowned shrine, into contributions for the Czech war. Other cases in which either service in the armed forces or a donation could be substituted for the more conventional acts of penance were also mentioned for the guidance of both the higher and the lower clergy.

By another, shorter bull, issued on April 21, Legate Rudolf was empowered to relieve of active service the poor and wounded crusaders and to absolve anyone who would hurt or kill a heretic in the combat.[469]

All together, the bulls of late April, 1468, marked a deliberate turn in the papal policy. After a consultation with the cardinals, Paul II postponed the Christian crusade against the Turks and gave priority to the execution of his sentence against the king of Bohemia. With Matthias prepared to move westward and the German princes admonished to attack George's positions from the opposite direction, no force was left on the continent of Europe that could be thrown across the Danube in concurrence with the naval operations, in which Pius II had reserved a major share for Paul's native city, Venice. Damages caused to some parts of Lower Austria by Victorin's forays, lacking any religious implication, were grossly exaggerated in order to create the impression that the Church and its faithful members had more to fear from "the most perfidious arch-heretic"—as George was designated in the bull for the Empire—than from the formidable leader of the Moslem hosts. Deeper in the background was the virulent opposition of the radical party in Breslau and such trifling incidents as the ruin of Cornštejn. Pius' grandiose scheme, for which Paul never burned with ardor, was thus overshadowed by another seemingly more urgent and laudable undertaking. Incensed by George's reluctance to bend his knee and to recant simply and humbly, Paul II gave the signal for a war in which, directly or indirectly, those parts of the continent were to be involved which otherwise could have served as bulwarks against the Turkish aggression.

When practical matters came under consideration, it was found advisable to open the campaign from Frederick's residence. Neither Paul II nor his chief advisers in the Czech affairs entertained any illusions as to the amount of help which could be expected from him. Frederick's title was worth more than his resources, and his court at Graz, though geographically remote, was in fact the administrative center of the far-flung Empire. Bishop Lawrence and also Fra Gabriel Rangoni chose it as temporary headquarters and arrived there, according to some indications, early in June, 1468. Along with Rangoni, Dean Hilarius reached Graz, and his knowledge of conditions of Bohemia was highly valued.

If Paul's bulls, dispatched either directly from Rome or from the residence of his two legates, Bishop Lawrence and Bishop Rudolf, had been only partially obeyed, George's prospects would have been dim indeed. It helped him considerably that no prince of the Empire offered his service to the Pope in organizing a crusade as designed by the bulls of late 1466. Even those princes who were not too friendly to George were aware of the risks involved in the campaign that the papal plenipotentiaries endeavored to initiate. The countries neighboring on Bohemia were even less inclined to be drawn into the new venture than the more distant areas, for fear of retaliation. Not princes, but leaders of marauding bands disguised as crusaders, heeded the appeals of fanatical preachers and penetrated into Bohemia and Moravia. They operated without centralized command in the territories left by the King and loyal lords without adequate protection. The civilian population suffered from their rapacity and stories of their brutality spread like wildfire among the

Utraquists, convincing even the half-hearted members that the salvation of their party lay in a resolute defense against any foe. The invaded areas were not large, and the bands, badly organized and poorly equipped, were unable to reach either the populous cities or the fertile and densely inhabited districts. The place reserved in the scheme of the anti-Hussite crusade for armies mobilized in Germany was never filled, despite repeated exhortations and generous offers of indulgences. Appeals to solidarity issued many times from Breslau stirred no sharper echoes than did the papal bulls.

Except for raids of predatory bands, the country would have been on the whole protected by the truce which was to last to the Feast of the Ascension, which occurred on May 26.[470] Matthias' advance, developing from his operation in Austria, brought about unforeseen complications and opened a struggle destined to be long and embittered. George hastened the preparations for a defense of Moravia, which was in immediate danger of invasions. To supplement the seasoned warriors in his pay, he levied men who had little knowledge of the art of warfare but could be used in mass encounters with the enemy. There existed a striking disparity between the opposing armies. The Hungarians excelled as light horsemen and were reluctant to get involved in a battle with the Czech forces, who used for their protection sturdy wagons which, if needed, could be converted into a moving fortress. As the Hungarians did not launch a mass attack, George saw no use in keeping the levies together. He retreated into Bohemia and kept only the mercenaries under his banner. Before he left, he instructed Victorin to keep under his control the fortified borough of Třebíč and from that stronghold to obstruct the Hungarian forays.

Foes and friends alike recognized Victorin's bravery; but he was too young and unexperienced to counteract effectively Matthias' strategy. As soon as Matthias learned of George's departure from Moravia, he moved his forces there almost unhindered and captured the borough of Třebíč by surprise. Victorin saved himself in the eleventh hour by a retreat to a spacious and fortified Benedictine convent on a hill dominating the surrounding countryside. But the Hungarian forces were strong enough to encircle the convent and to hinder the flow of supplies and the arrival of reinforcements.

The thought that his first-born son was in serious danger of falling into Matthias' captivity was unbearable to George. Troops were levied hurriedly in central Bohemia and rushed to the besieged convent. As soon as their march was noticed, the garrison split into three columns to break through the ring of the Hungarians and unite with the army of relief. The columns met with varying degrees of resistance and losses were heavy; but Victorin succeeded in reaching his kinsmen.

George's situation in the spring of 1468, though awkward, was not desperate. Although the truce was nominally valid until May 26, hostilities were reopened in many places before that date in order to heed Matthias' appeals for help. The city of Breslau moved ahead more eagerly than did the rebel lords in Bohemia. Matthias profited indirectly from such diversions, but he did not expressly sanction any irregular warfare and insisted that the Catholic forces be united with his army. The expedition into Moravia, since it dragged on without a decisive victory, drained the Hungarian financial reserves and caused the King a good deal of disappointment.

The spring was not far from ending when news from Cracow reached the rival kings. Due to various circumstances, not Rome nor Graz, but Cracow was for some time the center of feverish activities, on which the outcome of the conflict depended in no smaller degree than on the military operations in Moravia.

Traveling from Trnava after the conferences with the Hungarians, Bishop Tas reached the Polish capital late in April. He had two audiences with the King and endeavored to bring him into line with Matthias and the Bohemia Catholic opposition.[471] To dispel suspicions as to the motives of Matthias' expedition, Tas assured Casimir that no harm would come of it either to him or to his sons, as their claims to the crown of Bohemia would be respected. In the second private audience Tas went far beyond the original offer and opened before Casimir a broad vista of possible family connections. Tas was authorized to broach with the Poles the marriage of Casimir's eldest daughter, Jadwiga, to the widowed Matthias. The marriage of the younger daughter, Sophia, to Frederick's first-born son Maximilian, was also mentioned as a possibility to lure Casimir into the new coalition.

The Polish royal court was not fascinated by the prospect of such widely ramified connections. Rumors persisted that the Queen in particular refused to give her daughter to Matthias, who was not of royal blood. In political matters, Casimir pursued his traditional line by telling Tas that he neither had accepted nor rejected the crown of Bohemia, and could not make the final declaration before consulting the Diet of the realm, which was to meet late in August. Casimir also hinted at Matthias' meddling with the affairs of Bohemia, and in a straightforward statement expressed his displeasure with the Hungarian operations in the Spiš district as well as in the confines of Moldavia, a Polish vassalage. As a gesture of friendship, Tas was asked to attend the baptismal ceremony of a new-born prince and to have him baptized Frederick in honor of the Emperor.

The day after the Bishop's departure, Cracow greeted in its walls another guest. The best diplomat in George's service, Albrecht Kostka of

Postupice, arrived to assure Casimir of George's profound gratitude for his untiring efforts to bring about a peaceful solution.[472] Albrecht's instructions contained more than the recognition of Casimir's past services and an expression of George's readiness to comply with Casimir's suggestions. More than good will had to be pledged to preserve Casimir's friendship after the promulgation of the papal bulls against anyone maintaining contacts with Prague. Serious deliberations had apparently preceded Albrecht's departure for Cracow, and out of them emerged George's offer to facilitate the accession of one of Casimir's sons to the throne of Bohemia, when it should become vacant. Casimir's reply to Albrecht's speech was friendly and encouraging. More valuable than the formal statements was, undoubtedly, Albrecht's conviction that Casimir had no intention of exploiting George's embarrassment by attacking his flank.

Although Cracow was not too far away from Moravia, it took Tas several weeks to complete the return journey. He reported to Matthias in the camp near Třebíč. The King was surrounded by warriors and also by prominent personalities, clerics, and laymen. A group of Czech rebels present there was headed by Zdeněk of Šternberk. They were soon joined by Dean Hilarius, sent to Moravia from the imperial residence by the papal legate Rovarella. Tas's report caused disappointment, as it shattered the hope of a quick Polish attack which would have immensely aggravated George's position. Nor could Hilarius cheer up his countrymen, as he arrived empty-handed and could promise no other aid than the money to be collected in various countries for the support of a crusade.

Despite these reports, Matthias decided to continue the struggle. There existed no acute danger of invasion of Hungary by the Turks, and a sudden attack upon his advanced positions in Moravia by George's troops was also not very likely. Cold calculations gave Matthias a fairly strong hope that the Hussite party, if isolated by papal and other diplomats, would run out of resources and lay down their arms. While Matthias did not commit himself irrevocably to war as the only road to success, the Catholic rebels were resolutely opposed to any compromise, knowing that without the Hungarian troops they would not be able to deprive George of his throne. They intensified their efforts to keep the Hungarians in a bellicose spirit and ready to continue operations in other directions.

After Victorin's rescue, George withdrew to Bohemia and left the defense of Moravia in the hands of the loyal lords, among whom the family Tovačovský of Cimburk held pre-eminence. In keeping with George's general directives, the lords did not meet the invaders in an open battle, but protected their domains either from their castles or by hastily thrown up defenses. As they were scattered all over central and eastern Moravia, they were unable to hinder Matthias' penetration into the less protected areas bordering on the compact territory over which the Bishop of Olomouc reigned. The two cities in which the Moravian Diet used to hold its sessions, Brno and Olomouc, opened their gates to Matthias. In both instances the royal garrisons retreated to the two fortresses, Špilberk, towering over Brno, and the walled convent of Hradiště in the vicinity of Olomouc. As two other royal boroughs in southwestern Moravia, Jihlava and Znojmo, had joined the rebels before the war flared up, George held only the fifth of the royal boroughs, named also Hradiště, as the walled convent was called, but situated in the direction of Hungary. In addition to that, the royal captains controlled some less populous boroughs in northwestern Moravia, facilitating that region's connection with Bohemia.

As soon as the walled convent of Hradiště was encircled by the rebel forces, Olomouc was in no danger from the royal forces and Matthias moved his headquarters to that city. During the summer of 1468, George's implacable foes of long standing, and also the more recent deserters, gathered in Olomouc to ingratiate themselves with the king of Hungary, whose star was definitely in the ascendant. On several occasions the gate through the belt of fortifications opened to admit a foreign envoy clad in sumptuous clothes or in clerical garb.

Soon after his arrival at Olomouc, Matthias gave an audience to a delegation from Poland sent by Casimir both to him and to George in one more attempt at mediation.[473] Their visit was short, as they were anxious to explore the situation on George's side and get his terms first. More impressive was the entry into Olomouc late in July of the papal legate Roverella, accompanied by Gabriel Rangoni and by some Austrians. The agile monk had attempted to accomplish what other men had failed to do and by an urgent letter he put Bishop Rudolf in such an awkward position that the latter could no longer speculate on Casimir's candidature and therefore postpone his journey to Matthias' provisional court.[474] Rudolf arrived there about the middle of August, and as soon as the formalities were over, a conference was held to survey the situation on the scattered battlefields and the progress of the diplomatic negotiations.

Shortly before its opening, the League of Zelená Hora achieved a notable success: John of Rožmberk, for many years George's partisan, joined the rebels. His defection, although it meant a serious loss for the loyalists, did not come as a complete surprise. He was attached to the Roman Church and stood under persistent pressure from that side. The royal borough of České Budějovice, surrounded by the Rožmberk domains, also came under fire for its loyalty to George. When the mighty lord changed sides, the city council followed his lead. John did not attend the Olomouc parley, but sent his emissaries who were joined by a delegation from Budějovice. The past policy of that community was judged more leniently than was Rožmberk's case. Nobody had any respect for him and so he—as a contemporary chronicler said—remained "a weathercock and turncoat" to both parties.[475]

The temper of the assembled notables was unyielding and no serious thought was given to a policy of conciliation. The Polish envoys, when they returned from George's court, were heard out of respect for their master, Casimir. George's proposals, which they brought with them, were countered by requests which he could never grant without admitting sheer despair.[476] None of the legates participated actively in dealing with them. Persons inspired by the legates maintained that the Polish envoys should obtain from George a surrender of five of the foremost castles as a prerequisite to serious discussion of his terms: Prague, Karlštejn, Kladsko, Špilberk, and the royal borough of Hradiště. The enemy knew well where George's strength lay.

When the Polish envoys departed, arrangements were made for continuation of military operations. Toward the end of August the previous agreements between Matthias and the rebels were reinvigorated. With the fresh assurance of loyalty, Matthias left Moravia to attend to his duties in Hungary. At about the same time Bishop Roverella and Gabriel Rangoni went back to the imperial court to resume campaigning among German princes for pecuniary and military aid.

In Matthias' absence, Zdeněk of Šternberk acted as the supreme leader of the Catholic forces. He threw himself into the new task vigorously, in order to reconquer his own possessions lost to George in the initial stage of the war. His higher ambition was a concentration of the available forces so that the struggle could be closed by a decisive victory before the advent of winter.

After several months of war, George's position was distressing, as none of his neighbors dared to come openly to his aid. He had to use his resources prudently as not to exhaust them prematurely. No risky offensive could be undertaken by him, and therefore the initiative was mostly on the Catholic side.

When George learned of the failure of the Polish delegation to obtain reasonable terms, he levied fresh troops to bring relief to the loyal forces, located in strategic positions but threatened with exhaustion of reserves. Several columns were recruited in central Bohemia and sent from there in several directions, each with a specific assignment.

One urgent task was the defense of northwestern Moravia, since that territory served as a corridor from Bohemia to various positions in the eastern part of the kingdom. A column headed by Zdeněk Kostka of

Postupice advanced in that direction, but before anything significant could be accomplished, Zdeněk was so seriously wounded that no human help could save his life. Prince Victorin was sent immediately to Moravia to take over the command, but neither he nor Lord Ctibor Tovačovský of Cimburk, operating from his own domain, was able to supply the garrison in the walled convent of Hradiště. When it ran out of reserves it capitulated, to the great joy of the masters of Olomouc, in whose rear it had stood defiantly since the start of hostilities.

In Lusatia and Silesia George had lost two strategic positions before the Hradiště convent fell to the enemy. The Lusatian castle of Hoyerswerde, which had resisted for almost one year, capitulated when left entirely without supplies. The surrender of Frankenstein in Silesia on September 17 was even more lamentable an event, as it could be trumpeted to the world by Breslau leaders as convincing evidence of their superiority over George's forces.

In Bohemia, two Catholic strongholds fiercely resisted the King. The city of Plzeň, which had thrown off George's control as early as February, 1466, appeared to be impregnable; so George left it out of calculation when distributing, in September, 1468, his reorganized forces. Instead, he assigned one strong column to a perilous and costly expedition against the castle of Konopiště, at some distance from Prague, whose owner was his archfoe, Zdeněk of Šternberk, often called in contemporary sources Konopištský. The walls of Konopiště were so formidable that an attack, even if supported by heavy fire, appeared to be a desperate and useless gesture. Complete encirclement proved to be a less spectacular but safer method, and as the result the commander of Konopiště in December, 1468, capitulated. The news was greeted at George's court as evidence that the period of misfortune had happily ended and that new successes were bound to come in the spring of 1469.

Leaving military campaigns in the hands of experienced warriors, the political leaders carried on, in the fall of 1468, diplomatic negotiations to cement existing alliances and to win some neutrals for an active participation in the struggle. The most important event was the general Diet of Poland, opened at Piotrków by Casimir on October 9. Well aware of its significance, Bishop Rudolf sent there Canon Balthasar of Breslau with a request that Casimir permit the publication of the papal bulls against George and the preaching of the crusade in his kingdom.[477] George was represented by Provost Paul of Zderaz, who was well acquainted with the conditions at Casimir's court. The envoy most likely addressed the assembly in his mother tongue and supported his appeal for help by passionate reference to the ethnic kinship of the Czechs and of the Poles. Pressed from both sides, Casimir once more refrained from an irrevocable commitment, and promised to send distinguished delegates to Rome to make one more attempt at a peaceful settlement.

Casimir's unwillingness to be drawn into the war against George enhanced Matthias' prestige in the eyes of the clerical opponents of the Hussite king. He was indeed the only prince who was at war with George. As Hungary was in Roverella's sphere of influence, he attended the Diet at Pressburg (Bratislava) and tightened his connections with both the Hungarian prelates and the leaders of the warlike faction of the Hungarian nobility.

Roverella's presence at the general assembly of the Estates, as well as other friendly gestures from the papal legates or directly from the Pope, strengthened Matthias' belief that he could pursue his ambitious schemes, for which he would need both the Emperor's and the Pontiff's support.

The chances of Matthias' success seemed to be brighter than ever, for how could the Pope refuse to intervene in behalf of the only prince who brought effective help to the Catholic party in Bohemia? Moreover, Matthias was able to send to Rome the most distinguished representative that could be found—the Emperor himself.

Frederick III had toyed with the idea of a journey to Rome for several years. On various occasions he spoke of the vow he had made when in distress in 1462; in the fall of 1468 the time seemed ripe for its implementation. Matthias encouraged him in that proposition and promised to administer the Austrian lands during his pilgrimage. Negotiations between the two friendly courts were conducted in utmost secrecy. In the absence of reliable information, rumors circulated in Austria and elsewhere, according to which Frederick III had promised his junior ally effective help in a competition for the rank of the King of the Romans, coveted at one time by George of Poděbrady. Gregory of Heimburg, with his ear always sharp and attentive, claimed to have heard that Frederick III was prepared to go to extremes, hand over the imperial crown to Matthias, and take holy orders.[478]

Frederick III left his residence late in the fall and reached the eternal city on Christmas Eve. He was accorded the honors reserved traditionally for an emperor visiting the Pope. At the midnight mass, wearing the deacon's robe, he read from the Scriptures the passage concerning the edict issued by Caesar Augustus at the time of the birth of Christ in Bethlehem. A good deal of time was spent in religious ceremonies and formal sessions, but neither Frederick III nor Paul II wanted to miss the opportunity for a discussion of problems that were too delicate to be communicated in writing or confided to diplomats. Rome buzzed with rumors which the winds carried quickly across the Appenines and Alps to various political centers. It was believed in Poland that the Emperor, instead of promoting Matthias' interests, endeavored to obtain from the

Pope a sanction of the Habsburg claims to the crowns of both Bohemia and Hungary.[479] There is really no evidence of Frederick's serious occupation with Matthias' ambitious designs, and the Pope apparently also evaluated the Hungarian contribution to the campaign against George more soberly than did the King himself.

In Matthias' visions of things to come, the kingdom of Bohemia held a very prominent place. Occupied by his forces or at least controlled by a friendly ruler, it could serve as a stepping stone to higher dignities in Christendom. The assistance he had given in 1468 to the Catholic party was too important to be simply forgotten or written off. Even when kept busy by home affairs and negotiations with Frederick III, Matthias maintained contacts with his lieutenant in Bohemia, Zdeněk of Šternberk. From him he learned of the fall of Konopiště into George's hands. The winter season was usually regarded as unsuitable for military operations on a larger scale, but an exception was made when events seemed to be taking a sharp turn in George's favor. The conquest of Konopiště by the royal troops was to be avenged without too much delay, or else it could serve as a starting point for George's counteroffensive.

Late in January, 1469, Zdeněk of Šternberk visited Matthias' headquarters not far from the Moravian border and persuaded him to get ready for a renewal of hostilities.[480] Matthias hastened his preparations and early in February moved his forces across the border. Not expecting an invasion at such an early date, George was unable to rush his troops to Moravia, either to strengthen resistance of the loyal garrisons wherever they still existed or to meet the invader in the field. The castle of Špilberk was one of the few remaining strongholds held by the loyal forces, and as it could neither be relieved nor even supplied with victuals and ammunition, it fell into Matthias' hands. The Hungarian exploited this success and marched with his army from Moravia into Bohemia unhindered by George's troops or by the weather. His main objective was the city of Kutná Hora with its silver mines and the royal mint. He was joined by on the way rebel forces commanded by Zdeněk of Šternberk and other members of the League. Success of the combined operations depended largely on speed; therefore, no attempt was made to attack castles or walled boroughs as long as they could be neutralized by a siege or other device. Such a type of warfare was popular with Hungarian horsemen, whose forays caused immense suffering to the defenseless peasantry.

From his headquarters at Kutná Hora, George gathered his trained soldiers and also the levies as provided for such occasions by ancient laws. With the country invaded, no time could be spent in laborious preparations. Defects in equipment were compensated by the revival of religious fervor with which in 1420–31 the invasions of Bohemia by another king of Hungary, Sigismund, had been fought off. George himself made no attempt to mobilize the Utraquist party or to proclaim holy war against Rome and its instrument, the Hungarian king. He was too well aware of the repercussions which any admixture of religious motives into his program would have in Poland and other countries that he wanted to have on his side, or at least as benevolent neutrals. Other leaders, spiritual and temporal, were less circumspect. In their opinion, the time for negotiations was past and both the future of the kingdom and the fate of the Hussite cause depended on the swift concentration of forces and the ejection of the enemy from the country. From resolute Utraquist circles emerged a manifesto recalling the deeds of John Žižka and of his warriors.[481] Some of its passages directly attacked the Pope; others turned against the executors of his bans—the Germans and Matthias.

George could not remain unaware of the feverish agitation among people of his blood and faith, but he was not deflected from his course. He wanted to meet force with force. As soon as he had fresh troops under his banners, he moved at their head against Matthias. As the Czech captains were well acquainted with the terrain, they soon gained strategic advantages over the Hungarian commanders and pushed them into the densely wooded uplands of central Bohemia. From those unfavorable positions there was virtually no retreat, especially with snow covering the ground. Not only the subordinate leaders, but Matthias himself, were encircled and in danger of captivity.

The sequence of events was so rapid that they were not faithfully recorded by any contemporary writer.[482] Many engagements of the armed units occurred in thinly populated areas at a considerable distance from residential centers. Rumors cropped up and as they spread from their source to more distant places, they were colored by suspicions and recriminations. The center of attention was the Hussite king, personally controlling the movements of his troops while transacting political matters which arose from Matthias' quick advance. Another name, that of Albrecht Kostka, also aroused the chronicler's curiosity.[483] According to an unconfirmed report, Matthias succeeded in making contact with that diplomat and through him suggested to George a conference to be held in utmost secrecy. George was interested and met Matthias in a half-burned cottage. No document describing the interview was drawn, as Matthias, in view of the papal verdict, would have found the question of an appropriate title for George highly embarrassing, and George in turn could not attach his name to any charter omitting his own royal rank. As no witnesses were present—for Matthias was fluent in Czech—few people learned of the terms agreed upon. Bohemia and the neighboring countries buzzed with rumors concerning the private parley and its probable effects on the future course of events.[484]

The place of the conference and its secret character indicate that

George took this fateful step alone, without previous consultation with his political advisers or the captains commanding his forces. The royal army was swollen by recent arrival of men levied in the more distant areas, and by volunteers, primitively equipped but animated by fanatical zeal of the same intensity as during the Hussite war. It was generally regarded as superior to the invading forces and could throw them back without too much effort. George's decision to facilitate the enemy's retreat from what seemed to be a perfect trap stunned everybody, high and low. The resolute Utraquists freely vented their displeasure at the occurrence and the moderate elements were depressed by fears that George had put more trust in Matthias' oral pledges than was warranted by the latter's earlier record. George paid no heed to either consent or dissent on the part of his forces, and as soon as Matthias' troops withdrew from Bohemia, he disbanded the levies as if the country were free from danger. Truce was proclaimed to last until Easter Monday, which fell on April 3, 1469.[485]

It can be gathered from indirect evidence that George took his part of the treaty seriously. One of the terms apparently related to Matthias' ambitions in respect to the Empire. From conversation with him George most likely got the impression that both Frederick III and Paul II were prepared to grant Matthias the coveted rank. His duty now was to win over for this idea the princes with whom he maintained friendly relations. As on several other occasions, George turned first to Markgrave Albrecht Achilles. A special envoy, Span von Bartenstein, visited the Markgrave's residence and attempted to break his resistance.[486] George confidently expected that Albrecht would not only give his personal consent but get in touch with the Wettin princes and with his brother Frederick of Brandenburg, to orient them in the same direction.

The Czech envoy reported to the Markgrave what George knew from his own sources and from what Matthias had apparently confided to him to make his bid for the rank of King of the Romans more realistic. According to these reports, the Duke of Burgundy was considered by some princes as a candidate for the same dignity, especially by the dukes of Bavaria. Reference to them was made in the conversation with Albrecht Achilles, with particular emphasis on his strained relations with the leading representatives of the Wittelsbach house. The envoy also confided to the Markgrave that he was instructed to journey from Albrecht's residence to France and to deal there with King Louis XI. Most likely, the purpose of that mission was identical with that to the Markgrave, as the rivalry between Burgundy and France was no secret. Shrewd as usual, Albrecht Achilles did not take the envoys' message too seriously. He felt sure that Frederick III had no real intention of giving up the imperial crown. He was also convinced that the electors would be opposed to the candidature of a non-German prince either to the imperial dignity or to the lower rank of King of the Romans. It is not quite clear whether the envoy really proceeded from Albrecht's residence to France or whether he returned to Prague to tell George of the Markgrave's negative answer.

There is in the Markgrave's letter to his brother Frederick a vague reference to Matthias' promise to give back to George the captured castles as a compensation for his diplomatic support. Even if such a promise had been meant seriously, its execution would have been hindered by practical difficulties. The conquests were made not only by the Hungarians, but also by the rebels, including Breslau. These were not consulted before Matthias had decided to confer with George, and they were willing to observe the truce only out of deference to their powerful ally. This, in fact, was not a sacrifice, as the weather was still unfavorable. They did not object when an additional agreement was reached by which the truce was extended to the Feast of the Ascension, May 11, 1469.

The conference, at which both the kings and some of their advisers were to be present, was scheduled for March 24, but it was put off for two weeks. George, with Albrecht Kostka and other staunch followers, resided in the borough of Šternberk which, apart from its name, had no connection with the head of the Catholic league. Matthias in turn moved from Brno to Olomouc, to be as close to George's headquarters as possible.[487] In Matthias' splendid retinue were many clerics and laymen, notably the legate Roverella, Gabriel Rangoni, the Archbishop of Esztergom, and the Bishop of Eger, two envoys from the Emperor's court, Zdeněk of Šternberk, and other Catholic lords. Bishop Rudolf, escorted by two hundred horsemen, arrived directly from Breslau.

Negotiations opened on April 7, 1469, when George and Matthias conversed without witnesses in a tent, erected for that purpose in the countryside between Olomouc and Šternberk. The progress of the ensuing parleys was slow, partly because of the legates' refusal to tolerate the presence of George's plenipotentiaries in Olomouc. Instead of round table sessions, negotiations split into a number of private meetings which could be more easily arranged. George was anxious to meet *in camera* with the legate Roverella, but was apparently reluctant to open his mind to the Archbishop of Esztergom, who was delegated to substitute for the papal plenipotentiary. George also sent two of his trusted advisers to Zdeněk of Šternberk to attempt to change his adamantine attitude, but they did not accomplish anything worth reporting. Another, more solemn, meeting of George with Matthias took place on April 20, again in a tent, but with more people present. Its rather elaborate program, including a banquet and a contest between the royal jesters, failed to disguise Matthias' unwillingness to meet his rival halfway.

The papal legates and the Catholic lords viewed with distrust the royal personal conferences in which they did not participate. Immediately after the first meeting of the two kings, they got together and concluded that a wedge should be driven between the two rulers, so that they would not be able to agree on any compromise that would be unacceptable to the papal plenipotentiaries and the leaders of the Catholic party. Matthias' election was regarded as the best protection of Catholic interests and it was resolved to proceed quickly with the arrangements for that solemn act. Both the clerics and the lords found it advisable to get beforehand an assurance from Matthias that he would accept the offer of the Bohemian crown. Zdeněk of Šternberk was empowered to acquaint Matthias with the idea and got from him a binding promise on April 17. No wonder that Matthias in his conference with George three days later dodged all concrete issues and led George away from them to trivialities.

Not aware of Matthias' underhanded deal with the Catholic party, George was willing to carry on the exchanges. He did not take part personally, but left the matter in the hands of his most brilliant diplomats, Albrecht Kostka and Beneš of Veitmil. The gap between the terms drafted at an earlier date by Roverella and George's counterproposals was too wide to be bridged over by conventional methods.[488] But Matthias did not favor a flat refusal: therefore, he helped to hammer out a text which the opposing party could accept. As the papal legates would have vetoed even the slightest concession in religious matters, the basic issues were touched upon only lightly and prominence was given to practical matters, especially an armistice to last to the end of 1469. The agreement was oral and it was not George personally but his two envoys who confirmed it on behalf of the royal party.[489]

The Catholic opposition felt safe in the walled city of Olomouc and proceeded with their bold scheme. On May 3, 1469, the spiritual and temporal lords assembled in the Cathedral of Saint Wenceslas and unanimously elected Matthias king of Bohemia. The Archbishop of Esztergom and Bishop Rudolf administered the oath to him and the assembled electors swore fealty to him as their legitimate ruler. A sumptuous banquet, attended by about four hundred distinguished guests, climaxed the day. The burghers and the common folk were not forgotten. On the King's order, Hungarian wine was served generously. It flowed from a fountain and was carried through the streets in ingeniously constructed pipes.[490]

There was no coronation at Olomouc or anywhere else, as the crown and the other insignia were kept at Karlštejn, an impregnable fortress in George's control. Nonetheless, Matthias on the very day of his election appointed supreme officers of the realm, granting, as could be expected, the highest rank to Zdeněk of Šternberk, the same who in March, 1458, had been confirmed as the supreme burgrave by George.

Writing amidst the war and the kaleidoscopic changes arising from its ups and downs, Gregory of Heimburg remarked pithily: "Faith and oath are a joke, loyalty and honor are just about as much as to wish you good morning!" [491]

Keen observers of these momentous events noticed that the enthusiasm accompanying the election was not universal. In its preparatory stage, the two legates were not in agreement. Roverella hesitated to sanction the decision, maintaining that only Bishop Rudolf had powers wide enough to do so. Envoys from Poland, who on their way to Rome stopped at Olomouc and learned through their contacts of Zdeněk's negotiations with Matthias, reminded the Catholic leaders of their former proclamations in favor of Casimir or his son. In the end, the resolute elements got the upper hand and overrode all doubts or objections.

Bishop Rudolf left Olomouc shortly after the election to bring the glad tidings to his flock personally.[492] Preparations started at once for a solemn welcome of the new king. Matthias, escorted by over two thousand horsemen in splendid uniforms, moved from Olomouc through the mountainous borderland of Moravia and Silesia and approached Breslau on Friday, May 26. A delegation, accompanied by four hundred horsemen, with city banners and keys of the city gates, met him a mile away and, thus accompanied, Matthias entered the city. On the following Sunday its representatives knelt before him and gladly swore their allegiance.

Four days later, the feast of Corpus Christi was observed with unprecedented pomp and joy. Bishop Rudolf flanked by the Papal legate Roverella, and the Bishops of Eger, Lavant and Lubus, carried the Sacrament. The Archbishop of Esztergom was unable to attend on account of gout. On Matthias' right marched the Elector of Brandenburg, Frederick, who had arrived for negotiations with the new master of Silesia. Six princes carried the canopy. One of them was Frederick's son John, others were the vassal dukes from various provinces of Silesia. More than sixty lords from Brandenburg, Hungary, and Bohemia marched behind their sovereign. The triumph seemed to be complete. But the capricious weather failed to add to the splendor of the elaborate ceremony: a rain came from the heavy skies and interrupted the procession, so that the rites had to be completed in a spacious church nearby.

A KINGDOM DIVIDED AGAINST ITSELF

When notified of the Olomouc ceremony, George tried to remain calm and good-humored. According to an unconfirmed story, he said that he would arrange for the election of all Casimir's sons and that Bohemia then would have not two but six kings. Sarcastic remarks, whether authentic or fictitious, could not conceal George's discomfort.[493] The kingdom which he endeavored to consolidate was split, and the "two peoples" over which he desired to rule justly and peacefully faced each other as enemies.

No matter from which angle the recent events were viewed, the election and Matthias' acceptance had to be regarded as a national catastrophe and the King's personal humiliation. It showed how seriously George had blundered when he displayed magnanimity to his captured foe at Vilémov and when he entered into confidential negotiations with him. He should have insisted instead on the dissolution of the ties with the rebels and the speedy evacuation of all territories occupied by the Hungarian and rebel forces since the start of hostilities.

Disabused of many cherished illusions, George realized that damage could be undone and prestige restored only by a speedy mobilization of all available forces. What was ahead of him was no more skilful maneuvering, but rather a struggle for survival. He must move simultaneously in three directions, political, diplomatic, and military. The time from May, 1469, to Christmas of that year was, indeed, the most critical period in George's life, fraught with dangers, enervating, but bringing in the end hope and relief.

Reports coming to Prague in the summer months of 1469 from Silesia and the neighboring territories indicated that the majority of the German-speaking Catholics would sooner or later transfer allegiance from George to the "Olomouc king," as Matthias was often called. Not only the political leaders of the rebellion but also the clergy exercised influence on the irresolute elements in order to bring them to Matthias' side. The estrangement of the German-speaking population from the body of George's loyal subjects seemed unavoidable. The rift threatened to be no less perilous than during the Hussite wars, as the difference of faith only accentuated the racial antagonism.

The defection of the Czech Catholics, though not universal, caused problems no less painful than the Silesian and Lusatian separatism. In the course of his life George, who was approaching fifty, had often to deal with hostile individuals, factions, and leagues, and had gained experience in bargaining with political opposition and carrying on military operations against unruly elements. The Olomouc election surpassed the earlier acts of defiance in that it linked purely domestic issues with international problems. The earlier contacts of the Zelená Hora league with the Holy See or with the papal legates stationed in various capitals of Central Europe could be motivated by the need of an understanding with the supreme spiritual authority. An alliance with a foreign sovereign, no matter how cleverly masked, and finally his acclamation as king, were treacherous acts, which precluded resumption of the negotiations broken off late in April, 1469, by the secret accord of the rebels with Matthias. Capitulation or a defeat by arms were the only alternatives George could consider, without a loss of prestige, as the way toward restitution of unity among the Czechs.

Neither before the Olomouc election nor after it did the Czech Catholics act as a solid bloc. Their domains did not form a compact territory which could be constituted as an administrative unit. Opposition to the Chalice was an important factor in splitting the national body; but other forces, political, social, and economic, were in the play, reducing the effects of religious differences. On both sides the radicals formed a minority, whereas other sections of both the Catholic and Hussite parties were guided more by traditionalism than by fervent convictions. Doctrinal differences, when examined calmly, were not as significant as the controversialists maintained, and occasionally the decision for or against the Chalice depended on the priest administering the parish or serving as chaplain in a noble household.

Ever since George's accession to power, the peace and political stability had depended largely on the attitude of the aristocracy. In that class, which only a hereditary monarchy could curb in their lust for power, Utraquism never gained so much ground as to predominate. Up to the formation of the Zelená Hora league and, indeed, up to the Olomouc election, moderate elements among the lords supported George loyally. They dexterously resisted both the wooing by the Šternberk clique and admonitions by ecclesiastical authorities. After Matthias' election, the pressure from both sides increased, causing George loss of followers in all parts of Bohemia and Moravia. No less painful than the desertions were the illness or death of faithful followers, by which the reserves of potential mediators and envoys to Catholic courts were reduced. Replacements were usually difficult to secure, as the number of talented men was not inexhaustible. When the struggle entered its acute stage, many noble families shunned commitments to either party and passively awaited the outcome.

George's most faithful supporters came from the ranks of the lesser nobility. In that type of warfare which both he and his enemy preferred to all-out battles, experienced commanders of small units were particularly useful, as they were able to operate on their own and constantly harass the opposing party. By their social background as well as by their tactics, those leaders represented continuity with the times of the Hussite captains after Žižka's death. Men serving in such units came either from the lower strata of the townsfolk or from the countryside. Most of them were attached to the Chalice and in spiritual matters obeyed Rokycana and his priests. As time went on, they admitted into their ranks warriors of other than Czech nationality seeking adventure and willing to serve any master.

In the stormy years following the excommunication, George needed larger forces than before. Instead of hiring mercenaries of foreign blood, he accepted into his pay captains and men of Czech ancestry who had previously served foreign rulers, including Matthias. While operating abroad, many of them had lost contact with their native soil and had also returned to the fold of the Roman Church. The traditional term of "brotherhood" poorly disguised the true character of these bands who lost attachment to the patriotic cause, relaxed their discipline, and, when not firmly controlled, plagued both friend and foe. Another name used by their foes, "beggars," was in many respects more appropriate.

George did not have much sympathy with the captains of Czech origin serving abroad, as many of them caused him complications when in disagreement with their masters. However, when he was almost completely isolated from other reservoirs of manpower, he found it necessary to take in his service even some of the less reputable "brotherhoods," so as to increase his forces without too heavy an expenditure. He used them often for punitive expeditions against traitors and such sworn enemies as the city of Breslau and its associates. In the conduct of regular operations he endeavored to follow the traditional line, not giving too much prominence to the religious rift or national prejudices.

Coming after several weeks of personal contacts from which even the most intimate advisers were excluded, Matthias' perfidy blocked the road toward any compromise. George began to prepare for the impending struggle, regarding the consolidation of the home front as his primary duty. The illness of Prokop of Rabštejn and the vacillation of

some high-ranking officers of the realm made new appointments necessary. The most important of them was Prokop's replacement by Ctibor
Tovačovský of Cimburk. Ctibor was uniquely qualified to have the care
of the royal chancellery and to act as the King's prime minister. George
trusted him as a loyal citizen, and respected him for the profound learning which he himself had not been able to acquire. Ctibor's relatives,
adhering to the Chalice and owning large estates in Bohemia and
Moravia, were invaluable allies and held in the Poděbrady party about
the same place as had once belonged to the Kostkas of Postupice. The
Kostka family, once so close to the throne, had to be replaced, as
Albrecht, who headed it after Zdeněk's premature death, defected to the
"Olomouc king."

In view of Matthias' hurried attempts to lure away from George as
many Catholics as possible, it was of utmost importance to fill the
vacancies in the administrative system and convince the citizens that
they would gain more from continued loyalty than from its breach. The
national economy, once balanced, suffered from political disturbances.
One of the sorest spots was the gradual depreciation of the currency
which, in fact, had began at a much earlier date than the flare-up of
hostilities. The decrease of value of coins in circulation was one of the
grievances, aired for many years at the provincial Diets or informal assemblies of the nobles. It affected equally the Catholics and the Utraquists.
There were really few things as much needed as an energetic reform of
the debased monetary system.

George had also to give thought to the dwindling volume of foreign
trade. Paul II had issued in 1467 and 1468 several decrees forbidding
trade or any contact with the Hussites. As they were not dutifully respected, the Pope found it necessary to instruct his legates that they
reissue the ban on commerce with the Czechs and insist on its rigid
observation. The iteration of the sentence against George, made on
Maundy Thursday (March 30), 1469, was followed on April 9 by a
lengthy bull.[494] In it Paul II requested Bishop Lawrence, then his
legate in Germany, to compile and transmit to the Curia the list of all
persons maintaining friendly contacts with the Czech heretics and giving
them assistance. Pending a general condemnation of them, he was
authorized to proclaim excommunicated all those found guilty. What
else could serve better as an inducement to merchants and importers
risking excommunication than a stabilized currency?

In making a pledge to the Estates gathered in Prague early in June,
1469, to abstain from objectionable practices, George took upon himself
heavy obligations involving temporary sacrifices, but bound to bear fruit
in short time.[495] As he remained in possession of silver mines at Kutná
Hora and elsewhere, he was able to contemplate more than a partial

remedy. His reform was intended to undo the gradual deterioration of the monetary system which had taken place not only in his own time, but from the beginning of the Hussite wars—a period of about fifty years. Conditions prevailing under King Wenceslas IV (1378–1419) were to be restored by George's decision to strike at the sources of evil. The ratio of the Czech coin to the Hungarian florin was to be twenty-four grossi, as it had been under Wenceslas IV. The relation to the Rhenish gulden was also fixed as eighteen grossi to one gulden. A grossus was to be subdivided into twelve denars and those in turn into two hellers. All coins were to be produced of good silver. To avoid speculation and unwanted competition, George forbade circulation of foreign coins in his realm with only one exception, the grossi of Misnia, valid in the lands of his Wettin allies. The ratio was to be two Misnian grossi to one new grossus of Bohemia.

Technical details concerning the actual execution of the monetary reform are lacking, but it appears from scattered references to it that it proved to be an asset. Matthias did not move ahead in the same direction, but left that part of the kingdom of Bohemia which had come under his control in its chaotic situation. It did not take long to show the difference between the two portions of the kingdom. Matthias was by no means prepared to invest new resources in the newly occupied lands, maintaining that he has suffered heavy financial losses by his support of the rebels.

Another constructive measure of George's was his restatement of the principle of toleration. In doing so, he did not bring in any new ideas, as he had always regarded himself as the ruler of both the Utraquists and the Catholics. If at certain moments, as in the Saint Lawrence assembly of 1462,[496] he had manifested his adherence to the Hussite tenets, at other times he carefully maintained the idea of equality.

A good deal of tact and restraint were needed in those stormy days to keep apart political and religious issues. It was clear that George's principal enemies, the city of Breslau, the League of Zelená Hora, and the king of Hungary, acted in unison with the papacy, the prime mover of the combined campaign. The papal legates, Bishops Rudolf and Lawrence Roverella, were present both at Olomouc and Breslau when Matthias was invested with the royal title and when he received homage from the rebels. Other clerics, including Gabriel Rangoni, supported wholeheartedly the papal offensive and exerted themselves in inciting the princes and populations of the neighboring countries against the Hussites. The catalogue of epithets used against George in the papal documents, in letters and manifestoes, and in sermons by fanatical preachers, was long and awe-inspiring. The books of the Bible were eagerly searched for appropriate quotations to be inserted in the papal bulls and the sensitive reader could easily expect that sooner or later the earth would open and swallow up the "son of damnation." None of these fierce attacks stirred an echo in George's circle, and in his correspondence a reverent tone was observed whenever a reference was to be made to the Pontiff.

Even when the conflict reached its climax, no attempt was made on George's part to hinder the Bishops of Olomouc and Breslau in the discharge of their pastoral duties. Bishop Rudolf was of course shielded by his rank of papal legate, but Tas was a son of the kingdom and an avowed rebel, often absent from his see and serving Matthias as a diplomat. The metropolitan chapter of Saint Vitus, after the hasty retreat of its leading members from Prague in the spring of 1467, continued its activities from Plzeň. Its dean and administrator of the Prague Archdiocese, Hilarius, emulated the bishops of Olomouc and Breslau in that he was mostly absent from Plzeň. He also took an active part in political and diplomatic campaigns against the lawful king. He did not live to see that memorable turn of events, Matthias' election, as his life was cut short by an infectious fever in December, 1468.

The city of Plzeň had a Catholic administration and was surrounded by Catholic domains. It was thus sufficiently protected and it sheltered not only the leading Catholic clerics but apparently also some outstanding scholars. To Plzeň goes the primacy in the history of printing, as it was there and not in Prague that the first book, a Czech version of the Histories of Troy, was issued from the press in 1468.

The vacancy caused by Hilarius' death was soon filled by a less bellicose cleric, Hanuš of Kolovraty, a nobleman who had taken holy orders only after the death of his consort. He was assisted by Hilarius' successor in the deanship, John of Krumlov. Hanuš lacked experience and energy, nor was he interested in launching a polemical campaign against the Hussites. He was chiefly concerned with the application of the papal bulls as well as the instructions, received at times from the Bishop-legate Rudolf of Breslau, at other times from Bishop Lawrence Roverella. It was not an easy task to follow the official line, as practical considerations often proved stronger than legal precepts. In a letter to Bishop Rudolf he described his problems and summed up his exasperating position in this terse sentence: "What one party likes, the other dislikes; I close and you open"—alluding discreetly to the conflicting orders from the higher offices.[497]

The Utraquist leaders knew well that they would not ingratiate themselves with the King by the zealous propagation of their tenets. No significant writing in support of the Chalice came from their side after the stormy conference of 1465. Not only George's dislike of doctrinal controversies but also illness or death imposed limits on public discussion of unsolved issues. In April, 1468, one of the leading Utraquist theologians, Martin Lupáč, passed away. At that time not many people remembered that in 1434 he had been elected by the provincial Diet to be one of Rokycana's suffragans.

For the outside world, John of Rokycany towered as the archheretic and the chief opponent of the Hussite submission to the Pope. Similarly, most people on the Catholic side believed that communion in both kinds was the most formidable obstacle in the way of conciliation. Like all generalizations, this simple formula covered a variety of problems which only the experts were able to perceive. In this advanced period, Rokycana's confirmation by the Pope was tacitly omitted whenever the chances of peace were explored. He was not far from seventy and his health was somewhat uncertain. A slight defect in speech was attributed to a stroke which otherwise did not affect his general condition.

An anonymous Czech chronicler praised Rokycana as "a real hammer against the enemies of the Lord's chalice as well as against the Pikharts." [498] It was paradoxical that in the critical period for Hussitism Rokycana was compelled to desist from invectives against the Roman Church but that nobody curbed his efforts to suppress the "Pikharts," by which name were often designated the members of the Unity of Brethren from Bohemia and Moravia. To understand the situation, our attention must turn for a while from political developments to less spectacular but momentous events in the religious sphere.

The Unity, which came into existence when George was advancing from governorship to kingship, suffered in its infancy from the King's and Rokycana's disfavor. It survived, however, and for several years did not encounter danger. The ideological opponents of Hussitism, especially those who wrote in foreign countries, failed to realize the significance of the new movement, which for about a decade was protected by formal allegiance to Utraquism. When criticising conditions in Bohemia or attacking the dissenters, the polemical writers usually aimed their arrows at Rokycana or made stereotyped references to the multitude of heresies among the Hussites. The term "Pikhart," which occurred occasionally in controversial writings when the Unity came under attack, was not new and it was used indiscriminately as a label for any radicals among the Hussites. Its origin was rather obscure; some writers derived it from the Beghards, others from a group of dissenters who came to Bohemia from Picardy in 1418.

The papal bulls against George did not specifically mention the Brethren, as they mostly repeated the terminology of the earlier papal documents. Since no one of importance singled out the Unity as a target, George, too, did not insist that its members be ferreted out and punished.

True to their leading principles, the Brethren were not interested in casting their nets all around. Their number after ten years of precarious existence was not much larger than before the first persecution. Living mostly in secluded places, they were not too often molested by the Utraquist clergy. Since the original contacts with Rokycana, friendly or polemical, were suspended, the Brethren did not feel bound to consult him when they decided to take the bold step of separating from both the Utraquists and the Catholics.

The momentous decision was prepared by a careful study of historical and doctrinal problems, meditation, and prayer. At a clandestine meeting "in the Rychnov mountains" in 1464, the Brethren agreed on a summary of their teachings as well as on disciplinary articles, so that various groups scattered all over the country would stay together.[499] In general they recognized the idea of apostolic succession and they appreciated the friendly attitude of priest Michael, who had received the Roman ordination but was willing to perform religious services for them. Since they could not depend forever on his loyalty, they agreed that a more permanent solution must be made to give their community a solid basis. Sometime in the fall of 1467 a meeting of about sixty members was held in the village of Lhotka, which was so carefully prepared that it escaped the notice of both the secular and spiritual authorities. The procedure followed the example of the apostles. The delegates agreed on nine men qualified for the ministry and then lots were drawn and three candidates were finally chosen.

The election was only the first step toward the establishment of a priesthood. A question arose immediately who of the three should take the first place and by whom should the elected men be consecrated. In the second meeting, the lot fell on the youngest one, Matthias, who thus became the spiritual head of the Unity, although he was only twenty-five years old. In the consecration of the elected ministers priest Michael played the chief role. Under circumstances which the Brethren, for their own protection, wrapped in a shroud of mystery, co-operation of the Waldensians in confirming Matthias was sought and obtained. In connection with this contact, the name of a Waldensian bishop, Stephen, is usually mentioned, but the sources, obscure as they are, have little more to say about him than his name.[500]

By the creation of an independent ministry, the Brethren moved away from the Roman Church more resolutely than even such outspoken Hussites as Martin Lupáč and other priests of his orientation had ever done. George's occupation and the Catholic treatment of Rokycana provided a screen behind which the Brethren passed unnoticed. Not involved in the wars which plagued their homeland, they consolidated their ranks and solved the perplexing dilemma of priests duly ordained and yet not contaminated by wordliness.

After the establishment of their own order, the Brethren were more reluctant than before to obey local Utraquist priests. To avoid conflict, they turned to Rokycana, and explained to him the fundamental articles of their faith and revealed to him the existence of their priesthood. In a letter to the King they inserted a subtle allusion to a general Council in which their teachings could be examined. It is not quite clear whether Rokycana acted on royal orders or on his own initiative when in August, 1468, he issued a pastoral letter to his clergy warning them against the Brethren leaders and their tenets.[501] In doing so, Rokycana admitted that the Brethren held far more radical tenets than those of the Hussite faith. A period of stern measures against the Brethren set in after the promulgation of Rokycana's letter and no relief came to them from either the King or the Archbishop-elect.

It is very likely that George's information concerning the Unity was not too comprehensive and that he left the matter in Rokycana's hands. With the war in progress, George had little time for a study of problems arising from a new split among the Czechs and affecting less the Catholics than the Utraquist party. Letters with which the Brethren turned to him and to Rokycana were written in Czech and they probably never fell into the hands of the Catholic rebels to be used as a weapon when new attacks were launched either directly against George or the Hussites in general. Thus amidst bitter struggles there was born and consolidated a religious community that resolutely cut doctrinal and institutional ties with the Roman Church and felt connected through a thin thread of Waldensian confirmation with the uncorrupted community of early Christians.

When the dates relating to the Unity are compared with other memorable events of that time it becomes clear why the Brethren escaped suppression. Observing a passive attitude toward the state and its officers, they were far less dangerous than the Taborites against whom George once had turned with full force. Whether George understood the matters clearly or not, he saw no reason for a drastic action against the peaceful Brethren at a time of his involvement in the campaign against other, truly formidable enemies.

George's striving for peace among the theologians ran parallel with the general reorientation of his foreign policy. Without making much ado about it, he abandoned the scheme of conciliation with the Church through a general Council,[502] once suggested to him and propagated by Gregory of Heimburg. In 1469 the King thought more of the traditional channels—interventions in Rome by friendly ruling houses. He did not release Heimburg from his service, in view of the latter's popularity with some princes of the Empire and also with the learned opponents of excessive papal claims. When occupied by the war with Matthias, George listened to Heimburg less diligently than in 1466 and 1467. Heimburg was not a servile courtier, and he disagreed with George in the reorientation of Czech foreign policy, feeling that George should not pin all his hopes on Casimir and leave out of his calculations his Wettin and Hohenzollern relatives.

Depending in 1469 less on Heimburg's judgment than after his coming to Prague, George was able to analyze the new situation more realistically than in the early stage of the conflict and to turn his opponents' mistakes to his own advantage. Matthias' election was prepared hastily, as the lords of Zelená Hora wanted to present the Hungarian with a *fait accompli* and thus preclude his agreement with George. Matthias' acceptance was also not a premeditated act but an improvisation, the consequences of which were not altogether satisfactory. By assisting at it, the papal legates created problems which Paul II and the leading cardinals endeavored to avoid. With the exception of such zealots as Fra Gabriel, the Pope's advisers favored Casimir as the candidate for the crown of Bohemia and made several attempts to lead him away from association with the Hussite king. In the situation created by the hot-tempered lords, the papal diplomacy could not move ahead to obtain from Casimir more than nominal assurances of his attachment to the Holy See. On the other hand, Matthias could not be flatly rejected, as the papal legates, like the Czech lords, had a rather low opinion of his stability and feared that if antagonized, he might withdraw from the battlefield and seek a compromise with George.

The Pope's dilatory policy lent credence to rumors that he was broaching an even more elaborate scheme than a simple transfer of the vacated throne from one candidate to another. According to a rather prejudiced witness, Gregory of Heimburg,[503] Paul II studied a project whose originator had been one of his predecessors, Martin V. It called for splitting the kingdom of Bohemia into several principalities and counties, abolishing the royal title, and transferring the electoral dignity to another house, most likely the Habsburgs. This fantastic plan, whether treated seriously or not, did not guide the papal policy in the period following Olomouc. It was mostly a continuation of a subtle game in which both Casimir and Matthias were included as potential successors of the deposed Hussite king.

It was to Matthias' advantage that the papal diplomats were not in perfect accord in matters pertaining to the Bohemian succession. Fra Gabriel and some members of the Curia espoused his cause and worked for him indefatigably, contrasting his deeds with Casimir's procrastination. From the other center of political activities, the imperial court, Matthias received even less favor than from Rome. The Hungarian emissaries, seconded by other foes of Bohemia, urged Frederick III to use his imperial authority to rescind formally the charter of July 31, 1459, by which he had recognized George as the king of Bohemia and an elector of the Empire.[504] Their interventions, however, brought no results. Frederick III resented Matthias' quick decision, feeling that the latter should not have accepted the proffered crown without a previous consultation. Union of two large kingdoms was not an event which the ruler of comparatively small domains in their vicinity could accept without deep concern for his own future. Frederick III was not strong enough to protest the Olomouc election, but he was in no hurry to sanction it.

Rumors hinting at Frederick's displeasure with Matthias' aggrandizement quickly reached various princely courts. Encouraged by them, Albrecht of Saxony decided to undertake a diplomatic intervention on behalf of his father-in-law. In June, 1469, he journeyed to Graz to explore the ground.[505] The Emperor reacted in his traditional manner. He rendered Albrecht personal favors but made no commitments in matters pertaining to the war in Bohemia. The time for Albrecht's mission was not too well chosen. Frederick III was deeply involved in his own domestic troubles and he was aware of the weakness of the forces at his disposal. In a moment of crisis, Matthias could exercise potent influence on the Austrian affairs by either supporting the opposition or coming to Frederick's aid. Dilatory tactics to which Frederick had resorted in the past, when confronted with an awkward dilemma, seemed to promise more than a straightforward decision for George or Matthias. Under the existing circumstances, Frederick's indecision helped George, as it averted a demonstrative action which, if undertaken, would have shattered his position in the college of electors and among the princes of the Empire in general.

When Matthias extended at least a nominal control over the two Lusatias, he became a neighbor of the Wettin princes, Ernest and Albrecht. They were so well known for their attachment to George that it was highly unlikely that any offers would entice them. The danger that they would invade Upper or Lower Lusatia was negligible as long as George was not strong enough to pass from a defence of loyal territory to an offensive.

Another neighbor to the north of Lower Lusatia and Silesia, Frederick of Brandenburg, was to be treated with more consideration, as he held an important position in relation to both these provinces and to Poland. As a matter of fact, Matthias included Markgrave Frederick in his speculation long before the Olomouc election, at the time when in unison with George he had sought his promotion in the Empire. When the situation changed, he urged Frederick to come to Breslau for a frank exchange of views.[506] He was satisfied with the Markgrave's reaction, which was on the whole friendly. By attendance at various ceremonies, Frederick tacitly sanctioned the passing of Silesia and of the Lusatias under the new master. Encouraged by these acts of courtesy, Matthias offered him a treaty of alliance. Both the Hungarian and the papal diplomats supported the King, but met with a polite refusal.[507] Long experience had taught Frederick not to provoke aggression from the East, and at that juncture a pact with Matthias could easily be interpreted as an unfriendly gesture toward Casimir of Poland.

Matthias' diplomacy did not neglect the Wittelsbach princes ruling over the territories southwest of Bohemia. As the main strength of the Catholic party in that province was in the counties bordering on Bavaria, a combination of forces which could be supplied by the lords of Zelená Hora with Bavarian subsidies would have seriously jeopardized George's position. Two members of the Wittelsbach House, Lewis of Landshut and Albrecht of Munich, responded willingly to Matthias' overtures and induced their relative, Frederick of the Palatinate, to join the preliminary talks.[508] Their hands were not entirely free, as they all had on July 8, 1469, signed a treaty with Dukes Ernest and Albrecht of Saxony in which the two Wettin princes made friendly references to George.[509] Feeling that the relevant passage of the treaty was binding only for the Wettins, the Wittelsbachs went ahead in their negotiations with Matthias. They acted under various impulses: the pressure from Rome, a dislike of George's traditional ally, Albrecht Achilles, and last but not least, the desire to have Matthias' friendship in case of his ultimate victory over the Hussite king. Apart from the recognition of Matthias as king of Bohemia, the agreement signed on September 1, 1469, netted him little benefit, as it was defensive.[510] The Wettins and Casimir of Poland were mentioned among those princes against whom the Wittelsbachs did not want to undertake any hostile act.

Formal recognition by some neighbors of Bohemia and lack of aggressive designs among the Wettin princes gave Matthias a good deal of hope of being able to keep his forces together. There remained only one potential enemy, the king of Poland. Both Matthias and the lords of Zelená Hora were anxious to placate him. The latter felt particularly uneasy, as not so long ago they had requested him to take the crown of Bohemia personally or on behalf of his son Władysław.[511] No time was lost in designating envoys to Poland who would represent both Matthias and his Czech adherents. Headed by John Zajíc of Házmburk, who held the office of supreme chancellor from Matthias, the delegates endeavored to arrange matters by assuring Casimir that the election was not a demonstration of ill feeling against Poland.[512] A good deal of skill was required to hint at Casimir's dallying as one of the reasons for the election. The envoys strove earnestly to exculpate Zdeněk of Šternberk and also to promote friendship between the two kings. Among the other points mentioned in conferences with the Poles was the marriage of a

Polish princess to Matthias, which seemed to be a worthy compensation for the loss of Casimir's immediate succession in Bohemia. The King was not impressed by the solemn protestations of good will and showed no interest in an agreement by which his daughter would be given more prominence than the first-born son. However, he was not prepared for an armed intervention in the Bohemian imbroglio. He, therefore, gave the envoys a courteous but evasive answer.

Discarding his accustomed reliance on good luck, George resolved to thwart his foes' efforts by a formal offer of the crown of Bohemia to Władysław. As he wished to give weight to his message to Casimir, he put the problem of succession on the agenda of the same provincial Diet to which he announced the monetary reform.[513] He acquainted the notables with his decision not to favor the candidacy of his own sons but to work for Władysław's coming to Bohemia. The vote on this matter was taken immediately and was apparently unanimous. The leading members of the loyal Estates not only shared George's conviction that only a concrete proposal could frustrate Matthias' attempts to gain Polish acquiescence in his expansion, but they viewed with concern George's prospects. They were alarmed by the rapid deterioration of the King's health, which gave rise to doubts whether he would be able to conduct military operations as effectively as in the earlier years.

Assured of full support by his party, George appointed Ctibor Tovačovský of Cimburk as his spokesman and associated with him one of the ablest Czech diplomats, Beneš of Veitmil, and provost, Paul of Zderaz, who had been at Casimir's court on earlier occasions. The envoys had an audience with Casimir at Radom toward the end of June and solemnly offered the crown to the youthful prince.[514] It was understood that George would exercise royal power until his own death, and that Casimir would lend him military help and attempt a new mediation at the papal court. The envoys were also instructed to obtain from Casimir and Queen Elizabeth a promise that Władysław would be married to George's daughter Ludmila, then eleven years old and previously betrothed to George, son of the Bavarian Duke Lewis. Attached to these points were specific requests relating to the future status of George's consort, Johanna, and of his sons, and, in addition, the restitution of property to those of George's partisans who had lost it during the wars with Matthias.

Although the offer presented by Ctibor Tovačovský was more concrete than George's earlier proposals, Casimir did not accept it promptly and unreservedly. The most delicate point was the marriage of Władysław to Ludmila, as the Polish queen and the ranking Polish prelates were resolutely opposed to such a union. Casimir dismissed the Czech envoys courteously and appointed his own plenipotentiaries to go to Bohemia and seek milder terms from George.[515]

Casimir's dilatory answer did not noticeably change the situation in George's lands. Matthias drew some profit from the Polish policy, as it made highly improbable an invasion from there of Moravia or Silesia, or of both. Personally, George was more affected by Casimir's cunctation than was Matthias, as his offer was generous and deserved to be received more enthusiastically. He swallowed the bitter pill and was willing to see the Polish envoys for further discussions.

After several weeks of intensive diplomatic activities, George and Matthias reached the limits beyond which neither of them was able to move. Paul II had his hands tied by his earlier declarations favoring Casimir. Frederick III entertained a dislike of Matthias' intrusion into territories traditionally linked with the Empire. Casimir saw his hope of a smooth transfer of the crown of Bohemia to his son shattered by Matthias' usurpation. None of the three sovereigns received the emissaries from Hungary enthusiastically, but none of them—the Pope least of all—was prepared to give substantial help to the hard-pressed king of Bohemia. In view of their indecision and of general malaise affecting international life in those years, Matthias resolved to use his own forces more effectively so as to enlarge his sphere of influence within the boundaries of the newly acquired kingdom. Before the end of June, 1469, the Lusatias and most of Silesia were under his control, although in many cases only nominal. Highly satisfied with the pledges of allegiance received in his temporary residence at Breslau, Matthias moved from there early in July to Brno to receive homage from his Moravian and Bohemian partisans, invited there either by personal letters or by general appeals.[516]

Matthias' return to Moravia and his campaigning among the Catholics of the Czech tongue was a more serious challenge to George than his activities among the German-speaking inhabitants of Silesia and the two Lusatias. Although reluctant to unleash the furies of civil war, George had to admit that nothing but the sword could mend the ugly split. Nominally, he was bound to observe the truce until the New Year of 1470; [517] but he did not believe that after Olomouc the agreement concluded late in April had any validity. While Matthias feasted at Brno, George's forces reopened hostilities at many places. The King himself directed the operations in Bohemia, and Victorin established his headquarters in Moravia. The third center, the city and castle of Kladsko, served as the starting point for daring thrusts into the Silesian plains. The campaign was not too rigidly co-ordinated, but it was not entirely loose and haphazard. Its main purpose, at least in the initial stage, was to hit those boroughs and lords who had recently joined with the rebel bloc. The residences of the Zajíc family were among the principal targets of George's flying columns, as one of its members, John, held a high office in Matthias' government.

The center of gravity was for some time neither in Bohemia nor in the Kladsko region but in Moravia. Lords and lesser nobles who defied the "Olomouc king" readily joined hands with Victorin in order to recapture some of the lost ground. Fortified residences of such families as the Tovačovskýs served as rallying points and facilitated connection of the operating army with George's foremost stronghold in the direction of Hungary, the royal borough of Hradiště. When attempting late in July to bolster the resistance of the brave garrison, Prince Victorin was lured into a trap and fell into Matthias' hands.

No attempt was made to release Victorin from captivity by ransom or substantial concessions to Matthias. The King sent the prisoner to Hungary, although some of the Czech lords would have preferred to have him in their custody. The struggle went on with even more vigor than before; neither Matthias nor George had enough power to conquer the entire province of Moravia.

In Silesia and the Lusatias the Czech forces were comparatively small and it was unthinkable that they could undertake a systematic reconquest of those provinces. To make up for numerical weakness, the Czech captains resorted to tactics which in the second stage of the Hussite wars had proved highly effective. Instead of seeking battle, they attacked castles of the Silesian nobility, poorly defended boroughs, or even villages, and carried away booty of all kinds. To protect themselves against plundering and arson, the defenseless population gladly entered into agreements with the commanders, so that in addition to spoils a good deal of money was collected from the victims of aggression.

Parallel with forays into Silesia and the Lusatias, the campaign in Moravia was resumed early in the fall. There, too, no more could be done than to bring temporary relief to the loyal elements among the nobility as well as the common folk. Of special significance were well-timed advances toward isolated strongholds of the Poděbrady party. The most important of these was now, as before, the royal borough of Hradiště. Its reserves were running out, and if not replenished, the garrison would be forced to surrender to Matthias. To avert a painful loss, in October George organized a relief expedition. The first attempt to reach the garrison was frustrated by Hungarian forces, but George did not give up the idea. A more powerful army commanded by George's younger son, Henry, dashed through Moravia, broke the ring of Hungarian fortifications surrounding Hradiště, and moved in plentiful supplies. The Hungarian commanders, including Matthias himself, were misled by Henry's subsequent maneuvers into believing that having fulfilled his main task, he contemplated a retreat to Bohemia. They were caught unprepared when Henry suddenly changed direction and attacked them vigorously. The units, quickly mobilized to stop him, were put to rout and several prominent persons, Czech and Hungarian, fell into captivity. Encountering no organized resistance, the Czech warriors made forays into the valley of Váh and caused so much damage there that the population urged Matthias to suspend operations.

Military operations against Matthias and his adherents, though only partly successful, brightened George's prospects. He was able not only to hold ground but also to inflict losses on his enemies and force them to retreat from some of their outposts. Successes in the field encouraged hopes that diplomatic activities, rather disheartening in the few months following immediately after the Olomouc election, would yield more satisfactory results and dispel the danger of complete isolation. While in the time of depression the road to Poland seemed to be the only outlet, other combinations were attempted when the summer advanced and military operations in several parts of the kingdom got into a full swing.

Not depressed by Ctibor's report, George resumed dealings with Poland early in September, 1469. Knowing that Casimir liked to make important decisions at the general assembly at Piotrków, he appointed new envoys to go there.[518] The delegation was large and truly representative. At its head was the supreme chamberlain, William of Rýzmberk, and with him the representatives of all three Estates left Prague. Attached to them on account of his unique knowledge of conditions in Casimir's realm was again Provost Paul. Accompanied by two hundred horsemen, the envoys made a deep impression on the Polish-Lithuanian nobility attracted to Piotrków by Casimir's presence. They mixed easily with the secular members of the Diet but were looked upon coldly by the ecclesiastical dignitaries and their conservative allies. Success in social contacts failed to outweigh the adverse forces operating against them. The King himself was more cautious than on previous occasions, as he was impressed by the reports received shortly before the arrival of the Czechs from his delegates to Rome. The chief among them, Jacob of Dębno, told Casimir that they encountered at the Curia envoys representing Matthias and his Czech allies, and what they learned concerning their activities among the leading cardinals.[519] Assisted by Gabriel Rangoni, Matthias' emissaries endeavored to obtain from the Pontiff a confirmation of the Olomouc election and supplicated that he send their lord a new crown, as the ancient crown of Saint Wenceslas was in George's custody. Casimir used the report from Rome as evidence that in matters as delicate as the succession in Bohemia restraint was the best method. When addressed by the Czech envoys, he again gave them a dilatory answer. He told them that Paul II planned to send to Poland a special envoy for a thorough discussion of the problems concerning Bohemia and he did not think it advisable to make permanent commitments before the legate's arrival.

Gracious words, splendid presents, and vague assurances thinly masked Casimir's true face. The envoys were disheartened but did not break off the contacts, knowing well that an angry gesture would not bring help. On their journey home they made a stop at Cracow and paid homage to the princes who did not follow their father to Piotrków. Władysław's personal charm and sound judgment made a favorable impression on the lord of Rýzmberk and his companions so that they did not return to their master's residence in a pessimistic mood.

The contacts with Poland had a concrete objective, the dynastic union of the kingdom of Bohemia, after George's resignation or death, with the Polish-Lithuanian Commonwealth, and they were fostered by both George and his leading Czech advisers. If Casimir had resolved to take the risks which undoubtedly were involved in an alliance with an excommunicated king, it would not have been too difficult to hammer out the details of a definitive agreement with Bohemia. The King's reluctance to precipitate a conflict with the Pope, though not followed by an unfriendly gesture toward Prague, served George as a warning not to neglect entirely other princes in the Empire and beyond its western boundary.

Reviews of the international scene in 1469 inspired less hope than at the outbreak of the conflict with the Papacy. Princes of the Empire, willing to maintain friendly contacts with Prague, could really be counted on one's fingers. Even if they succeeded in winning some noncommitted elements for the same policy, they would have been too weak to prevail on the Pope to lift the ban and seek a more elastic formula to settle the conflict with Bohemia. A more powerful monarch had to be found to take the initiative and to form a coalition of princes jealous of clerical interventions in political affairs.

Whenever such an idea emerged from conferences at the Prague court, the talents and experience of Gregory of Heimburg came to be more highly valued than at the time of concentration on the Polish candidature. Apart from him, George employed either permanently or for specific tasks other diplomats of Austrian or German origin. One of them, George of Stein, a native of Upper Swabia and formerly chancellor of Duke Albrecht of Austria, proved to be especially useful, as he shared Heimburg's ideas concerning the relations between the spiritual and secular powers and his sympathy for the Hussite king. Stein was in conflict with Frederick III and, although put under the ban by the Bishop-legate Roverella, he could travel more freely than Heimburg, repeatedly included in the Maundy Thursday excommunication.

In the early part of 1469, George used Stein in minor diplomatic missions and, as he found him competent, later entrusted him with the rather delicate task of finding out whether any of the West European sovereigns would be inclined to come to Bohemia's aid.

It can be assumed that men as well versed in international problems as Heimburg and Stein had at least a vague knowledge of the current developments in lands beyond the western frontiers of the Empire. The Franco-Burgundian hostility transcended the local boundaries, affected to some extent the relations of the two rivals with the Holy See, and offered opportunities for diplomatic maneuvering. Former experience with France, and a strong opposition among the French notables to an alignment with Bohemia, made success of renewed sounding at the court of Louis XI highly improbable.

It is quite likely, though direct evidence is not available, that soon after the Olomouc election George formally dissociated himself from the scheme of Matthias' promotion in the Empire, and that he notified the French and Burgundian courts of the changed situation. This did not cause embarrassment to anyone, as the plan had few supporters when conceived, and it did not get out of the exploratory stage in any case. A disqualified candidate was dropped, but the idea of attaching somebody to Frederick III, which had been ventilated on several previous occasions, did not lose its attractiveness. When the new circumstances were sized up, there emerged as the most suitable candidate for the title of King of the Romans the ambitious duke of Burgundy, Charles the Bold.

Reports concerning Charles's ambition to obtain the royal rank undoubtedly reached Prague through some friendly court. The size of his territories and his wealth seemed to justify this ambition. A benevolent attitude on the part of some German courts could be anticipated; others were to be won by diplomatic intervention or promises of compensation. In 1469 George was in a more awkward position than at the time of his contacts with the Duke of Milan [520] but, the papal bulls notwithstanding, he was still respected as the leading member of the group of secular electors. Preliminary conferences resulted in the conclusion that contacts with Burgundy be established without previous consultation with the Emperor.

Early in July, 1469, George of Stein left Bohemia with a detailed offer to Charles the Bold and soon reached the Duke's residence.[521] Following his instructions, he assured Charles that chances of his election as King of the Romans were brighter than ever before. King George was ready to prepare the ground for that solemn act and believed that three other electors would go along with him, if properly approached and compensated: the Archbishop of Mainz, Duke Ernest of Saxony, and Frederick of Brandenburg. George's contacts with Frederick of the Palatinate were rather strained, but his help was not so much needed in view of the earlier friendly relations between Burgundy and the Palatinate. Neither could George be of much help in dealings with the Archbishops of Cologne and Trier, but not all details were to be settled at once.

George's offer was well calculated. In addition to diplomatic support in any future attempts to settle the conflict with Rome, George expected from Charles a rather large sum of money, two hundred thousand Rhenish florins, partly to improve his financial position and partly to compensate the other electors. Charles apparently considered the matter seriously and requested Stein to prepare a document embodying the terms proposed by George.

Stein's report from Burgundy seems to have been encouraging. George instructed him to pursue the matter further and obtain more concrete promises of co-operation from the electors mentioned in the original proposals. Stein's correspondence and visits to various courts were to be kept secret and there is little contemporary evidence concerning their course and outcome. The Elector of Brandenburg was apparently reluctant to give his consent to a scheme which directly or indirectly affected the Emperor. Stein found it advisable to turn for help to the Elector's brother, Albrecht Achilles, who was known for his sincere attachment to George's cause.[522] It was expected that Albrecht Achilles would soon move higher, as Frederick was seriously occupied with the thought of resignation and retreat from public life.

George's diplomacy scored several successes in combatting the offensive conducted by Matthias in co-operation with the papal diplomacy. The results accomplished were not astonishing and had little immediate effect, but their moral value could not be measured by normal standards. When correlated with the outcome of the military operation in Moravia and elsewhere, they showed both friends and enemies that the Olomouc election did not seal George's doom. His position continued to be precarious and called for vigilance and patriotic sacrifice. But it was not hopeless, as Matthias' expansion was stopped at a line which, though far from satisfactory, made possible the concentration of the loyal forces as soon as the danger of an immediate catastrophe could be averted and some help, in manpower or at least in supplies, would be secured abroad.

THE HORIZON BRIGHTENS

George's German relatives were not shaken in their attachment to him when everybody else pondered the risks of solidarity with an excommunicated person. The Wettins, Albrecht and Ernest, enhanced by their benevolent attitude the sense of security along the northwestern boundary of the kingdom and could be included as friends in any diplomatic combination. Services rendered by them to George directly were surpassed only by the advice and assistance he obtained from Markgrave Albrecht Achilles, father-in-law of the second-born Poděbrady prince, Henry.

Six years older than George, the Markgrave could talk to him as to his equal, dissuading him from impulsive reactions and recommending protective measures of the conventional type. It seems very likely that in talks with Stein or in direct contacts with George the Markgrave suggested a step which he believed to be a prerequisite of any diplomatic campaign in the Empire. He recommended that George issue an appeal to German princes for a collective intervention at the papal court. Anyone acquainted with the current trends of political life could see that no international project in which George would be involved, either as the initiator or as a benevolent partner, could lead to success as long as he was under the papal ban. The number of princes who were willing to risk papal displeasure for dealing with an excommunicated ruler was not large, and even they preferred to reduce the contacts to an inoffensive minimum.

George accepted Albrecht's hint and prepared a manifesto for the princes and the free cities of the Empire, dating it on the first of January, 1470.[523] Composed probably with the help of Gregory of Heimburg, the letter recapitulated the conflict with the Papacy and the rise of opposition among the Czech nobles. The King pointed out his fruitless attempts to bring together representatives of both spiritual and secular authorities, whose verdict he was willing to accept. He complained

that his striving for a peaceful settlement had not been adequately supported by the imperial Estates and that his kingdom was drawn into un-
provoked and devastating wars. Not without justification, George stressed
his close links with the Empire and hinted at a danger of separation, if
the traditional ties should be loosened by indifference on the part of the
princes and the free cities to the fate of one of the electors. The letter
culminated in a request that the Estates support more earnestly George's
effort to get a hearing before an international tribunal or that they pro-
pose other methods by which justice would be done and peace restored.

The appeal had a more modest but a more concrete objective than
the campaign launched, with Heimburg's help, in 1467,[524] in that it was
intended for the imperial Estates only. It was written in moderate language, so that neither the Pontiff nor the Emperor could feel offended
if it reached their hands. It was probably delivered to most of its addressees as, in addition to George's own agents, Markgrave Albrecht
Achilles circulated it among his friends. Although direct evidence is lacking, it may be assumed that George's complaints were received sympathetically by the opponents of papal interference in imperial politics, and
that their number was by no means small.

Friendly reactions to the voice from Prague did not crystallize into a
program of action. Not an individual, but a group of energetic leaders,
would have been needed to orient the policy of such an unwieldy body
as the imperial Estates in the direction to which George had pointed.
No such group was formed under Albrecht Achilles' aegis and, indeed,
it was not even attempted. The level to which the Empire had been reduced since Frederick's election was too low to be changed by appeals
to patriotism and similar slogans.

Instead of waiting for a collective intervention, George's son-in-law,
Albrecht of Saxony, resolved to initiate a less spectacular action. Full of
enthusiasm, he announced his intention to go to Rome and plead for
George personally. He won Prince Otto of the Upper Palatinate for his
idea. The two princes learned probably soon that such an idea was not
practicable on account of many formal and technical problems. Instead
of undertaking the mission, Albrecht sent to Rome John Weissbach, a
native of Misnia. The learned cleric was instructed to stay there as long
as he deemed necessary and to explore quietly the conditions under
which serious negotiations could be begun.[525]

Under the existing circumstances, the presence in Rome of a neutral
cleric was the maximum that George or his friends could achieve. The
sentence of excommunication was neither lifted nor modified and a direct approach from Prague would have most likely been flatly rejected.
Observers on the spot, if keen and discerning, could notice that around
Christmas, 1469, the atmosphere in the highest circles was relaxed, though

not to such a degree as would permit resumption of contacts. Early in December, 1469, Cardinal Carvajal, the most ardent advocate of an anti-Hussite crusade, died. None of his colleagues, not excluding the Bishop of Pavia, Jacopo Ammanati, was so strongly opposed to any compromise with the Czechs. The most respectable figure among the cardinals, Bessarion, was not as deeply involved in Central European affairs as Carvajal had been, because his stay there had been too short and far from reassuring. Bessarion's chief concern was the Balkans. The Pope himself could not remain indifferent to the setbacks suffered by the Christian forces in Albania.

The slight decrease in the original fervor could be ascribed also to other circumstances than the Turkish advances and Skanderbeg's death. For about a decade the city of Breslau acted as the protagonist of a hostile policy against George. Its agents in the eternal city established contacts with persons of influence and created the impression that Breslau would spare no funds or energies to bring about the Hussite king's downfall. The hasty retreat from Frankenstein, coupled with other misfortunes, had its effects on both the community and the leaders. It ushered in a period of mutual accusations and caused in the end a reorientation of the city's policy. The masses who originally responded eagerly to fiery sermons and calls for war against the Czech heretics were sobered up when affected in their daily lives by the consequences of the prolonged warfare. They pressed the senate that mercenaries be hired to drive the Czech "brotherhoods" from Silesia. As the crafts and merchants suffered from disruption of normal contacts with Bohemia and Poland, the senate hesitated to overstrain the expenditure on the soldiery and appealed to patriotic sentiments of the populace. Results, however, fell far below their expectation.

The rebellion, even when carried on in co-operation with the Czech lords and Matthias, proved to be a harder task than its fanatical instigators had anticipated. Canon Nicholas Tempelfeld, one of the fiercest opponents of the Czech heresy, on one occasion ruefully admitted that he had underestimated George's power.[526] He withdrew from preaching and devoted himself entirely to his duties as precentor of the chapter. The bishop-legate, Rudolf, too, slowly realized that he had not seen clearly enough the perplexities of the Silesian situation when he first arrived in Breslau and had accepted the view current there that the Czechs must be crushed by force. Correspondence of the senate with Rome, at one time very lively, was reduced to a mere trickle and lost its impetuosity.

Disillusionment with the meager results of the campaign waged in the summer and fall of 1469 spread from the capital to other parts of Silesia. Princes, lesser nobles, and boroughs allied with Breslau, who were as a rule more vulnerable than the walled capital, felt that neither Breslau leaders nor Matthias concerned themselves sufficiently with their plight to send them re-enforcement. They saw that the less committed rebels entered into pacts with George's captains and for tribute in either money or in kind secured for themselves at least a temporary relief. The league of George's foes, formed hastily during Matthias' stay in Silesia, was weakened by altercations and mutual accusations, and only the fear of Matthias' vengeance kept its lukewarm members from defection.

The situation was aggravated by Matthias' employment of Czech Catholic warriors for the Silesian warfare. Their supreme commander, František of Háj, who after a rift with George had joined the Hungarian forces, was held in high esteem by Matthias for his experience and disregard of danger. He and his men did not plague only the enemy. On one occasion the bishop-legate himself complained of heavy burdens imposed by Háj on the ecclesiastical domains at Nisa and sighed that peace with the heretics would be more bearable than these exactions.[527]

An episode recorded by the Breslau secretary, Peter Eschenloer, reflected the discontent among the laymen with the fanatical preachers. At a sumptuous feast in the Convent of Trzebnica in middle January, 1470, Duke Conrad the Black, up to June one of George's staunchest adherents, volunteered his opinion on the causes of all troubles. When one of the guests ascribed the calamities to an unfavorable position of planets, the Duke interjected that the two planets mostly to be blamed could be found in Breslau, namely the provost of the chapter, John Düster, and the precentor, Nicholas Tempelfeld. On other occasions people recalled the moderating influence exercised in the early stage of the conflict by Bishop Jošt and Bishop Tas; the latter, of course, had deviated from his earlier viewpoint and had joined hands with George's enemies.[528]

Matthias' role in the crusade against the Czechs had undergone, since the Olomouc election, changes of which perhaps not even his intimate collaborators were fully aware. In his dealings with the Czech lords and the Breslau burghers he could resort, as their king, to harsher methods than at the time of the alliance. To whom could they appeal if at odds with a ruler whom they had voluntarily accepted?

In the second year of the struggle, clashes of armed forces, even if the units were small, aroused more attention than the slow changes of its general pattern. In the winter of 1469–70 the war lost much of its original character of a citizens' revolt against their legitimate ruler and resembled more a conflict between two neighbors, frequent in all periods of history. The immediate reasons for Matthias' march against the Czechs lost much of their validity. Nominally, he still acted as the chief instrument of the papal campaign against an incorrigible heretic, but since the acceptance of the royal title of Bohemia, his objectives had reached far beyond the original intentions. The new dignity, apart from his claims to George's entire territory, offered opportunities for intervention in the affairs of the Empire, since as king of Bohemia Matthias could claim admission to the electoral college of the Empire. He had spent a good deal of time outside Hungary and was by no means inclined to write off the amount of money invested in the anti-Hussite campaign.

Since early November, 1469, Matthias had dwelt again in Hungary and was fully occupied with the problems that had accumulated there. The Hungarian nobility was not solidly behind him when, early in 1468, he resolved to make an alliance with the Czech and Silesian rebels. Those who resented his absences from the kingdom and the excessive occupation with Bohemian affairs became bolder and more articulate in the summer and early fall of 1469. The Turkish menace could no longer be regarded as merely a nightmare haunting the inhabitants of the border areas; it became a stark reality. The Turks were, in 1469, not prepared to launch a powerful offensive against their northern neighbor, but made thrusts west and northward. In June, 1469, the southern domains of Frederick III were victimized, and in September the rich provinces of Slavonia adjoining southern Hungary suffered the same fate. After these events, Matthias was unable to pretend that no danger of invasion existed in southern Hungary. It would have been risky to disregard the anxiety of the Hungarian population. He therefore returned to Buda before the arrival of frost and snow.

Assisted by the officers of the realm, he prepared for a Diet and opened it around Christmas.[529] The Turkish acts of aggression came up for discussion, but Matthias probably also stressed the danger from Bohemia, using the Czech raids into the Váh valley as concrete examples. The Diet proved co-operative and accepted Matthias' interpretation of the recent events in the south and the northwest regions of the kingdom.

Assured of adequate financing of the military operations when the weather would permit them, Matthias resorted to diplomacy to improve his position in the west. His first objective was an agreement with the Emperor to settle the accumulated grievances. While Matthias could not get reconciled to Frederick's reluctance to recognize the changed situation in Bohemia, the Emperor believed himself to have valid reasons for criticism of Matthias' conduct. The King neither took energetic measures against the Turks when they were plaguing the southern fringes of the Habsburg patrimony nor did he come to Frederick's help when a league of noblemen, headed by Andrew Baumkircher, rose in arms and harassed his loyal forces. According to some indications, Matthias was more keenly interested in the conference than was Frederick III.

It took place in Vienna in February, 1470, but was attended only by a handful of princes from Germany. In Matthias' splendid retinue were Zdeněk of Šternberk and other Czech lords. Their presence stirred up rumors that a concerted action against George would be high on the agenda. In fact, Matthias was more interested in matters that, if settled successfully, would enhance his prestige. Among other things he insisted that Frederick III definitely give up the title of the king of Hungary which he had begun to use after the death of Ladislav Posthumus. Another request was for the hand of the Emperor's daughter Cunegonde.[530]

The Emperor was friendly and entertained his Hungarian visitor splendidly. Envoys from Milan and Venice sojourning in Vienna believed that an agreement about the betrothal and a settlement of other problems was reached. In fact, Frederick III dallied, straining his guest's patience to the utmost. When a month elapsed and no public confirmation of oral assurances was made, Matthias gave orders that a boat be prepared for him at once; on March 11, 1470, he departed for Pressburg without taking formal leave of his august host.[531]

Papal diplomats attempted to heal the rift, but succeeded only in averting an outbreak of hostilities. Preserving a semblance of correct relations, Frederick III veered from a close alliance with Hungary to seek contacts with other rulers. His new policy was bound to damage Matthias' position and to play directly or indirectly into George's hands.

Under the new circumstances, the Burgundian project, as outlined by George of Stein, lost its importance.[532] It would have been preposterous to pursue negotiations with Charles the Bold without Frederick's participation, as they could not be kept secret indefinitely, and as they would, when uncovered, only increase his irritation. People so well acquainted with current affairs as Stein or Heimburg could not be unaware of Frederick's connection with the Burgundian court, intensified in 1469 at the insistence of Sigismund of Tyrol. They also could see that Frederick III, if disposed to be friendly, could offer Charles the Bold more than could their master. Indeed, in 1470, Frederick was willing to consider the royal title for the Duke, but instead of agreeing to his election as King of the Romans, he thought of connecting the higher rank with one of Charles's possessions. A treaty of marriage between Prince Maximilian and Charles's daughter Mary was mentioned by the mediators as the best way toward the alignment of the two houses. The idea was never abandoned, but the marriage was not celebrated until 1477.

With the abandonment of Stein's project, George's contacts with German princes resumed their normal course. It was no longer necessary to contemplate territorial compensations to the Hohenzollerns and the Wettins—an idea George entertained in moments of depression in 1469.

No faction among the imperial Estates raised demands that George be expelled from the electoral college and replaced by Matthias. Even those princes who, like the Wittelsbachs, recognized Matthias as king of Bohemia, were not too enthusiastic about supporting his ambitions in the Empire. Markgrave Albrecht Achilles impressed many indifferent princes by his conviction that even when in conflict with the Papacy, George was more acceptable than the Hungarian king. Albrecht's opinion was more respected than in the past, as in April, 1470, he took over from his brother Frederick the mark of Brandenburg as well as the electoral dignity.

By his hasty departure from Vienna, Matthias created a situation from which George, if on the watch for opportunities, could derive a good deal of profit. It was to his advantage that the two neighbors of Bohemia, instead of reaching a more effective agreement, were at odds. Some benefit also came to George from Albrecht Achilles' effort to dispose the Emperor favorably to the transfer of Brandenburg.[533] While in the past the Markgrave participated in various schemes which Frederick III resented, in 1470 he courted his favor and thus put in better light his Czech ally and relative.

Another hopeful sign of improvement was the Emperor's decision to seek closer contacts with Poland. After the estrangement of Matthias, he feared isolation, and had to admit that an attack on Austria from Hungary might be launched. Fear of Matthias' retaliation was so widespread that no Austrian lord was willing to go to Poland with the offer of a pact. Frederick confided this delicate mission to a Polish nobleman, Raphael Leszczyński, who had been in his service for some time and who could, if captured by Matthias' agents, conceal more successfully the purpose of his journey than could an Austrian. The Emperor's gesture made a good impression on Casimir and his councillors and it was decided to appoint Polish envoys for further exploration of the terms under which an alliance could be concluded.[534]

As the regrouping of the European powers was in its initial stage, it helped George only indirectly to reduce the danger of an anti-Czech coalition. As long as the sentence of excommunication was in force— Paul II had reiterated it on Maundy Thursday (April 19), 1470 [535]—none of the friendly princes dared to send military forces to operate with George's troops. It was necessary to tap the local reserves and to increase the internal revenue. Those of the Estates who adhered to him acceded without murmur or hesitation to his demand for fresh troops. At the provincial Diet of Bohemia in March, 1470, they approved an elaborate agreement concerning levies in the loyal areas.[536] The figures mentioned in the dietal resolution are not complete, but an approximate calculation results in a total of five thousand men on foot, several hundred horsemen, a fairly large number of wagons, and all kinds of equipment. By approving this extraordinary contribution, the Estates did not preclude the King's appeal for the traditional type of levies for purely defensive purposes. For the upkeep of hired troops, George had various sources of income, above all the continuous flow of money from the silver mines of Kutná Hora, not as rich as in the pre-Hussite period, but nevertheless significant.

The outbreak of hostilities which George anticipated occurred when the weather permitted. Soon after Easter, which came late in 1470, the two kings moved ahead without knowing of each other's strategy. Matthias' chief concern was Silesia, from which he received bad news while staying in Hungary. On the other hand, George's thoughts were fixed on Moravia and in that province primarily on the besieged borough of Hradiště. He sent a strong army to its relief, forcing Matthias to put off the march into Silesia and to move instead from the Slovak-inhabited Váh region into Moravia.

Although the armies were large, reorganized, and well equipped, their commanders resorted to cautious tactics instead of seeking a direct trial of force. Matthias felt a need of reinforcements to outnumber George and to crush him by sheer weight. The Silesian leaders were disappointed when, instead of the long-expected help, they received a request that they send their troops to Moravia.[537] Pending their arrival, Matthias operated in the vicinity of Hradiště, forcing the bulk of George's forces at one moment to retreat to the southeastern corner of Moravia around Hodonín. George, too, found it necessary to enlarge his army and designated the borough of Německý Brod, not far from the boundary of Bohemia and Moravia, as the gathering place of the freshly recruited troops.

At the head of an imposing mass of people, George crossed the border early in July and proceeded toward Brno, which had been under Matthias' control for some time. When informed of George's progress, Matthias moved from Hodonín westward. He did not, however, carry out his plan, as upon hearing that the Czech troops intended to withdraw from southeastern Moravia and move westward to unite with the army brought by George from Bohemia, he reversed his original orders so as to prevent the Czech concentration. Near the village of Kralice, in the central Moravian lowlands, he scored a victory over the marching Czech columns, trumpeted immediately to the world as a catastrophic defeat for George. In many churches in Silesia, upon the reception of the exaggerated reports, a solemn *Te Deum* was sung.[538] In fact, only a minor part of the Czech forces was captured, while others, protected by the chain of wagons, retreated to a safer position.

As George showed no intention of leaving his camp near Brno, Matthias moved some of his troops there and made connections with the garrisons in the city and at Špilberk. At the moment when a direct encounter appeared to be unavoidable, George made a startling offer. He proposed to his rival a duel to save the armies from suffering and losses. Realizing that his body, afflicted by disease, was too heavy to make possible quick turns or brusque movements, he suggested that a narrow and suitable field be chosen for the combat. As an alternative, he mentioned a battle for which the forces of both sides, now scattered all over Moravia, would prepare for four days by an undisturbed concentration at a selected place.[539]

Neither of these proposals was accepted by the Hungarian. The troops moved slowly from the Brno area eastward, George advancing and Matthias following slowly and cautiously. Opposed only by minor forces, George relieved Hradiště of the ring of improvised Hungarian fortresses and their garrisons and moved supplies into that principal stronghold and into other fortresses nearby. About the middle of August, strong armies commanded by George and Matthias faced each other near Olomouc. Then again the commanders, instead of plunging into a bloody battle, gave orders by which the scene changed surprisingly.

George was tempted by prospects of an easy advance into Upper Silesia, where he had sympathizers among the local princes and the population, Slavic by an overwhelming majority. When Matthias noticed the preparation for such an expedition, he turned quickly from Olomouc toward Bohemia. The columns of Hungarian horsemen quickly reached the Bohemian territory, by-passing whatever obstacles they encountered. They did not contemplate systematic occupation of the country, but resorted to pilfering of the unprotected territory and its inhabitants. Fresh troops were levied in Bohemia and with Queen Johanna at their head, they stemmed the tide of the Hungarian invasion. George, too, gave up his intended drive into Upper Silesia and hastened to Bohemia. Matthias did not move in stronger forces, but ordered his horsemen to retreat to safer positions in Moravia. When August ended, no major operation was undertaken to follow the evacuation of Bohemia by the Hungarians.[540]

As the spring and summer campaigns did not lead to a decisive battle, both parties had to make provisional arrangements for the winter period of reduced military operations. George's position was in some respects more advantageous, as Bohemia was his homeland and he fought for its reunion. By proving his ability to resist Matthias' aggression and to regain some of the lost ground, George not only made himself popular with his subjects, including some of those who had temporarily left his party, but enhanced his diplomatic prestige. The papal ban notwithstanding, he was regarded by other princes as one of them; chances of his conciliation with the Pope were debated in 1470 more frequently than in the previous two years.

The improvement, though in general auspicious, did not tangibly affect George's vital problems—the succession to the throne and the welfare of his family. The envoys who returned from Poland late in 1469 undoubtedly reported that Casimir was reluctant to take a resolute step before hearing the special envoy from the papal court.[541] Under such circumstances, it would have been futile to insist on a clarification of the Polish policy. George found some compensation for the Polish deadlock in the contacts with the princes of the Empire but did not retract his offer of the crown to Władysław.

The winter over, the roads became passable again, permitting a special papal emissary to proceed northward. His name was Alexander Numai, and shortly before his new assignment he had been elected Bishop of Forli. He met with Casimir at Nowy Korczyn and conferred also with the members of the royal council.[542] His proposal was not straightforward and not specially favorable to the Poles. He endeavored to explain that the Pope could not leave the Hungarian king out of his calculations, for he had gone to war with the Hussites and had scored several victories over them. Not daring to criticize the Polish king for his past policy, the envoy urged him to join hands with Matthias and to cement the alliance by a marriage to him of one of the Polish princesses. Apart from that, the envoy made suggestions which remain rather obscure for lack of direct evidence. Some of the most delicate points could not be put in a written document for fear of interception, and even to present them orally would have been rather risky. It can be surmised that at least some papal diplomats would have felt relieved if Casimir, either by force or by negotiations, had overcome George's reluctance to step down from the throne. In a situation thus created it would have been easier for those who in principle favored Casimir to resist pressure from the other group of prelates dominated by Gabriel Rangoni. Only when such a hypothesis is assumed is it possible to understand Alexander's cryptic statement that he would be prepared to deal even with George, if he could promote Casimir's interests thereby.[543]

Assuming that Alexander reached Nowy Korczyn in May, it must be admitted that several weeks had passed before Casimir made up his mind and appointed Jacob of Dębno and Stanisław Szydlowiecki as his envoys to George.[544] They traveled through the war-torn country and found the King at his headquarters near Malenovice in Moravia. They were instructed not to waste time in generalities but to secure George's binding promise that he would prepare immediately for Władysław's coronation. The sources are silent on another delicate point, namely, Ludmila's marriage to the future king. It is very likely that not much was said concerning it by the Poles, as their attitude had not changed. The envoys were more outspoken when other problems were canvassed. They promised Casimir's intervention in Rome to get from the Pope a confirmation of the Compacts, the lifting of the sentence of excommunication, and the sanction of Władysław's election to the throne of Bohemia.

Casimir enjoined his representatives to make contact not only with George but with the Catholic lords siding with Matthias. This idea emerged probably in discussions of Bishop Alexander's message from Rome. It would have been really of great advantage for Władysław if both George and the rebel party agreed that the Polish candidature would be the best solution of the problem of succession. An attempt to reach the Catholics was made, probably with George's knowledge, but a joint session could not take place. The answer given by Matthias and Zdeněk of Šternberk to an exploratory letter contained conditions which, if accepted, would have nullified the envoys' accord with George. The Poles were requested by the Catholics to recognize, in their application for safe conduct, Matthias as king of Bohemia; but if they had done so, they would have wrecked the agreement with George.[545]

A promise of Casimir's intervention in Rome transmitted to George by Jacob of Dębno could not surprise anyone, as it would have been in the Poles' interest to have the Pope's consent to Władysław's election. The reference to the Compacts cannot be so easily harmonized with Casimir's cautious policy. The question arises whether the document, which had been repudiated by Pius II in 1462,[546] was mentioned explicitly or only in vague terms in the conference near Malenovice. The only source in which it occurs are the papal letters addressed to Matthias, Casimir, and Bishop Roverella, and those merely echoed what had been reported to Rome by Matthias' agents soon after the conference, with the evident purpose of denigrating the Poles.[547]

Be it as it may, no visible progress toward conciliation was made in the summer or fall of 1470, when the envoys were expected to return to their homeland and report. Several months were to pass before Casimir took the next step by appointing his representatives for further dealings with the Pope. George, from his side, made no attempt to speed up the Polish intervention.

Compared with the bleak days after the Olomouc election, George's situation by the end of the summer of 1470 was so hopeful that he saw no reason for offering excessive concessions to the neutrals. The Wettin and Hohenzollern friends, and also princes who were less committed to his support, believed that he had succeeded in extricating himself. In the light of recent developments, his affairs were considered benevolently at a conference at Villach held under the Emperor's sponsorship, late in July, 1470.[548] In that gathering of crowned heads or envoys from several countries, including those of Burgundy and Poland, there was no discussion of George's expulsion from Bohemia, but rather of the means and ways by which his protracted conflict could be settled. Rumors were heard that an Austro-Czech-Polish coalition had been considered in private talks as a means of stopping Matthias' expansion. In fact, Frederick III was not yet prepared to offer an olive branch, but at least he did not oppose other princes in their search for a formula which both the Pontiff and George could accept.

Some improvement of George's position could also be ascribed to continued negotiations between Frederick III and Casimir. These proceeded slowly, as both parties traditionally disliked hasty measures. The fear of Matthias' aggression proved to be a stronger incentive than other reasons for a friendly pact. The first concrete product of the written and oral exchanges was an offer, with which the Polish envoys returned late in 1470, to Casimir's temporary residence at Poznań. Casimir's reaction to the tenor of the proposed agreement was favorable, but he took exception to Frederick's title, in which was included also the royal dignity of Hungary. He felt that by recognizing the Emperor's claims to that crown he would prejudice his own aspirations. His refusal to endorse the imperial draft made further negotiations necessary. The refusal was made tactfully, since Casimir was careful not to hurt Frederick's feelings and thereby break off contacts with him.[549] The latter's hostility would have been an unpleasant complication, as he could delay the formal confirmation of Władysław's rule in Bohemia.

Matthias' failure to secure a footing in Bohemia was far less serious than his neglect of the Silesians and other allies. When the balance sheet of his activities in 1470 was drawn, the lack of concern for the northern provinces was conspicuous. Much of his laxity originated in his conviction that the rebels should mobilize their resources to assist him in operations to which he assigned priority, instead of expecting that he would march to their rescue.

Reports from Moravia that in late September Matthias had departed for Hungary cast gloom over the northern provinces, especially those areas close to the Czech outposts. Silesia seethed with fear that, free from other obligations, George would attack it with full force.[550] Rumors were also heard that the dukes of Oleśnica had secretly requested Casimir to reconcile them with George. To combat dissatisfaction, Bishop Rudolf called a provincial Diet to meet on October 25, 1470.[551] No skill could disguise the concern of the Estates that the Czech troops were operating without effective opposition in many parts of the country. The Breslau senate and many of the patricians in walled boroughs in the Duchy of Świdnica-Jawor stressed the need of resistance, but the landowners and peasantry preferred agreements with the Czech captains. Two courses were open before the assembled notables, both rather awkward and risky. The radicals recommended a request to Matthias, urging him to assert his authority by coercing those of his subjects who established contacts with the Hussites. The more moderate elements would have favored contacts with George, so that local agreements could be replaced by a general truce. No one, however, was bold enough to plead for the latter policy for fear of ecclesiastical censures.

Before a resolution could be adopted, news arrived at Breslau that Zdeněk of Šternberk, to whom Matthias had left the supreme command, had attacked with notable success several Hussite strongholds in Bohemia.[552] Impressed by Zdeněk's victories, the assembled leaders rejected the idea of sounding out George and appointed delegates to Matthias. They departed without delay, but several weeks were needed to cover the distance between Breslau and Buda. And again several weeks were to pass before they could return to Breslau to give the report of the King's answer, which was neither kind nor reassuring.

When observed from a shorter distance than Breslau, Zdeněk's victories appeared to be far less significant than the city leaders believed. There are no documents left from which it would be possible to study Zdeněk's intentions and reactions. He was a captive of his own ambitions and dreams of aggrandizement, but not altogether deprived of critical abilities. Perhaps the whispering campaign following his meetings with Bohuslav of Švamberk was not entirely unfounded. It went on for some time, making many people believe that Zdeněk, disillusioned with Matthias, was exploring chances of a return to George's obedience.

Citizens of the kingdom of Bohemia, whether obeying George or Matthias, could get so involved in local clashes as to believe that their plight would be over if the two kings sheathed their swords and reestablished their former peaceful relations. The resources of the two rulers seemed equal and neither found powerful allies with whose help he would be able to defeat the other. Judged superficially, the conflict was no more than a spectacular duel in which the rivals held equally strong positions and each attempted in vain to uncover his opponent's most vulnerable point. In fact, the two rivals could not go too far in searching for ways toward conciliation without a previous reorientation of the papal policy. George was under the sentence of excommunication and Matthias would have risked grave consequences if he had attempted to extricate himself from the manifold obligations he had eagerly taken upon himself in 1468. The war in Bohemia was not a mere conflict between two secular rulers and their armies, but had the character of a crusade in which the Pontiff was also involved.

While Paul II, chiefly on Carvajal's advice, fulminated against George, Albania was the only territory in which the Turks conducted offensive operations. Their troops were tied up by Skanderbeg, and other targets of their aggressive policy seemed to be out of danger. In that atmosphere it was possible to give credence to the inflated reports from Central Europe depicting the strength and resolution of the Catholic elements in Bohemia as well as the sad condition of the Hussite king. As Hungary was not directly threatened by the Turks, Paul II overcame his hesitation as to the advisability of Matthias' involvement in the affairs of Bohemia, seeing no other monarch who would be willing to head the anti-Hussite crusade. The war, instead of being short and decisive, dragged on unpleasantly and its third year dashed hopes of its timely and successful conclusion.

In the spring of 1470 Paul II showed no sign of vacillation and gave evidence of his firmness by the bull of Maundy Thursday.[553] Like other foes of the Hussite king, he too rejoiced in Matthias' temporary success in Moravia and mentioned it when writing to Hungary on another subject,[554] but the joy aroused by the exaggerated reports did not last long. News coming from the Balkans to Venice and to Rome sharply contrasted with the information concerning Matthias' advances. A powerful army commanded by Mohamed II himself, as well as a strong fleet, advanced toward Greece. On July 12, 1470, the principal stronghold of the Venetians in the Aegean, known as Negroponte, fell into Turkish hands.[555] Other losses were to be feared. Questions could be raised, though few people would dare to do so loudly, whether papal diplomacy did not confuse the basic issues confronting Christendom by putting the Hussite cause above the Turkish menace.

The Pope's immediate concern was for the termination of quarrels among the Italian states so that a league could be formed for general defense of the peninsula against the Moslems. Venice, the chief victim of their aggression, not only looked toward Rome and other Italian courts but also northward. In co-operation with papal diplomacy, the Republic approached Matthias to secure his participation in an amphibious campaign to be launched in the spring of 1471.

It was expected in Venice and Rome that Matthias would accept the role to be assigned to the king of Hungary whenever the plans of a collective action against the Turks were developed. Who else should regard it as his primary duty to hinder the Turkish advances if not the ruler of a fairly large and prosperous kingdom bordering on the Turkish-dominated Balkans? Matthias was not deaf to the appeals for help, but demanded a heavy price for it—the surrender by the Venetians of whatever they possessed in Dalmatia. That maritime province was traditionally regarded as the third part of the triune kingdom of Croatia and its reunion with Croatia and Slavonia appeared to be an appropriate compensation to the king of Hungary for his substantial help against the Turks.[556]

The Venetians' reluctance to give up their scattered possessions on the eastern Adriatic was not the only impediment the diplomats, endeavoring to organize a mighty anti-Turkish alliance, encountered in late 1470 and early 1471. Matthias' entanglements in Bohemia were no less perplexing and onerous, even for those who originally had welcomed his attack on George. His armed forces and financial resources were to be split, and he was unable personally to keep together his party in the provinces of the kingdom of Bohemia and to head effectively the crusading army in the Danubian area. The papal diplomacy labored under disadvantages greater than those met in its normal tasks.

Information concerning Poland pointed unwaveringly in one direction—Casimir's determination to get the crown of Bohemia for his oldest son, to found a Jagellonian secundogeniture. The Emperor and other members of the Villach conference [557] agreed to such a solution of the Czech problem, as it appeared to be less harmful to their interests than a personal union of two kingdoms in Matthias' hands. Paul II did not shut the door to Polish envoys seeking his help and endeavored to keep up Matthias' spirit by other signs of friendship.

Late in 1470 two clerics from Hungary reached Rome to acquaint the Pope with the recent developments in Central Europe and to secure favors for their king.[558] Paul II got a rather vague and unduly optimistic report, most likely from them, that the Emperor had returned to his former policy and concluded an agreement with Matthias. Not waiting for a confirmation of the glad tidings, Paul II wrote on January 14, 1471, to Frederick III approving his policy and urging him to make the accord definitive, if he had not already done so. He also informed the Emperor that Fra Gabriel Rangoni would soon arrive at his court and give him a more detailed account of the current developments.[559] Paul's joy over the conciliation of the two rulers, whose participation in the anti-Turkish alliance was highly desirable, was rather premature, as the negotiations with Frederick III conducted in Matthias' name by the supreme chamberlain, John Rozgonyi, made no visible progress.

It was undoubtedly known in Rome that Matthias' expenditure since the start of his war with George was out of all normal proportions and that requests for additional contributions fomented discontent among the secular lords and the highest clerics. The primate of Hungary, John Vitéz, and the learned Bishop of Pécs, Janus Pannonius, came to be regarded as the foremost critics of Matthias' policy, which had unduly drained the financial resources of the kingdom, so that even the ecclesiastical possessions had to be heavily taxed. The King's staunchest supporter among the hierarchy was John Peckenschlager (Bechenslocr), a native of Breslau and, since June, 1467, Bishop of Eger. In him Fra Gabriel and the other two papal legates, Bishops Lawrence and Rudolf, had their most faithful ally.

To alleviate the burden of financial obligations and to mitigate the increasing dissatisfaction, Paul II dispatched several letters directly to Hungary and to his plenipotentiaries elsewhere, and instructed Fra Gabriel what steps to undertake immediately after his return to Buda. One letter, rather vague in promises of future compensation, was destined for Archbishop Vitéz.[560] Another, addressed to Bishop Lawrence, was more specific, as it empowered him to use money collected in Poland and in the Catholic parts of the kingdom of Bohemia to send whatever remained, after covering his own expenses, as subsidies to Bishop Rudolf and to the king of Hungary.[561] In addition to that, Paul II granted Matthias eighteen thousands ducats from the papal funds to enable him to bring the anti-Hussite war to a successful end.[562] This sum, added to the earlier subsidies, did not cover all the costs Matthias had incurred, but could not be belittled when both the advantages and inconveniences arising from a close alliance with the Holy See were weighed and contrasted.

Money set apart for Matthias was to be sent to Bishop Lawrence for safe transmission, but the two emissaries were not allowed to leave Rome empty-handed. The Pope resolved to honor Matthias by presenting him with a hat and a sword, consecrated solemnly on Christmas Day, in recognition of his loyalty to the Holy See.[563] Fra Gabriel, who apparently joined the two Hungarians, carried another precious object—the red hat for Stephen de Varda, Archbishop of Kalocsa, created cardinal on an earlier occasion. The ceremonial transmission of the hat never took place, as Stephen died before Fra Gabriel had placed a foot on Hungarian soil.[564]

Distances between Rome and the Central European capitals retarded contacts, especially in the winter. Matthias' patience, tried by the Pope's hesitancy to confirm his election and to send him a crown for his coronation in Bohemia, was further strained by the failure of his envoy in Vienna. The Pope's resolutions, made around Christmas, 1470, and the letters referring to them, dated in January, 1471, could not become known in Hungary before the middle of February. Before they had reached Buda, Matthias took a step which startled both his friends and enemies: he made known his desire to liquidate his Czech venture and make peace with George. His initiative apparently caused more excitement in Poland than in Bohemia, as it has been recorded more vividly in the Polish than in the Czech documents. The terms mentioned by the chronicle of John Długosz were so attractive that nobody could outbid the Hungarian.[565] He was willing to leave the entire kingdom of Bohemia to George as long as the latter should live. He promised also to set Victorin free and grant him the title of markgrave of either Silesia or Moravia. Matthias also hinted that if he remained without legitimate descendants, provisions would be made for the succession of George's sons to the throne.

According to Długosz, the Hungarian offer was taken seriously and a conference was held early in 1471 at Polná, a borough on Šternberk domains in southeastern Bohemia. The Catholic party was represented by Zdeněk of Šternberk, Bishop Tas, and Albrecht Kostka of Postupice, while George sent three of his ablest councillors, William of Rýzmberk, Peter Kdúlincc, and Beneš of Veitmil. The principal points under discussion related to the exercise of royal power and succession to the throne, and the delegates considered the danger, if George died suddenly, of an armed intervention from Poland, the purpose of which would be a swift occupation of the territories held since 1468 by Matthias. They also believed that with Matthias' strong support it would be easier to get acceptable terms from the Holy See than with the Poles as intermediaries.

As only one report concerning these negotiations is available, it is impossible to say to what extent the Hussite king had become committed. The offer, as recorded by Długosz, was highly attractive and additional arrangements could be made after its acceptance in principle. The weakest spot in the sensational maneuver was Matthias' notorious laxity in keeping his pledged word. Could George forget the events from Vilémov to the Olomouc election?

John Długosz reported the Polná conferences and added tersely that Provost Paul of Zderaz was once more instructed to saddle horses and journey in the midst of winter to Lithuania, where Casimir was reported to reside. Preparations for the onerous mission were apparently in progress, but did Paul have to endure the discomfort of such a long trip?

On Saint Valentine's Day, 1471, an assembly was held in Prague to debate the report from Polná. The session, again according to Długosz,[566] was interrupted by the unexpected appearance of Jacob of Dębno and his companion, Abbot Michael of the Holy Cross. They were en route to Rome, conveying the decision of the conference near Malenovice, and stopped in Prague to get more information. Realizing, to his great surprise, that serious consideration was being given to a deal with Matthias, the Lord of Dębno sternly reminded the assembled notables of their former commitments to Casimir and Władysław. If Długosz' report is to be believed, the envoy's speech made such a deep impression that the assembly resolved to discontinue negotiations with Matthias.

Długosz made no attempt to exonerate the Hussite king or to search for reasons for the latter's sudden turn. As neither Matthias nor George publicly revealed his motives, it is possible to offer conjectures, but no positive answer, as to Matthias' unexpected gesture. It was made, apparently, in the absence of satisfactory assurances from Rome that Matthias would be confirmed in his acquisitions in Bohemia and that Władysław's candidature would be unequivocally rejected. George's mild interest could be motivated by growing impatience with Casimir's dilatory tactics. It was most likely Provost Paul's primary task to obtain from Casimir an immediate decision. Be it as it may, neither Matthias nor George suffered harm from the dramatic interruption of hostilities and from the hastily convened conferences. At least there was an opportunity to show the easy-going Pole that both direct negotiations with Prague and the intervention in Rome must be speeded up.

The situation in Hungary was not visibly affected by Matthias' *volte face*, which he himself regarded as so insignificant that he made no reference to it in his correspondence with Rome. He gratefully accepted the insignia granted him by the Pontiff and advised him of his intention to send envoys to Rome for a discussion of outstanding problems.[567]

Public life in Bohemia also went back to its former course. The traditional constellation reappeared on the horizon: Casimir, the Wettin princes, Albrecht Achilles, and the Emperor in a not too conspicuous position. The roles were divided according to previous experiences. The Polish envoys were to promote in Rome the political objectives: the sanction of the peace of Toruń, and the Pope's consent to Władysław's rule in Bohemia. The more delicate task of George's conciliation with the Pope was undertaken by the Saxon princes, Albrecht and Ernest. It was agreed that the Saxon envoys would also second the Polish petition on Władysław's behalf. The assignment of the roles appeared to be sound, as the Saxon princes were less tainted than either the excommunicated Albrecht Achilles or the none-too-cooperative Casimir. Moreover, they had personal reasons for their intervention. Duke Albrecht was George's son-in-law, and another family link was to be forged in the not distant future.[568]

The princes, probably informed by Dr. Weissbach of the trends prevailing in Rome, carefully prepared their instruction for the envoys so that their proposals could not be flatly rejected. It is very likely that George was asked to express his own opinion of it. His preference was for a simple formula, avoiding painful details and personal humiliation. The princes apparently knew that such a solution had no chance of acceptance. Instead of working out a rigid instruction, they left it to the discretion of their plenipotentiaries to submit as a definitive proposal a set of articles to be compiled in Rome after consultation with high ranking clerics of the papal court.[569] The envoys left home some time in February and passed through the gates of the eternal city around the twentieth of March, 1471.

Although the mediation was planned as a political act, with princes and not theologians as its originators, religious problems could not be left out. The stumbling block was a statement attributed to George, but denied by him categorically, that the Chalice was necessary for salvation.[570] Without investigating whether or not George had used these words, the Saxon envoys proposed that he make a statement disclaiming the necessity of the communion in both kinds for laymen. Though in the earlier schemes a special papal legate had usually been mentioned as the chief architect of conciliation, the Saxon mediators reserved the key position for the archbishop to be appointed to the see of Prague. No mention was made either of Rokycana or of a Catholic prelate of George's choice. It would be the archbishop's primary obligation to bring Church life into harmony with the pattern prevailing in the Roman orbit. A special reference was made to the administration of the Eucharist to infants, as practiced by many Hussite priests. It was suggested that it be tactfully suppressed. The envoys recommended in general that the change from the Hussite rites to the elaborate ceremonies and pomp of the Roman ritual be slow and smooth. They hinted at a restitution to the Church of the confiscated domains and to other sources of income. They did not pledge a general abandonment of the Chalice, but indicated that its adherents should be permitted to follow the accustomed practice to the end of their days. In the final article, they postulated that all sentences against George be lifted and that his royal dignity be reconfirmed; once this was done, he would feel obliged to accord to the Pontiff honors and services rendered by the other Christian princes.

Compared with the earlier proposals that had emanated from George's circle, the Saxon scheme came nearer to the official Roman point of view. The envoys scored a modest success in so far as their initiative was not totally rejected. Paul II accepted their scheme as a basis for exploration and enjoined the cardinals to comment, after a close study, on its specific points. The cardinals took the matter seriously and attached to each article remarks and questions to which, before the final acceptance, George would be expected to give precise answers, in order to avoid controversies, or even relapse into errors, in the future.[571]

Although intensely concerned with the Turkish menace, the Pope was in no haste to release George from obligations incurred by his failure in 1466 to comply with the cardinals' citation and the ensuing papal bulls. The cardinals, with perhaps some exceptions, persisted in their intransigence and the Saxon envoys left Rome without any manifest success. The circles hostile to George were satisfied when, in the summary condemnation of the enemies of the Church on Maundy Thursday (April 11, 1471), Paul II again included George of Poděbrady and Gregory of Heimburg.[572]

The text of the bull, following documents of the same type promulgated in the earlier years, did not express accurately the Pope's intentions in the spring of 1471. Nor did it correspond to the events in Bohemia of which the Curia could not be informed, as the communication with Prague was infrequent and slow. The Pope's chief preoccupation was the Turkish advance and the consolidation of Western Christendom for an effective counteraction. After the formation of a general alliance of the Italian states, he looked with hope to the imperial Diet which Frederick III convened to Regensburg. To show the Emperor and the imperial Estates how much importance the Holy See attached to their assembly, Paul II bypassed Bishop Lawrence, residing in Germany as his legate, and appointed as his special representative Francis Cardinal Piccolomini, a nephew of Pius II.[573] He believed that the envoy's rank and his kinship with Pius II would make him more acceptable than Roverella, who had been too deeply involved in the organization of the anti-Hussite expedition and had made enemies among the princes. In view of the Emperor's desire to have Central Europe at peace, it would have been preposterous to exclude beforehand any other way toward that goal than an unconditional surrender by George. On April 8, 1471, three days before Maundy Thursday, Paul II resolved that Cardinal Francis should be acquainted with both the Saxon proposals and the cardinals' recommendations in order to use them in his negotiations with the princes at Regensburg.[574] On the date of the papal resolution, the cardinal was already on his way northward, having left Rome on March 18.

Dominated by the desire to compose the long-standing enmities, Paul II responded graciously to the overtures from the Brandenburg court. Since he succeeded his brother Frederick, Markgrave Albrecht Achilles regarded as a handicap the sentence of excommunication which he had incurred by consenting to the marriage of his daughter Ursula to Henry of Poděbrady. The Pope considered the case benevolently. He knew the brave prince personally, having met him in 1459 at Mantua. Memories of that assembly, in which Albrecht Achilles had received from Pius II the same insignia by which recently the Hungarian king was honored, guided the Pope when he concerned himself with the Regensburg assembly and began to think concretely of which princes more could be expected than vague assurances. The course of the Diet showed that Paul II, when authorizing Cardinal Francis to lift the excommunication from Albrecht Achilles, acted wisely.[575] Both the Elector of Brandenburg and Elector Ernest of Saxony seconded the papal legate and organized troops for participation in the anti-Turkish crusade.

In the winter of 1470–71, when the Saxon mediation was undertaken, one obstacle, which had formerly proved unsurmountable, ceased to block the way. No protest from the Utraquist ranks was heard when John of Rokycany was left out of the conciliation scheme as a candidate for the Prague See. He was now over seventy, and his health showed distinct symptoms of decline. He died in Prague on February 22, 1471, and was buried at the Týn church. Queen Johanna, the princes, prominent Utraquist lords, and many members of the lesser nobility attended the funeral.[576]

Soon afterwards, the Prague population witnessed another, more cheerful ceremony. The third of George's sons, Hynek, then nineteen, was married to Catherine of Saxony, a daughter of Prince William who ruled over Weimar and the surrounding territory.

George's absence from Rokycana's funeral, noticed by attentive observers, was not a calculated act of cautiousness but a fact which even the ardent Utraquists had to recognize as serious. The King was not in good health, and attendance at a long and elaborate ceremony would have caused him a good deal of pain and embarrassment. Zdeněk of Šternberk did not exaggerate when he remarked that the "deposed king would not live to touch the colored Easter eggs."

The King himself did not view his condition as critical and worked no less intensely than in previous years. He knew of the journey of the Polish envoys and of the Saxon mission and expected good results. Another vital problem, the re-establishment of friendly contacts with Frederick III, was moving toward a solution. On March 9, 1471, George was able to report to Albrecht Achilles that a letter had just been received in Prague indicating that the Emperor would attend the imperial Diet at Regensburg and act in George's favor.

As the prospects of peace with the two highest authorities steadily improved, George expected that his struggle with Matthias would soon be terminated. More than anybody else, he trusted the reports from Hungary concerning Matthias' conflict with some of the prelates and lords. Indications of Matthias' preparedness for a new campaign in the spring could not be dismissed as a mere hearsay, but George apparently regarded the reports of Matthias' troubles as more important. Full of optimism, he expressed, in a letter to Markgrave Albrecht Achilles of March 9, 1471, his firm hope that as "Matthias had drunk with him Czech beer, so would he, George, with God's help taste with him the Hungarian wine." [577]

George was active in conferring with his councillors and attending such current duties as the sanctioning and signing of official correspondence. But no human help could stop the rapid decline of his health. He suffered from dropsy, and the swelling of legs, which had been observed previously, was spreading to the upper part of his body. Lack of movement, coupled with other physical handicaps, seriously affected George's system, especially the liver. A gallstone formed, causing him undoubtedly a good deal of discomfort. On Friday, March 22, 1471, two hours after sunset, death came to relieve George of all worries and pain and to close his life at a not very great age. He was a little over fifty.

Recording the memorable events of his period, an anonymous Czech chronicler wrote: [578]

"In the same year King George died at night from Friday to Saturday, before the Sunday *Laetare*, soon, only four weeks, after Master Rokycana. The latter defended the Lord's chalice by word, the former by the sword. And the king was buried on the day of the Annunciation to the Holy Virgin, in the new choir in the Prague castle at the side of King Ladislav, in the direction of Saint Václav's chapel; but his bowels were put in a barrel and deposited at the side of Master Rokycana's tomb at the Holy Virgin of Týn. He [the King] was found steadfast in the Christ's truths, in taking the Lord's most precious blood until his death. He died amidst those great wars. O Lord, be merciful to his gracious soul."

Gregory of Heimburg reported George's death to the dukes of Saxony. According to him, the King died on Friday and the body lay in state in the royal court on Saturday and Sunday. On Monday it was transferred to the Cathedral and buried there with the assistance of priests and monks from both sides, Catholics and Utraquists, whom he had protected and shielded graciously until his death.[579]

THE KING'S LEGACY

Signature and seal, which George of Kunštát and Poděbrady appended in January 1440 to the "letter of peace" could well be regarded as his first significant step toward the pacification of Bohemia.[580] Coming after twenty-five years of storms and wars, the "letter of peace" manifested the desire of the Czech nobility to terminate the political and religious struggles that had broken out soon after the martyr death of John Hus, and to give Bohemia peace and stability. For thirty-one years George pursued steadfastly the policy outlined in the "letter of peace," striving both for a solution of the political problems and for the coexistence of the Catholic and Utraquist parties. In his political program he was guided by the example of King Charles IV, who by several charters had regulated the relations between Bohemia and the four incorporated provinces. As a basis for religious peace, George accepted the Compacts, negotiated in 1436 by the delegates of the Council of Basel and the spokesmen of the Czech Utraquists. Sanctioned by King Sigismund, the Compacts were included among the basic laws of the kingdom.

Convinced that monarchy was the most appropriate system of government for his country, George participated in negotiations with Frederick III, the custodian of the infant prince, Ladislav, concerning the latter's claims to the crown of Bohemia. In 1453, Frederick III released the Prince from his tutelage and sent him to Prague for coronation. Four years of Ladislav's reign can be rightly included in the period of the thirty-odd years which some historians call summarily "the Poděbrady era," as George held the first place in Ladislav's council and guided his hand when important decisions were to be made. No serious opposition in 1458 marred George's bid for the supreme position in the kingdom—the royal throne.

Friends and foes alike have formed a high opinion of George's personal qualities, recognizing gladly or invidiously his political talents. His competence in the conduct of public affairs was matched by his

strength of mind and his dedication to the national cause. He was skillful and assiduous in negotiations, but both partisans and foes soon
learned that it was rather risky to strain his patience or to oppose obstinately the measures upon which he had set his mind. He apparently
attracted people with whom he came in contact by his native charm
and simple manners. Many friendships and alliances formed when he
was rising to prominence withstood pressure in the period of adversity
and were broken only by his death. As John Długosz remarked when
commenting on his premature end, George was not quick in causing
bloodshed, and that endeared him to his people.[581]

As an elected king, George was supported by the Czech population
of Bohemia and Moravia so that he possessed enough power to overcome opposition in some parts of the kingdom. In his effort to get his
title generally recognized, he felt himself somewhat handicapped by
his family background, nationality, and steadfast adherence to the Hussite tenets. Not only was he himself elevated to kingship from the aristocratic ranks, but both his first and second wives were of Czech origin
and of Hussite faith. Consequently, they could not help in reducing the
gap between the Poděbrady house and other dynasties. Sensing danger
from one side or another, George was more interested in such symbolic
acts as the coronation or recognition by the Emperor than a prince of
royal blood would have been under similar circumstances.

George's relations with Frederick III were not at all times friendly
and smooth, but the differences of interest which in 1463 caused an
estrangement never led to a violent conflict. In order to safeguard his
position against the Emperor or a coalition of German princes, George
submitted to ceremonies, such as the investment with the regalia, stipulated by the ancient charters. He deliberately tightened the ties between
Bohemia and the Empire, which had been considerably weakened during the period of the Hussite wars. On various occasions, he stressed
his solidarity with the other princes of the Empire, especially the electors,
among whom he, as the king of Bohemia, held a prominent place. Although his knowledge of German was hardly more than rudimentary,
he maintained personal contacts or correspondence with his German
allies and occasionally attended their meetings. Treaties of marriage by
which his family came to be linked with the Wettins and Hohenzollerns
fitted well into his program. They lessened the danger of isolation or
of coalition of foreign rulers with the dissatisfied elements within the
kingdom.

The crucial test came when George resolved to seek a solemn sanction
of the Compacts. The chance of success was slight, because of the basic
disagreement on the significance of that document. George believed,
like the other Utraquists, that the Compacts created a legal basis for

the recognition of the Hussite party as a specific unit within the orbit of the Roman obedience. Memories of their acceptance by the delegates from Basel and by King Sigismund were not fading and could be reinvigorated, if necessary, by the display of the original document, one of the most treasured items in the Crown archives.

One point remained somewhat obscure, but the lack of explicit evidence did not worry the Hussite leaders too much. They believed that Pope Eugene IV approved the steps taken by the Council of Basel in order to reach an agreement with the Czechs. According to vague indications, the Hussites possessed some documents which they interpreted in their favor. The matter is so intricate that no answer can be given other than a simple statement that the Papacy did not accept the Hussite interpretation of whatever document they may have had. Statements pertaining to these problems, whenever made by Pius II or his successor, were unequivocal. They saw in the Compacts a reminder of the conciliar era and did not feel bound to abide by them. Their attitude in this particular point is consonant with the general lines of their policy to introduce into the entire Church uniformity both in doctrine and liturgy.

It could be adduced by the Hussites that Eugene's successors, Nicholas V and Calixtus III, dealt with the Czech envoys without any explicit objection to the Compacts. George himself shared the common view that the Compacts had proved their usefulness in facilitating contacts between Prague and Rome. He felt that his coronation oath, containing a pledge of obedience to "the Roman, Catholic and Apostolic Church," could be harmonized with his sincere adherence to the Chalice. Viewing his main problems from the political angle, George hoped that on the basis created by the participation of the Hungarian bishops at the coronation rites and the recognition of his royal rank by Pius II, his relations with the Holy See would develop smoothly and to the satisfaction of both the parties concerned. In this hope he accepted the help of papal diplomacy in allaying the Breslau opposition, thus permitting Rome's intervention in the affairs of his own kingdom.

In the absence of direct evidence, nothing but conjectures can be offered concerning George's decision to close the period of his subtle maneuvering by a request for a sanction of the Compacts. Did he reach by his own speculation, or under the influence of his intimate advisers, the conclusion that, out of consideration for the political aspects of the Hussite cause, Pius II would be willing to substitute a formal approval of the Compacts for tacit toleration? The request was not preceded or accompanied by a truculent gesture, but it was made firmly and with an appropriate representation of the Utraquists among the envoys. When all circumstances are taken into account, it can be concluded that George was confident of success, but that he fatefully misjudged Pius' intentions.

The Pope did not see in George's petition a good opportunity for diplomatic bargaining in matters pertaining either to Bohemia or to his cherished project of an anti-Turkish crusade. Instead, he made use of his spiritual authority and repudiated the Compacts as incompatible with the restoration of the absolute unity of Christendom. Papal contacts with Prague, not too friendly before 1462, were further strained and the consequences could not be immediately foreseen.

George's foes at the papal court, in Breslau, and elsewhere, headed by Cardinal Carvajal, saw to it that the line adopted by Pius II in March, 1462, would be followed consistently. Rigid precepts of the canon law served as directives for the papal court, and in a situation thus created, George's political strategy or occasional interventions by friendly princes bore no fruit.

As the Hussite king had only sporadic contacts with Rome, he failed to see the chasm between his endeavors and the papal offensive. Relying on such advisers as Gregory of Heimburg, George placed excessive hope in rulers and statesmen who were in actual conflict with the Papacy or at least manifested their anticlerical leanings. Limited in personal contacts with foreign courts, George failed to see clearly the limits to which even the most resolute of his friends were ready to go. His efforts to link the Hussite cause with the general problems of relationship between the secular and spiritual powers came to nothing. By advocacy of the general Council, despite the Mantua decree of 1459, he added fuel to the flame and hardened the Pope in his resolution to suppress the Hussite movement by the application of all coercive measures.

The heaviest charge against George was the statement, supposedly made at the Saint Lawrence gathering in 1462, that the communion in both kinds is necessary for salvation. As the evidence supporting this accusation was flimsy, it would not have been too difficult to exonerate George on that point. Not trained in theology, the King had no intention of passing judgments on the problems of doctrine. However, he believed simply but firmly that by denouncing the Chalice he would be found personally guilty before other Utraquists and before God. He could not be induced to take such a fateful step publicly, and he would have found secret abjuration no less distasteful. The conflict, when narrowed down, centered on the problem of papal authority, to which all Christians, irrespective of their position in wordly affairs, were expected to yield obedience in matters of religion. In George's case the situation seemed to be clear and simple, in view of the coronation oath which the Popes interpreted in their favor, repudiating resolutely any attempt to give it a different meaning.

Problems with which George was faced after his election made impossible the separation of religion from politics. The closest juncture existed in Breslau. George's conduct in that affair resembled his preparations for the coronation, as in both instances George acted in the hope that subsequent developments would at least partly relieve him of the accepted commitments. In his dealing with the rebel city, he permitted the papal legates to act as mediators and acquiesced in a temporary agreement which had to be implemented within three years, a period seemingly long enough to improve George's position in all respects.

Trusting his luck and experience in negotiating with hostile factions, George accepted an imperfect accord, but the ensuing events taught him a lesson that came too late to permit a thorough change of policy. A formal defect, which under more propitious circumstances could have easily been rectified, became a source of trouble when George strained his relations with the Papacy. The rich and proud city, which had defied George in the early stage of his reign, rekindled the spirit of opposition as soon as its leaders perceived the symptoms of crisis. It failed to swear the oath of allegiance when the period of three years had expired, and in March, 1463, put itself under the papal protection. The first breach in the order George had laboriously established was followed in 1465 by the emergence of an opposition among the Czech Catholic lords and by a gradual consolidation of the enemy ranks. Foreign support, which George endeavored to eliminate by friendly contacts with his neighbors, did not come from the German-speaking countries related to Breslau by ethnic kinship and an attachment to the Holy See, but from Hungary, governed by George's one time friend and son-in-law.

Although in the last year of his life George considerably improved his position, he was still far from his ultimate goal when attacked by an incurable disease. Death came for him before the Saxon mediation had made visible progress. The papal ban had not been lifted, but the clerics administering Saint Vitus Cathedral did not oppose the King's burial at the side of King Ladislav. The treaty with Poland, although agreed on in principle, was not formally concluded and internationally recognized. Matters particularly dear to George—such as the financial security for his consort and Ludmila's marriage—were not settled. It fell to other peoples' lot to take over the King's cherished ideas and to attempt their realization.

At the time of George's death, Prince Victorin was in Hungarian captivity. His brother Henry, although distinguished in campaigns against Matthias, did not command as much authority as was needed in those troubled times; and George's other sons were even less qualified than Henry. Under these conditions, the Supreme Chancellor, Ctibor Tovačovský of Cimburk, assumed leadership of the Poděbrady party and continued negotiations with Poland. His task was difficult, for Duke

Albrecht of Saxony coveted the throne and used his kinship with the Poděbrady family as a justification for his activities. Spokesmen of all candidates attended the provincial Diet at Kutná Hora, which was stormy but not too long. The majority followed Lord Ctibor and elected the Pole. Prince Henry was appointed the supreme captain of the realm.[582] A delegation headed by Lord Ctibor left immediately for Cracow and obtained from Władysław (whose name from this point on will be given in the Czech form of Vladislav) a solemn sanction of the ancient privileges and freedoms of the kingdom, including the Compacts.

Duke Albrecht realized that his chances were slim and withdrew from the contest. Matthias was more tenacious and resolved to carry on the struggle from positions in Moravia and elsewhere that he held at the time of George's death. The Hungarian forces were scattered and not strong enough either to capture Prague or to obstruct Vladislav's journey from Cracow through Upper Silesia and Kladsko to Bohemia. On August 22, 1471, the elected king was crowned by three Polish bishops with the ancient crown of Saint Wenceslas in the Cathedral of Saint Vitus. Although the ceremony followed the *Ordo coronationis*,[583] an exception was made in it—at the coronation mass Vladislav ostentatiously took the sacrament in one kind only (bread), to the grief of his Utraquist supporters.

The loyal party slightly increased its membership as some Catholic lords from Bohemia, impressed by the coronation, joined it. Far more was, however, needed than local shifts to expel Matthias from the incorporated provinces and bring them under Vladislav's control. As Casimir IV was unable to send strong forces to Bohemia to add to his son's prestige, chances of reconquest were very small indeed. An attempt to overthrow Matthias with the help of his opponents in Hungary foundered on poor co-ordination between the rebels and the Polish troops. Matthias dispersed his Hungarian foes, and was encouraged by the poor showing of his rival in attempting to seize the control of Bohemia by force.

The struggle went on with varying intervals for seven years. Vladislav's army was strong enough to protect Bohemia, but in Moravia and other provinces Matthias exercised royal prerogatives without much opposition. Unable to defeat each other with forces at their disposal, the conflicting parties appealed to other powers. Pursuing the new course of his policy, inaugurated in the spring of 1470, Frederick III sympathized with Vladislav. No effective help came to Bohemia from Frederick's lands, but it was of some importance that in 1477 the Emperor confirmed Vladislav as king.[584]

The papal diplomats supported Matthias and their reports to Rome impressed the Pontiff more deeply than the assurances made by the Polish envoys in the name of their sovereign. The new Pope, Sixtus IV, elected in August, 1471, followed the advice of Bishop Roverella and other partisans of the Hungarian king. He placed both Casimir and Vladislav under the ban, as well as the bishops who had performed the coronation ceremony.[585] No steps were taken, however, to enforce the sentence of excommunication and it was allowed to fall into oblivion. Contacts between Cracow and Rome were re-established after a relatively short time, as co-operation of the three kingdoms, Poland, Hungary, and Bohemia, was desirable in view of the rising Turkish menace. But the formal recognition of Vladislav as the king of Bohemia was granted only in 1483 by Innocent VIII.[586]

The resources from which the two rival kings could draw were approximately equal and in neither case were they inexhaustible. After several years of vain attempts to settle the conflict by force, advocates of a peaceful solution gained ground on both sides. In December, 1478, Vladislav's envoys met with those of Matthias at Olomouc, and accepted a compromise by which Bohemia was left to Vladislav. Matthias was confirmed in the possession of the incorporated provinces, which could be redeemed by Vladislav only by the payment of an enormous sum of four hundred thousand ducats.[587] The accord of Olomouc was followed by an agreement between Casimir IV and Matthias that no help could be expected from Poland in case of Vladislav's decision to upset the settlement.[588]

The division of the kingdom, with all its grave consequences, lasted for more than ten years. After Matthias' death in April, 1490, the Estates of the incorporated provinces manifested a desire to unite with Bohemia. The course of events in Hungary made easier the return to normalcy. A strong party among the Hungarian nobility decided to support Vladislav's candidature to the Hungarian throne. After his election in Hungary, Vladislav was able to remove the last obstacle by cancelling the clause concerning the payment of four hundred thousand ducats. His action caused a good deal of displeasure among the Hungarian magnates who maintained that the sum was due not to the King personally but to the entire kingdom of Hungary.

By a series of legal measures the reunion of Moravia, Silesia, and both Lusatias with the heart of the kingdom of Bohemia was effected. No opposition against Vladislav arose after 1490 on account of either his dynastic aspirations or his religious affiliation. The ties between Bohemia and the incorporated provinces were strengthened by various supplementary agreements. Though the tension between the Czech and the German elements in the kingdom never completely disappeared, waves of rage and hatred that had run so high during George's reign fell to a low ebb.

The presence in the kingdom of a ruler who was of royal blood and of Catholic religion helped to bridge the divisions which at one time had threatened to break the political and constitutional links. Vladislav's personal attachment to the Roman Church did not seriously affect Matthias' partisans. The young prince owed his position more to the Utraquists than to those Catholics who had sided with George or at least observed neutrality—they were too weak to play an important role.

In view of this situation, it would have been inconsiderate of him or his father to question the validity of the Compacts as one of the basic laws of the kingdom. The papal displeasure, even if manifested by a rigid sentence, was less disturbing than would have been a dispute with the Utraquist nobles. The diagnosis made in the initial stage proved to be confirmed by subsequent developments. Neither Sixtus IV nor any of his successors entered into conflict with Vladislav on account of the Compacts. The King's only son and successor, Lewis, followed the same subtle line of retaining the good will of the Utraquists without incurring the wrath of the pontiff.

Trusting that the new king would adopt a friendly attitude, the Utraquist leaders moved ahead to fill the vacancy caused by Rokycana's death. At a provincial assembly of the clergy and the laity, Václav Koranda was elected as administrator of the "Lower Consistory." The Diet abstained from designating Koranda as the incumbent of the See of Prague, as his confirmation by the Pope was even more unlikely than that of Rokycana.[589] The new administrator acted with authority and encountered no organized opposition among the Utraquist clergy. He held quist administration, Koranda held a prominent position at the University and on two occasions he served as its rector. Even when relieved his office for over twenty-five years. Apart from his service in the Utraof public functions on account of declining health, he was respected by his party as the dominant figure until his death in 1519, at the advanced age of ninety-four.

Koranda's election, although less provocative than the decision for Rokycana at the provincial Diet in 1435,[590] complicated the problem of church administration in Bohemia. The Utraquists clung to the idea that any appointment to the See of Prague should be made in the spirit of the Compacts. A candidate rigidly following Pius' sentence in that matter [591] was automatically ruled out. Without reversal of Pius' verdict, nothing could be done to satisfy both the Holy See and the Utraquists. Vladislav had his own candidate, the canon and chronicler John Długosz, but an agreement on him between the Catholics and the Utraquists proved to be just as difficult as on any other prelate devoutly attached to Rome.

Vladislav did not exert himself to secure a speedy settlement of the Church affairs in Bohemia. His position was rather awkward as, personally, he disliked the Hussite rites, including the communion in both kinds, but in political matters he could not antagonize the Hussite party. On the other hand, the papal legates and other prelates, including Bishop Tas, stood by Matthias and showed no inclination to change their political orientation. Neither the Olomouc pact of 1478, nor the reunion of all provinces in 1490, created conditions in which an accord on a candidate for the vacant see could be reached. In fact, no archbishop of Prague was appointed before 1561.

In the absence of a strong hand, the Estates of Bohemia continued to exercise great influence on church life, continuing the practice begun in the Hussite era. The Catholic and Utraquist lords shared the conviction that the Estates were entitled to intervene in ecclesiastical affairs. If the issue of restitution of church property had been raised seriously, the Catholic landowners would have been most likely just as deaf to appeals for surrender of the domains seized during the Hussite wars or obtained as compensation for services rendered to King Sigismund, as the Utraquist peers.

Failing to overcome Vladislav's reluctance to get involved in religious problems, the Utraquist leaders took matters in their own hands, as they were accustomed to do in politics. The congress of the Utraquist party in August, 1478, was so well attended that no hall could be found in the Carolinum for its plenary sessions and the overflow filled the corridor as well as the courtyards.[592] Neither the King nor the Catholic lords could close their eyes to this manifestation of strength. Speculation that Utraquism could be worn down by persistent pressure and liquidated at an opportune moment proved to be fallacious. The Utraquist party had to be taken into consideration as a factor co-determining the course of public life. This conclusion was not reached immediately after the Utraquist congress in 1478, but only after some futile efforts to curb the resolute elements among the Utraquists, without whom the rank and file would have been helpless. Insidious maneuvers launched by the aggressive Catholic wing, not without the King's knowledge, failed to split the Utraquist ranks and had to be abandoned. The moderate elements on both sides got the upper hand and helped to create an atmosphere in which peaceful co-operation could be achieved. With the King neutralized, the representatives of the two parties hammered out the terms of pacification adopted at Kutná Hora in March, 1485.[593]

Coming after several decades of struggles, the Agreement of Kutná Hora opened a period of peace and mutual respect. The two parties reaffirmed the Compacts as one of the basic laws of the country and accepted the existing division. Each party was to be content with the parishes and churches under its control at that time. The clergy were enjoined to abstain from polemics and aggressive sermons, and freedom to communicate according to the Catholic rite or in both kinds was guaranteed to both the upper classes and the peasantry. Attempts of either party to extend the sphere of influence at the expense of the other were forbidden, and the line separating one faith from the other was to be respected. The Agreement of Kutná Hora was to last until 1516. Four years before its expiration, in April, 1512, it was renewed as of perpetual duration.

Viewed from the political angle, the position of Utraquism under the Catholic Jagellonians was no less favorable than under the Hussite king. The popes who followed after Paul II did not insist on the eradication of Hussitism, as they were amply occupied with other affairs, ecclesiastical and political. The agreement with the Catholics and the comparative security after 1485 did not act as incentives to revival of the original fervor. In fact, Václav Koranda was the last surviving representative of the Utraquist interest in religious controversies, and in his writings he turned more often against the Unity of Brethren than against the Catholic party.

Under Koranda's administration, Utraquism was not shaken by internal dissensions, but it suffered from its chronic weakness more distressingly than under Rokycana. Regarding themselves as full members of the universal Church, the Utraquists required from their clergy ordination by duly consecrated bishops. Difficulties of obtaining the holy orders increased considerably after Pius' repudiation of the Compacts in 1462, and as time passed, illness and death decimated Rokycana's generation. Some vacancies were filled by clerics who defected from their Catholic party to serve the Utraquists. For example, the priest Michael, a Pole of noble origin, who settled in Bohemia and served a Utraquist congregation in Prague for over thirty years, was not an isolated case. However, priests of Polish or other origin were not too numerous and few of them could measure up to Michael the Pole in their steadfastness and popularity among their flocks. The lack of pastoral care continued to trouble the Utraquist community and little could be done to remedy it.

Temporary aid came in 1482 after some search for a way out of the perplexing dilemma. An Italian cleric, Augustin Luciano, titular Bishop of Santorino, who in the earlier times had disregarded the papal decrees concerning consecration of the Czech candidates for priesthood, arrived in Bohemia and settled down there for the rest of his life (d. 1493).[594] The King was not opposed to his activities, but no agreement with the "Upper Consistory" regarding him could be reached, since Augustin came on his own initiative and was reprimanded by the Pope for his ministration to the Utraquists. The Bishop's ambivalent position gave rise to unpleasant complications. Shunned by clerics of his own faith, he drew closer to the Utraquists, but was not found by Koranda and other leaders to be rigorous enough in the discharge of his priestly obligations. The mutual relation never became cordial, but as Augustin found his road to Italy blocked and the Utraquists needed his services, a compromise was arranged. The Bishop was permitted to reside at the Týn church and after his death his body was buried there.

After an interval of more than ten years, in 1504, another Italian, Philip de Novavilla, the titular Bishop of Sidon, came to Bohemia. He was rather advanced in years when he left the comforts of Modena and set out on the journey across the Alps.[595] Informed of his sudden departure, Pope Julius II addressed urgent requests to Emperor Maximilian I and King Vladislav to capture the lost sheep; but the old man, accompanied by a youthful guide, safely reached the city of Tábor and was escorted from there to Prague. As on the previous occasion, King Vladislav acquiesced in the Bishop's doings; but the King's good will did not save the Bishop from the same problems and worries that had afflicted his predecessor. After two years of friction with the Utraquist clergy, annoyed by the Bishop's occasional application of "Welsh and German tricks"—that is, disciplinary measures against the recalcitrants—Philip found a more pleasant abode at Kutná Hora. In that rich mining town he closed his days late in October, 1507.

The two Italian bishops were unable to give the Utraquists more than temporary relief. Whenever they attempted to gain influence over the Utraquist clergy, they met with firm opposition. The Utraquists did not ask for more than consecration of their candidates for priesthood. The number of young clerics thus prepared for the pastoral service is not known, but apparently the "Lower Consistory" was able to fill the vacancies wherever they occurred. Only a short period separated the death of Bishop Philip from Luther's attack on the indulgences.

Vladislav's accession to the throne brought instant relief to the third religious party, the Unity of Brethren. In an amnesty, granted by the new ruler on the day of his coronation, were included those members of the Unity who had been imprisoned by George's order in 1468 or thereafter. The act of clemency did not change the position of the Unity in relation either to the King or to the Utraquist party. The Brethren were not accorded legal protection and were not included in the Kutná Hora agreement of 1485. Occasionally a Catholic controversialist hurled invectives against them, but more often they were attacked by the Utraquists. Václav Koranda opposed them more resolutely than Rokycana had done, and censured their teachings in public disputations and in polemical writings. The Utraquist lords were, on the whole, more conciliatory than the quarrelsome clerics, and they protected the Brethren living in their domains.

While the King was fully occupied with political problems, the Unity, not troubled by royal officers, developed along the lines adopted in 1467. It did not grow rapidly in numbers, as the Brethren insisted on complete conformity of personal morals to the demands of the Gospel. As long as Brother Gregory, the founder of the Unity, lived (d. 1474), the Brethren rigidly followed his precepts. The Unity kept its agrarian character and only small groups of their members lived in Prague or in other boroughs. Gregory feared contamination with the world more than persecution, and permitted only agriculture and some specific crafts as suitable occupations for the Brethren.

In about fifteen years following Gregory's death, the Unity achieved a transformation in its teachings and its social structure. The number of Utraquists who learned of the Unity and wished to join it was growing, and its leaders found it increasingly difficult to adhere to the original precepts determining admission. Some of the mighty lords possessed not only rural areas but urban communities. Some of the latter were small; others competed successfully with the royal boroughs and differed from them only in legal status. Questions arose whether the Brethren living in towns should participate in the local administration, engage in commerce, or in such crafts as had originally been suspect. There also appeared among the Brethren men with higher education, some with training in the liberal arts, and their presence soon began to be felt.

Problems accumulating in the course of some fifteen years came to a head in 1490, the year of King Matthias' death. Unhindered by secular or spiritual authorities, the Brethren held at Brandýs an assembly of priests, deacons, and judges to settle the disputes concerning some articles of faith and their practical application.[596] Bishop Matthew sympathized with the defenders of the original concepts, but his authority was not great enough to keep the Brethren together. As a matter of fact, the advocates of the new, broader, and more tolerant attitude to the state and society gained the majority in the first open clash and assumed the leadership. The struggle went on so that it was found advisable in 1494 to hold a new assembly for a more thorough discussion of the controversial issues.[597] Bishop Matthew saw that he had lost ground, but did not follow the staunch advocates of complete separation from the world who had seceded and constituted themselves into the "minor party." He kept his office and continued to ordain candidates for the ministry, but the spiritual leadership passed into the hands of the "learned men," among whom the most prominent was Lucas of Prague. After Matthew's death in 1500, the Brethren elected four bishops (or seniors) to reside in various centers in Bohemia and Moravia.

The new orientation facilitated the numerical growth of the Unity as well as its literary activities. Lucas and other "learned men" used the presses that were established early in the sixteenth century in some centers of the Unity to instruct the Brethren in the matters of doctrine and to fight off attacks from outside. Around 1500, Václav Koranda displayed less zeal in combatting the Unity than in the earlier decades of his service as administrator; but new opponents, humanists of Catholic orientation, entered the arena. Their literary campaigns portended hard days for the Unity, and a heavy blow, indeed, came in 1508 after some scattered local outbursts of an intolerant spirit. The Brethren ascribed their plight to Vladislav's consort Anne, who came of the princely house of Candal-de Foix, remotely related to the French royal family, and soon came to be known in Bohemia for her bigotry. The provincial Diet approved, on July 25, 1508, an earlier royal edict against the Unity.[598] As the vote of the Diet was entered in the Land Registers and was never formally rescinded, it could be invoked by either Vladislav or his successors whenever the Unity appeared to be dangerously raising its head.

The "Saint James mandate," as the document is usually called, was legally valid only in Bohemia, whereas in Moravia the provincial assembly introduced less rigid measures. In Bohemia, the mandate was applied rigidly in royal domains and boroughs and on the estates of its aristocratic sponsors. Other lords, both Utraquist and Catholic, soon realized that persecution or expulsion of the Brethren would cause them considerable economic losses, and they relaxed restrictive measures. Vladislav's death in 1516 closed, in fact, the period of adversity. Several months later, early in 1517, Lucas appealed to the Brethren under his spiritual care to rely on the divine protection and again to resume public services.

Only a detailed study of the local conditions would make possible an estimate of the respective strength of the Catholics and Utraquists in Bohemia and Moravia. In the Agreement of Kutná Hora they appeared as equal partners; but such a recognition does not necessarily mean numerical equality. The Utraquist percentage was most likely higher in Bohemia than in Moravia. In Bohemia the most compact Utraquist area was in the central and the northeastern zones, whereas western Bohemia with the city of Plzeň and several Catholic domains had an intense Catholic concentration. Two regions were only lightly touched by the rise of Hussitism—the domains of the Bishop of Olomouc, and the possessions of the Rožmberks in southern Bohemia. The latter with the delightful town of Krumlov as its center existed, in fact, as an autonomous territory and maintained lively contacts with both Austria and Bavaria. Connected by good roads with those countries, and through them with the more distant parts of Catholic Europe, Krumlov was the gateway through which Renaissance influences could reach Bohemia.

The enemies of the Unity, especially the humanists, largely overestimated its membership, easily creating the impression of its wide diffusion. Modern scholars, taking critically into account all available evidence, are inclined to believe that around the year 1500, the number of the Brethren was not much above ten thousand, living partly in Bohemia, partly in Moravia, under the benevolent protection of such families as the Kostka of Postupice, Krajíř of Krajek, and Ctibor Tovačovský of Cimburk. The time for a solemn admission to full membership of some of their aristocratic benefactors came two years after Lucas' death in 1528, but some members of the lesser nobility had joined the Unity individually at various dates.

The Poděbrady family, to which Utraquism owed much of its strength, retreated from the front line soon after George's death. One of his daughters, Zdeňka (Sidonia), was by her marriage to Duke Albrecht brought back to the Roman obedience while her father was still alive. She gave birth to three sons, two of whom held the paternal throne: George in direct succession to Albrecht, and Henry for two years following his brother's death (1539–1541). Zdeňka survived her husband by ten years and died in 1510. Her grandson, Henry's son Maurice, rose above his relatives from the Ernestine line and as a compensation for services rendered to Charles V obtained the rank of elector. His descendants ruled over Saxony until 1918.

A more modest position was accorded to Zdeňka's younger sister, Ludmila, whom George wished to see on the royal throne as Vladislav's consort. She was married to Duke Frederick of Legnica, and having survived her husband, she died in 1503. In her case, too, it is necessary to assume that she conformed to her husband's religion, as nothing could be found in the available sources contrary to this hypothesis.[599]

After George's death, Queen Johanna moved to the castle and borough of Mělník, which served traditionally as the residence of the queen-dowagers. From there she exercised an extensive influence on public affairs in Bohemia. After some wavering, in 1471, Johanna adhered to the loyal party and maintained through her Catholic brother, Lev of Rožmitál, friendly contacts with King Vladislav. She remained faithful to the Utraquist teachings and publicly advocated stern measures against the Brethren. No wonder that in their traditions she was linked with other implacable enemies, and even historians of the Unity writing after her death (1474) seldom referred to her in appreciative terms.

The Silesian principality of Münsterberg, which George had once obtained from King Ladislav along with Kladsko, held a higher rank than the family domains of Poděbrady. Prince Henry, who actually ruled over Münsterberg, and also his brothers, put that name into their respective titles. In the situation created by George's premature death, Prince Henry, along with his mother, represented the family in both private and political affairs. One of his brothers, Boček, was mentally incapacitated and never played an active part in public life. Victorin was in Hungarian captivity, and Hynek was still rather young.

In the hope that Victorin could organize an opposition to Vladislav, Matthias permitted him in February, 1472, to travel to Bohemia. Victorin met with other members of the family and agreed on a division of the family domains. Leaving Münsterberg and Kladsko to Henry, Victorin took over the Duchy of Opava and some property in Bohemia. The estate of Litice, the cradle of the Unity of Brethren, was assigned to Boček (d. 1496), whereas to Hynek went the home of the family, the castle of Poděbrady.

Few people knew that Victorin, while in Hungary, renounced the Chalice and was received into the fold of the Church by the bishop-legate Roverella. The conversion was held secret so that it would not lower Victorin's prestige in the eyes of his late father's partisans. New religious orientation, even when it became known, affected Victorin's relations with the Utraquist lords far less seriously than his dependence on Matthias. Even when released from captivity, Victorin felt obliged to render friendly services to Matthias. The sum demanded by Hungary as his ransom was too high, and to meet his obligations Victorin was forced to cede some of his estates in Bohemia, to the displeasure of Vladislav's partisans. With the surrender of these properties, Victorin lost his foothold in Bohemia and lived on his domains at and near Opava. From there he established connections with the princes of Upper Silesia and to one of them, Casimir of Těšín, he married his daughter. At the castle of Těšín, while visiting his relatives, Victorin died in August, 1500, at a less advanced age than that of his father.

If conditions had been favorable for an establishment of succession in the Poděbrady family, Prince Henry would have been a more competent condidate than his older brother. His personal qualities and his marriage to Ursula of Hohenzollern would have given him better chances of recognition at home and abroad. For some time after his father's death, Henry played an active role in the Poděbrady party. In the spring of 1472 he retreated to Kladsko, which was allotted to him with Münsterberg and some estates in Bohemia when the Poděbrady patrimony was partitioned. As a consequence of this deal, Henry's position was rather delicate, for part of his property was in Bohemia, while Münsterberg was in Matthias' sphere of influence. As one of the lords of Bohemia, Henry often appeared among Vladislav's partisans but succeeded in preserving Matthias' goodwill.

Henry's political manoeuvering was facilitated by his detached attitude toward religious problems. Under the influence of his wife and his brother Victorin, Henry renounced the Chalice orally, so that the fact did not come immediately to the notice of the Utraquist nobles. Henry was apparently not too zealous in public attendance on Catholic services and even after several years of frequent association with this faction, he was regarded by other Utraquist nobles as a member of their party. He resented statements or acts vilifying his father's memory. An episode enlivens the story of his life. The abbot of the Convent of the Holy Virgin at Breslau had a fresco painted in his chapel representing the Last Judgment. When Henry learned that among other figures the fresco depicted two devils carrying the body of the Hussite king to hell, he threatened to burn all the villages of the convent.[600] Thereupon, George's figure was promptly obliterated from the painting.

Three sons were born of Henry's union with Ursula of Hohenzollern: Albrecht, George, and Charles. They were married in January, 1488, to three daughters of Duke John of Żagań (Sagan) who once had sided with the Hussite king. Henry, too, failed to reach an advanced age and died in 1498, two years after his oldest brother, Boček, and two years earlier than Victorin.

George and his wife had given a good deal of attention to the preparation of their sons for public careers. The princes were brought up in chivalrous ideas and acquired skills and manners required of men of their social rank. Knowing from his own experience the handicaps arising from inadequate education, George gave his sons tutors who instructed them in both religion and liberal arts. Some of these tutors were known for their attachment to humanism, which movement had its champions among both Catholics and Utraquists. On several occasions the princes visited the university halls and witnessed academic ceremonies or disputations.

The youngest of the boys, Hynek, found more pleasure in learning than his brothers and combined it with a keen interest in public affairs. After his father's death, Hynek vacillated in his political orientation and could be found once at Vladislav's court and then again in Matthias' entourage. At about the same time that Henry abjured the Chalice, Hynek used the services of his chaplain in making peace with the Roman Church to the satisfaction of his Wettin relatives.

His instability caused displeasure among members of the Poděbrady party. Those of its leaders who retained the memory of George's embitterment against Matthias keenly resented Victorin and Hynek's journey in 1476 to the Hungarian court to attend Matthias' wedding to Beatrice of Naples. Younger and more enthusiastic than Victorin, Hynek joined the group of Hungarian nobles who departed for Naples and formed an honorary escort to accompany the bride through central and northern Italy to her new homeland.

Matthias' conciliation in 1478 with Vladislav eased Hynek's position. From his residence at Poděbrady he maintained lively contacts with

Vladislav and held a high position in court circles. He won distinction at a splendid tournament, held in August, 1482, at the Old Town Square under Vladislav's patronage, but eventually the palm of victory in that contest went to the Utraquist leader, John Tovačovský of Cimburk.

Public functions required of Hynek by the King were not onerous, and he had enough time to pursue literary interests. Through contacts with the Czech humanists, or more likely during his sojourn in Italy, Hynek became acquainted with the current or earlier literary productions in that country, and in his spare time used his knowledge for translations. He turned into Czech selected tales from Boccaccio, adjusting some passages to the capacity of his readers.[601] Hynek's productive talent was limited and his attempt to compose a novel in Boccaccio's style was not too successful. He achieved better reputation as a poet. His *Verses concerning a Lover,* and a related composition, *May Dream,* circulated in manuscripts and eventually were printed, some time in the first half of the sixteenth century.[602]

Although the youngest of George's children, Hynek was destined to die first. He was afflicted by a long and wearisome illness, which chained him to bed at Poděbrady, and he expired in July, 1492, at the age of forty. His daughter Anne was married a year after his death to Lord Henry of Hradec, who was already advanced in age and of a somewhat lower social rank. Among Hynek's illegitimate children from a liaison with Catherine of Strážnice, the oldest was a son named Frederick, who inherited one of Hynek's residences in the fertile plains of central Bohemia.

Compared with George, his sons appear inferior in both character and statesmanship. None of them, not even the ablest, Henry, rose significantly above the level of the contemporary aristocratic society. Their pliancy in matters so dear to their father and mother as the communion in both kinds is one of the most striking phenomena, and cannot be ascribed merely to the desire to conform to the religious views of their wives or more distant relatives. If abjuration of the Chalice had been a matter of conscience, and not an outcome of opportunistic considerations, it would not have been kept in secrecy but made openly. Vacillation between Matthias and Vladislav can also be attributed to opportunistic disposition, not uncommon among contemporary princes and nobles. The youngest and intellectually most gifted, Hynek, presented the sharpest contrast to his father. The style of his life conformed more to the Renaissance mode than to the conventional ways of Hussite society.

At one time, people who remembered the old days could believe that George's personal charm and political acumen became reincarnated in one of his grandsons, Prince Bartholomew, Victorin's son. He was brought

up by close relatives at the castle of Těšín and made his first public
appearance in 1509 when the infant prince Lewis was brought from
Buda to Prague and crowned king of Bohemia. Bartholomew attached
himself to the Jagellon family and rendered Vladislav valuable services.
He endeavored to curb the ambitions and activities of an aristocratic
clique, who during Vladislav's prolonged residence in Hungary virtually
controlled Bohemia. Supported by some members of the lesser nobility,
and even more effectively by the royal boroughs, Prince Bartholomew
endeavored to re-establish the traditional balance of power, upset dangerously by aristocratic usurpations. On special occasions he served in
diplomatic missions and distinguished himself by his dexterity and fine
manners. He won the favor of Emperor Maximilian I and at one time
was considered for a high position in the imperial armies.

Early in the spring of 1515, Prince Bartholomew attended the splendid
assembly at Bratislava (Pressburg) and facilitated communications between the Emperor and the Jagellonians—Sigismund of Poland and
Vladislav of Bohemia and Hungary. One trip from Vienna proved to be
fatal. The barge plying the Danube and carrying Bartholomew lost its
way in the darkness. It foundered on a rock near Heimburg and as the
river was deep at that point, Bartholomew's body sank to the bottom
and was never recovered.

The Bratislava assembly was a long overture to a congress of princes
and courtiers which took place in Vienna in July, 1515. Maximilian's
guests were Vladislav, his son Lewis, and Sigismund of Poland. As the
ground had been prepared by earlier negotiations, the monarchs quickly
settled their conflicting views and interests. The agreement was corroborated by treaties of marriage between the Habsburgs and the cadet
branch of the Jagellonian house.

The destinies of the kingdom of Bohemia were predetermined by the
betrothal of Maximilian's daughter Mary to Lewis, and by the arrangements by which Lewis' sister, Anne, was to be married to a Habsburg
prince. It was not decided immediately who would be the bridegroom.
After some months, not Charles but his younger brother, Ferdinand, was
designated for succession in Austria. His wedding to Anne was celebrated
at Linz in May, 1521.

Friendly relations between the Jagellonians and the Habsburgs, which
Frederick III had inaugurated in 1470 by negotiations with Casimir IV,
were intensified when their common enemy, the Ottoman Turks, resumed
their aggressive policy. The Turkish offensive launched by Suleiman the
Magnificent was under way when Ferdinand's and Anne's hands were
joined before the altar. Princess Mary, who attended the festivities, left
Linz soon afterwards for Hungary and reached the royal residence two
days before Lewis' departure for his military headquarters in southern

Hungary. On August 29, 1521, the fortress of Belgrade fell into Turkish hands and the road to the invasion of Hungary was open. After five years, on August 29, 1526, Lewis' short life came to a sudden end. He died in bloody battle at Mohács, leaving vacant the thrones of both Bohemia and Hungary.

After lengthy negotiations with the Estates of Bohemia, Ferdinand I was able to secure for himself and his descendants the crown which once George had worn. Maintaining that the family treaties of 1515 were not submitted to the provincial Diet for sanction, the Bohemian nobles contested their validity and claimed the right to a free election of their king. Among the candidates considered by Ferdinand as opponents was a grandson of the Hussite king, Charles of Münsterberg, the eldest son of Prince Henry. Charles's partisans were not numerous enough to give him a fair chance of victory. Ferdinand emerged from the contest as the winner and inaugurated the Habsburg dynasty in Bohemia which lasted, with two short intervals, from 1526 to October, 1918.

Two statues, one on the ancient stone bridge over the river Vltava, the other in a niche among the Gothic spires of the Church of the Holy Virgin at Týn, reminded the Czechs of the Poděbrady era. It is not quite clear when and under what circumstances the statue representing George on horseback disappeared from the bridge.[603] The removal of the other monument was more spectacular and, indeed, symbolic. Three years and some weeks after the victory of Ferdinand II over the Protestant Estates of Bohemia, orders were issued by Catholic authorities of the Old Town to take down from the Týn towers the gilded Chalice which had been placed there at Rokycana's order, and the statue of the Hussite king. The date was January 24, 1624. That act did witness more convincingly than any written mandates or decrees the ultimate suppression of the Hussite and Reformation spirit in Bohemia and its incorporated provinces.

NOTES

In writing this book I consulted not only the standard works on the Hussite movement and the Poděbrady era but also a large number of monographs and articles in learned journals. Their titles appear in my bibliography especially under the names of František Palacký, Václav V. Tomek, Rudolf Urbánek, Adolf Bachmann, Hermann Markgraf. Most of these writings are in Czech or in German, in some instances still valuable, in others antiquated by more recent publications.

When preparing my manuscript for the press I saw two ways open, both theoretically justifiable and technically feasible: continual confrontation of my statements with the views set forth by the recognized authorities, or a general evaluation of the available critical literature followed by a selective bibliography. After a good deal of reflecting not only on scholarly problems but also on practical consequences, I adopted the second approach. The decision in principle, once made, determined the type of the annotations to my text. Instead of copious footnotes with innumerable references to publications mostly out of the reader's reach, and of extensive quotations from them, I have compiled a list of references to significant documents which I have evaluated critically, while drafting the text, and used in corroboration of my interpretation and conclusions. Scholars interested in the complete text of the documents or in relevant passages from contemporary sources will be directed to the depositories of original materials or to printed collections of sources.

In this connection, it is necessary to say that there are numerous gaps in the archival and other collections and that some documents, mentioned in the narrative sources or in other records, are lost forever and can be reconstructed only from such allusions or fragments. In some particularly interesting instances references will be made to contemporary chronicles, pamphlets, or literary compositions reflecting the atmosphere of the Poděbrady era. The earlier scholars, like Palacký or Tomek, though in general dependable, occasionally omitted references to their source materials and gaps thus caused could seldom be filled by additional research.

No reader is *a priori* excluded from the use of the attached footnotes. It is, however, anticipated that they will be consulted primarily by scholars familiar with late medieval sources and the critical literature pertaining to them. Therefore, the references will be short and to the point. Names of the authors and titles of their works listed in the bibliography will be abbreviated in the conventional manner. In deciding for this simplified documentation I have been guided by several examples, especially by my former colleague at Columbia University, the late Professor Garret Mattingly in his chef d'oeuvre, *The Armada*.

CHAPTER I

1. František Palacký published Concordata in Egra de iudice in Basilea in his Urkundliche Beiträge zur Geschichte des Hussitenkrieges (UBGH) Prague, 1873, vol. II, pp. 281–83. Another edition by F. D. Mansi, Sacrorum conciliorum nova et amplissima collectio, Venice, 1792, tomus XXX, col. 145–46 (to be quoted as Mansi).

2. Our translation of the four articles follows a simplified version in František Palacký's Dějiny národu českého (Dějiny), third edition, Prague, 1877, vol. III, pt. 1, p. 399. Cf. with S. H. Thomson, Czechoslovakia in European History, 2nd ed., Princeton, 1953, pp. 85–86, and R. W. Seton-Watson, A History of the Czechs and Slovaks, London, 1943, p. 62.

3. Palomar's admonition occurs in Johannes de Segovia, Historia gestorum generalis synodi Basiliensis, ed. by Ernest Birk, in Monumenta conciliorum generalium saeculi decimi quinti. Concilium Basiliense. Scriptorum tomus II (MC. Basiliense), p. 433.

4. The best critical edition of the Compacts was prepared from several manuscripts by F. Palacký and published in Archiv český (AČ), Prague, 1844, vol. III, pp. 398–444. The first draft of Nov. 30, 1433, is there in Czech and Latin, pp. 398–404.

5. Prokop's letter to Sigismund in E. Martène, Veterum scriptorum et monumentorum . . . amplissima collectio (Martène), Paris, 1733, vol. VIII, p. 134.

6. Ordo ad coronandum regem Bohemorum (also Ordo coronationis regum Bohemorum), published by J. Loserth in Archiv für österreichische Geschichte (AÖG), vol. 54, pp. 9–36.

7. Revelation, XII, 3. Cf. with Laurentius de Březová, Chronicon Hussitarum, Fontes rerum bohemicarum (FRB), Prague, 1893, vol. V, p. 360.

8. S's letter to Oldřich from Parma, May 22, 1432, and O's reply of May 31, 1432, in Blažena Rynešová, Listář a listinář Oldřicha z Rožmberka (Listář), Prague, 1929, vol. I, pp. 146–47; S's full powers for Oldřich, Feb. 28, 1434, ib., pp. 166–69.

9. F. Palacký, Dějiny, III, 3, pp. 153–54.

10. S's charter in AČ, III, pp. 428–31.

11. The provost of St. Florian at Koblenz reported S's cynical remark to Aegidius Carlerius. See MC. Basiliense, Scr. I, p. 597.

12. A record of the election in AČ, III, pp. 436–37.

13. A detailed description of negotiations between the delegates of the Council and Sigismund, held late in December, 1435, and early January, 1436, in MC. Basiliense, Scr. I, pp. 676–98.

14. A reference to their pledge in MC. Basiliense, Scr. I, p. 769. The date was June 20, 1436.

15. The text of the charter in AČ, III, pp. 442–44.

16. A reference to the proclamation in a Czech account of the Jihlava diet in AČ, III, p. 444. Also in a Latin account in Palacký's UBGH, II, pp. 456–57.

17. S's charter of July 13, 1436, in AČ, III, pp. 445–46.

18. The charter of July 20, 1436, in AČ, III, pp. 446–49.

19. The pact with Tábor of Oct. 16, 1436, in AČ, III, pp. 450–51. S's charter elevating Tábor to the rank of a royal borough, Jan. 25, 1437, in Jaromír Čelakovský, Privilegia královských měst, Prague, 1948, vol. III, pp. 167–71.

20. S's sentence concerning the seats in the provincial court, Jan. 27, 1437, in AČ, III, pp. 451–52.

21. Referred to by Johannes de Turonis, MC. Basiliense, Scr. I, p. 852.

22. Eugene's bull in MC. Basiliense, Scr. II, pp. 1033–40; the relevant passage on p. 1039.

23. MC. Basiliense, Scr. II, p. 1112.

Chapter II

24. Václav Hrubý, Archivum coronae regni Bohemiae (ACRB), Prague, 1928, vol. II, Nos. 58, 59, 60, 61, on pp. 57–67.

25. Especially in No. 61 as above.

26. S's charter to Albrecht, Oct. 1, 1423, in B. Bretholz, Die Übergabe Mährens . . . AÖG, vol. LXXX (1894), pp. 346–49.

27. By a letter of May 10, 1439, in Ryněšová, Listář, vol. II, pp. 30–33.

28. V. Hrubý, ACRB, vol. II, No. 51, pp. 43–47.

29. Ibid., No. 124, pp. 142–54; Charles's charter for John of Moravia, Sept. 27, 1355, in Codex diplomaticus et epistolaris Moraviae (Codex Moraviae), vol. VIII, Brno, 1874, pp. 253–58.

30. The charter of Feb. 10, 1364, in Codex Moraviae, vol. IX, pp. 257–59; the charter of March 26, 1366, ibid., pp. 326–32.

31. See A. F. Kollar, Analecta monumentorum omnis aevi Vindobonensia, Vienna, 1761, vol. II, pp. 845–50.

32. Full text in AČ, I, pp. 245–49.

33. See note 28.

34. AČ, I, B III, Nos. 4, 6, pp. 263–65.

35. Palacký published in AČ, I, the following documents: (a) articles presented by Czech delegates to Frederick III in Oct., 1443, pp. 275–77; (b) F's tentative answer, pp. 277–78; (c) F's second answer, pp. 278–89. He published in AČ, III, p. 528, only an abstract of F's final answer given on October 24, 1443.

36. Its text has not been found by either Palacký or Urbánek. References to it were made by Oldřich in his letter to Frederick's councillors, March, 1444. See Ryněšová, Listář, II, pp. 309–12. Cf. with AČ, I, 284–85.

37. The statement comes from an allegorical writing in Czech by Ctibor Tovačovský of Cimburk, Hádání Pravdy a Lži (A Dispute between the Truth and the Lie), of which there is no modern edition.

38. See note 20.

39. Letters like the one in AČ, IV, No. 14, p. 8, were apparently sent to many addressees.

40. A report of the Diet in AČ, I, 294–96. A good deal of information is contained in Oldřich's letter to Juan Cardinal Carvajal of Dec., 1446, in Ryněšová, Listář, III, pp. 169–73.

41. Several documents relating to the Diet in AČ, II, pp. 209–18; one of them, an abstract of the instruction for the delegates to Vienna is on pp. 212–13.

42. A special messenger, Václav of Krumlov, was sent to Vienna as it appears from F's letter to Oldřich, dated Jan. 16, 1447, in Ryněšová, Listář, III, pp. 176–77.

43. A. F. Kollar, Analecta, II, pp. 1312–14.

44. See note 41.

45. Palacký published in AČ, II, pp. 229–32, a contemporary Czech translation from Latin of a complaint against Frederick III, dated March 3, 1448.

46. The agreement in Czech has been preserved in a manuscript in the Nationalbibliothek in Vienna, No. 4935, fol. 31ᵃ–32ᵃ. See Tabulae codicum, vol. III, Vienna, 1869, p. 427.

47. E.g., in a document, dated Sept. 29, 1448; its abstract in AČ, III, No. 515, p. 539.

CHAPTER III

48. See note 32.

49. See note 19. The agreement dated November 16, 1436, was inserted in Joannis de Lukavecz et Nicolai de Pelhřimov Chronicon Taboritarum (Ch. T.) published by Constantin Höfler in Fontes rerum Austriacarum (FRA), I, Scriptores, vol. VI, p. 728.

50. Quoted by R. Urbánek, Věk Poděbradský (Věk), III, 1, p. 765, without reference to the original.

51. An abstract of Ptáček's letter in Ch. T., FRA, Scr., vol. VI, p. 731.

52. Resolution adopted at Kutná Hora, Oct. 4, 1441, published by Zdeněk Nejedlý, Prameny k synodám strany pražské a táborské, pp. 32–38.

53. Staří letopisové (St. l.), ed. by F. Palacký, No. 365, p. 129.

54. Přibram's letter concerning its sessions, dated July 21, 1443, in Nejedlý, l.c., pp. 42–44. See also Ch. T., FRA, Scr., VI, pp. 749–51.

55. The resolution of Jan. 31, 1444, in Nejedlý, l.c., pp. 107–16.

56. Ch. T., FRA, Scr., VI, pp. 731–820.

57. Palacký, Dějiny, IV, 1, pp. 109–10, reproduced a record of the assembly from an original in the Rožmberk archives at Třeboň.

58. Only the Pope's letter to Oldřich and his associates, May 15, 1445, has been preserved; an abstract in Rynešová, Listář, III, No. 25, p. 18.

59. Accusations of Rokycana were sent to Rome several times and it is not always easy to separate one version from another and to fix the date of origin. One version, most likely from 1445, in Z. Nejedlý's article Mládí Jana z Rokycan, Čas. Čes. Musea, vol. 73 (1899), pp. 532–34.

60. See note 40; the passage concerning Rokycana in AČ, I, p. 296.

61. See note 41. A summary of discussions concerning the archbishopric in AČ, II, pp. 213–17.

62. Its Czech version in AČ, II, pp. 217–18.

63. It was published, as stated in note 40, in Rynešová, Listář, III, pp. 169–73.

64. Documents concerning the Czech mission to Rome, including the papal resolution in AČ, II, pp. 233–36.

65. The text of the agreement, Concordata inter Fridericum III et Nicolaum V in K. Zeumer, Quellensammlung zur Geschichte der deutschen Reichsverfassung, Leipzig, 1904, pp. 221–24.

66. A contemporary description of C's visit has been published by Gomez Canedo Lino in his Un español . . . as appendix III, El cardenal Carvajal en Praga: 1448, pp. 304–11.

67. Ibid., p. 305.

68. St. l., p. 152.

69. The agreement, dated Nov. 16, 1448, was inserted in the manual of the Old Town of Prague, No. 993 from which it was quoted by Urbánek, Věk, III, 2, p. 303.

Chapter IV

70. The text of the agreement in AČ, II, pp. 244–46.

71. Dated April 30, 1450, in Rynešová, Listář, IV, No. 247, pp. 184–87; see also George's letter to Oldřich, ibid., No. 318, pp. 222–3.

72. Oldřich's defense in Rynešová, Listář, IV, No. 332, pp. 228–30.

73. The armistice concluded at Vildštejn, June 11, 1450; AČ, II, pp. 274–79.

74. Documents relating to it in AČ, II, pp. 287–95.

75. Their names and instruction in AČ, II, 295–301.

76. A contemporary Czech translation of F's instruction in AČ, II, pp. 303–4.

77. Prokop's translation in AČ, II, pp. 304–7.

78. Enea wrote a lengthy letter to Juan Cardinal Carvajal, dated August 21, 1451; published by R. Wolkan in FRA, II Abt., vol. 68, pp. 22–57.

79. This description comes from Enea's Historia Friderici III. Imp. in A. F. Kollar, Analecta, vol. II, p. 181.

80. It is contained in a treatise In libros Antonii Panormitae poetae de dictis et factis Alphonsi regis memorabilibus commentarius, lib. II, 17, in Aeneae Silvii Piccolomini Opera, Basel, 1571, p. 480.

81. See note 19. Cf. with FRA, Abt. II, 68, p. 25.

82. In the absence of direct evidence these negotiations can be reconstructed with the help of a detailed instruction for Oldřich's envoys to Frederick III in F. Palacký, Urkundliche Beiträge zur Geschichte Böhmens und seiner Nachbarländer im Zeitalter Georg's von Podiebrad, in FRA, Abt. II, vol. XX (to be quoted henceforth as FRA, XX), pp. 36–38.

83. Rokycana's letter to Capistrano inviting him to a disputation, and the monk's reply, both written in Sept. 1451, in Johannes Cochlaeus, Historiae Hussitarum libri XII, pp. 370–73. Cf. with Amandus Hermann, Capistranus triumphans, Köln, 1700, p. 345 ff. This book has also other documents relating to C's sojourn in Bohemia.

84. The papal bull for Cusa, Dec. 29, 1450, in O. Raynaldi, Annales ecclesiastici, (Raynaldi) Colonia Agrippina (Köln), 1694, XVIII, p. 369. Cusa's aggressive letter to the Czechs, June 27, 1452, in Cochlaeus, l.c., pp. 384–87.

85. See note 64.

86. At least one example should be quoted: a letter from Prague to Venice, July 10, 1420, in which a reference is made to the churches "Graecorum, Indorum et aliorum regnorum orientalium"; see Palacký, UBGH, I, p. 40.

87. Antonin Salač, Constantinople et Prague . . . published, pp. 28–39, a confession of faith (λιβελλος) presented to Gennadios and other Greek clerics by Constantine Platris.

88. The letter in Salač, l.c., pp. 16–19; the confession of faith, ibid., pp. 40–61.

89. Its text in Salač, l.c., pp. 63–64; also in FRA, XX, pp. 51–53.

90. The letter of Nov. 14, Salač, l.c., 65–66.

91. Its record, dated April 27, 1452, in AČ, pp. 309–13.

92. AČ, II, p. 311.

93. Some documents relating to the surrender of Tábor have been preserved in the Třeboň archives; for reference see F. Palacký, Dějiny, IV, 1, p. 269, note 257.

94. AČ, III, p. 551, Nos. 598 and 599.

95. No record of this important assembly has been found in printed sources. Its course and resolutions were reconstructed from other sources.

96. See note 90.

CHAPTER V

97. Joseph Chmel, Materialien, II, pp. 26–27.

98. Some information concerning its proceedings in Aeneas Silvius, Historia Frederici III, A. F. Kollar, Analecta, II, p. 405.

99. Quoted by F. Palacký, Dějiny, IV, 1, p. 283, note 275, from a MS in the Nationalbibliothek, Vienna, No. 4975, fol. 380.

100. L's confirmation, dated May 1, 1453, AČ, IV, pp. 416–19; his letters for George, May 1 and May 2, in AČ, XV, pp. 212–13.

101. The German version of L's oath in Palacký, Dějiny, IV, 1, p. 294, note 282; its Czech translation in AČ, IV, p. 419.

102. Published by Melchior Goldast, Zwo rechtliche Bedencken, Frankfurt, 1627, Beilage 63.

103. Published by I. Zahradník from a Vatican MS under the title Ladislava Pohrobka sborník latinsko-německo-český dle rukopisu Palatinského č. 1787 ve Vatikánu. Prague, 1905.

104. See note 24.

105. The records of the coronation Diet in AČ, IV, pp. 419–23. Cf. with an anonymous writing De factis regni Bohemiae publ. by J. Loserth, Mittheilungen des Vereines f. Gesch. d. Deutschen in Böhmen, XVIII, pp. 301–6.

106. See note 100.

107. E. M. Lichnowsky, Geschichte des Hauses Habsburg, VI, pp. CCXXII.

108. A commission to survey the transfers which had taken place since the death of King Wenceslas IV was created by the coronation Diet in Nov., 1453. It resumed its work in 1454. Its records in AČ, I, pp. 494–546; AČ, II, pp. 175–208 and 444–81.

109. In his account of these events Urbánek, Věk, III, 2, p. 815, followed a book by Ctibor Tovačovský, Pamět obyčejů . . . known simply as Kniha Tovačovská, chapter 7.

110. Eschenloer, Geschichten . . . , I, p. 13.

111. The text of the oath in German, Dec. 11, 1454, in Scriptores rerum Silesiacarum (SRS), vol. XII, p. 67.

112. On Dec. 26, 1454, SRS, XII, p. 68.

113. A brief description of the royal visit in P. Eschenloer's Historia Wratislaviensis, SRS, VII, pp. 7–8.

114. St. l., p. 155.

115. St. l., p. 493.

116. By a letter, Jan. 10, 1454, FRA, XX, pp. 71–73.

117. Using some documents from unprinted manuscripts R. Urbánek described the two synods in Věk, III, 3, p. 25 ff.

118. For references to Mandatum sacerdotibus regis Ladislai see Urbánek, Věk, III, 3, p. 35.

119. Johann Joachim Müller, Reichstagstheatrum (Müller, RTT), I, pp. 473–88 has a collection of documents relating to the Frankfurt Diet.

120. A brief reference to G's offer in a letter sent by the delegate from Saxony to Elector Frederick, March 20, 1455, Müller, RTT, I, p. 532.

121. The most important of them was Enea's speech to Pope Calixtus III. See below, note 123.

122. Mansi, Orationes, vol. I, p. 336 ff.

123. Published by Mansi in Pii II . . . Orationes, pp. 352–83.

124. Capistrano's letters, one of March 24, 1456, to Calixtus III, the other of April 7, 1456, to Enea Silvio in a book by Amandus Hermann, Capistranus triumphans, pp. 398–400.

125. St. l., p. 163.

126. See his letter to Peter von Schaumberg, Nov. 18, 1453, and a letter to Piero da Noceto, FRA, Abt. II, vol. 68, pp. 361 and 385. Cochlaeus, l.c., p. 403 vividly described L's aversion to Rokycana.

127. Quoted by Urbánek, Věk, III, 3, p. 212.

128. St. l., p. 167.

Chapter VI

129. See notes 28, 29.

130. See note 30.

131. V. Hrubý, ACRB, II, pp. 45–46.

132. Only a brief account of the Diet has been preserved in St. l., p. 169; modern authors (Palacký, Urbánek) corrected, with the help of other documents, the date given by the chronicler as January, 1458.

133. R. Urbánek published the relevant passage from that short pamphlet in a collection of documents relating to G's election, O volbě . . . , p. 40. Some authors (V. Novotný, F. M. Bartoš) maintain that the succinct compilation dates from 1438, not 1458. Its full text, Krátké sebranie, published by Ant. Polák in Věstník král. české spol. nauk, 1904, č. III.

134. Aeneas Silvius, De Bohemorum . . . origine . . . historia (ed. 1687), p. 181.

135. Published by Urbánek, O volbě, pp. 43–45.

136. R. Urbánek, Dvě studie o době poděbradské, p. 173, refers to an unpublished report by dr H. Leubing to his master William of Saxony, March 5, 1458.

137. No contemporary chronicler described the election Diet in detail. Letters to various addressees relating to it and short accounts are now accessible in Urbánek, O volbě, pp. 55–67.

138. See note 6.

139. His letter to Calixtus III concerning the conference, Aug. 9, 1458, in SRS, vol. VIII, p. 7.

140. This is one of the most important documents relating to G's reign. A contemporary copy of the original which the Hungarian bishops took with them was sent by King Matthias, in November, 1466, to Rome. It is deposited in the Vatican archives, Archivum arcis, Arm., I–XVIII, No. 639. The text was published by many authors, e.g., Raynaldi, XVIII, p. 515. The best version in A. Theiner, Monumenta historica Hungariam sacram illustrantia (Theiner, Hung.), vol. II, Rome, 1860, No. 580, pp. 405–6. See note 385.

141. Reference to Frederick's agreement with George, October 2, 1458, in Jos. Chmel, Regesta. . . . Frederici IV . . . , p. 362. Cf. with Urbánek, Věk, III, 3, p. 434.

142. FRA, XX, p. 164.

143. The breve of May 13, 1458, in the Vat. archives, Arm., XXXIX, tom. 7, fol. 172ᵛ. Cf. with Raynaldi, XVIII, p. 514.

144. Their copies in Vat. arch., Arm., XXXIX, tom. 7, fol. 173. Cf. with Raynaldi, vol. XVIII, pp. 511–12.

145. Urbánek, Věk, III, 3, p. 400, quotes from the Pope's letter, dated May 17, 1458, but has no reference to the source.

146. Pii II. P. M. Commentarii, ed. 1614, pp. 430–31. (This book is quoted by modern historians differently; some give the Pope's name, others refer to Gobelinus. We shall use an abbreviated title Pius II. Comm.) Ludwig Pastor, who searched the papal registers thoroughly did not find C's letter and is inclined to question its authenticity. See Geschichte der Päpste (1955), vol. I, p. 755. In our opinion the absence of either the original or of an authentic copy does not necessarily mean that a letter with the royal title for G was a forgery, fabricated either in Rome or in Prague.

147. Matthias' letter was dated Aug. 7, Carvajal's, Aug. 9, 1458, in SRS, VIII, pp. 6–8.

148. Its author was probably Gregory of Heimburg; C. Höfler, Das kaiserliche Buch, p. 97.

149. The letter of Oct. 1, 1458, in M. Goldast, De Bohemiae regni . . . , appendix, pp. 102–3; the letter of Jan. 20, 1459, in FRA, XX, pp. 165–66.

150. The text of oath made by Rabštejn in SRS, VIII, p. 12.

151. A letter sent to Pius II from Breslau, March 23, 1459, in SRS, VIII, pp. 13–15; see also the complaints presented to the Pope in Siena, ibid., pp. 16–20.

152. A fragmentary report concerning Cheb in FRA, XX, pp. 177–78. The original copy of an agreement between George and Frederick, April 15, 1459, in the Crown archives of Bohemia. See Ant. Haas, Archiv koruny české, vol. VI, katalog listin z let 1438–1526, Prague, 1958, p. 60, No. 8.

153. Seven originals are in the Crown archives in Prague; cf. with Haas, l.c., Nos. 87 (1), 85 (2), 84 (3), 90 (4), 89 (5), 86 (6), 87 (7); the numbers in brackets are those given by Palacký in FRA, XX, p. 179. William's renunciation, April 25, 1459, in FRA, XLII, p. 274.

154. A lengthy letter of April 30, 1459, in SRS, VIII, pp. 20–24.

155. Urbánek, Věk, III, 3, pp. 523–24 has a reference to these negotiations.

156. Cf. with Urbánek, l.c., p. 524, note 1.

157. The letter for George in L. Pastor, Ungedruckte Akten, pp. 103–5; the one for Breslau in SRS, VII, 46.

158. An abstract of the papal breve, June 12, 1459, in Pastor, Geschichte, II, p. 719. Full text in the Vat. arch., Arm., XXXIX, tom. 9, fol. 49.

159. As reported by George to the mayor and council of Prague on July 31, 1459; see AČ, V, p. 279. The original of the imperial charter in the Crown archives; cf. with Haas, l.c., No. 94. Published by Goldast, De regni Bohemiae . . . app. No. 84. The treaty of alliance between Frederick III and George Aug. 2, 1459, in the Crown archives, no. 95.

160. Text of George's oath, July 31, 1459, FRA, XLII, p. 284.

161. The original of the treaty signed by George and Lewis on Oct. 16, 1459, in the Crown archives; cf. with Haas, l.c., No. 110. Abstracts of other documents relating to the Plzeň conference in FRA, XX, pp. 192–94.

162. The Cheb ceremony was recorded briefly by an anonymous chronicler, St. let., pp. 172–73; other details in a letter, Nov. 23, 1459, in FRA, XLII, 296–97.

163. See note 154; other letters in SRS, VIII, p. 25 ff.

164. SRS, VII, pp. 91–92.

165. Dated Oct. 20, 1459, in FRA, XLII, pp. 287–94.

166. This was the gist of Archbishop Jerome's speech in the Senate's session on Nov. 13, 1459, SRS, VII, pp. 65–71.

167. SRS, VII, p. 89.

168. Eschenloer included in his Historia not only an account of the negotiations (both in Breslau and in Prague) but also the text of the agreement between Breslau and the king; SRS, VII, pp. 90–98.

169. George's contacts with Sforza can be reconstructed with the help of an exhaustive account given to the King at the end of the mission by Martin Mair; see FRA, XX, pp. 201–16. Some other documents pertaining to these matters, ibid., pp. 198–200.

Chapter VII

170. Information concerning various editions of these two bulls in Pastor, l.c., II, p. 78, n. 1, and p. 80, note 2.

171. Raynaldi, vol. XIX, p. 43.

172. Vat. archives, Arm., XXXIX, tom. 9, fol. 97; cf. with FRA, XX, pp. 196–97.

173. See note 169; the passage relating to the forthcoming assembly at Nurnberg on pp. 213–16.

174. Only one letter, i.e., the Pope's reply to George, March 28, 1460, was published in FRA, XX, pp. 217–18; the original in Vat. archives, Arm., XXXIX, tom. 9, fol. 174–75.

175. Arm., XXXIX, tom. 9, fol. 175–76.

176. FRA, XX, pp. 221–22.

177. Ibid., pp. 227–28.

178. Ibid., pp. 228–30.

179. Abstracts of these documents, dated May 8, 1460, in FRA, XX, pp. 224–25.

180. Palacký, Dějiny, IV, 2, p. 149, refers to the original which he saw in the family archives at Oleśnica (Oels).

181. Dated September 12, 1460, in SRS, VIII, pp. 47–48.

182. Abstracts in FRA, XX, pp. 232–34; the original copy of the agreement between George and Lewis in the Crown archives; A. Haas, l.c., No. 132.

183. C. Höfler, Das kaiserliche Buch, pp. 52–65.

184. Matthias' acceptance of George's proposals, dated Nov. 25, 1460, in FRA, XX, pp. 234–36.

185. A declaration of Zdeněk of Šternberk and other envoys for a treaty of friendship in FRA, XX, pp. 236–38.

186. J. J. Müller, RTT, II, pp. 1–6, used contemporary documents for his description of the Cheb congress.

187. The bull against Sigismund of Tyrol, Nov. 10, 1459, in Raynaldi, XIX, p. 50. The bull announcing to the mayor and senate of Nurnberg the excommunication of Gregory of Heimburg, Oct. 18, 1460, in Aeneae Sylvii . . . Opera, quae extant omnia, Basel: 1571, pp. 932–33.

188. J. J. Müller, RTT, II, pp. 6–16.

189. To preserve his good will George sent on November 1, 1460, another message to Rome, mentioning Bishop Tas and Prokop of Rabštejn as his envoys to be sent around the Feast of the Purification. SRS, VIII, p. 49.

190. Vat. archives, Arm., XXXIX, tom. 9, fol. 196.

191. Raynaldi, XIX, pp. 61–62.

192. J. J. Müller, RTT, II, p. 7, has a passage from the Pope's letter to Prokop.

193. The names are in Thomae Ebendorferi Chronicon Austriacum (Pez, Scriptores rerum Austriacarum II), p. 938.

194. Dated June 5, 1462, in A. F. Riedel, Codex diplomaticus Brandenburgenis, II. Hauptteil, vol. II, pp. 63–64. For original in the Crown archives see A. Haas, l.c., No. 148.

195. The Pope's letter announcing the appointment to the Prague chapter was published by T. J. Pešina, Phosphorus septicornis, p. 242.

196. See note 117.

197. See note 123; the passage relating to the Polish priests in Mansi, Orationes, I, p. 368.

198. Published by Bidlo, Akty Jednoty bratrské, II, pp. 242–54.

199. Bidlo, l.c., pp. 254–55, published a short description of the wagon as well as an interpretation of its meaning.

200. O původu Jednoty bratrské (published by O. Odložilík), p. 63.

201. Ibid., pp. 62–63.

202. The permission was, undoubtedly, given orally; the early historians of the Unity (Brother Lukáš of Prague, Blahoslav, l.c., 65) date it 1457.

203. See note 140.

204. See note 189.

205. FRA, XX, pp. 243–44.

206. The reference is most likely to Charles' edict of 1376; published by M. Goldast, Zwo rechtliche Bedencken, Beilage no. 49.

207. Several sources refer to them; e.g., a letter most likely by Řehoř to Valečovský, Bidlo, l.c., I, p. 555.

208. Its full text in Bidlo, Akty, I, pp. 585–87.

209. St. l., p. 176.

210. Published from the original in the Crown archives by Josef Kalousek, České státní právo, p. 568; cf. with A. Haas, l.c., No. 138.

211. FRA, XLIV, p. 147.

212. See note 204.

213. See note 181. A Czech translation of Marini's letter, Aug. 8, 1461, was published by Palacký in Časopis spol. vlast. museum II (1828), pt. 3, pp. 21–24. On June 30, 1461, Pius II issued a safe-conduct for George's envoys to be valid for eight months. AČ, XV, pp. 236–37.

214. The silence concerning Rokycana was not generally known. An anonymous annalist believed that the envoys' task was to request confirmation both of the Compacts and of Rokycana. St. l., p. 177.

215. His name was Wolfgang Forchtenauer.

216. Published by A. Patera in AČ, VIII, pp. 322–54.

217. The King reported his decision to Pius II on Nov. 27, 1461; cf. with Pastor, l.c., II, p. 110.

218. Koranda's report in AČ, VIII, p. 324.

219. Forchtenauer's speech in Latin, AČ, VIII, pp. 355–56.

220. Koranda has a general reference to, but not the text of, the formula. AČ, VIII, p. 328. Another account of the session sent from Rome to Breslau early in April, 1462, in SRS, VIII, pp. 25–26.

221. Its Czech version in AČ, VIII, pp. 328–36; a contemporary Latin translation, ibid., pp. 356–60.

222. It is available only in Koranda's Czech (abbreviated) translation; AČ, VIII, pp. 336–42.

223. AČ, VIII, p. 341; see above, note 23.

224. Both meetings were described by Koranda; AČ, VIII, pp. 342–47.

225. Its Latin version in AČ, VIII, pp. 360–63; a better text in Mansi, Orationes II, pp. 93–100.

226. The proclamation in FRA, XX, p. 269.

227. In AČ, VIII, p. 353. Conclusiones datae oratoribus regis Bohemiae, ibid., pp. 363–64.

Chapter VIII

228. See note 12.

229. See note 185.

230. The text of the Głogów agreement, May 27, 1462, in SRS, VIII, pp. 97–100.

231. The matter is rather complicated. The Czech envoys (excluding Rabštejn) left Rome on April 3, 1462. Fantino followed after a week or so. Later the Curia maintained that the Czech envoys asked that Fantino be sent to Prague as the Pope's representative. See FRA, XX, p. 380.

232. He carried with him letters from Pius II to various Catholic personages as well as for the cities of Plzeň and Breslau; cf. with Urbánek, Věk, III, 4, p. 536, note 51.

233. SRS, VIII, pp. 107–11.

234. Palacký published in FRA, XX, two accounts of the assembly, one (A) on pp. 272–74, on the whole sympathetic to George, the other (B) on pp. 275–77, unfriendly. B was inserted in a letter from Breslau to Rome, Aug. 28, 1462, and as such it was published in SRS, VIII, pp. 123–26. J. J. Müller, RTT, II, pp. 244–46 published a report destined for Duke William of Saxony. Shorter reports are listed by Urbánek, Věk, III, 4, p. 561, note 87. Cf. with Raynaldi, XIX, p. 115.

235. See above 234. The relevant words which later served as a justification of stern measures against George run as follows: . . . "nec credimus aliam esse viam salutis animarum nostrarum quam sub eisdem (i.e., Compactatis) mori et utraque communione uti juxta Salvatoris institutionem."

236. Gregory of Heimburg inserted a statement in his Apologia accusing Zdeněk of a breach of faith and of malevolent intentions; FRA, XX, p. 650.

237. The speech is not available; abstracts both in A and B accounts; FRA, XX, pp. 273–74, 276–77.

238. This, indeed, was one of the most significant points on which the Curia and the Hussites differed. Neither Pius II nor his successor showed any intention to accept the Czech interpretation. The Hussites translated Eugene's bull into Czech and this version appeared in AČ, III, pp. 441–42. For the bull of Sept. 18, 1437, see note 22.

239. When presenting the Czech cause to Calixtus III; see note 123.

240. Most of these details originated in sources hostile to George and reached Rome via Breslau or otherwise. They influenced the Pope's policy. See Pius II . . . Commentarii, pp. 434–35.

241. A lengthy report of it (from the Catholic side) in SRS, VIII, pp. 133–35. Palacký published in FRA, XX, p. 278, a letter by the Catholic administrator Hilarius of Litoměřice urging the priests under his jurisdiction to attend the convocation. It can be assumed that Rokycana issued a similar order.

242. See notes 176 and 178.

243. Dated August 8, 1461; see note 213.

244. See note 230.

245. Several authors (Markgraf, Jorga, Bartoš, et al.) endeavored to examine the origin of Marini's scheme and to sketch the progress of his negotiations. My story follows closely the pertinent chapter in Urbánek, Věk, III, 4, p. 576 ff. A contemporary copy of Marini's draft has been preserved in a manuscript (15.606) at Munich; see Urbánek, l.c., p. 583, note 25.

246. A report of the session in FRA, XX, pp. 289–90.

247. Not available. Cf. with Urbánek, l.c., p. 569, note 110. The Pope's letter to George, Sept. 14, 1462, in SRS, VIII, p. 130.

248. As reported by George to Pius II, Oct. 27, 1462; SRS, VIII, pp. 146–47.

249. His name was Andreas Baumkircher; he was reported to cover the distance from Vienna to Prague in three days. Cf. with FRA, XX, p. 283.

250. A. Bachmann reproduced its terms from an unprinted charter, Dec. 2, 1462, in Deutsche Reichsgeschichte I, p. 341.

251. The agreement of Dec. 8, 1462, FRA, XX, pp. 284–85.

252. Frederick III issued two charters of the same contents, one, Dec. 11, 1462, sealed with wax, the other, Dec. 21, 1462, with his golden seal. See A. Haas, l.c., no. 156 and 158. An abstract in FRA, XX, pp. 285–86.

253. George referred to this charter in his speech at the provincial Diet, Sept. 25, 1465; AČ, IV, p. 109. Cf. with Jos. Kalousek, České státní právo, p. 184.

254. Its text in J. Sommersberg, Silesiacarum rerum scriptores, Leipzig 1729, vol. I, p. 1077; cf. with Jos. Chmel, Regesta No. 3952, p. 397.

255. Frederick's charter was dated Dec. 8, 1462. Abstract in Chmel, l.c., No. 3953, p. 397; George's pledge of help of the same date in Chmel, l.c., Anhang, p. CXLIX.

256. The Emperor's message was delivered to Pius II by a special emissary, the court chaplain Gallus; the Pope replied on Dec. 31, 1462. FRA, XX, pp. 287–89.

257. See note 168.

258. His reports dated April 6, 1462, in SRS, VIII, pp. 87–89.

259. Kitzing's later reports as well as other correspondence in SRS, VIII, under various dates.

260. By a bull of Sept. 24, 1462; SRS, VIII, pp. 136–37.

261. He arrived on Nov. 15, 1462; SRS, VII, p. 102.

262. The Senate's letter to Pius II, Nov. 26, 1462; SRS, VIII, pp. 148–51.

263. His letter dated March 3, 1463, in SRS, VIII, pp. 171–72.

264. Fantino wrote on March 13, Francis of Toledo on March 15, 1463; SRS, VIII, pp. 173–75; the papal bull, ibid., pp. 183–86. Cf. with Raynaldi, XIX, pp. 145–47.

265. SRS, VIII, pp. 186–87.

266. Ibid., p. 187.

267. Published from an undated copy in SRS, VIII, pp. 193–94.

268. Ibid., pp. 204–6.

269. Undated and addressed to Pius II in FRA, XX, pp. 302–6. Jošt's letter addressed to prominent Czech lords, May 27, 1463, in AČ, IV, pp. 99–100; his correspondence with Pius II and Carvajal in FRA, XX, pp. 302–8.

270. Documents relating to negotiations between Archbishop Jerome, Bishop Jošt, and the Breslau Senate in SRS, VIII, pp. 207–17.

271. The stormy scene was described by Eschenloer, Geschichten, I, pp. 212–13.

272. Their text in SRS, VIII, pp. 219–22.

273. Ibid., pp. 225–27.

274. This was reported to the Pope by the Breslau Senate on June 29, 1463, SRS, VIII, pp. 237–38.

275. The Breslau Senate had its correspondents in Brno. Their reports, hostile to George, were summed up in a letter to Pius II, Aug. 4, 1463, SRS, VIII, pp. 258–60.

276. Ibid., pp. 257–58.

277. Andreas, a priest from Budějovice, whom George sent to Frederick's court, traveled from there with the Emperor's letter and arrived in Rome early in September, as reported by a Breslau agent Weinrich; SRS, IX, p. 6.

278. Reference to this decision in the Pope's letters, July 18, 1463, to Breslau, Archbishop Jerome, Frederick III, and Bishop Jošt. SRS, VIII, pp. 247–49.

279. Letters under various dates to Pius II and other addressees in SRS, IX, p. 17 ff.

280. Letter from Breslau, January 2, 1464, SRS, IX, pp. 25–26.

281. Their names were Beneš of Veitmil and Prokop of Rabštejn. They arrived in Wiener Neustadt early in March, 1464. Cf. a contemporary writing De Georgio Bohemiae rege in C. Höfler, Geschichtsschreiber III, p. 219.

282. Abstracts of several documents from late August, 1463, in FRA, XX, pp. 312–13.

283. Published by Palacký without Mair's name in FRA, XX, pp. 313–19.

284. See note 245.

285. Abbé Lenglet du Fresnoy published it as an appendix to his edition of Philippe de Comines Mémoires, vol. II, pp. 424–31. F. M. Bartoš with the help of other copies established a better text and published it in Jihočeský sborník historický, XII (1939) and also separately. The above summary follows Bartoš' edition. More recently Polish historians discovered in the records of the royal chancellery in Warsaw a copy of "tractatus pacis toti Christianitati fiende," sent to the Polish king by Marini on June 14, 1463. This copy has, according to preliminary reports, a much better text than Abbé Lenglet's edition.

286. FRA, XX, pp. 290–91.

287. The appointment of an emissary was reported to the Senate of Breslau by their agent Merboth on March 15, 1463. SRS, VIII, p. 179. The letter to Duke Philip was dated July 2, 1463.

288. Bessarion's reports, July 20 and July 29, 1463, in Pastor, Geschichte der Päpste, II, pp. 737–41.

289. Papal confirmation of Oct. 22, 1463, has the original text of July 19, 1463. See A. Theiner, Monum. Hung., II, pp. 382–91.

290. Ibid., II, pp. 380–82.

291. Pius II . . . Commentarii, pp. 329–31.

292. Aeneas Silvius, Opera (1571), pp. 914–23; for other references see Pastor, l.c., II, p. 258, note 1.

293. It is not quite clear how many speeches prepared beforehand de Lelli was able to deliver. The most significant of them, the third, has been preserved in two manuscripts in the Vatican Library, Ottoboniana, cod. 233, fol. 23 ff. and Vatic. Lat. 5315, f. 35 ff.

294. See note 281.

295. Their appeal to Frederick III in SRS, IX, pp. 49–50.

296. The legate's answer in FRA, XX, pp. 325–28.

297. Vatic. Arch. Reg. 518, fol. 149–50.

298. Ibid., Reg. 519, fol. 34–35 and fol. 37–38.

299. Palacký knew Prokop's letter from a contemporary copy; cf. with Dějiny, IV, 2, p. 262, note 194. Urbánek, Věk, III, 4, p. 663, note 217 expressed disagreement with Palacký and suggested that the letter was written in 1463.

300. The text of the treaty, April 14, 1464, in Katona, XIV, pp. 712–15; Marini made a reference to the bishops' threat in his speech before the king of France; cf. with AČ, VII, p. 435. See below note 302.

301. The copy of Marini's "tractatus" of June 14, 1463 (see note 285), shows that he resumed negotiations with the Polish court after his return from Venice.

302. A member of Albrecht's retinue, known simply as Knight Jaroslav, described in Czech their journey to France and included abstracts of the speeches. Published by Jos. Kalousek in AČ, VII, pp. 427–45.

303. Goldast, Commentarii (Frankfurt 1627) App., documentorum, pp. 112–15.

304. Breslau's new agent Fabian Hanko presented to Pius II a new petition of the Senate; SRS, IX, pp. 54–57.

305. The Pope's breve, Apr. 23, 1464, in SRS, pp. 65–66.

306. SRS, IX, Nos. 250, 252, pp. 75–77.

307. These documents (the advocate's speech, the Pope's reply, and the bull of citation) in SRS, IX, pp. 77–87. The editor, H. Markgraf, attached a copious footnote to the bull of citation; it contains excerpts from contemporary sources indicating that the bull, though approved and prepared for expedition, actually was not despatched to the prospective addressees. See also C. Höfler, Geschichtsschreiber III, pp. 220–21.

CHAPTER IX

308. Rohrbacher's report of his mission sent to Prokop of Rabštejn on Feb. 15, 1465, in FRA, XX, pp. 337–40.

309. Hanko's report of Paul's election, Sept. 2, 1464, in SRS, IX, p. 94; after that, he wrote to Breslau several times, Sept. 29, Oct. 21, Nov. 22, 1464; ibid., pp. 96–98, 100–2; 103–4.

310. Hanko reported his appointment on Jan. 14, 1465, SRS, IX, pp. 105–6.

311. Also reported by Hanko, l.c., p. 105.

312. Rudolf's letter to Tas, Jan. 21, 1465, in FRA, XX, pp. 336–37. A longer and sterner letter to the Estates of Moravia, March 18, 1465, in T. Pešina, Mars Moravicus, p. 737.

313. See note 308.

314. It was dated Prague, March 7, 1465; published in Pešina, Mars Moravicus, p. 739; a letter by George to Bishop Rudolf, April 11, 1465, ibid., p. 740.

315. Both Hilarius and Rokycana described the convocation. H's Disputatio cum Rokycana coram Georgio, rege Bohemiae, was published several times. R's Contra propositiones frivolas doctorum apostatarum (i.e., Hilarius and Křižanovský) circulated also in a Czech translation. The Czech version was published by Fr. Šimek, Traktát M. Jana Rokycany o přijímání krve in

VKČSN, I. tř., 1940, sect. II. Using various sources of information Raynaldi, XIX, pp. 175–78, described the disputation from his point of view.

316. An abstract of their first letter, Feb. 23, 1465, in SRS, IX, p. 114.

317. Legate Rudolf addressed on March 18, 1465, a letter to the clergy of Bohemia and Moravia forbidding the Catholics to participate in the Cornštejn expedition. FRA, XX, pp. 342–44; Tas's reply, March 27, ibid., p. 344.

318. Beneš carried George's letter to Bishop Rudolf of April 1; see FRA, XX, pp. 345–46. On March 7, 1465, the King wrote directly to Paul II; ibid., pp. 340–42.

319. The legate wrote concerning this unexpected complication on April 17, 1465; FRA, XX, pp. 350–51.

320. His lengthy letter of April 17, 1465, in FRA, XX, pp. 349–52.

321. An abstract of this letter, April 21, 1465, in SRS, IX, p. 121.

322. The letter was sent in mid April, 1465; SRS, IX, pp. 118–19.

323. Václav Koranda included a copy of Jošt's writing in his Manuálník. The entire text of Manuálník was published by Josef Truhlář. See in that edition, pp. 203–5.

324. See above, note 318.

325. FRA, XX, pp. 354–56.

326. See note 319.

327. An abstract of Hanko's letter, July 4, 1465 in SRS, IX, p. 130; cf. with note 307.

328. An abstract of Paul's bull, July 11, 1465, ibid., p. 132.

329. Ibid., p. 134.

330. Ibid., pp. 135–39.

331. FRA, XX, pp. 362–64.

332. Palacký has a passing reference to Elias' letter, Dějiny, IV, 2, p. 310, No. 227.

333. FRA, XX, p. 345; cf. with note 317.

334. The proclamation dated Aug. 19, 1465, in AČ, IV, p. 102.

335. The list of grievances, ibid., pp. 102–5.

336. Ibid., pp. 105–9.

337. Ibid., p. 110.

338. Its text and signatures in AČ, IV, pp. 110–14.

339. Ibid., pp. 118–19.

340. See note 319.

341. Tomek, Dějepis, VII, p. 109, gives the essential points of Tas's memorandum without quoting the source.

342. Katona, XV, pp. 135–36; "sive ergo in Bohemos, sive in Turcos opus est, ecce Matthias simul et Hungaria."

343. This he reported to Tas on Oct. 17, 1465, and to King George on Feb. 26, 1466; see Teleki, XI, pp. 145 and 153.

344. It was dated Oct. 21, 1465; SRS, IX, pp. 142–43.

345. Reference to them in Palacký, Dějiny, IV, 2, p. 319, note 234; Mair also drafted letters which the addressees were expected to send to Rome.

346. The most recent edition of an English translation by M. H. I. Letts appeared in 1957. See the bibliography.

347. See note 302.

348. This was most likely a supplement to the letter of Oct. 21, 1465; cf. with note 344 and FRA, XX, pp. 384–85.

349. Neither Lewis' instruction for Bernbeck nor Bernbeck's articles presented to the Pope have been found; they must be reconstructed from the papal bull to Lewis dated February 6, 1466. See below note 357.

350. See note 331.

351. SRS, IX, pp. 143–45.

352. The legate's letter is not available; the lords' reply to it, Nov. 30, 1465, in FRA, XX, p. 371.

353. See note 347.

354. SRS, IX, pp. 147–49.

355. Ibid., p. 146.

356. These events were reported to Breslau by Hanko; cf. with SRS, IX, p. 150.

357. See note 344. The text of the papal answer SRS, IX, pp. 150–54.

358. Ibid., pp. 156–63.

359. SRS, IX, p. 164.

360. See note 342.

361. He wrote on March 28, 1466; SRS, IX, p. 165.

362. Hanko's reports, May 1 and 30, 1466; ibid., p. 165 (abstracts only).

363. Two documents concerning Rožmberk's change of orientation in AČ, IV, pp. 123–24 and 127–29.

364. AČ, IV, pp. 131–32.

365. SRS, IX, pp. 167–68.

366. Ibid., pp. 168–69.

367. According to the Senate's report to the Pope, June 16, 1466, SRS, IX, pp. 173–75.

368. This can be concluded from various references in Heimburg's letter to George, July 18, 1465, FRA, XX, pp. 407–9.

369. See note 187.

370. Heimburg's letter, dated Sept. 8, 1465, at Würzburg, in FRA, XX, pp. 366–69. Carvajal's answer from Rome, Dec. 3, 1465, ibid., pp. 377–82.

371. This happened for the first time in 1463, as shows the Vatic. Reg. 518, ff. 214–18. See note 400.

372. See note 327.

373. See note 344.

374. SRS, IX, pp. 181–90.

375. See note 354.

376. This can be gathered from a copious footnote attached by H. Markgraf to the text of George's letter to Matthias. SRS, IX, p. 190.

377. Markgraf published in SRS, IX, pp. 192–95, both the text suggested by the royal chancellery and its modification by the princes; an abstract of the Pope's answer, ibid., p. 198.

378. Palacký has 1467 as a tentative date of its compilation; he published the Apologia in FRA, XX, pp. 647–60.

379. Cardinals Bessarion, Carvajal, and Erolo reported this to Bishop Rudolf on July 17, 1466; SRS, IX, pp. 179–80.

380. Paul II announced his intentions to Frederick III on October 2, 1466; SRS, IX, p. 197.

381. Published with a tentative date Oct.-Dec., 1466, in SRS, IX, pp. 203–10.

382. SRS, IX, pp. 200–1; Gabriel Rangoni, a Franciscan (Ordinis minoris) acted as Rudolf's deputy.

383. Długosz, Historia Polonica, tomus 2, Leipzig 1712, col. 394–95.

384. Several letters exchanged between Matthias, King George, and Prince Victorin in Teleki, XI, pp. 177–81, 183–87, 191 ff.

385. A. Theiner, Mon. Hung. II, 405–6; cf. with note 140.

386. It was held at Nurnberg; J. J. Müller, RTT, II, pp. 211–19, published selected documents relating to that session.

387. Müller, RTT, II, pp. 216–17, has a list of those present at Nurnberg, including Fantino.

388. His letter to Breslau, Nov. 21, 1466, SRS, IX, p. 199.

389. FRA, XX, pp. 415–18.

390. FRA, XX, p. 425.

391. Dated Jan. 25, 1467, in FRA, XX, pp. 424–25.

392. See note 381.

393. SRS, IX, pp. 210–13.

394. Ibid., pp. 213–14.

395. An example of his activities, a letter to the municipal council of Zhořelec (Görlitz), Jan. 19, 1467, in FRA, XX, pp. 423–24.

396. AČ, IV, pp. 334–35.

397. Palacký, Dějiny, IV, 2, p. 370, note 277, refers to an unprinted report from Prague to Zhořelec, dated Feb. 24, 1467.

398. Abstracts of his messages to Breslau, March 12 and 16, 1467, in SRS, IX, pp. 220–21.

399. FRA, XX, pp. 435–36.

400. The relevant passage from the bull in SRS, IX, pp. 222–23; cf. with note 371.

401. The bull Execrabilis; cf. with note 170.

402. Its text in FRA, XX, pp. 454–58. An abstract in SRS, IX, p. 226.

403. H. Finke, Acta concilii Constanciensis, vol. II, Münster, 1923, p. 606: . . . "statuimus, ut deinceps saltem de decennio in decennium generalia concilia . . . celebrentur."

404. Published by Julius Pažout in AÖG, XL, pp. 357–71.

405. See notes 285 and 302.

406. See note 393.

CHAPTER X

407. St. l., p. 184.

408. Responsiones christianissimi regis Franciae were included in the Czech envoy's report AÖG, XL, pp. 365–69; see above note 404.

409. See note 406.

410. SRS, IX, pp. 226–28.

411. SRS, VII, pp. 126, 129–30; a letter of the Zelená Hora League requesting closer cooperation, ibid., pp. 127–29.

412. Ibid., p. 129.

413. See note 364.

414. George's letter to Zdeněk, April 20, 1467, announcing the imminent start of hostilities, in AČ, IV, p. 139.

415. Długosz, l.c., cols. 399 and 405–6.

416. This can be gathered from Paul's letter to Bishop Rudolf, May 14, 1467; SRS, IX, pp. 229–30.

417. On June 1, 1467, Paul II sent him to Nurnberg to represent the Holy See at the Diet to be held there; Reg. Vat. 519, fol. 244–48.

418. Ibid., fol. 235 and 250.

419. SRS, IX, pp. 230–31.

420. Ibid., p. 231.

421. Ibid., pp. 232–33.

422. Ibid., pp. 233–36.

423. These full powers were granted to Rudolf by two letters of the same date as the bull of appointment, ibid., pp. 236–37.

424. Ibid., pp. 237–38.

425. Ibid., pp. 239–40.

426. A short record of these events in Eschenloer's Historia; SRS, VII, pp. 134–35.

427. Mentioned by Długosz (originale decretum), l.c., col. 407.

428. The most important source concerning the Cracow conferences is Długosz, l.c., cols. 407–9.

429. See note 417.

430. J. J. Müller, RTT, II, pp. 260–90; the list of those present on pp. 261–62. Cf. with FRA, XX, pp. 472–74. One of the two noblemen, Jan Kocovský, made a speech in German in which, among other charges and exhortations he admonished the assembled princes: "If you wish to defeat the Turks crush first the enemies at home who are worse than the Turks." F. Dvorský published a Czech version of Kocovský's speech in AČ, XX, pp. 542–50. He also published a Czech translation of a letter sent by the Czech delegation to the papal legate; ibid., pp. 550–53.

431. A letter to the Polish king, June 3, 1467; FRA, XX, pp. 460–62. Palacký, Dějiny, IV, 2, p. 409, note 215, referred to George's unprinted letter to John of Rožmberk to which was attached a copy of the royal letter to friendly princes. Its form and contents can be established with the help of George's letter to Albrecht Achilles; AÖG, VII, pp. 44–46; the date May 5, 1467, suggested by C. Höfler, is not correct and should be June.

432. J. J. Müller, RTT, p. 269. Albrecht reported to George, Aug. 14, 1467; AÖG, VII, p. 49.

433. J. J. Müller inserted this document into his account of conferences of the princes in the Bavarian capital, Landshut, RTT, II, pp. 297–310. Other correspondence pertaining to this matter is also included.

434. Długosz, l.c., cols. 411–13; cf. with a report by the Poles to Bishop Rudolf, Nov. 30, 1467, in FRA, XX, pp. 500–2.

435. George's reply (in Latin), Oct. 26, 1467, in SRS, VII, pp. 148–51; the original Czech version in AČ, IV, pp. 146–50.

436. Zdeněk's reply given at Jihlava, Nov. 2, 1467, in SRS, VII, pp. 151–53. When presented with this declaration, George made a statement of his policy, Nov. 11; SRS, VII, pp. 153–55 (Czech version in AČ, IV, pp. 150–53); Zdeněk answered it promptly; SRS, VII, pp. 155–56.

437. SRS, VII, p. 159.

438. A succinct account of these events by Eschenloer in SRS, VII, pp. 159–60. Palacký published in FRA, XX, pp. 503–12, a diary of a Lusatian observer, J. Frauenburg.

439. By a letter, Dec. 27, 1467, in SRS, IX, pp. 250–51.

440. The letters were sent on Feb. 1, 1468; SRS, IX, pp. 257–59.

441. SRS, IX, pp. 271–72. See also A. Theiner, Mon. Polon., vol. II, No. 195, pp. 158–59.

442. SRS, VII, p. 169. Two letters sent to George from Strzelin by Polish legates, Dec. 27 and 28, 1467, in FRA, XX, pp. 515–18.

443. SRS, VII, pp. 175–76.

444. Fra Gabriele was active in campaigning against George, prior to the Breslau congress. He undertook a refutation of Heimburg's Apologia (see above note 378) and organized his writing as a fictitious speech to be held before the Emperor, kings, princes and assembled people. He relied heavily on Bishop Rudolf's lengthy letter to King Matthias which Eschenloer inserted in his Latin Historia. For information concerning the date of writing and other problems see SRS, IX, pp. 209–10. Fra Gabriele's invective, Perditi nominis Georgii de Podiebrad . . . refutatio, was published by Paul Joachimsohn, Die Streitschrift des Minoriten Gabriel v. Verona (see the bibliography); cf. with note 446.

445. George's reply, dated Jan. 11, 1468, in AČ, IV, pp. 153–55; a covering letter addressed to the Polish mediators, ibid., pp. 155–57. The text of the agreement on truce in SRS, VII, pp. 173 and 179. Other correspondence relating to the same matter in AČ, IV, pp. 160–64.

446. Palacký published in FRA, XX, pp. 512–15, a document drafted by Fra Gabriele and presented to the Polish envoys in the name of the League of Zelená Hora. Heimburg or another of George's advisers attacked that letter. A contemporary Czech translation from Latin in AČ, IV, pp. 157–60.

447. Victorin's letter, Dec. 4, 1467, in Teleki, XI, pp. 289–90.

448. It was dated Feb. 9, 1468, and referred to Prokop's failure to undertake the journey; Teleki, XI, pp. 306–7.

449. George's promise of help to Stein in SRS, IX, pp. 248–49.

450. Victorin's challenging letters to Frederick III, dated Dec. 29, 1467, and Jan. 8, 1468, in SRS, IX, pp. 252–54.

451. Ant. de Bonfinis, Rerum Hungaricarum decades, dec. IV, liber I. et II. has a description of the Eger Diet. Included is a speech (fictitious) by Matthias, justifying the decision to go to war against George; in a modern edition by I. Fógel–B. Iványi–L. Juhász, Budapest, 1941, vol. IV, pp. 20–25.

452. While at Pressburg on April 8, 1468, he pledged allegiance to Matthias personally and also in the name of the Catholic lords; SRS, IX, pp. 263–64. On the following day he gave Bishop Rudolf a report of his mission to Hungary; FRA, XX, pp. 523–24.

453. Palacký inserted the main part of it (from a contemporary copy) into his Dějiny, IV, 2, pp. 441–42. Latin version, undated in Teleki, XI, pp. 327–29.

454. See note 289.

455. SRS, IX, pp. 262–63; also Katona, XV, p. 294.

456. See note 443.

457. The breve dated Feb. 23, 1468, in Reg. Vatic. 540, fol. 44–45; cf. with A. Theiner, Mon. Hung., II, No. 581, pp. 406–7.

458. The bull, April 22, 1468, in Reg. Vatic. 540, fol. 55–56.

459. A passage from it concerning George in SRS, IX, pp. 264–65; full text in Reg. Vatic. 540, fol. 21–26.

460. SRS, IX, pp. 261–62.

461. Ibid., pp. 270–71.

462. Ibid., p. 264.

463. Ibid., p. 272.

464. Reg. Vatic. 528, fol. 180–81.

465. Ibid., fol. 209.

466. Ibid., fol. 181–83; a detailed instruction how to collect the contributions, ibid., fol. 184–85.

467. Reg. Vatic. 518, fol. 207–8; printed in SRS, IX, pp. 265–67.

468. Reg. Vatic. 518, fol. 235–38; printed in SRS, IX, pp. 267–69.

469. Reg. Vatic. 519, fol. 266.

470. See note 445.

471. Długosz, col. 421–23.

472. Ibid., col. 423–25.

473. Ibid., 430.

474. Rangoni's letter was dated at Olomouc, Aug. 2, 1468; SRS, IX, pp. 289–90.

475. St. l., p. 191.

476. Długosz, l.c., col. 430.

477. Długosz, l.c., col. 435.

478. C. Höfler, Das kaiserliche Buch, p. 218.

479. Długosz, l.c., col. 439.

480. The meeting was reported from Olomouc to Breslau; SRS, IX, p. 302.

481. Published in AČ, XX, pp. 557–63.

482. An anonymous chronicler of the fifteenth century treated the campaign as an insignificant episode; see St. l., pp. 197–98. See also a contemporary rhymed composition concerning the war with the Hungarians, ibid., pp. 488–91.

483. St. l., p. 197.

484. E.g., the captain of Jindř. Hradec wrote to Zdeslav of Šternberk that the truce was to last till Easter; AČ, VII, pp. 376–77.

485. As reported to the municipal council of Zhořelec by their agent. FRA, XX, pp. 564–65.

486. These conferences can be reconstructed with the help of Albrecht's detailed report to his brother Frederick, March 23, 1469, FRA, XX, pp. 567–69.

487. Palacký published fragments of a diary of a Lusatian observer at the conference, covering April 7–May 3, 1469; see FRA, XX, pp. 371–82.

488. FRA, XX, pp. 569–70.

489. SRS, IX, pp. 304–5.

490. A Lusatian reporter described the ceremony in his diary, FRA, XX, pp. 581–82; cf. with SRS, VII, p. 202; St. l., p. 199.

491. In a letter to his brother-in-law, Aug. 22, 1469; see Höfler, Das kaiserliche Buch, p. 215.

492. A description of these events in SRS, VII, pp. 202–4. The text of the bull of allegiance, ibid., p. 204.

CHAPTER XI

493. Höfler, Das kaiserliche Buch, p. 204.

494. The bull of Maundy Thursday in Reg. Vatic. 540, fol. 56–62; the bull of April 9, 1469, ibid., fol. 63–64.

495. The royal decree concerning the monetary reform, June 5, 1469, in AČ, IV, pp. 437–40.

496. See note 234.

497. His letter to Bishop Rudolf, Nov. 19, 1469, in FRA, XX, pp. 608–9.

498. St. l. (ed. F. Šimek–M. Kaňák), p. 281.

499. Included in Acta Unitatis Fratrum (unprinted), vol. V, fol. 260–61; the main points reproduced in J. Th. Müller, Geschichte der böhmischen Brüder, I, pp. 101–8.

500. Jaroslav Goll devoted to the contacts with the Valdensians the first part of his Quellen und Untersuchungen zur Geschichte der böhm. Brüder,

Prague, 1878. Later J. Th. Müller, F. M. Bartoš, R. Říčan, et al., attempted to shed more light on the origin of priesthood among the Brethren.

501. Published by Jar. Bidlo, Akty Jednoty bratrské, II, pp. 11–17.

502. See note 403.

503. C. Höfler, Das kaiserliche Buch, pp. 215–17.

504. See note 159.

505. C. Höfler, Das kaiserliche Buch, p. 215.

506. Ibid., pp. 191–94.

507. Długosz, l.c., col. 442.

508. FRA, XX, pp. 600–1.

509. FRA, XLVI, pp. 664–67.

510. E, J, Kremer, Geschichto des Kurfürsten Friedrichs 1. von der Pfalz (Urkunden), No. 145, pp. 401–3.

511. At their meeting at Jihlava, June 1467; see note 426.

512. Długosz, l.c., col. 443.

513. Early June, 1469; see note 495.

514. Długosz, l.c., col. 445–46.

515. According to Długosz, col. 446, their names were Johannes Tarnowski Woynicensis et Stanislaus Watrobka Sandecensis castellani.

516. There are only brief references in contemporary sources to Matthias' travels in July, 1469; the Diet was short, as can be gathered from the King's letter to Bishop Rudolf, July 21, 1469, in FRA, XX, p. 599.

517. See note 489.

518. Długosz, l.c., col. 452.

519. Długosz, l.c., col. 451.

520. In 1459–60; see note 169.

521. For references to Stein's mission see Commines (ed. Godefroy), IV, p. 378.

522. These negotiations can be at least partly reconstructed from Stein's memorandum for Markgrave Albrecht, Jan., 1470; cf. with FRA, XX, pp. 616–19.

CHAPTER XII

523. Its German version in FRA, XX, pp. 610–15.

524. See note 402.

525. Ermisch, Neues Archiv für sächsische Geschichte, Bd. II, p. 35.

526. Eschenloer, Geschichten, vol. II, p. 195.

527. On Dec. 26, 1469, when consecrating the Abbot of St. Vincent; see SRS, VII, p. 219.

528. Eschenloer, Geschichten, II, pp. 194 and 196.

529. Matthias included the resolutions of the Diet in his charter issued early in January 1470; Katona, XV, pp. 418–25.

530. Teleki, IV, pp. 164–71; Długosz, l.c., col. 455.

531. Długosz, l.c., col. 455.

532. See note 521.

533. Frederick III confirmed him in the possession of Brandenburg on Dec. 12, 1470; an abstract of this charter in Chmel, Regesta, II, No. 6159, p. 598.

534. Długosz, l.c., col. 455–56.

535. Reg. Vatic. 540, fol. 93–96.

536. A record of this memorable assembly in AČ, IV, pp. 441–44.

537. Matthias' representatives headed by Fra Gabriele arrived in Breslau on June 10, 1470. See SRS, VII, p. 226.

538. SRS, VII, p. 228.

539. He sent to Matthias a group of noblemen headed by William Jr. of Rýzmberk to agree on the terms of the duel; their instruction, July 22, 1470, in AČ, I, pp. 485–87; Matthias' answer (negative), July 24, ibid., pp. 487–89.

540. On Oct. 2, 1470, Henry of Poděbrady sent to his father-in-law Albrecht Achilles a lengthy account of military operations in Moravia and Bohemia in the spring and summer of that year; FRA, XX, pp. 635–37.

541. See note 518.

542. Długosz, l.c., cols. 454–55.

543. Ibid., col. 455.

544. Ibid., col. 456.

545. Ibid., col. 456. A letter of the Polish envoys to Zdeněk protesting the request for an explicit recognition of Matthias, Aug. 11, and Zdeněk's reply, Aug. 16, 1470, in SRS, XII, pp. 24–26.

546. See note 226.

547. Copies of these letters in the volume of breves issued by Paul II in the Vatic. archives, Arm., XXXIX, vol. 12, fol. 64–66; publ. by A. Theiner, Mon. Hung., vol. II, Nos. 590, 591, and 592, pp. 415–17.

548. Only a short report of the Villach conference is available; see C. Th. Gemeiner, Regensburgische Chronik, vol. III, pp. 470–71.

549. Długosz, l.c., col. 460.

550. SRS, VII, p. 232.

551. Ibid., p. 233.

552. Ibid., p. 234.

553. See note 535.

554. A. Theiner, Mon. Hung., vol. II, No. 590, p. 415.

555. Długosz, l.c., col. 461, remarked that the loss of Negroponte "non secus quam Byzantina fatalis Catholicis visa est."

556. Długosz, l.c., col. 461–62.

557. See note 548.

558. Their names were Ladislaus de Zara, provost of Buda, and Nicholaus, lector of Vácz.

559. Theiner, Mon. Hung., II, No. 597, p. 419. T. by mistake speaks of Ferdinand.

560. Theiner, l.c., No. 593, p. 417.

561. Theiner, l.c., No. 594, pp. 417–18.

562. Theiner, l.c., No. 595, p. 418.

563. Theiner, l.c., No. 596, pp. 418–19.

564. Theiner, l.c., Nos. 598 and 601, pp. 419–22.

565. Długosz, l.c., cols. 463–64.

566. Ibid., cols. 464–65.

567. The letter with a rather confused date in Katona, XV, pp. 468–69.

568. A marriage of George's son Hynek to Catherine, daughter of Prince William of Weimar.

569. Raynaldi, XIX, pp. 224–25 and J. J. Müller, II, p. 431 ff.

570. George and his followers blamed Zdeněk of Šternberk for spreading this accusation. See note 236.

571. The Pope referred to the arrival of the envoys from Saxony and of

their proposals in his letter to Cardinal Francis, April 28, 1471. Vatic. archives Arm., XXXIX, vol. XII, fol. 129–30; cf. with Raynaldi, XIX, p. 225.

572. Vatic. archives Reg. 540, fol. 116–19.

573. The date of his appointment was Feb. 18, 1471; cf. with Pastor, l.c., II, p. 408, note 1. The Pope's letter to Bishop Lawrence, Feb. 24, 1471, announcing the intention to send the cardinal to Regensburg, Feb. 13, 1471, in Theiner, II, No. 599, pp. 420–21. In another breve, Feb. 24, 1471, Paul II instructed Bishop Lawrence to attend the Diet; Theiner, l.c., No. 600, p. 421.

574. See note 571.

575. The ban was lifted on May 21, 1471; cf. with Pastor, l.c., II, p. 438, note 1. Pastor, l.c., II, p. 778, published an abstract of Paul's letter to the markgrave, July 20, 1471.

576. St. l., p. 202.

577. Priebatch, Politische Correspondenz, I, pp. 218–19.

578. St. l., p. 203.

579. Heimburg's letter to the princes of Saxony published by C. Höfler, Böhmische Studien, AÖG, XII, pp. 347–48.

Chapter XIII

580. See note 32.

581. Długosz, l.c., col. 465: "in sanguine humano fundendo non agebat se praecipitem."

582. J. J. Müller, RTT, II, pp. 439–45, published some documents relating to the Diet, e.g., the speech of the Polish representative. Cf. with Długosz, l.c., col. 466–67. A modern edition of a contemporary description of the Diet by Jan Kozlík in ČČM, XXI (1847), pt. 2, pp. 186–95.

583. See note 6. Vladislav's confirmation of the privileges of the kingdom in AČ, IV, pp. 451–55.

584. Published by M. Goldast, Zwo rechtliche Bedencken, Beilagen 65, 66.

585. The bull dated March 2, 1472, for Cardinal Marcus in Theiner, Mon. Hung., II, No. 613, pp. 471–73.

586. To obtain it Vladislav sent one of his envoys, Jan Hasištejnský, to Rome; cf. with Raynaldi, XIX, p. 386.

587. The final act of Olomouc was prepared by negotiations at Brno and Buda. Palacký published in AČ, IV, pp. 481–87, the first draft of the agreement approved at Brno; the version approved at Buda, ibid., pp. 488–95. The text of Olomouc proclamation in AČ, V, pp. 377–87. The Latin text of the Buda agreement in Theiner, Mon. Hung., II, pp. 460–66.

588. Katona, XVI, pp. 188–93, has the text of an agreement between the kings of Poland and Hungary, dated April 2, 1479.

589. Some documents concerning the Diet in AČ, V, pp. 375–77; a survey of its session was included in the Liber decanorum facultatis philosophicae and printed in Monumenta Historica Universitatis Carolo-Ferdinandeae Pragensis, t. I, pars. II, Prague, 1832, pp. 133–40.

590. See note 12.

591. That is the repudiation of March 31, 1462; see note 225.

592. See note 589.

593. Palacký published important documents in AČ, V, pp. 418–27.

594. His arrival was reported by an anonymous chronicler; see St. l., 224–45.

595. St. l., 268.

596. Portions of a report of the assembly, compiled by a member of the majority in Jaroslav Goll, Chelčický a Jednota v XV. století, pp. 213–15.

597. No contemporary record of an assembly at Rychnov, in 1494, is available. Its progress can be only partly reconstructed from later sources. Conclusions adopted in 1495 in Goll, l.c., pp. 209–11.

598. Reprinted from the Land Register in AČ, VI, pp. 391–93.

599. Theiner, Mon. Polon., II, No. 234, p. 215, published a breve by Sixtus IV, Oct. 14, 1480, granting Ludmila permission to attend on Fridays divine service in the Carthusian church outside the city walls of Legnica.

600. Eschenloer, II, p. 274.

601. A collection of these tales in Czech was published by Antonín Grund under the title Hynek z Poděbrad: Boccaciovské rozprávky, Prague, 1960.

602. A modern edition of them (and some other contemporary compositions) was published by Zdeňka Tichá, Veršované skladby Neuberského sborníku, Prague, 1960.

603. R. Urbánek collected and analyzed all available evidence pertaining to these statues in an article K ikonografii Jiřího krále in his collection of minor studies, Z husitského věku, Prague, 1957, pp. 235–48.

BIBLIOGRAPHY

I. The Progress of Research on King George and His Times

It is rather surprising that George of Poděbrady did not find a man with adequate training in liberal arts and with a good style of writing who could produce either a reliable biography or a comprehensive description of public life in Bohemia from 1420 to 1471. None of the Hussite clerics of Rokycana's circle undertook a task which would have been both onerous and rewarding. The most gifted among George's foreign advisers, Gregory of Heimburg, readily drafted letters and manifestoes; whenever necessary, he defended his master against calumnies and false accusations. But Heimburg's *Apologia*, though brilliant and forceful, is of limited usefulness as a historical source since it related only to George's conflict with the Papacy.

In the last years of his life, George had in his service a man who earned several academic degrees but actually was shallow and mediocre in whatever he attempted to produce. His name Paul was usually connected with a sobriquet Žídek (Little Jew), originating in rumors that, as a child, he was kidnapped from his family home and baptized. At the King's request Žídek compiled a theoretical treatise concerning government and the qualifications of an ideal ruler, entitled *Spravovna*. The book in three parts was a hotch-potch of historical reminiscences, details concerning social conditions in the author's lifetime, food, manners and costumes; all this was interspersed with impertinent remarks, addressed to the King, or, more often, to Queen Johanna. A question can be asked whether George ever did find time to peruse this weird mixture of knowledge and charlatanism from Žídek's pen.

In the time of adversity George was loyally supported by Ctibor Tovačovský of Cimburk, one of the mightiest of the Utraquist lords. Trained in law and political theory, Ctibor was predestined for high positions in public service. In one of them, as a provincial captain, he administered Moravia with distinction and success for twenty-five years. Sensitive to the problems plaguing his country, Ctibor wrote in Czech and dedicated to George an allegorical dialogue, *Hádání pravdy a lži*, etc. (The Truth Disputing with Falsehood Concerning the Clergy's Property and their Domination). Some of its passages refer explicitly to current affairs or have allusions to them; but the bulk of Ctibor's lengthy composition has little connection with either political or military events.

More gifted and skillful than the Utraquist layman was George's diplomatic adviser, John of Rabštejn, Catholic by birth and expert in canon law. When George's conflict with the Papacy entered its critical stage, the learned provost of the Vyšehrad chapter retired from active service to the King and devoted a good deal of time to writing a fictitious conversation among four Czech noblemen concerning the war against George, called inaccurately *Dialogus.*

Rabštejn's Latin work summed up admirably the causes of unrest in Bohemia. It told the author's Italian friend, Giovanni Grasso, and other readers, little about George himself, but portrayed vividly his chief enemy, Zdeněk of Šternberk. Other partners in the conversation were the supreme chamberlain William of Rýzmberk and Rábí and John of Švamberk, Grandmaster of the Knights of the Cross, both presented more sympathetically but less effectively than Zdeněk.

John of Rabštejn undoubtedly possessed the greatest literary talent among the distinguished noblemen who served George in permanent functions or on occasional missions, but he showed no interest in biographical studies or in a systematic recording of the events. Although personally attached to George, Rabštejn would have faced an awkward dilemma if he had attempted to pass from discussion of home affairs to the international aspects of George's case, as nothing worth while could be accomplished in that wide field without reference to the policy of the Holy See.

Research in the Poděbrady era cannot be limited to narrative sources, but has to include official and private correspondence, records of theological disputations, polemical tracts, and other manifestations of interest in religious problems. Compared with other types of historical evidence the narrative sources for 1440–1471 are rather fragmentary and poor both in content and form.

Early in his scholarly career František Palacký made copies of short chronicles or annalistic writings in the Czech language. He published them in his own arrangement in a volume entitled *Staří letopisové čeští* (Old Czech Annalists). Scholars working after Palacký (Josef V. Šimák, Rudolf Urbánek, František M. Bartoš, František Šimek) contributed critical studies of these annalists, but have not succeeded in preparing a more satisfactory edition than Palacký's. The quality of these minor writings varies according to the individual's intellectual ability or access to the sources of information, but it never reaches a high level. Some details recorded by the anonymous authors could not be found elsewhere, but none of them was competent enough to marshal multifarious facts and interpret the great issues of George's reign.

Later the Czech Brethren were careful to leave accounts of the reasons for separation from the Utraquist party and for the steps leading to the foundation of the Unity and the establishment of their own clergy. References were made in such writings, historical or apologetical, to trials and persecutions experienced by both the leaders and the flock. It is no wonder, therefore, that George, if mentioned at all, appears in an unfavorable light. With even less favor the Brethren viewed Queen Johanna whom they suspected of implacable hostility toward their communion. Little that was worth while, indeed, could be culled from the writings of the early Brethren or from the chronicles of the sixteenth century that would help to complete the story of George's reign.

Although primarily occupied with the destinies of his native Bohemia and of the Czech Utraquists, George could not avoid involvements in problems pertaining to the German-speaking areas of the kingdom. As a matter of fact, the hostile attitude of the city of Breslau and its allies became the touchstone of George's statesmanship. Silesian materials of the Poděbrady era are no less numerous and important than the sources of Czech origin. Apart from the official documents, private letters, sermons and invectives, two historical narratives are available to modern historians. Their author, Peter Eschenloer, a native of Nurnberg, served as a secretary in Breslau from 1455 to his death and through his hands passed most of the senate's foreign correspondence. Originally, he intended to write an account of the negotiations of 1458–60 in Latin, but as the conflict continued, Peter resumed writing and carried the narrative on to January 1472. At one time, probably in 1467, Peter decided to produce a German version of his story. As this work got under way, the author apparently became more interested in the German text and carried it beyond January, 1472. While the Latin version, *Historia Wratislaviensis*, in its second part is a mechanical arrangement of official documents, connected loosely by Peter's own words, the German story, *Geschichten der Stadt Breslau*, is more original and subjective. Peter made no secret of his hostility toward the Hussite king and of his own attachment to Matthias; he wrote deliberately in German to reach wider circles of laymen than a Latin book could do. Although he gave a good deal of attention to the struggle with George, he did not neglect other aspects of public life in the populous city and the surrounding territory.

Similarly, his Polish contemporary, Johannes Długosz, allotted only a modest portion of his comprehensive work, *Historiae Polonicae libri tredecim*, to the affairs of Bohemia. Loyal to his sovereign, Canon Długosz favored Casimir's alignment with Bohemia but made no attempt to analyze George's political program or his motives for such bold steps as the appeal of April 14, 1467. Passages devoted by Długosz to the Polish diplomatic negotiations with Prague and vice-versa have considerable value as they contain details not mentioned elsewhere. George's portrait as drawn by Długosz is somewhat brighter than Eschenloer's, but his aversion to Hussitism was so strong that it tipped the balance in George's disfavor.

It is beyond any doubt that none of George's contemporaries wielded the pen as ably as his one-time admirer and ultimately bitter foe, Aeneas Silvius Piccolomini, bishop, cardinal, and for six years head of the Roman Church as Pius II. Aeneas' letter to Cardinal Carvajal of August 21, 1451, reflects vivid impressions gained in Bohemia, and the passage relating to confidential talks with George is particularly effective. On the other hand, not much can be gleaned from Aeneas' historical writings, *Historia bohemica* and *Historia Frederici III imperatoris*, since the former covers the earlier period up to 1458, and the latter deals with the problems of the Empire.

Viewed from Bohemia, Pius II appeared to be one of the key figures in the history of that kingdom from his coronation with the tiara to 1464. He himself did not see events in the same light and he treated the conflict with George as one of the many problems of his pontificate. Consequently, he did not spend too much time in recording it in his autobiographical *Commentarii rerum memorabilium*. More often than in the first part of this work, prepared by the Pope himself, George's name occurs in the continuation of the *Commentarii* and in the polemical tracts of Bishop Rudolf Rüdesheim and Fra Gabriele Rangoni directed against Heimburg's *Apologia*. There are few factual details in these writings which could not be found elsewhere, but they are not without interest for modern historians as they show how vigorous and bitter was the opposition of the protagonists of the Catholic cause against the two leaders of the Czech Utraquism, George, and even in a higher degree, John of Rokycany.

In modern times George's personality, ideas, and deeds have attracted scholars of various nationalities, creeds, and convictions. Those who were able to detach themselves coolly from the problems of his life and political career can be counted on one's fingers. The struggles in which, indeed, he had been *magna pars* were diagnosed as medieval prototypes of the conflicts harrassing George's homeland in the nineteenth and twentieth centuries.

In the ambitious plan of *Dějiny národu českého v Čechách a v Moravě* (History of the Czech People in Bohemia and Moravia) evolved by František Palacký (1798–1876) after his appointment as the official historiographer, George of Poděbrady figured prominently both as governor and as king; his epoch was to be treated in detail. In fact, the fourth of the five volumes of the *Dějiny* had been devoted to George's lifetime. In its first part, Palacký sketched the interregnum after the death of Albrecht II and the reign of Ladislav Posthumus, giving high prominence to the youthful Hussite leader. In the second part, the historian portrayed, with fine understanding and sincere sympathy, George as a king. The fourth volume was written in the eighteen-fifties, in the era of soulless absolutism, and its compiling alleviated the depression that preyed upon Palacký since the failure of the constitutional experiment in 1848–49.

The fourth volume of Palacký's *Dějiny*, published simultaneously in Czech and German, attracted many attentive readers in Bohemia and abroad. One of them was J. G. Droysen who in his *Geschichte der preussischen Politik* paid a good deal of attention to the relations of Brandenburg with Bohemia. In the passages describing the chaotic conditions in the Empire the name of George was mentioned in connection with both the Emperor Frederick III and the Hohenzollern princes, especially Albrecht Achilles. One of Droysen's pupils in Berlin, Max Jordan, compiled a monograph, *Das Königthum Georg's von Podiebrad* (1861). Inspired by both Palacký and Droysen, the young scholar, who later distinguished himself in the history of fine arts, conceived his book as a contribution to the knowledge of the growth of secular states in opposition to the Catholic Church.

With both Palacký's *Dějiny* and Jordan's book at hand a French student of Central European affairs, Saint-René Taillandier, wrote for the *Revue des deux mondes* a series of chapters on the appealing aspects of George's life and included them later in his book *Bohême et Hongrie* (1869). His skillful confrontation of critical comments on George's policy was distinctly more favorable to Palacký than to Jordan, in whose thought he detected strong and somewhat intrusive leanings toward Hegelianism.

Palacký's *Dějiny* encountered vigorous opposition among his German contemporaries. In general, the German scholars in Bohemia were stiffer in their attitude than the critics living in the more distant learned centers. Historians of Protestant origin and of enlightened philosophical orientation showed little enthusiasm for Palacký's idyllic picture of the early Czech society, but wrote with respect of the sections dealing with the high and late Middle Ages. Palacký's interpretation of the Hussite movement stirred up a violent storm in conservative circles. Constantin Höfler, Johann Loserth, and some lesser lights concentrated on the life of the Reformer, John Hus, so as to invalidate Palacký's evaluation of his originality and importance. Other polemical writers chose John Žižka or the Hussite king as their targets.

The Poděbrady era was the field of specialization of Adolf Bachmann who began to lecture at the Carolo-Ferdinandean University, Prague, while Palacký was still alive. Bachmann turned away from the line marked by such moderate critics of George's policy as Hermann Markgraf and set out to revise Palacký's views. After some minor studies Bachmann published, in 1878, a book *Böhmen und seine Nachbarländer unter Georg von Podiebrad, 1458–1461*, dealing with George's endeavors to consolidate Bohemia internally and to make it safe against any danger from abroad. The German scholar made no secret of his antipathy to George as well as of his disagreement with Palacký, not in minute details but in the crucial points. Bachmann's sketch of George's life (in *Allgemeine deutsche Biographie*, vol. VIII) had the same undertones as his monographic studies and it foreshadowed his final account in the second volume of his *Geschichte Böhmens* (1905). Although written in Prague, Bachmann's works were marked by reflections of the Breslau struggles and echoed the animosities of George's fifteenth-century adversaries in Silesia.

Václav Vladivoj Tomek, who was for some time closely connected with Palacký as his research assistant and tutor of his children, viewed the Hussite movement from a different angle. Brought up in Catholic schools and loyal to the ruling dynasty, Tomek resented instinctively any revolutionary tendencies in politics no less than in religion. He wrote in his *Dějepis města Prahy* (A History of the city of Prague) with far more restraint than Palacký when dealing with John Hus and the Hussite theologians. Tomek's outline of Žižka's life and the relevant sections in the *Dějepis*, while not enthusiastic, were sympathetic, putting Žižka's statesmanship and simple belief in the righteousness of the Hussite cause higher than his military genius and successful campaigns. Tomek wrote in the same vein when he advanced in his story to the perplexities of the Poděbrady era. The sixth book of the *Dějepis*, dealing with the period 1436–1460, followed simply after its predecessor. To the seventh volume, devoted to the years 1460–1478, Tomek wrote a preface, sober and quiet in words but firm in its positive evaluation of George's reign. No name was mentioned, but Tomek's readers were versed enough in the contemporary production to interpret his innuendos and to fill in the names.

Tomek explained George's interventions in the affairs of the Empire by his deep concern for the welfare and security of Bohemia. He also dissociated himself discreetly from George's severe judges in a matter so delicate for a true son of the Church as George's coronation oath and its implications. Viewing George as a layman and statesman, Tomek absolved him of the charge of perjury and obstinacy—the Compacts were regarded by the Hussites as valid and the majority of the Czechs adhered to them so faithfully that George, if attempting to placate Rome, would have run into a deadly conflict with the very kernel of his own people. George, as portrayed by Tomek, was a worthy successor of the earlier rulers of Bohemia from the Přemysl and the Luxemberg houses, a restorer of peace and prosperity after two decades of war and devastation, a national king.

In the same year as Bachmann's study of George's reign in 1458–61, there appeared in Paris a book *Huss et la guerre des Hussites*. Its author, Ernest Denis, of Huguenot ancestry, submitted to the Sorbonne also a Latin thesis *De Antonio Marini*, an attempt to elucidate the activities of a French diplomat for many years in George's service. It is possible to assume that Taillandier's book, *Bohême et Hongrie*, revealed to Denis the dynamic elements in George's policy.

The first indirect contact with the Hussite king was soon followed by more thorough studies, for which Denis equipped himself with the knowledge of both German and Czech. He spent three years in Prague (1872–75), was introduced to the study of Hussite sources by Palacký, and came to know also the one-time student of the Ecole des Chartes, V. V. Tomek. In the first part of his *Fin de l'indépendance Bohéme* (Paris, 1890), Denis assigned to George the dominant place as the unifier of the kingdom after the loosening of the traditional ties by wars, religious dissensions, and racial antagonism. The French author felt no obligation to stress the national interests weighing on Palacký's and Tomek's minds, but took a broader view and investigated George's conflict with the Papacy. Discreet but critical references to the relevant passages in Ludwig Pastor's *Geschichte der Päpste,* corrections of Bachmann's severe verdict, and mild polemics with the biographer of Pius II, Georg Voigt, placed Denis among the sympathetic judges of the Hussite king. Refraining from a mechanical projection of modern issues and terminology into the remote eras, Denis concluded (using the English saying) that George was "the right man in the right place." He compared him with Henry IV of France when pointing out his tolerant spirit and concern for the unity of the kingdom of Bohemia.

Denis' *Fin de l'indépendance* was soon translated into Czech. The translator, Jindřich Vančura, not only did justice to the rhetorical style of the original but supplemented the author's critical notes by materials drawn from the less accessible sources and from secondary pieces of evidence. The Czech readers accepted Denis' work as a sequel to Palacký and Tomek. In fact, Denis' lively and captivating sketch of the Poděbrady era had a wider appeal among the Czech readers than Tomek's plain and not too inspiring prose or Palacký's monumental but rather archaic narrative.

The Czech version of the *Fin de l'indépendance* had on the title-page 1893 as the year of publication. This was little more than a decade since the division of the Carolo-Ferdinandean University (as that ancient institution was called under the Habsburg regime) and five years since Tomek's retirement from active service. Among the historians teaching at the Czech university, Jaroslav Goll, though not senior chronologically, held the most prominent position. To his initiative has to be attributed the foundation of a seminar in which he trained young talents for research and scholarly production. It was Goll's great and noble ambition to keep together his pupils as a "school" and to undertake with their help a systematic revision of the works of the Romantic generation. In view of its enormous popularity and undiminished appeal to the reading public, Palacký's *Dějiny* seemed to deserve a thorough reexamination more urgently than any other book. In the early nineties Goll assigned to his students several topics relating to the Poděbrady era and inspired some minor studies or publications of sources. He himself was keenly interested in the early development of the Unity of the Czech Brethren, but apart from critical studies of that subject he did not show much interest in the latter part of the fifteenth century.

Not the master Goll himself, but one of his most gifted pupils, Václav Novotný, passed from preliminary studies to writing a new history of the Czech people according to the precepts and methods acquired in Goll's seminar. The *České dějiny* (Czech History) as Novotný modestly entitled his work, aimed at two goals: the replacement of Palacký's five volumes by a more up-to-date survey, and a continuation of the latter's story to extend to modern times. Novotný reserved for himself the early part, up to 1436, and invited three congenial scholars to do the rest. One of them, Rudolf Urbánek, accepted a comparatively light assignment, the period from 1437 to Palacký's terminal point, 1526. Conceived in a hopeful atmosphere and inaugurated in

1912 with its first volume, Novotný's project was destined to remain incomplete. Its originator and chief editor reached only 1273, in his painstaking description of Czech national life in the Middle Ages, so that a wide gap separated the finished portion from Urbánek's starting point, 1437, to be filled, partly at least, by new collaborators, Josef V. Šimák, Josef Šusta, and František M. Bartoš.

Prepared by earlier research in the sources of the fifteenth century and complete mastery of the critical literature, Urbánek produced the first volume of *Věk Poděbradský* (Poděbrady era) in 1915, and started at once on the second one, so that it was published in 1918. A longer interval separated that date from the appearance of the third volume in 1930. The causes of an even longer delay were various and need not be retold in this connection. The fourth volume, and the last that was completed by Urbánek, was published in 1962, several weeks before his death. The description of the Poděbrady era filled four large books with almost four thousand pages but it did not cover it completely. The author did not go beyond the year 1464, regarding the death of Pius II as a turning point in George's fortunes.

Brought up in the positivist school, Urbánek genuinely believed that he would be able to write a definitive study of George's life and reign if he explored all the sources of information and re-examined in their light the long-standing controversies. He worked with devout concentration and hardly anything connected with the topic, directly or indirectly, escaped his notice. He published several monographs on such intricate problems as the death of King Ladislav in 1457, so that he would not be obliged to dwell on all minutiae in his general survey; but while reducing the load, he spent more time in the critical excursuses than he had foreseen in the preliminary estimate.

In the busy decade following the appearance of the second volume, Urbánek produced a succinct biography of his hero and called it *Husitský král* (The Hussite King). It was published in 1926. In the selection of the title Urbánek followed Alois Jirásek, a novelist of boundless popularity among Czech readers, who drew inspiration for his historical tales from the original documents as well as from the scholarly works of Palacký and Tomek.

With the *magnum opus* unfinished, the biography of the *Husitský král* can be used as a source of information concerning Urbánek's point of view. Endeavoring to observe the principle of objectivity, Urbánek nevertheless came under the spell of a story so fascinating and tragic as George's phenomenal rise from the aristocratic circles to governorship and kingship, followed, after a bright interlude, by his inextricable involvement in the conflicts with opposition in his own kingdom, with the son-in-law and one time ally, Matthias of Hungary, and above all with the Papacy. Of all the ideas and schemes propounded by his hero, Urbánek valued most George's effort first to administer the kingdom and later to rule over it as a head of two peoples, the Czechs and the Germans, inhabiting the five provinces of the kingdom of Bohemia, as well as the Hussites and the Catholics. While the narrative in the four volumes of *Věk Poděbradský* suffered from frequent digressions—the longest and the most important one is a detailed account of the Unity of the Czech Brethren in George's lifetime—and from meticulous exploration of all biographical details, *Husitský král* has sound proportions and reads well.

It is of some interest that, writing in Czech, Urbánek uses as a rule the diminutive form of the king's name, Jiřík (instead of Jiří), the English equivalent of which would be "Georgie." In doing so, he followed the sources in

Czech, German, and Latin, in which the diminutive (Girzig, Georgius alias Gersicus) was inserted because it was commonly used among the King's followers and became so common that even his opponents adopted it. In employing it for his own writings, Urbánek expressed more eloquently than any panegyric could do his admiration for the King's winning personality, for his firmness in religious convictions, dexterity in negotiations, and optimistic disposition in adversity as well as in good fortune. Had the *Věk Poděbradský* been completed, it would have been the worthiest monument to the Hussite king that a human hand could accomplish.

The research in the Poděbrady era was not always oriented toward a biography of the King's dominant figure. A good deal of attention was given to religious problems of the middle and late fifteenth century. Two themes tempted both the Czech and foreign scholars: the notable, often disturbed career of the spiritual head of the Hussite party, John of Rokycany, and the rise of the Unity of Czech Brethren under George. Less work has been done in other fields, social, economic, and intellectual. George's governorship and reign restored to Bohemia its former administrative and constitutional order and gave it considerable prestige in international relations; but it did not stimulate scholarship, literature, and fine arts in any remarkable way. Economic prosperity, which had set in soon after the suppression of religious and private feuds and which continued, despite George's wars with the rebels and their Hungarian ally, prepared the ground for the spread of humanism in Bohemia and for the revival of Gothic art, especially architecture. Those activities, however, really began only after George's death.

The efforts to elucidate the Poděbrady era turned in various directions. Contemporary sources, narrative as well as documentary, are mostly available in earlier but not too satisfactory reprints, or in modern editions. One omission is rather distressing. A large collection of George's correspondence, often referred to as *Cancellaria regis Georgii* and preserved in several manuscripts, has not been published as a whole. Palacký and other scholars included selected documents in their editions, but none attempted to arrange the material for publication in a single volume.

George's modern biographers have today at their disposal a large number of minor texts, as a rule introduced by a critical study. They are scattered in learned periodicals. The same is true of analytical studies, articles, and critical remarks on George and his contemporaries. A careful sifting of all such publications has to precede any attempt to compile a critical bibliography. Similarly, the titles of general works on Europe in George's time and of monographs touching only lightly on the subject have to be chosen conscientiously to avoid a merely mechanical arrangement but rather to separate distinctive studies from the mass of derivative contributions. It is, after all, the purpose of a selective bibliography: not to confuse but to guide the reader from a comprehensive work to which it is appended, to the detailed studies of the various facets of the subject.

II. Selected Bibliography *

A. SOURCE MATERIALS

Aeneas, Silvius Piccolomini, Pii Secundi P. M. Commentarii rerum memorabilium . . . a R. D. Joanne Gobelino . . . compositi. Quibus hac editione accedunt Jacobi Piccolominei, cardinalis Papiensis commentarii . . . eiusdemque epistolae. Frankfurt, 1614.

Aeneas, Silvius, Historia Bohemica (many editions).

Aeneas, Silvius, Historia rerum Frederici III. imperatoris. In: Kollar Ad. Fr., Analecta monumentorum omnis aevi Vindobonensia, vol. II. Vienna, 1762.

Bachmann, Ad., Briefe und Akten zur österreichisch–deutschen Geschichte im Zeitalter Kaiser Friedrich III. FRA, 2 Abt., vol. XLIV. Vienna, 1885.

Bachmann, Ad., Urkunden und Aktenstücke zur österreichischen Geschichte im Zeitalter Kaiser Friedrichs III. und König Georgs von Böhmen (1440–1471). FRA, 2 Abt., vol. XLII. Vienna, 1879.

Bachmann, Ad., Urkundliche Nachträge zur österreichisch–deutschen Geschichte im Zeitalter Kaiser Friedrich III. FRA, 2 Abt., vol. XLVI. Vienna, 1892.

Bidlo, Jaroslav, Akty Jednoty bratrské. Vol. I, II. Brno, 1915, 1923.

Čelakovský, Jar., Traktát podkomořího Vaňka Valečovského proti panování kněžskému. Zprávy o zasedání Král. české spol. nauk. Tř. I. Prague, 1881.

Chmel, Jos., Urkunden, Briefe und Actenstücke zur Geschichte der Habsburgischen Fürsten K. Ladislaus Posthumus, Erzherzog Albrecht VI. und Herzog Siegmund von Österreich, 1443–1473. FRA, 2. Abt., vol. II. Vienna, 1850.

Cochlaeus, Joh., Historiae Hussitarum libri duodecim. Mainz, 1549.

Comines, Phil. de, Mémoirs (nouvelle édition augmentée par M. l'abbé Lenglet du Fresnoy). Vol. II, III, IV. Paris, 1747.

Daňhelka, J., Husitské skladby budyšínského rukopisu. Prague, 1952.

Długosz, J., Historiae Polonicae libri tredecim. Leipzig, 1711, 1712. (A modern edition by Alex. Przezdziecki in J. Długosz Opera omnia, vol. XIV, Cracow, 1878.)

Dogiel, M., Codex diplomaticus regni Poloniae et m. d. Lithuaniae. Vol. I. Wilno, 1758.

Fraknói, V., Matthiae Corvini . . . epistolae ad Romanos pontifices datae et ab eis acceptae. In: Monumenta Vaticana Hungariae, ser. I, vol. VI. Budapest, 1891.

Fraknói, V., Mátyás király levelei. Külügyi osztály. Vol. I (1458–1479). Budapest, 1893.

Gemeiner, C. Th., Regensburgische Chronik. Vol. III. Regensburg, 1821.

Goldast, Melchior, Commentarii de regni Bohemiae incorporatarumque provinciarum iuribus ac privilegiis. Frankfurt, 1719.

Goldast, M., Zwo rechtliche Bedencken der Succession und Erbfolge . . . in beiden Königreichen Hungarn und Böheimb. Frankfurt, 1627.

---

* Abbreviations: AÖG = Archiv für Kunde österreichischer Geschichtsquellen; Archiv für österreichische Geschichte. FRA = Fontes rerum Austriacarum (Österreichische Geschichtsquellen).

Gragg, Fl. A., and Gabel, L. C., The Commentaries of Pius II. In: Smith College studies in history. Vols. XXII, XXV, XXX, XXXV, XLIII. Northampton, Mass., 1937–1957.

Höfler, C., Das kaiserliche Buch des Markgrafen Albrecht Achilles, 1440–1470. In: Quellensammlung für fränkische Geschichte. Vol. II. Bayreuth, 1850.

Höfler, C., Geschichtsschreiber der hussitischen Bewegung in Böhmen. Vol. II. (Containing among others N. de Pelhrzimow Chronicon Taboritarum.) FRA, 1. Abt. (Scriptores), vol. VI. Vienna, 1865.

Hrdina, C., Commentarius brevis et iucundus itineris atque peregrinationis . . . susceptae . . . a . . . Leone, libero barone de Rosmital et Blatna. Prague, 1951.

Hrdina, K., and Ryba, B., Píseň o vítězství u Domažlic od Vavřince z Březové. Prague, 1951.

Hrubý, V., Archivum Coronae Regni Bohemiae. Prague, 1928–1935.

Joachimsohn, P., Die Streitschrift des Minoriten Gabriel v. Verona gegen den Böhmenkönig Georg Podiebrad vom Jahre 1467. In: Programm zum Jahresbericht des k. Real-gymnasium zu Augsburg 1895/6. Augsburg, 1896.

Kaprinai, St., Hungaria diplomatica temporibus Matthiae de Hunyad, regis Hungariae. Vol. II. Vienna, 1771.

Katona, St., Historia critica regum Hungariae stirpis mixtae. Vol. XIII, XIV, XV. Kalocsa. 1790–1792.

[Kelcz, Imre], Epistolae Matthiae Corvini regis Hungariae ad pontifices, imperatores, reges, principes aliosque viros illustres datae. Cassovia (Košice), 1764.

Kremer, C. J., Geschichte des Kurfürsten Friedrichs des Ersten von der Pfaltz. Vol. II (Urkunden). Frankfurt-Leipzig, 1765.

Kunisch, J. G., Peter Eschenloers Geschichten der Stadt Breslau, oder Denkwürdigkeiten seiner Zeit vom Jahre 1440 bis 1479. Breslau, 1827/8.

Letts, M. H. I., The Travels of Leo of Rozmital through Germany, Flanders, England, France, Spain, Portugal, and Italy, 1465–7. Cambridge, 1957.

Lewicki, Anatol, Codex epistolaris saec. XV. Vol. III. In: Monumenta medii aevi historica res gestas Poloniae illustrantia. Vol. XIV. Cracow, 1894.

Loserth, J., Die Denkschrift des Breslauer Domherrn Nikolaus Tempelfeld von Brieg über die Wahl Georgs von Podiebrad zum König von Böhmen. AÖG, vol. LXI. Vienna, 1880.

Mansi, J. D., Pii II. olim Aeneae Sylvii Piccolominei . . . orationes politicae et ecclesiasticae. 1755–7.

Markgraf, H., Historia Wratislaviensis von Mag. Peter Eschenloer. In: Scriptores rerum Silesiacarum, vol. VII. Breslau, 1872.

Markgraf, H., Politische Correspondenz Breslaus im Zeitalter Georgs von Podiebrad. In: Scriptores rerum Silesiacarum, vol. VIII, IX. Breslau, 1873, 1874.

Müller, J. J., Des Heiligen Römischen Reichs Teutscher Nation Reichstagstheatrum . . . Vol. I, II. Jena, 1713.

Nagy, I., and Nyáry A., Magyar diplomácziai emlékek Mátyás királý korából. In: Monumenta Hungariae Historica, Acta externa. Vol. I, II. Budapest, 1875, 1877.

Nejedlý, Z., Prameny k synodám strany pražské a táborské v letech 1441–1444. Prague, 1900.

Neumann, Aug., Francouzská hussitica. In: Studie a texty k náboženským dějinám českým. Vol. IV. Olomouc, 1925.

Odložilík, O., Jan Blahoslav: O původu Jednoty bratrské a řádu v ní. Prague, 1928.

Palacký, Fr., Archiv český. Vol. I–VI. Prague, 1840–1872.

Palacký, Fr., Staří letopisové čeští od roku 1378 do 1527. In: Scriptores rerum Bohemicarum. Vol. III. Prague, 1829.

Palacký, Fr., Urkundliche Beiträge zur Geschichte des Hussitenkrieges in den Jahren 1419–1436. Vol. I, II. Prague, 1872, 1873.

Palacký, Fr., Urkundliche Beiträge zur Geschichte Böhmens und seiner Nachbarländer im Zeitalter Georgs von Podiebrad. FRA, 2. Abt. vol. 20. Vienna, 1860.

Pastor, L., Ungedruckte Akten zur Geschichte der Päpste. Vol. I (1376–1464). Freiburg i. Br., 1904.

Patera, Ad., Poselství králo Jiřího do Říma k papeži r. 1462. In: Archiv český. Vol. VIII. Prague, 1888.

Priebatsch, F., Politische Correspondenz des Kurfürsten Albrecht Achilles (1470–1474). In: Publicationen aus den k. Preussischen Staatsarchiven. Vol. LIX. Leipzig, 1894.

Raynaldi, Odorico, Annales ecclesiastici. Vol. IX, X. Lucca, 1752, 1753.

Ryba, Boh., Jana z Rabštejna dialogus. Prague, 1946.

Rynešová, B., Listář a listinář Oldřicha z Rožmberka. Vol. I–IV. Prague, 1929–1954.

Šimek, Fr., M. Jan Rokycana obránce pravdy a zákona božího. Prague, 1949.

Šimek, Fr., Staré letopisy české. Prague, 1937.

Šimek, Fr., and Kaňák M., Staré letopisy české. Prague, 1959.

Tadra, Ferd., K pobytu Jana Kapistrana v zemích českých. In: Věstník Král. čes. spol. nauk Tř. I. Prague, 1889.

Teleki, József, Hunyadik kora Magyarországon. Vol. X, XI. Budapest, 1853, 1855.

Theiner, Aug., Vetera monumenta historica Hungariam sacram illustrantia. Vol. II. Rome, 1860.

Theiner, Aug., Vetera monumenta Poloniae et Lithuaniae . . . historiam illustrantia. Rome, 1860.

Tobolka, Z. V., Hilaria Litoměřického traktát k panu Janovi z Rozenberka. Prague, 1898.

Tobolka, Z. V., Mistra Pavla Žídka Spravovna. Prague, 1908.

Tovačovský, z Cimburka C., Hádání Pravdy a Lži o kněžské zboží a panování jich. Prague, 1539.

Truhlář, Jos., Manuálník M. Václava Korandy. Prague, 1888.

Urbánek, Rud., O volbě Jiřího z Poděbrad za krále českého. Prague, 1958.

Wolkan, Rud., Der Briefwechsel des Eneas Silvius Piccolomini. FRA, 2. Abt. Vol. LXI, LXII, LXVII, LXVIII. Vienna, 1909, 1912, 1918.

Wratislaw, A. H., Diary of an Embassy from King George of Bohemia to Louis XI of France in the Year of Grace 1464. London, 1871.

B. SECONDARY WORKS

(a) General Histories

Aubin, H. (ed.), Geschichte Schlesiens. Vol. I (1526). Breslau, 1938.

Bachmann, Ad., Deutsche Reichsgeschichte im Zeitalter Friedrich III. und Max. I. Leipzig, 1884–1894.

Baronio, Cesare, Annales ecclesiastici. Vol. XVIII, XIX. Köln, 1693, 1694.

Calmette, Jos., and Déprez, E., L'Europe occidentale de la fin du XIVme siècle aux guerres d'Italie. In: Glotz G. Histoire du moyen âge. Vol. VII. Paris, 1939.

Dąbrowski, J., Dzieje Polski średniowiecznej. Vol. II (1333–1506). Cracow, 1926.

Długoborski, W., Gierowski, J., and Maleczyński, K., Dzieje Wrocławia do roku 1807. Warszawa, 1958.

Droysen, J. G., Geschichte der Preussischen Politik. Vol. II, pt. 1. 2nd ed. Leipzig, 1868.

Dvornik, Fr., The Slavs in European History and Civilization. Vol. II. New Brunswick, 1962.

Fessler, J. A., Die Geschichte der Ungern und ihrer Landsassen. Vol. IV, V. Leipzig-Wien, 1816, 1822.

Gilmore, Myron P., The World of Humanism 1453–1517. In: The Rise of modern Europe, vol. II. New York, 1952.

Grünhagen, C., Geschichte Schlesiens. Vol. I. Gotha, 1884.

Hóman, B., and Szekfü, Gy., Magyar történet. Vol. II. Budapest, 1936.

Huber, Alf., Geschichte Österreichs. Vol. III. Gotha, 1888.

Kalousek, Josef, České státní právo. 2nd ed. Prague, 1892.

Kraus, Victor, Deutsche Geschichte im Ausgange des Mittelalters. Vol. I (1438–1486). Stuttgart, 1905.

Lützow, Fr. Count, Bohemian Literature. London, 1899.

Manteuffel, T., Grosfeld, L., and Leśnodorski, B., Historia Polski. Vol. I. Warszawa, 1955.

Pastor, L., Geschichte der Päpste seit dem Ausgang des Mittelalters. 12th ed. Vol. I, II. Freiburg-Rome, 1955.

Previté, Orton C., and Brooke, Z. N. (eds.), The Cambridge Medieval History. Vol. VIII. Cambridge, 1936.

Thomson, Harrison S., Czechoslovakia in European History. 2nd ed. Princeton, 1953.

Uhlirz, K., and Uhlirz, Math., Handbuch der Geschichte Österreichs und seiner Nachbarländer Böhmen und Ungarn. Vol. I. Vienna, 1927.

(b)　Books on King George and His Times

Bachmann, Ad., Böhmen und seine Nachbarländer unter Georg von Podiebrad, 1458–1461. Prague, 1878.

Bachmann, Ad., Geschichte Böhmens. Vol. II. Gotha, 1905.

Bartoš, F. M., Literární činnost M. Jana Rokycany, M. Jana Příbrama, M. Petra Payna. Prague, 1928.

Brock, Peter, The Political and Social Doctrines of the Unity of Czech Brethren. The Hague, 1957.

Čapek, J. B., Jiří z Poděbrad v české literatuře. Prague, 1940.

Denis, E., De Antonio Marini et de Bohemiae ratione politica. Angoulême, 1878.

Denis, E., Fin de l'indépendance Bohéme. Vol. I (George de Podiébrad. Les Jagellons). Paris, 1890.

Düx, J. M., Der deutsche Kardinal Nicolaus von Cusa. Regensburg, 1847.

Fraknói, V., Matthias Corvinus. Freiburg, 1891.

Goll, Jar., Chelčický a Jednota v XV. století. Prague, 1916.

Gómez, Canedo Lino, Un español al servicio de la Santa Sede Don Juan de Carvajal. Madrid, 1947.

Heymann, F. G., John Žižka and the Hussite Revolution. Princeton, 1955.

Hocks, Else, Pius II. und der Halbmond. Freiburg i. Br., 1941.

Hofer, Joh., Johannes von Capestrano. Innsbruck, 1936.

Joachimsohn, P., Gregor Heimburg. Bamberg, 1891.

Koebner, R., Der Widerstand Breslaus gegen George von Podiebrad. Breslau, 1916.

Lützow, Fr. Count, The Hussite Wars. London, 1914.

Meulen, Jacob ter, Der Gedanke der internationalen Organisation in seiner Entwicklung. Vol. I (1300–1800). The Hague, 1917.

Mohler, Lud., Kardinal Bessarion als Theologe, Humanist und Staatsman. Paderborn, 1923.

Müller, Jos. T., Geschichte der Böhmischen Brüder. Vol. I. Herrnhut, 1922.

Müller, Jos. T., and Bartoš, F. M., Dějiny Jednoty bratrské. Prague, 1923.

Palacký, Fr., Dějiny národu českého v Čechách i v Moravě. Vol. III, IV. 3rd ed. Prague, 1877.

Palacký, Fr., Geschichte von Böhmen. Vol. III, IV. Prague, 1845–1860.

Palacký, Fr., Zeugenverhör über den Tod König Ladislaw's von Ungarn und Böhmen im Jahre 1457. Prague, 1856.

Picotti, G. B., La dieta di Mantova e la politica de' Veneziani. Venice, 1912.

Říčan, Rud., Die Böhmischen Brüder, ihr Ursprung und ihre Geschichte. Berlin, 1961.

Říčan, Rud., Das Reich Gottes in den böhmischen Ländern; Geschichte des tschechischen Protestantismus. Stuttgart, 1957.

Saint-René, Taillandier, Bohême et Hongrie. Paris, 1869.

Schwitzky, H., Der europäische Fürstenbund Georgs von Podiebrad. Marburg, 1907.

Šimek, Fr., Učení M. Jana Rokycany. Prague, 1938.

Tomek, V. V., Dějepis města Prahy. Vol. VI, VII. 2nd ed. Prague, 1906.

Urbánek, Rud., Dvě studie o době poděbradské. Brno, 1929.

Urbánek, Rud., Husitský král. Prague, 1926.

Urbánek, Rud., Konec Ladislava Pohrobka. Prague, 1924.

Urbánek, Rud., Lipany a konec polních vojsk. Prague, 1934.

Urbánek, Rud., Věk Poděbradský. In: České dějiny. Vol. III, 1,2,3,4. Prague, 1915, 1918, 1930, 1962.

Urbánek, Rud., Vladislav Varnenčik. Prague, 1937.

Urbánek, Rud., Z husitského věku. Prague, 1957.

Voigt, G., Enea Silvio de Piccolomini als Papst Pius II. Berlin, 1856, 1863.

(c) Articles

Bachmann, Ad., Ein Jahr Böhmischer Geschichte. Georgs von Podiebrad Wahl, Krönung und Anerkennung. AÖG. Vol. LIV. Vienna, 1876.

Bachmann, Ad., Die Wiedervereinigung der Lausitz mit Böhmen (1462). AÖG. Vol. LXIV. Vienna, 1882.

Bartoš, F. M., Návrh krále Jiřího na utvoření svazu evropských států. Jihočeský sborník historický. Vol. XII. Tábor, 1941.

Cibulka, Josef, Český řád korunovační. Časopis katolického duchovenstva. Prague, 1934.

Ermisch, Hubert, Studien zur Geschichte der sächsisch-böhmischen Beziehungen in den Jahren 1464–1468. Neues Archiv für sächsische Geschichte und Alterthumskunde. Vol. I. Dresden, 1880.

Ermisch, Hubert, Studien . . . in den Jahren 1468–1471. Neues Archiv . . . Vol. II. Dresden, 1881.

Fink, K. A., Der Kreuzablass gegen Georg Podiebrad in Süd- und Westdeutschland. Quellen und Forschungen aus italienischen Archiven. Vol. XXIV. Rome, 1932–3.

Heymann, F. G., City Rebellions in 15th century Bohemia and their ideological and sociological background. The Slavonic and East European Review. Vol. XL, no. 95. London, 1962.

Heymann, F. G., The Death of King Ladislav: Historiographical Echoes of a Suspected Crime. The Canadian Historical Association. Report 1961.

Heymann, F. G., John Rokycana—Church Reformer between Hus and Luther. Church History. Vol. XXVIII. 1959.

Höfler, C., Böhmische Studien. AÖG. Vol. XII. Vienna, 1854.

Jorga, N., Un auteur de projets de Croisades Antoine Marini. In: Études d'histoire du Moyen Age dediées à Gabriel Monod. Paris, 1896.

Kalina, Tomáš, Václav Křižanovský. Český Časopis Historický. Vol. V. Prague, 1899.

Kalina, T., Hilarius Litoměřický. Český Časopis Historický. Vol. V. Prague, 1899.

Kaminsky, H., Pius Aeneas among the Taborites. Church History. Vol. XXVIII. Chicago, 1959.

Loserth, J., Die Krönungsorder der Könige von Böhmen. AÖG. Vol. LIV. Vienna, 1876.

Markgraf, H., Das Verhältniss des K. Georg von Böhmen zu Pius II (1462–1464). Forschungen zur deutschen Geschichte. Vol. IX. Göttingen, 1869.

Markgraf, H., Über Georgs von Podiebrad Project eines christlichen Fürstenbundes zur Vertreibung der Turken aus Europa und Herstellung des allgemeinen Friedens innerhalb der Christenheit. Historische Zeitschrift. Vol. XXI. 1869.

Nejedlý, Z., Česká missie Jana Kapistrana. Časopis musea království českého. Vol. LXXIV. Prague, 1900.

Novotný, Václav, Über den Tod des Königs Ladislaus Posthumus. Věstník Král. české spol. nauk Tř. I. Prague, 1906.

Odložilík, O., Bohemia and Poland in Medieval Plans of European Organization. Bulletin of the Polish Institute. Vol. I. New York, 1942/3.

Odložilík, O., George of Poděbrady and Bohemia to the Pacification of Silesia, 1459. University of Colorado Studies. Vol. I, no. 3. Boulder, 1941.

Odložilík, O., Problems of the Reign of George of Poděbrady. Slavonic and East European Review. Vol. XX. 1941.

Papée, Fr., Polityka Polska w czasie upadku Jerzego z Podiebradu. Polska Akad. Um. Rozprawy . . . wydzialu hist.-filoz. Vol. VIII. Cracow, 1878.

Paulová, Milada, L'Empire Byzantin et les Tchèques avant la chute de Constantinople. Byzantinoslavica. Vol. XIV. Prague, 1953.

Pažout, Jul., König Georg von Böhmen und die Concilfrage im Jahre 1467. AÖG. Vol. XL. Vienna, 1869.

Polišenský, Jos., Bohemia, the Turks and the Christian Commonwealth (1467–1620). Byzantinoslavica. Vol. XIV. Prague, 1953.

Polišenský, Josef, Problémy zahraniční politiky Jiřího z Poděbrad. Acta Univ. Palackianae Olomucensis, Fac. Philosophica. Historica. Vol. I. Olomouc, 1960.

Polišenský, Jos. (ed.), Sborník přednášek věnovaných životu a dílu anglického husity Petra Payna-Engliše. Univ. Carolina. Vol. III. 1957–(IX) Historica. Prague, 1957.

Ryba, B., Ozvuk královské volby Jiříkovy na universitě Karlově. Časopis Matice Moravské. Vol. LXVII. Brno, 1947.

Salač, A., Constantinople et Prague en 1452. Rozpravy čsl. akademie věd. Vol. LXVIII, no. 11. Prague, 1958.

Schmidt, O. E., Des Böhmenkönig Georg von Podiebrad Lösung von Kirchenbann und sein Tod. Neues Archiv für sächsische Geschichte. Vol. LIX. Dresden, 1938.

Solovjev, Alex., Corona Regni. Przewodnik historyczno-prawny. Vol. IV. Lwów, 1933.

Spinka, M., Peter Chelčický, Spiritual Father of the Unitas Fratrum. Church History. Vol. XII. 1943.

Tobolka, Z. V., Styky krále českého Jiřího z Poděbrad s králem polským Kazimírem. Časopis Matice Moravské. Vol. XXII. Brno, 1898.

Urbánek, Rud., K historii doby Jiskrovy na Slovensku a ve východní Moravě. Věstník Král. čes. spol. nauk. Tř. I. Prague, 1939.

Urbánek, Rud., K historii husitské Moravy. Časopis Matice Moravské. Vol. LXIII–LXIV. Brno, 1939–40.

Urbánek, Rud., První utrakvistický humanista Šimon ze Slaného. Listy filologické. Vol. LXV. Prague, 1938.

Urbánek, Rud., Prvních sto let utrakvismu (1419–1526). In: Československá vlastivěda. Vol. IV. Prague, 1932.

Urbánek, Rud., Volba Jiřího z Poděbrad za krále českého. Sborník příspěvků k dějinám hl. města Prahy. Vol. V. Prague, 1932.

Urbánek, Rud., Ženy husitského krále: Kunhuta ze Šternberka a Johana z Rožmitála. In: Královny, kněžny a velké ženy české. Prague, 1940.

Wallner, J., Iglaus Widerstand gegen die Anerkennung Georgs von Podiebrad. Mitteilungen des Vereins für Geschichte der Deutschen in Böhmen. Vol. XXII. Prague, 1884.

POSTSCRIPT

Several books and articles dealing with King George and his period appeared while my manuscript was in the printer's hands. I add the most important titles to the above list:

The Universal Peace Organization of King George of Bohemia. Prague, 1964.

Heymann, Frederick G., George of Bohemia, King of Heretics. Princeton, 1965.

Macek, Josef, K zahraniční politice krále Jiřího. Československý časopis historický, Vol. XIII. Prague, 1965.

INDEX

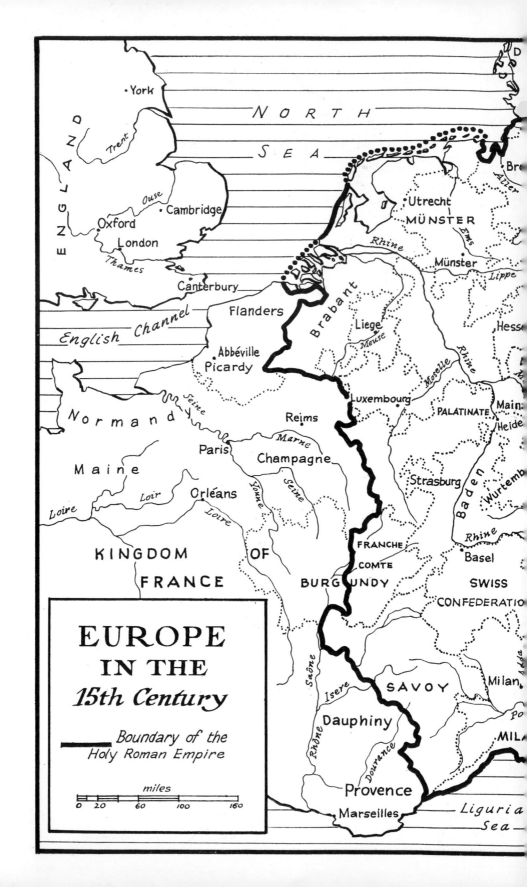

York

N O R T H

S E A

ENGLAND

Trent

Ouse

Cambridge

Oxford

London

Thames

Utrecht

MÜNSTER

Münster

Rhine

Ems

Lippe

D

Br

Aller

Canterbury

Flanders

Brabant

Liege

Meuse

Hesse

Rhine

English Channel

Abbéville

Picardy

Seine

Luxembourg

Moselle

Rhine

Main

Normand

Reims

Marne

Champagne

Seine

PALATINATE

Heide

Strasburg

Baden

Wurtemb

Paris

Maine

Loir

Orléans

Loire

Yonne

Loire

OF

Rhine

Basel

Loire

KINGDOM

FRANCE

FRANCHE

COMTE

BURGUNDY

SWISS

CONFEDERATIO

EUROPE

IN THE

15th Century

Boundary of the
Holy Roman Empire

Saône

Isère

SAVOY

Milan

Rhône

Dauphiny

Po

MILA

Durance

miles

0   20   60   100   160

Provence

Marseilles

Liguria

Sea

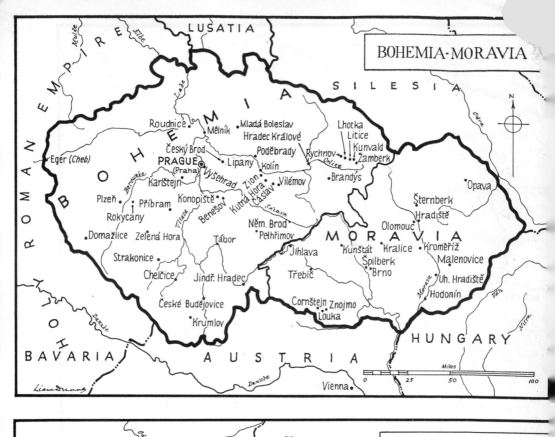

BOHEMIA-MORAVIA

LUSATIA

HOLY ROMAN EMPIRE

B O H E M I A

S I L E S I A

Roudnice
Mělník
Mladá Boleslav
Hradec Králové
Lhotka
Litice
Eger (Cheb)
Český Brod
Poděbrady
Rychnov
Kunvald
Žamberk
PRAGUE (Praha)
Lipany
Kolín
Brandýs
Vyšehrad
Zion
Vilémov
Plzeň
Karlštejn
Konopiště
Kutná Hora
Čáslav
Opava
Příbram
Benešov
Šternberk
Rokycany
Hradiště
Domažlice
Zelená Hora
Něm. Brod
Olomouc
M O R A V I A
Strakonice
Tábor
Pelhřimov
Kunštát
Kralice
Kroměříž
Chelčice
Jihlava
Špilberk
Malenovice
Jindř. Hradec
Třebíč
Brno
Uh. Hradiště
Hodonín
České Budějovice
Cornštejn
Znojmo
Louka
Krumlov

HUNGARY

BAVARIA
AUSTRIA

Vienna

Miles
0   25   50   100

SILESIA-LUSATIA

Warta

Havel
Berlin
Poznań (Posen)
Gniezno

HOLY ROMAN EMPIRE

LOWER LUSATIA
Nysa Łuz
Odra
P O L A N D
Warta

Głogów (Glogau, Hlohov)

Cottbus (Choćebuz)
Żagań (Sagan, Zaháň)
Hoyerswerda
UPPER LUSATIA
Trzebnica (Trebnitz, Třebnice)
Oleśnica (Oels, Olešnice)
Prosna
Warta

Legnica (Liegnitz, Lehnice)
Jawor (Jauer, Javor)
S I L E S I A
Brzeg (Brieg, Břeh)
Świdnica (Schweidnitz, Svídnice)
Strzelin (Strehlen, Střelín)
Opole (Oppeln, Opolí)
Frankenstein
Münsterberg
Nysa (Neisse, Nisa)

Ohře
Labe
Kladsko (Glatz, Kłodzko)

Berounka
Orlice
Prague (Praha)

B O H E M I A
Sázava
Cieszyn (Těšín, Teschen)

Olomouc
M O R A V I A
Hungary

Miles
0   25   50   100